Capitalism and the Senses

HAGLEY PERSPECTIVES ON BUSINESS AND CULTURE

Roger Horowitz, Series Editor

A complete list of books in the series is available from the publisher.

Capitalism and the Senses

Edited by Regina Lee Blaszczyk
and David Suisman

UNIVERSITY OF PENNSYLVANIA PRESS

PHILADELPHIA

Published by
University of Pennsylvania Press
Philadelphia, Pennsylvania 19104-4112
www.upenn.edu/pennpress

Printed in the United States of America on acid-free paper
10 9 8 7 6 5 4 3 2 1

Hardcover ISBN: 978-1-5128-2420-9
eBook ISBN: 978-1-5128-2421-6

A catalogue record for this book is available from the Library of Congress.

CONTENTS

SERIES EDITOR'S FOREWORD

For thirty years the Hagley Center for the History of Business, Technology, and Society has assembled events and programs that bring creative empirical scholarship to the attention of the academic community. As an archives and library, Hagley has ever sought to expand the range of scholars in many fields who can find materials pertinent to their interests in our collections. Hundreds of scholars have availed themselves of our research and residential grants to dig into the extensive records we hold pertaining to American enterprises and their impact on the world.

Conferences have been an important component of our promotional efforts. For many years the Hagley Center has solicited papers for annual thematic conferences organized around a call for papers, with the intent of attracting the interest of any scholar intrigued by the conference's theme and questions. To ensure that the conferences engage with issues animating current scholarship, the program committee developing the call for proposals and selecting papers have always included members outside of Hagley staff who are engaged with the conference's topic, often having worked in our collections. The conference themes have been as diverse as the scholarship Hagley's collections supports; but they share a commitment to identify cutting edge scholarly trends that could encourage those so interested with pursuing research in our collections.

In 1999 the Center initiated a book series, the Hagley Perspectives on Business and Culture, to serve as a vehicle for edited collections that built on successful conferences. Philip Scranton and Roger Horowitz served as founding series editors and were joined in 2001 by Susan Strasser. (With Scranton's and Strasser's retirement, Horowitz is now the sole series editor.) The series began under the imprimatur of Routledge and moved to the University of Pennsylvania Press in 2005 where it has prospered, thanks to the press's strong support and the skilled guidance of Robert Lockhart. The volumes aspired to capture and disseminate the fresh scholarship presented at our conferences, informed and improved by the insights of commentators, editors, and outside readers. From the beginning these collections were not imagined as conference proceedings, simply reproducing all the conference papers with only minor editing. Instead, the volumes developed the conference themes, including only some of the papers presented, and with the editors recruiting additional original essays that they felt complemented the volume.

This volume has a similar lineage. Our research grant program has brought a steady stream of scholars to Hagley interested in understanding the relationship between business, commerce, and the history of the senses. One of these researchers, Regina Lee Blaszczyk, asked if we would be interested in a conference on capitalism and the senses. Blaszczyk was well-known to us at Hagley as an indefatigable researcher and prolific author, including prize-winning books that draw from our collections. We were intrigued, and so asked David Suisman from the University of Delaware if he would be interested in joining this initiative. Suisman also had used Hagley collections for his prize-winning book on sound. Indeed, both he and Blaszczyk had previously edited books in the Hagley Perspective series, so we were familiar with their editorial skills as well.

The connections involved in creating this volume, and the scholarly base on which it stands, are worth noting. What stands out to me is the intertwined presence of the Hagley Library and University of Delaware graduate Hagley Program going back many decades. It seems no accident that volume coeditor Regina Lee Blaszczyk and contributor Ai Hisano are both graduates of the Hagley Program, albeit separated by three decades; that Susan Strasser and David Suisman overlapped as faculty for Hagley Program graduate students; and that Blaszczyk, Suisman, and Hisano all made extensive use of Hagley Library collections in their own research. Less obvious to readers is the importance of the Business History Conference generating the networks that have accentuated the new directions reflected in this collection. Blaszczyk, Suisman, and Hisano each received the Hagley Prize for the best book in business history from the Business History Conference for their first book and have served as trustees of this organization. The foundation for these networks is in many respects the business collections of the Hagley Library, assembled over fifty years, that offer the raw data from which scholars are now tracing the interaction between capitalism and the senses.

The result is the volume you are reading, a quintessential product of the Hagley conference and Perspectives on Business and Culture series. We hope you find it engaging, and perhaps even transformative. And if it inspires you to look more into the relationships between business and culture, we hope you will consult our research collections to see if we have something for you.

Roger Horowitz
Director, Center for the History of Business, Technology, and Culture

INTRODUCTION

REGINA LEE BLASZCZYK AND DAVID SUISMAN

You have probably never heard of the food scientist Louise Slade, but you likely have eaten the soft ice cream, chewy cookies, and crisp potato chips that she developed during her twenty-five-year career at two American companies, the General Foods Corporation and its later parent company, Kraft Foods, Inc. As noted in her obituary in the *New York Times*, Slade's research on the natural polymers in food led to innovations that insured every single Oreo-brand cookie is held to exacting standards, retaining its distinctive shape and texture through production, distribution, storage, and ultimately, dunking into a glass of milk. Together with her research and life partner, Harry Levine, Slade developed the new field of "food polymer science," which today is involved in the creation of 75 percent of all processed foods. Food polymer science focuses on standardizing everyday foods without sacrificing their structure, texture, or taste.[1]

Researchers like the late Louise Slade are among the countless scientists, marketers, and other experts who, over the course of the long twentieth century, built careers that forged relationships among science, technology, markets, and the human senses. Eager to make connections between academic science and American industry, these sensory specialists laid the foundation for the modern practice of exploiting the senses for commercial purposes. They created new fields of study such as food polymer science, psychophysics, and motivational research, and incorporated sensory experience into existing practices such as branding, marketing, and industrial and interior design. Collectively, these little-known sensory experts built on the observations of the nineteenth-century political economists who acknowledged the intimate connection between the productive capacities of industrial capitalism and the fundamental role of the senses in consumer experience. Perfume manufacturers had always relied on individuals with a strong sense of smell to detect subtle differences in aromas, but with the rise of advanced capitalism, a "nose," or an expert in scent, could become a specialist in "olfactory branding."[2]

This collection is the first edited book to explore the sensory history of capitalism—the ways that seeing, hearing, tasting, smelling, and touching have shaped, and been shaped by, business enterprise from the turn of the twentieth century to our own time. From the stench of the stockyards to the saccharine sounds of Muzak, everyday sensory environments have been made and remade by capitalism, and as portals through which we take in knowledge of the world, the senses have been subject to manipulation, exploitation, and commodification. If, as Karl Marx contended in 1844, the senses have a history, then that history is intertwined with the development of capitalism, which has drawn on the embodied power of the senses and, in turn, influenced how sensory experience has changed over time.[3] This book draws on the innovative scholarship in the history of the senses and as well as established fields such as anthropology, business history, cultural history, and science studies to offer a new perspective on modern capitalism.

The seed for this volume was planted at a workshop organized by Ai Hisano at the Harvard Business School titled "Capitalism and the Senses" in June of 2017, and it was sown at an online conference of the same name sponsored by the Hagley Museum and Library in November of 2020 which attracted more than 200 participants.[4] The Hagley call for papers, issued the previous spring, solicited contributions on a range of related themes: the construction of knowledge about the senses; the creation of sensory standards and measurements for trade and commerce; the development of new forms of sensory labor; the rise of sensory manipulation in the workplace; the impact of industrial research and innovative technologies on sensory products; the use of sensory appeals in marketing, advertising, packaging, and selling; and the manipulation of commercial products to augment their sensory appeal. The conference call attracted proposals from academics in fields ranging from art history to hospitality management. Sixteen papers were selected for delivery at the one-day symposium. The program included presentations on the sensory life of an eighteenth-century craftsman, the nineteenth-century trans-Pacific tea trade, and interspecies relationships in early twentieth-century China. To give coherence to this volume, we have selected for publication a group of papers that focus on the American experience, with some reference to developments in Great Britain and continental

Europe.[5] The result is a book offering an innovative blending of the history of capitalism and the history of the senses.

Understanding the Senses

Historicizing the senses faces two great challenges: first, establishing that the senses *have* a history, and second, clarifying what *the senses* involve. On the face of it, the human sensorium might seem an incongruous or paradoxical historical subject, for the ways that we see, hear, touch, smell, and taste are so intimate and so fundamental to how we know the world that it would be easy to think them timeless—unchanging, hard-wired, and outside history—which is how thinkers from Aristotle to John Locke saw them. Since the nineteenth century, however, a range of writers have challenged this assumption, probing ways that sensory experience is, to a substantial degree, socially and culturally constructed and mutable over time. As early as 1844 Karl Marx wrote, "The *forming* of the five senses is a labor of the entire history of the world down to the present." In the twentieth century, Georg Simmel identified sensory overload as a signature element of urban modernity in his now-classic reflection on daily life in the city, "The Metropolis and Mental Life" (1903). A quarter century later, Walter Benjamin likewise posited that sense experience was historically contingent in his landmark essay, "The Work of Art in the Age of Mechanical Reproduction." Sensory perception, Benjamin suggested, was the dialectical outcome of biological constants and shifting historical circumstances. Shortly thereafter, the *Annales* historian Lucien Febvre proposed that exploring the alterity of affective and sensorial experience in earlier epochs could lead to new historical insights.[6]

Only in the 1980s did historical analysis of the senses get purchase, however, beginning with the work of Alain Corbin, whose pioneering study of smell, *The Foul and the Fragrant: Odor and the French Social Imagination* (1982 in French; English translation 1986), showed how judgments about pleasant and noxious scents changed from the eighteenth to the nineteenth century in relation to the dramatic restructuring of French society.[7] Since then, a growing number of historians, art historians, literary scholars, anthropologists, and others have become attuned to ways that historical conditions have shaped vision, hearing, and the other senses. In so doing, they have both expanded and honed the analytical and methodological toolkit available for studying and explaining how people's sensory apparatuses have shifted from one era to another and how such changes have been meaningful. They have shown, for example, how deeply ideas about health and illness have been intertwined with the senses—from the rise of auscultation (diagnostic listening to bodies through stethoscopes) in the nineteenth century to color and music therapy in the twentieth century. Other scholars have mapped how the senses have informed hierarchies of class and race (the lower classes and non-whites being associated with coarseness and dissonance, the upper classes and whiteness being linked to polish and refinement). They have tracked how the senses have been used to police social boundaries. They have revealed how the senses have become sites of religious conflict and contestation. Together, these and other innovative studies have called attention to a previously overlooked facet of historical change.[8]

Arguably, there is something inherently interesting in denaturalizing the senses and puzzling over ways that people's sensory worldviews are historically contingent. How often did a medieval French peasant see the color purple? How frequently did an eighteenth-century English factory worker taste sweetness? But there is more at stake in this work than an antiquarian cataloguing of sensations. Rather, the thrust of this work has been to explore how and why the senses have *mattered* historically.[9] It has shown the ways in which ideas, debates, and conflicts connected to sensory perception and experience have been historically consequential—and by extension, they complicate and enrich what we know and think about the past and the present. In some cases, we may gain new perspectives on the threshold of perception of this or that sensory phenomenon, and the meanings associated with this awareness. In other cases, we come to understand how efforts to shape sensory experience (either one's own or that of others) have been drivers of historical change. In both, we gain a new understanding of ways that both discursive and behavioral practices related to the senses have reflected and inflected larger historical developments.

The second challenge in historicizing the senses is definitional and requires that we disentangle "the senses" from the welter of cognates derived from the Latin *sentire*, to feel—a number of which have incommensurable or contradictory meanings. Some of the kindred terms and phrases denote rationality, intelligibility, and consciousness (*make sense*, *come to one's senses*). By contrast, others signify physicality, corporeality, feeling, and emotion (*sensual*, *sentient*, *sentimental*). Further, some uses suggest reflexive or involuntary response (*sensation*), while others entail discrimination or interpretation (*sensibility*, "*in one sense, . . .*"). Most of this language revolves around individuals (*intuitive sense*) but some has a clear social dimension (*common sense*). Notably, in the eighteenth century, *sensibility* connected the two, signaling, as Raymond Williams noted, "a personal appropriation of certain social qualities."[10]

Amid this jumble, we find *the senses*, a term designating something distinctly or inherently corporeal, an embodied means of perceiving the world, often in reference to what were once called the "sense organs." Since Aristotle, these have generally been understood in the West as a pentad—a five-way split of physiological affordances distributed across vision, hearing, smell, taste, and touch. In fact, the number five is neither universal nor fixed. Plato counted only four. (Aristotle added touch.) Many contemporary scientists and philosophers also include perception of temperature, pressure, balance, body position, and other phenomena as senses. By contrast, anthropologist Ian Ritchie has suggested that Hausa-language speakers in West Africa recognize principally two senses, sight and a complex of all non-visual senses. And yet another picture emerges when we look beyond humans, as many non-human animals have other faculties, such as perception of electricity or magnetic fields.[11]

Recognizing the number five as a construct, we have tried not to lean too hard on this convention. The book was not conceptualized (as many works in the field of sensory studies are) around what David Howes wryly referred to as the "pentarchy" of the five senses, and while some of the chapters that follow focus on specific senses, others cut across multiple faculties or are concerned with the senses in a more general way.[12] Together, these essays are less concerned with the significance of specific pathways than they are, as Mark S. R. Jenner put it, with "how sensory perception *worked* in particular historical settings." Or, put differently, they are interested in "explor[ing] the senses as a form of practice, which is both situated and intersensorial."[13]

Understanding the senses as a form of practice, these essays present a direct challenge to the assumption that the senses are automatic, autonomous, and ahistorical. Doing so, this work may recall an influential article on the history of emotions by Monique Scheer. Emotions, she posits, are located in our bodies as well as our brains. They are at once physiological and cognitive phenomena—just as the senses are. And emotions are *historical* phenomena to the extent that our bodies are inseparable from the temporality of society. To explain this, Scheer draws on Pierre Bourdieu's theorizing of *habitus*—"schemes of perception, thought, and action"—extending his proposition that habitus is "embodied history, internalized as a second nature and so forgotten as history" to argue that emotions are most productively apprehended as a kind of practice or action, grounded in historically positioned bodies. This book approaches *its* subject in much the same way. If emotion is, as Scheer puts it, "something people *do*, not just *have*," that doing always takes place, through bodies, in particular historical circumstances.[14] And so with the senses.

Understanding Capitalism and the Senses

Appreciation of the senses as an analytic category is a relatively recent development in scholarship on the history of capitalism and its related field of business history. Studies of capitalism are necessarily engaged with the writings of Karl Marx, both critiquing his limits and recognizing his insights. As a prescient observer of nineteenth-century industry and finance, his views on the unequal distribution of wealth and power among business owners and factory workers and his arguments about the evolving nature of capitalism became the basis for an enormous body of scholarship—focused above all on production. Following from this, for many decades scholars of capitalism have tended to explore the relationships between economy and polity, labor and capital, and state and society far more than they have probed capitalism's cultural dimensions.

Marx himself believed that sensory experience was debased by capitalism but would ultimately be redeemed. On the production side, Marx saw a distinct sensory dimension of nineteenth-century factory labor: "Every sense organ is injured in an equal degree by artificial elevation of the temperature, by the dust-laden atmosphere, by the deafening noise, not to mention danger to life and limb among the thickly crowded machinery."[15] For the most part, however, capitalism degraded and suppressed sensory experience in Marx's estimation, not only for the proletariat but also for the bourgeoisie, who, he believed, regularly forwent sensual satisfaction in favor of ever greater capital accumulation. Conversely, following the utopian socialist Charles Fourier, Marx imagined sensory liberation as part of capitalism's transcendence. The abolition of private property, he wrote, would lead to "the complete *emancipation* of all human senses." As the "richness of man's essential being" unfolded, "the richness of . . . *human* sensibility (a musical ear, an eye for beauty of form—in short *senses* capable of human gratifications, senses confirming themselves as essential powers of *man*) [would be] either cultivated or brought into being."[16]

What Marx did not anticipate, however, was that before that apotheosis, the senses would become *more* important to capitalism, not less.[17] This was evident especially (but not exclusively) in the realm of consumption, to which he devoted far less attention than he did to production. Focused on "the factory and the stock market," David Howes has pointed out, Marx "neglected an equally salient development—the *presentation* of commodities in the department stores and world exhibitions that sprang up in the mid-nineteenth century."[18] By the turn of the twentieth century, the cultural and economic value of goods was becoming increasingly linked to the ways that they were marketed, packaged, and displayed. In the decades that followed, what the senses meant for the circulation and accumulation of capital grew ever more pronounced. The result was, as this book shows, that over the twentieth century there developed a distinct capitalist *sensibility*—in the dual sense of a disposition (a general way of thinking or feeling), and a sensitivity or sensory responsiveness.

In this new era—the age of what Ai Hisano calls "aesthetic capitalism" in Chapter 1—producers paid unprecedented attention to the sensory appeal of the design and packaging of products and the means by which they were sold, and the control and manipulation of sensory experience came to bear on the operations of capital as never before. Manufacturers, marketers, and merchants understood that how goods looked, felt, and, in some cases, sounded, smelled, and tasted had a lot to do with whether or not a potential purchaser would buy them. At the turn of the century, when foodstuffs once purchased in bulk began to be sold prepackaged, consumers who could no longer inspect, sniff, feel, and sample before buying had to be convinced of value and quality by other means. Thus, as Susan Strasser has shown, the visual appearance of packaging was not an afterthought; it was essential to many products' marketability. A label or carton was not an advertising medium, a 1913 advertising textbook stressed, it was "an integral part of the commodity itself."[19] Over the course of twentieth century, visual marketing grew to encompass everything from illustrated magazine advertisements and billboards to skywriting and television commercials.

Breaking with the structuralist approach of pioneering business historian Alfred D. Chandler Jr., a cohort of researchers concerned with other aspects of American enterprise took inspiration from social and cultural history and engaged with novel types of evidence to understand these cultural processes linked to commerce.[20] One of the best known of these culturally oriented business historians, Roland Marchand, analyzed corporate imagery in his studies of modern advertising and public relations as a means to understanding how they disseminated myths and stereotypes.[21] In another corner of the academic universe, art historians in the emerging field of visual culture studies turned away from the canon of fine art—architecture, paintings, and sculpture by recognized masters—to consider American popular culture, including photography and advertising graphics. Patricia Johnston's analysis of objectification and sensuality in the advertising snaps of Edward Steichen, a fashion and fine-art photographer who did studio work for J. Walter Thompson of Madison Avenue in the interwar years, was a pioneering study of how modern enterprise manipulated visuality, female sexuality, sensual pleasure, and the senses for profit.[22]

The work of Marchand and Johnston on the visual and sensual dimensions of American business culture did not directly engage with the history of the senses but it overlapped with and helped to advance a dramatic shift in the study of capitalism and its business institutions. In the 1990s, the Chandlerian worldview was vigorously challenged anew by a younger generation of business historians, who, influenced by the rise of cultural history and cultural studies, pioneered a new approach to the study of commercial enterprise. This "cultural turn" in business history was informed by scholarship in a range of disciplines—anthropology, literature, African American studies, design history, gender studies, historical sociology, material culture studies, social history, visual culture studies, and others. The new generation explored topics untouched by the Chandler school and included subjects such women in business, African American entrepreneurs, industrial design, consumer society, advertising, marketing, retailing, and small family firms.[23] One particular research thread, focused on enterprise and consumer culture, highlighted the efforts of advertising creators, product designers, and marketing experts to "imagine" the needs of particular market segments, be it homemakers or children, and scrutinized business efforts to accommodate, shape, or manipulate their desires.[24] In her work on color, volume coeditor Regina Lee Blaszczyk showed how American enterprise, including some of the firms deemed central by Chandler, purposefully developed business-to-business systems for selecting the colors and color combinations in product design that would stimulate a surefire emotional response in consumers.[25] Collectively, the new culturally informed business history, most rigorously theorized by Kenneth J. Lipartito, revealed how interdisciplinary thinking, combined with scrutiny of activities within the confines of the firm, the trade association, or the industry, could illuminate the internal operations of American capitalism.[26]

Visual presentation was not the only sensory aspect of twentieth-century consumer society, however. Consider the commodification of sound, for example. As volume coeditor David Suisman has shown elsewhere, in the United States the music churned out by the "popular song factories" of Tin Pan Alley (as the *New York Times* called them in 1910) was itself nothing if not a commercial product: made to make money through the sale of sheet music, the songs were literally advertisements for themselves. In the 1920s, commercial radio was born when broadcasters introduced aural advertising, including jingles, to their programming, so the adman's pitches now resounded in the intimate space of people's living rooms. Then there was the business of phonograph records, which "stockpiled" the labor of professional musicians in the grooves of sound recordings (as theorist Jacques Attali memorably put it). On the eve of the Great Depression, the phonograph industry enjoyed revenues of nearly $100 million a year. Taken together, these industries showed how, by the 1930s, "selling sounds" had become big business.[27]

In the sensibility of aesthetic capitalism, sensory experience ceased to be merely a byproduct—something that "just happened" to a consumer when a product was used—and instead became a conscious, sometimes explicit, part of the way that capitalism as a system worked. The senses are among "our best salesman," argued the industrial designers Roy Sheldon and Egmont Arens in their 1932 treatise *Consumer Engineering*. As its title suggests, their book expanded on the concept of "engineering" consumers, recently advanced by Earnest Elmo Calkins, one of the pioneers of modern advertising. A key aspect of his proposition, they explained, was factoring sensory experience into the design of goods, for considerations like shape, feel, and touch affected a product's ultimate commercial value. "After the eye," they wrote, "the hand is the first censor to pass upon acceptance [of a product], and if the hand's judgment is unfavorable, the most [visually] attractive object will not gain the popularity it deserves. [Conversely,] merchandise designed to be pleasing to the hand wins an approval that may never register [consciously] in the mind but which will determine additional purchases." Thus, they exhorted product designers, "*Make it snuggle in the palm*"—after which they extrapolated to hearing, tasting, smelling, and seeing. "Scrutiny of the other sensory systems in the light of the new psychology," they asserted, "would lead to similarly stimulating suggestions for the modern business man."[28]

As the essays in this volume demonstrate, numerous factors explain why this new sensate capitalism emerged when and as it did. Technology was a big part of the story. The capacity of scientists and engineers to isolate, measure, and, in some cases, synthesize specific sensory phenomena enabled manufacturers and merchants to fine-tune the appeal of their products—some of which had been marketed for centuries, like perfumes and textiles, and others of which were wholly new, like Wrigley's chewing gum—to a far greater degree than had been possible in Marx's lifetime (he died in 1883). This sensory sea change, however, should not be understood as the result of technological determinism, for several other factors besides technology mattered just as much. First was the creation of a capital-dependent infrastructure capable of collecting, studying, and analyzing concrete information about consumer response. This included the establishment of dedicated research-and-development laboratories, whether as independent firms or as part of large chemical corporations, and standalone market research firms, such as Ernest Dichter's Institute for Motivational Research, to provide systematic feedback on all kinds of consumer attitudes and behavior.[29]

Second, the senses became important to capitalism when and as they did because of the specific ideological conditions in which heightened attention to sensorial response was manifest, making it seem like an organic extension of existing economic activity. If technological innovation produced new potentialities and infrastructure made possible standardized experimentation, both were underpinned by the intensified logic of rationalization in production and marketing in the late nineteenth century. Of course, some degree of sensorial attunement informed commercial exchange long before the rise of modern capitalism, especially in relation to foodstuffs and luxury goods. There is nothing particularly capitalistic about buyers valuing some sensory characteristics and denigrating others—avoiding goods that look spoiled or smell rancid. Yet around the turn of the nineteenth into the twentieth century, every aspect of both manufacturing and selling goods was brought under the microscope of calculation.[30] One of the best known examples of this phenomenon lay in the rise of scientific management, which externalized the analysis of efficiency, abstracting the search for the "one best way" in every productive or commercial process.[31] The same spirit animated aesthetic capitalism, in which sensory response came to be seen as an independent variable in consumer marketing, not inherent in the goods but extrinsic and manipulable. The new common sense, as it were, among manufacturers, marketers, and merchants—as well as among many scientists, engineers, consultants, bankers, accountants, and others—urged never-ending refinement in every aspect of business, including the pursuit of ever-cleverer ways to build or capture markets. If capitalism reified the imperatives of the market, increasingly elevating commercial relationships above all others, then commercializing the sensorium grounded that abstract impulse in the materiality of bodies. In that environment, seeing the senses—the channels through which bodies relate to the physical world they live in—as just another commercial relationship takes on a sheen of naturalness and inevitability.

In This Book

If there is a political economy of the senses, it has been manifest not only in marketing but at many points in the processes of production, distribution, and consumption. Accordingly, the twelve chapters in this edited volume explore how the trajectories of the history of capitalism and the history of the senses have intersected across a wide range of practices and effects. The volume is divided into four sections that move from the big picture to the telling details, beginning with an exploration of broad concepts and ending with meticulous analysis of the nuts and bolts of marketing. Focusing on subjects ranging from product design to measurements and standards, from supply chains to the practices of end users, the individual chapters "flesh out" the corporeal, sensorial dimensions of making, selling, and buying across the modern cultural and economic landscape. Through this work, we come to appreciate capitalism not merely as a set of relationships governing where and how goods are made and circulated but also as a phenomenon bearing on, and filtered through, sentient human bodies. In spaces as diverse as laboratories, department stores, feed lots, hotel rooms, and the hulls of 100,000-ton container ships, people who make, measure, move, and market commercial products have manipulated sensory experience for commercial gain. Through clinical testing, focus groups, product displays, meetings of trade associations, and other means, they have sought to rationalize, quantify, and commodify the sensorium.

Part I of the book, "Framing Capitalism and the Senses," raises broad theoretical questions. It begins in Chapter 1, "'Use Not Perfumery to Flavor Soup': The Science of the Senses in Aesthetic Capitalism," with Ai Hisano's contention that in the late nineteenth century a new kind of "aesthetic capitalism" emerged which made sensory judgment integral to business strategies, with far-reaching ramifications for the norms and expectations of ordinary people (consumers) in daily life. Hisano uses the sensory philosophy of Aristotle as a springboard for exploring how aesthetic, or sensory, judgement became an integral part of business strategies in consumer-product development among managerial firms at the center of the economy. By incorporating philosophical and historical studies of emotion and the senses into business history, she argues that the creation of aesthetic capitalism grew out of the translation of aesthetics and scientific investigation into industrial sensory science. Consequently, consumer-goods companies constructed a new kind of aesthetics, which became not only an industry standard in product design and marketing but also a social norm. Certain sensations became acceptable while others became disgusting. Consulting firms like Arthur D. Little, Inc., helped raise sensory awareness and enhance sensory experience by creating new sensations, but at a cost of diminishing more traditional, localized senses.

In Chapter 2, "Chasing Flavor: Sensory Science and the Economy," Ingemar Pettersson examines the emergence of food sensory science in the twentieth-century

United States. He considers how scientists and engineers within and around the food industry attempted to turn the individual and elusive property of flavor into an object of scientific inquiry. Pettersson posits that the scientific objectification of flavor corresponded with the evolution of the economy and argues for two major changes that evolved in tandem: the senses and sensory impressions were "economized" and, concurrently, the economy was "sensitized." The concept of the "economization of the senses" refers to the process by which industrialization transformed consumers' understanding of flavor qualities and to the mechanisms involved in the standardization of sensory attributes. The concept of the "sensitization of the economy" refers to the process through which consumers and producers developed a greater awareness of the taste, tactile qualities, sounds, smells, and appearances of industrially produced goods.

Next in "Richer Sounds: Capitalism, Musical Instruments, and the Cold War Sonic Divide" (Chapter 3), Sven Kube looks at the impact of musical equipment from the capitalist West on the soundscapes of popular music in the Eastern bloc during the Cold War. Specifically, he probes why pop, rock, and dance music from the United States, the United Kingdom, and continental Western Europe had such broad and powerful appeal in Communist countries and analyzes how amateur and popular musicians there sought to imitate the instruments and sounds from across the Iron Curtain. Kube argues that the sonic properties of Western popular music (associated with instruments such as Fender guitars) made popular music a Cold War battleground distinct from lyrical themes and generic conventions. The result, he suggests, was that the *sound* of popular music from the capitalist countries penetrated deep into the aural consciousness of Eastern bloc nations and made Western popular music an audible signifier of capitalism.

Part II, "Resisting Rationalization," explores the elusiveness of the senses for those who have sought to harness their commercial potential and the refusal of the senses to conform to the logics of capital. Chapter 4, "Altered States and Gustatory Taste: The Sensory Synergies of Whiskey Marketing in the Mid-Twentieth-Century United States," by Lisa Jacobson takes on the intoxicating effects of alcohol consumption—a subject that complicates both marketers' and consumers' efforts to pinpoint consumer preferences. Focusing on the postwar era, she draws on advertisements for alcoholic beverages and market studies conducted by Ernest Dichter's Institute for Motivational Research, a business-to-business consulting firm, to consider the interactive role between producers and consumers in the construction of knowledge about the sensory experience of drinking. The focus on alcoholic beverages allows Jacobson to consider a consumer product that stimulated all of the senses—sight, taste, touch, sound, and smell—while altering the user's state of mind and their sensory perceptions. She demonstrates how mid-century market researchers and advertisers became ever more inventive in the ways they blended messages about the pleasures of gustatory taste with more covert messages about the pleasures of altered states.

In "The Psychophysics of Taste and Smell: From Experimental Science to Commercial Tool" (Chapter 5), Ana María Ulloa probes the ambiguities and contradictions in the industrial measurement of sensory experience. Self-assured scientific pronouncements notwithstanding, connoisseurship, expertise, and judgment about the senses have never rested on firm ground, Ulloa argues, and the professionalization of taste experts cannot be disentangled from the variability and subjectivity inherent in their instruments and metrics. Drawing on extensive ethnographic fieldwork at the Monell Chemical Senses Center, an independent research institute in Philadelphia, Ulloa explores the domain of commercial psychophysics to document how chemosensory scientists and flavorists manufacture a contested and unstable kind of sensory expertise.

David Suisman, a coeditor of this book, flips the script in Chapter 6, "Sky's the Limit: Capitalism, the Senses, and the Failure of Commercial Supersonic Aviation in the United States," which is concerned with the impact of ear-splitting, bone-rattling sonic booms in the development of an American supersonic transport (SST) in the 1960s and 1970s. Suisman's study turns our attention to sensory experience as an unwanted byproduct of commercial activity—what economists would call a negative externality. When the U.S. government and the American aviation industry sought to design and build a commercial airplane that would fly faster than the speed of sound, the sonic booms caused by supersonic flight proved so disruptive that they, along with other several other factors, forced Congress to abandon the project in the early 1970s. This chapter shows how industry leaders, government officials, scientists, engineers, and political activists each perceived the sonic boom issue through a different lens, and refracts the tensions that emerged over prioritizing different kinds of outcomes. If, in the preceding chapter, Ulloa explores the limits of scientists to produce standardized sensory outcomes, Suisman shows sensory experience as a different kind of challenge: as an *obstacle* to commercial development—not a practice to be manipulated but a problem to be suppressed or avoided.

The auditory dimensions of globalization are the subject of Chapter 7, "Sounding Maritime Metal: On Weathering Steel and Listening to Capitalism at Sea" by Nicholas Anderman. This author begins with a provocative question, "What does the global economy sound like, and how might we hear it?"

The nuanced answer he develops emerges from his listening to the "metallic sonorities" of a fully loaded French container ship slicing through the northern Pacific Ocean at twenty knots, including both the creaking hull of the boat and the "social content" of the specific steel alloy from which shipping containers are made. He anchors this work in a reexamination of Max Weber's notion of the "iron cage of civilization," which, Anderman proposes, is better understood as a steel container and concludes with a proposition that attentiveness to the ways we think about sound may unlock doors to thinking outside of capitalism.

Part III, "Production," looks upstream at processes of engineering and design in two very different settings. In Chapter 8, "Making Human Trash Tasty: A History of Sweet Cattle Feed in the Progressive Era," Nicole Welk-Joerger examines the industrial engineering of the taste of animal feed, which underpins a substantial portion of the human food supply in the United States. She chronicles how the taste of sweetness has been used strategically by farmers and feed companies since the Progressive Era to induce dairy and meat cattle to eat as much as possible. Her detailed, stomach-churning findings reveal how the widespread practice of habituating cattle to eat "unnatural" products has transformed the American food supply. Humans have used their own sense of what constitutes a "good taste," including sweetness, to inform the investigation and development of livestock flavoring. These flavor additives, ranging from molasses to "candy apple" powder, have encouraged cattle to eat various materials to the benefit of different nonagricultural mass consumer industries.

The histories of design and of the senses are linked in Chapter 9, "Getting a Handle on It: Thomas Lamb, Mass Production, and Touch in Design History," by Grace Lees-Maffei in her study of a man widely known in creative circles as the pioneer of Universal Design. The chapter considers how Lamb engaged with the senses as he reimagined the shapes of commonplace consumer products like cups and teapots. Lamb's decision to use his own hands as a "standard" form of measurement risked universalizing his personal experience at the expense of potential users who were of different sizes, genders, or abilities. The essay raises important questions that link capitalism and the senses: How "universal" was Lamb's concept of Universal Design? How did he benefit from a design process that depended on touch as well as sight? What did he learn by engaging with haptic experience as he reimagined everyday tableware and other prosaic objects? This chapter is unique among the contributions in this collection for its engagement with design theory and its use of artifacts as evidence.

Finally, Part IV, "Marketplace," considers sites, spaces, and conditions of contact between merchants, manufacturers, products, and consumers. In Chapter 10,

"Fragrance and Fair Women: Perfumers and Consumers in Modern London," Jessica P. Clark uses a single event—the "All-British Shopping Week" in London's West End in 1911—as a case study to interrogate the relationship between commercial modernity, capitalism, and smell in early twentieth-century Britain. Her essay considers how London retailers meshed ideas of national identity with exciting new sensory experiences to expand their sales in the domestic market during a peak period in British international expansion. The focus on perfumes allows for the analysis of exclusion and "othering" in the creation of a highly nationalistic smellscape by retailers and other economic actors. This study is distinctive for its deep analysis of historical texts about smells and for its use of that evidence to unpack the British experience of modernity.

The global textile and apparel business is a complex industry whose engagement of sensory marketing has not been considered in depth. In Chapter 11, "Sold on Softness: DuPont Synthetics and Sensory Experience," volume coeditor Regina Lee Blaszczyk homes in on the American textile business during the early to mid-twentieth century, a large industry whose supply chain extended from the chemical companies who made the fibers to the retailers who sold the fashions. The chapter looks at the DuPont Company, a chemical manufacturer that ventured into fiber production in 1920 to become the dominant global player by 1970. Blaszczyk explores how DuPont, a science-based company, embraced psychological research on the senses as it tried to get a handle on the markets for man-made fibers in the interwar years and for the new synthetic fibers—nylon, polyester, acrylic, and spandex—in the postwar era. Here, we see how a Fortune 500 company known for its investment in science, technology, and management looked to develop its capacities in marketing, and how sensory analysis figured into that effort.

In Chapter 12, "Feminine Touches: The Sensory World of Lady Hilton," Megan J. Elias focuses on "Lady Hilton," a promotional program created in 1965 by Hilton Hotels International as a marketing device to attract a new customer: the woman traveling on business. It places the Lady Hilton experiment within the context of the broader sensory landscape of the booming American hotel industry of the postwar era, considering how hotel managers orchestrated and navigated the smells, colors, textures, and tastes of commercial hospitality. Hilton's venture into sensory management involved a range of strategies, from the creation of enclosed rooms for cigarette smoking to the aesthetics of interior decorating and menu planning. Elias links the history of capitalism to the history of the senses by focusing on the marketing of a unique sensory package by Hilton, a major mid-twentieth-century player in commercial hospitality.

* * *

Taken together, the twelve chapters in this book offer us new purchase on the ways that people experienced twentieth-century capitalism through their bodies and the ways that corporeal experience has been socially, culturally, and economically constructed. If the senses are the channels through which we know and interact with the world, the work in this book shows the degree to which such knowledge and interactions are historically situated, both shaped by and shaping the circumstances of particular times and places. Since the end of the nineteenth century and the start of the twentieth century, those circumstances have increasingly involved the economic valuation of sensory response. This collection, then, focuses our attention on the unprecedented ways the logic of the market has been brought to bear on the senses and on the wide range of social actors who have sought to control the pathways connecting us to the world for commercial ends. To date, however, bringing the senses under capitalism's yoke has been difficult to achieve. These essays are representative not only of a subtle but profoundly important shift in the design and selling of consumers goods but also the obstacles in reducing the expansive poetry of the sensorium to the crude lexicon of the market.

PART I

Framing Capitalism and the Senses

CHAPTER 1

"Use Not Perfumery to Flavor Soup"

The Science of the Senses in Aesthetic Capitalism

AI HISANO

"Use not perfumery to flavor soup." So wrote Aristotle in his discussion of sense perception, quoting the comic poet Strattis, who warned against mixing perfume with lentil soup.[1] In ancient Greece, it was a common practice to add perfume, often derived from herbs and other plants, to flavor dishes.[2] Yet Aristotle, agreeing with Strattis, contended: "Those who nowadays introduce such flavors into beverages deforce our sense of pleasure by habituating us to them, until, from two distinct kinds of sensations combined, pleasure arises as it might from one simple kind."[3] Aristotle believed that mixing two different kinds of odors from food and perfume would not generate pleasant sensations. Rather, as people became accustomed to such artificially created sensory stimuli, the phenomenon would trigger what could be understood as sensory alienation.

If mixing two sensations was disagreeable to the great philosopher of ancient Greece, the practice became a crucial means for modern business to mobilize the senses in marketing.[4] Since the late nineteenth century, with the emergence of what the historical sociologist Steven Shapin has called the "aesthetic industrial complex," manufacturers, scientists, designers, and marketers in the industrialized world together created a dizzying array of products, ranging from cosmetics and toiletries to food and fashion, with different colors, shapes, smells, textures, and tastes.[5] Consumer-goods companies combined multiple sensory stimuli to complement each sense and stir consumers' sensations.

In a hypersensual world of goods, marketers now needed to determine the right color, texture, flavor, and taste for their products. This aesthetic judgement in product development was crucial as consumers would not accept, for example, ice cream with "off" flavor or "discolored" meat. It required complex processes to distinguish good enough, or acceptable, sensations from those considered "off."[6] Researchers and marketers employed diverse methodologies, including the quantification of color and the establishment of standardized lexicon for flavor characteristics, to develop a sensory threshold and keep sensory properties within an acceptable range. But the most important end result of this development was not merely a new marketing strategy. Business began reshaping how people perceived the world through their senses, creating "aesthetic capitalism"—a mode of capitalism that rested on, and was fueled by, creating and appealing to sensory and emotional experience.

I use the term "aesthetics" to refer to holistic human perception and sensations rather than simply the domain of art, beauty, or visual elements, following the original definition derived from the ancient Greek word *Aisthesis*. In this sense, I use "sensations" almost interchangeably with feelings, entailing both sensory and emotional perceptions.[7] Aesthetics is a form of knowing, or feeling-knowing, through physical and psychological stimuli.

As historical studies on the senses and emotions have demonstrated, aesthetic experiences are not given or ahistorical.[8] Aesthetic capitalism thus needs to be understood in a specific historical context, namely, industrialization, mass production, mass consumption, and scientific and technological advancement from the late nineteenth century onward. The emergence of aesthetic capitalism was complex and dynamic processes involving a wide range of agents in diverse businesses, including designers, architects, scientists, and business consultants. Its impact was also broad, reaching almost every corner of the globe. New materials, such as aluminum and plastics, and new professions like industrial designers and advertising agents were key to the creation of a new aesthetic world.[9] Walter Benjamin, for example, illustrated in his *Arcades Project* how iron transformed not only production methods and architectural design but also the entire cultural atmosphere of the city of Paris with its arcades, exhibition halls, train stations, and gas lights enabled by the new material.[10]

I analyze aesthetics not only as a design feature of consumer products but also as a social process. In this regard, the philosopher Gernot Böhme and the sociologist Andreas Reckwitz, who employ the term "aesthetic capitalism" in their respective works, provide the theorization of aesthetics in capitalist development.[11] The present chapter is in a way revisionist with regard to their formulation of aesthetic capitalism. In the following narrative, I will first situate the history of aesthetics in broader theoretical and historiographical discussions of emotion and the senses, then provide my definition of aesthetic capitalism in the form of a critique of Böhme and Reckwitz, particularly on three points: (1) periodization, (2) the role of aesthetics, and (3) social aestheticization. The last two sections of the chapter turn to the development of sensory science as one of the building blocks and driving forces of aesthetic capitalism, focusing on the mid-twentieth-century United States, which was instrumental in the development of the new science of the senses. Sensory science refashioned the aesthetic aspects of products and, more importantly, helped depersonalize consumers' experience in buying and using goods. The chapter will conclude with the implications of historical studies on capitalism and the senses. Not only can historians help illuminate how aesthetic experience changed over time but they can also bring emotions and senses back to the personal.

Emotions and Senses

In analyzing aesthetics as sensory and emotional perceptions, I draw on insights from historians of the senses and emotions. Reformulating sensations as aesthetic experiences can in turn provide an intellectual means to bridge the history of the senses and the history of emotions—two academic fields that share common grounds in terms of methodologies, analytical frameworks, and research objectives but have often been studied separately.

In their 2020 work, *Emotion, Sense, Experience*, Rob Boddice and Mark Smith, two historians who have engaged largely with the history of emotions and the history of the senses respectively, asserted the significance of analyzing emotions and the senses holistically: "[I]t may no longer be useful or justifiable to think in terms of emotions, senses and even cognition (or mind, or soul) as discrete elements of human experience, but rather to see them all as culturally contingent and dynamically connected parts of a whole."[12] For a fuller understanding of human experience in the past, the authors proposed the "re-entanglement of emotions and senses, mind and body." What is critical for this "new history of experience," according to Boddice and Smith, is a collapse of an "artificial divide" not only between emotions and senses but also between science and humanities. Calling for interdisciplinary "dialogue" between historians and neuroscientists, they argued that historians could contribute to and benefit from a new approach to emotion and sensory research that could defy biological reductionism and undergird historical contingencies.[13]

As Boddice, Smith, and others suggest (see, for example, Jan Plamper's proposed "coalition" between neuroscientists and humanities scholars), research in psychology and neuroscience could be important sources for historical studies of sensory and emotional experience.[14] In cognitive psychology and neuroscience, the dominant discourse about emotions has held that sensations are reactions created in a distinct area of the brain such as the amygdala—a group of nuclei in the brain traditionally associated with fear.[15] Over the last few decades, however, new research in these fields have provided a different understanding of brain mechanisms, maintaining that emotions are neither hardwired nor activated by certain structural elements in the brain.[16] The neuroscientist Lisa Feldman Barrett, for example, has argued that "emotions are not reactions to the world"; rather the "brain constructs meaning and prescribes action."[17] Nor are people's perception and feelings universal or inevitable constructions as a result of evolution. Emotions emerge as a combination of the physical properties of the body, the physical environment, and the broader culture. In this approach, emotion is not a system separate from cognition. While there has been no definite agreement, scientists have in the past commonly viewed cognition and emotions as separate mental phenomena.[18] In contrast, the work of Barrett and others has demonstrated brain function as complex, context-dependent, and flexible.[19] Cognition is embodied, embedded, and enacted.

A cross-disciplinary "coalition" may have a potential to help historians reframe the working of the body in aesthetic experience. As the historian Barbara Rosenwein notes, looking at fMRI scans (images created by a technology known as function magnetic resonance imaging) of emotional activity in the brain, for example, "[does not] tell us what love means." Yet electronic signals generated by nerves and muscles can still tell us something, which Rosenwein dubs "affective potential." This "potential is universal, but it manifests itself in different ways at different times in response to the conditions, assumptions, values, goals, and everything else that makes up human society and political life."[20] The historian William Reddy likewise argues that any "attempt to theorize emotions as pure discursive constructions appears doomed to failure."[21] Bodies—both physical and discursive—are agentic in their ability to shape people's experience. In other words, emotions and senses are both embodied, bodily experiences and culturally discursive practices.

The assertions by Rosenwein and Reddy also point to the importance of historicizing natural science research. Not only are bodies a historical product, but science that investigates the body is also embedded in culture. It is crucial to understand the contingency of development in scientific knowledge, including the recent rise of the so-called psychological constructionist approach proposed by Barrett and others.[22] Doing so can provide a key to analyze how and why, for example, agents of aesthetic capitalism, such as scientists, marketers, and product designers, understood consumers' bodies and perceptions, and how their scientific knowledge in turn formalized the aesthetics of products and marketing.

In this regard, the proposal by Monique Scheer, a historical and cultural anthropologist, to think of emotions as a "practice" is useful. Drawing on Pierre Bourdieu's practice theory, Scheer conceives emotions as a "practical engagement with the world." By foregrounding the body in the historical inquiry into emotions, Scheer argues that emotions are always an "embodied" experience and emerge from bodily dispositions conditioned by a social context. Emotions are, she writes, "something people experience *and* something they do. We *have* emotions and we *manifest* emotions."[23] In contrast to affect studies scholars, such as Brian Massumi, who consider "affect" entirely unconscious and physical, Scheer regards emotions as conscious and unconscious practices through the "manipulation of body and mind," and even when unconscious, they are not naturally ingrained in the body but a learned practice—hence, something people *do*.[24]

Boddice has approached the role and place of the body in the history of emotions rather differently than Scheer. Although both Boddice and Scheer view the body as a historical construction, they each place it in a different terrain. For Scheer, the body is a site and agent that represents or embodies emotions while also creating them. Boddice is more interested in materialistic and anatomical aspects of the body. Emphasizing the importance of historical contingency and cultural dynamics that shape human experience, he takes a "biocultural" approach to integrate physiological discussion of the body into cultural narratives of emotions.[25]

The work of both Scheer and Boddice is productive for studying the history of aesthetics as a material and cultural process. The materiality of creating new aesthetics, including formulating designs, employing new materials, and buying and using products, is crucial for understanding the physical impact of new aesthetics on people's bodies. At the same time, narratives that shaped aesthetic experience help analyze how and why certain aesthetics emerged in a particular time and place. As shown in the later sections, marketers and sensory scientists conducted their market and scientific research based on the Cartesian dualism separating mind and body as they built primarily on the dominant discourse in biological and neuroscience studies at the time. Emotion and sensory studies could together clarify the working of the body as a biological organism and a cultural narrative in aesthetic capitalism.

Aesthetics in the History of Capitalism

Aesthetics was born as a discourse of the body, as the cultural critic Terry Eagleton put it.[26] In his 1735 thesis, the German philosopher Alexander Gottlieb Baumgarten introduced the term "aesthetics" as a philosophical discipline, defining it as the "science of sense cognition (the theory of the fine arts, the lower doctrine of knowledge, the art of thinking beautifully, the art of the analogy of reason)."[27] Following the rationalist account of knowledge based on the dual understanding of upper and lower cognitive systems, Baumgarten contended that sensory perception had lower cognitive capability than intellectual knowledge. But he reconceptualized the relations between the sensible and the intelligible—the sensible as a crucial, if inferior, form of cognition that served for logic. Baumgarten also indicated emotional arousal as a crucial element in aesthetic experience.[28]

Although Baumgarten conceived of his theory of aesthetics primarily within the realm of beauty, his conceptualization of sense perception and emotions is insightful for analyzing aesthetics in the context of capitalist development. Beginning in the nineteenth century, social theorists and philosophers came to see change in people's aesthetic knowing of the world. Karl Marx, who, according to Eagleton, was one of the "greatest 'aestheticians' of the modern period," described the devastating impact of the capitalist system on emotional and sensory experiences.[29] Marx argued that the proletariat was stripped of sensory pleasure when exposed to the unpleasant working conditions of the modern factory, where "the artificially high temperatures" and "the deafening noise" injured "every sense organ."[30] The bourgeoisie, too, lost rich sensory experience under capitalism. Marx wrote: "The less you eat, drink and read books; the less you go to the theater, the dance hall, the public-house; the less you think, love, theorize, sing, paint, fence, etc., the more you *save*—the greater becomes your treasure which neither moths nor dust will devour—your *capital*. The less you *are*, the more you *have*; the less you express your own life, the greater is your *alienated* life."[31] What Marx suggests as aesthetic alienation differs from what Aristotle had in mind. For Aristotle, aesthetic alienation meant the loss of pleasant sensory experience as a result of artificially created sensations (like the mixture of perfume and soup). Marx saw the loss of aesthetic experience as social alienation. For him, aesthetics constituted a crucial part of one's identity and life in the capitalist system.

Marx was interested primarily in the working and consequences of industrial capitalism, emphasizing, perhaps overly, the capitalist obsession with accumulating money. However, as later scholars, some of whom built on Marx, have shown, what Marx saw as sensory alienation for capitalists was not necessarily or solely a result of capital accumulation. Rather than simply saving money, capitalists (and others—who would be later called "mass consumers") did appreciate a new aesthetic world of goods and commercial space. They immersed themselves in the visual, olfactory, and aural sensations by, for example, strolling around the city, gazing at store windows, and shopping at department stores. This was the case with the flâneur described by Charles Baudelaire and later Walter Benjamin, and new types of sensual experience detailed by the French novelist Émile Zola.

In his 1971 study, *Critique of Commodity Aesthetics*, the philosopher Wolfgang Fritz Haug explored the "new theory of culture and ideology" in modern capitalist society, and in doing so, underscored the importance of aesthetics in the consumption of goods. He saw the technological and economic system that created a new aesthetic environment as the "technocracy of sensuality." Commodity aesthetics, according to Haug, meant the new capitalist-begotten "beauty developed in the service of the realization of exchange-value, whereby commodities are designed to stimulate in the onlooker the desire to possess and the impulse to buy." Sensuality thus became "the vehicle of an economic function."[32]

For Haug, commodity aesthetics was a visual illusion, a mirage created solely for the purpose of selling commodities in capitalist society. For the selling and buying of goods, until the transaction is completed, the commodity's "promise of use-value" is the only value that matters because "something that is simply useful but does *not appear* to be so" would not sell, while "something that *seems* to be useful" would sell. Hence, to sell goods, the "appearance of use-value," or "what is the use-value appears to be," becomes of prime importance.[33] The rise of modern packaging and advertising put even more stress on the aesthetic promise of use value. Along these lines, brand names and trademarks came to convey the quality and usefulness of a particular commodity by appealing to consumers' sensuality. Consequently, the aesthetics of the commodity became detached from the object itself.

Advancing Marxist discussion of exchange value, Haug helps clarify how aesthetics became a dominant force in capitalist society. His conceptualization of commodity aesthetics and the technocracy of sensuality in particular foregrounds change in people's sensory understanding of the world. Yet his analysis focuses largely on visual elements and the quality of beauty. Besides, he envisioned the aestheticization of commodities primarily for the sake of successful transaction.

In expanding Haug and other theorists, Böhme offered a broader conceptualization of aesthetics in his *Critique of Aesthetic Capitalism* and related works. According to Böhme, aesthetic capitalism is the phase that "comes after the development of capitalism through the economic saturation of the private sphere."[34] One of its distinctive features is the importance of what he called "staging value," which is a third value independent of the Marxist concepts of use value and exchange value. At this "particular stage of development of capitalism," where basic human needs for foods, clothes, and shelter are met, capitalism enters the next phase where most commodities are no longer intended for consumption, but for the staging of one's life. Status display and lifestyle choices are part of this staging. In this interpretation, aesthetics thus becomes an essential part of the economy. According to Böhme, this shift in capitalism initially took hold in the 1950s and 1960s in the United States and Europe.[35]

I agree with Böhme's proposal for a "new aesthetics," which describes not only the appearance of things but also applies to the entire sensorial experience and the individual's understanding of surrounding environments. But I would argue that the rise of the "aesthetic economy" occurred much earlier than the 1950s and 1960s. By the late nineteenth century, aesthetic elements of goods had already become an important part of manufacturing and marketing strategies in capitalist societies.[36] The "aestheticization" of the capitalist economy was a significant part of the Second Industrial Revolution when consumer products were becoming standardized. An increasing number of Americans, for example, enjoyed domestic products like pottery and glassware embellished with elaborate patterns and colors.[37]

What Böhme calls "staging value" is certainly an important element of commodity aesthetics, as other scholars, including Thorstein Veblen and Jean Baudrillard, previously suggested.[38] However, aesthetic factors are important not just for "staging" one's lifestyle or the satisfaction of desires which, according to Böhme, comes after basic needs are met. People pursue aesthetics in their lives even in times of difficulty.[39] For example, in the United States, women did not discard their makeup during World War II, and the beauty industry proved to be resilient throughout the conflict. The United States government even declared that the production of lipstick was a wartime necessity.[40] This does not mean that all women splurged on makeup simply to beautify themselves, but rather that the government used makeup, as well as the female body, as part of its propaganda during the war. Aesthetic experience is not necessarily a luxury available only to people with economic means. As the lipstick example shows, it is also an apparatus that can empower people while simultaneously being used as a political tool.

Social Aestheticization and De-Aestheticization

Reckwitz's accounts on aesthetic capitalism shows aesthetics as a social process by employing two seemingly contradictory concepts: social aestheticization and de-aestheticization. The former involves the integration of aesthetics into political, economic, and social spheres. In aesthetic capitalism, aesthetics became important not only in the realm of art but also in a wide range of industries and institutions, including media, design, education, consultation, fashion, and architecture.[41] The other side of aesthetic capitalism, "de-aestheticization," is, according to Reckwitz, a process that caused "atrophy and inhibition" of the senses and emotions.[42] In the case of Marx, for example, capitalist forces drove sensory and social alienation, as noted above. Marx and others believed that rationalization, industrialization, and technological advancement de-aestheticized society by robbing people of rich sensory and emotional experiences.

In Reckwitz's view, until the last third of the twentieth century, aestheticization had been marginal, except for three "early forms of the later aesthetic economy": fashion, advertising, and design.[43] I would argue, however, that the emergence of aesthetic capitalism can be traced back also to other industries. Foods and automobiles, for example, played a significant role in facilitating the importance of aesthetics and transforming people's sensory and emotional experience, well before the late twentieth century.[44] As mentioned earlier, aestheticization had already been a part of industrialization in broad sectors from the late nineteenth century at least.

In addition, the pervasive force of social aestheticization should be examined not only through products and industries that were themselves sensory and emotional, such as fashion, advertising, and design, but also through products and industries for which sensory experience was a secondary characteristic. The extensive use of new materials, including plastics, nylons, and aluminums, in the late nineteenth and early twentieth centuries transformed the visual, tactile, and aural characteristics of products, as compared to those made of woods or papers. Vibrant colors, milliard shapes, and smooth texture of plastic-made products, for example, were new sensations that many consumers had never experienced before.[45] Although the primary objective of employing these new materials was not necessarily or always the creation of sensory appeals, they nonetheless altered how consumers felt in using them.

To delineate the rise of aesthetic capitalism, it is also necessary to historicize the processes of "social aestheticization" and "de-aestheticization." Reckwitz carefully discusses them as twinned processes in modernity rather than as parts of a linear shift from one to the other. But he sees the rationalization of social practice as a driver of de-aestheticization, while associating social aestheticization with the irrational. The "current economy cannot be understood in rational or cognitive terms," argues Reckwitz, because "its main processes are not rational or cognitive but, rather, sensuous and affective—processes of the aestheticization of the economy."[46]

This divide between rational and irrational, and the association of sensuous and emotional experience with irrationality, should not be considered givens since this division and this association are historical constructions. It was only in the early nineteenth century that a category of "emotions" was created, in opposition to reason, intellect, and will.[47] As Boddice argues, feelings were, and are, "not rationality's 'other' after all, but part of a relatively stable understanding of sympathy between body and mind, *ratio* and *passio*."[48] De-aestheticization was part and parcel of aesthetic capitalism—that is, there was no clear line between de-aestheticization and aestheticization but instead different forms of aestheticization.

This does not necessarily mean that historical agents viewed aesthetics as rational. In fact, aesthetic capitalism depended on a search for "rational" and "objective" knowledge and technological innovations to control what marketers believed to be "irrational" factors like sensuality and emotion. Sensory marketing in general and sensory science in particular, for example, rested on the premise that emotional and sensory factors were irrational. What is important here is to historicize, and not to assume, the understanding of aesthetics and aestheticization, situating them in a certain time and place.

Mind and Body in Sensory Marketing

The catch phrase "sensory marketing" has gained popularity among a wide range of industries over the last few decades.[49] It is a concept based on the belief in a mind-body duality. This dualism was useful and convenient for marketers in formulating business strategies. By analyzing marketers' and scientists' understanding of the human body and sensory and emotional experiences, this and the following sections examine how their research contributed to creating a new kind of aesthetic world. Here I use the term "sensory marketing" to indicate broad marketing activities, including not merely advertising and selling but also the design and development of products, to appeal to consumers' senses and emotions.

Sensory marketing scholars assert that appealing to the senses is a means to treat "customers in a more intimate and personal way than was achieved with mass and relationship marketing before."[50] The sensory marketing scholar Aradhna Krishna argues, "sensory aspects of products . . . affect our emotions, memories, perceptions, preferences, choices, and consumption of these products," and "creating new sensations or merely emphasizing or bringing attention to existing sensations can increase a product's or service's appeal."[51] In her view, multisensory experiences designed to evoke memories and emotions can provide consumers with personalized and individualized perceptions, products, and services.

The increasing interest in sensory marketing has contributed to the growing body of scholarship in the field. Be that as it may, if we step back from the vantagepoint of marketing researchers and practitioners, a broader view of sensory marketing emerges. The prime objective of sensory marketing was, and is, not necessarily the creation of personalized experience but the *de*personalization of senses and emotions. Rather than providing a unique experience for each consumer, product designers and marketers sought to create what they believed to be an ideal aesthetic feature for the mass market.

Depersonalization was necessary for controlling sensory and emotional, or what marketers considered "irrational," factors in marketing. In their 2009 book, *Sensory Marketing*, the marketing scholars Bertil Hultén, Niklas Broweus, and Marcus van Dijk proclaimed the importance of appealing to consumers' five senses and emotions for successful marketing. They wrote, the "treatment of the customer should be based on logic and rationality as well as emotions and values to create brand awareness and establish a sustainable image of a brand. This image is the result of the sensory experiences an individual has of a brand."[52] For these scholars, emotions and the senses are the polar opposites of "logic and rationality." While some neuroscientists, philosophers, and historians of the human experience have been increasingly questioning the real or perceived divide between mind and body, as well as borders between the rational and the irrational, dualism is still persistent in many fields and institutions. Business marketing is no exception. Marketers intentionally distinguish corporeal sensations from cognitive processes, reducing the senses to "passive receiving channels." This divide between "consumer mind and body" has sustained research departments and corporate practices in recent decades.[53] For example, Hultén, Broweus, and van

Dijk contended that it "is in the human brain, in both the left and right hemispheres, that the mental flows, processes, and psychological reactions take place that result in an individual's sensory experience."[54]

Criticizing marketers' conceptualization of human perception in sensory marketing, Timothy de Waal Malefyt, a business school professor trained as an anthropologist, has contended that "marketing and anthropological approaches to the senses" assume "fundamentally different concepts of agency between objects in relation to the body, mind, and senses." For anthropologists, "agency is located in social interaction and is highly contingent on context." For marketers, agency is in "the strategic deployment of brand qualities that evoke a desired response from consumers." As such, sensory marketing is not actually aimed at consumers, but it is primarily concerned with how companies strategically engage the senses "to 'perform' their products, brands, and services to consumers, in expectation of eliciting greater response from [consumers]."[55]

Echoing Malefyt, the anthropologist David Howes has asserted that the concept of the senses providing "direct links" to the brain is "fundamentally flawed." Neither marketers nor marketing scholars recognize the senses as social construction. For them, "it is all a happy matter of biology and evolution."[56] As shown by Howes and likeminded anthropologists and historians, how past actors experienced and understood the senses, and what meanings were evoked by sensations, were contingent on historical circumstances. In the case of sensory marketing, it is the marketing campaigns themselves, including the rhetoric and imagery in advertisements, that construct consumers' sensory experience and perception. Nonetheless, through the "fetishization of the asocial, ahistorical paradigms of Behaviourism and, more recently, Neuroscience," marketers naturalize sensory experience and consumers' engagement with the senses without realizing their role as mediators between the senses and the consumer.[57]

Marketers' and scientists' conscious or unconscious reliance on the mind-body duality was (and still is) apparent in a wide range of business practices. One of the prominent examples is the development of sensory science in the food industry. The next section turns to how this science of the senses helped depersonalize consumers' aesthetic experience in the mid-twentieth-century United States.

Depersonalized Aesthetics in Sensory Science

"Sensory evaluation is a child of industry," argued the sensory science professors Harry T. Lawless and Hildegarde Heymann.[58] The field of sensory science or sensory evaluation is generally defined as "a scientific discipline used to evoke, measure, analyze and interpret reactions to those characteristics of foods and materials as they are perceived by the senses of sight, smell, taste, touch and hearing."[59] The development of sensory science was contingent on the emergence of mass production and the growth of consumer-goods industries in the early to mid-twentieth century. As food scholar Jacob Lahne noted, the techniques were "biased in a way that support[ed] a particular system" of production and consumption.[60] Building on what Lahne dubs the "assumptions of homogeneity and contextual portability," I argue that standardization, decontextualization, and deskilling became crucial to the success of sensory science.[61]

Sensory scientists believed that consistency and predictability were essential to product development, whether it was a box of breakfast cereal, a cake of soap, or a bottle of perfume. Back in 1927, researchers at Arthur D. Little, Inc. (ADL), a Boston-based consulting and research firm specializing in sensory science, claimed that it would "soon be possible to specify numerical values and variation limits for the odors of commercial materials." The result would be "greater uniformity and satisfaction with such materials as preserved food, flavors, cheeses, soaps, and perfumers' goods and industrial liquids, such as gasoline, oils, denatured alcohols, and the solvents used for pyroxylin lacquers."[62] Sensory evaluation, the ADL researchers believed, would help not only standardize finished products but would also provide a universal means to investigate sensory qualities of products under development, from food to perfume to gasoline.

The establishment of formulas, recipes, and procedures for making new products was one way to standardize sensory qualities. In a project to improve the flavor of pea soup, for example, ADL scientists suggested the amount of salt should be "between 5.5 and 6 parts by weight per 100 parts of soup" to maximize the flavor. In addition, ADL researchers suggested the most effective way of mixing the soup ingredients: "It is our belief that mixing should occur in three steps" and that all "blending is best done in horizontal, spiral agitator mixers."[63] The standardization of product formulas, manufacturing procedures, and finished products helped manufacturers to make goods that were consistent, economical, and predictable. The consumer in turn learned to expect certain qualities from certain merchandise or specific brands.

Standardization delivered consistent sensory experiences. But, in reality, each consumer was an individual who might react to the same stimulus differently. Here was the great contradiction. Sensory science was supposed to offer consistent results to as many consumers as possible—or to the imaginary "average" consumer. As such, in product development, sensory science necessarily targeted the anonymous, depersonalized consumer, rather than catering to each individual's personal satisfaction.

This standardization of consumer products and consumers' sensory experience was enabled, in part, by the decontextualization of aesthetic factors. Sensory science rested on the assumption that the intrinsic qualities of products could be detached from the context in which they were consumed. In short, scientists believed that "true" stimuli existed, regardless of the consumption environment.[64] To investigate these stimuli, scientists often conducted sensory research in a laboratory where the environment was standardized. At ADL's labs, for example, the evaluation of the "fresh aroma" of coffee, the flavor of artificial cinnamon, and the taste of dog food took place in a strictly controlled environment using standardized temperatures, lighting, and fixtures.[65]

Decontextualization was inherent in the nature of sensory science research. As Howes noted, the science of sensory evaluation rested on a "fundamental paradox." Most sensory aspects of products could "only be measured well, completely, and meaningfully by human subjects." Meanwhile, human subjects were supposed to "behave as much like scientific instruments as possible."[66] Since no two persons would respond to a given sensory stimulus, such as flavor, color, and texture, in exactly the same way, there were discrepancies in data measurement among researchers. To minimize variations and errors on the part of individual researchers, it was necessary to control all testing methods and conditions, which often differed sharply from the actual situation in which the product was used or consumed. As it developed in laboratories like that of ADL, the science of the senses investigated corporeal stimuli by severing the actual consumer's body from context. By doing so, sensory science allowed for the reproduction of consistent sensory qualities and the creation of new sensations.

Recent studies have shown, however, how contexts influence the ways people feel sensually and emotionally when they use products.[67] For example, people may feel the taste of food differently in the context of eating alone at home versus eating with close friends, even when they eat the same food. Sensory science may be useful for quantifying and categorizing sensory stimuli but may not be for understanding actual consumer experiences which are contingent on various contexts.[68]

As the scientific investigation of sensory qualities developed and technologies to reproduce sensory factors advanced, decontextualization became a crucial aspect of modern consumer society filled with artificially created sensory objects and places. Such products as deodorants which had the smell of "fresh air" and the sound of "ocean waves" used as relaxation music became standardized and detached from their temporal and spatial contexts. At the same time, theme parks and restaurants like Disney World, SeaWorld, and Rainforest Cafe created entirely simulated sensory environments providing consumers with a world detached from the everyday context.

The industrial production of sensory experience in consumer goods, which was enabled by standardization and decontextualization in the laboratory, also produced a kind of "deskilling" of consumers. That is, it reduced or even eliminated the special skill or knowledge needed in, say, cooking. An apt example would be packaged cake mixes, which became popular in the late 1940s and 1950s in the United States. Sensory science, along with the development of food technology and chemistry, enabled the creation of this magical product, which required no know-how, expertise, or special ingredients. "Anyone could bake a perfect cake without fail" was a catch line that cake mix manufacturers like General Mills and Pillsbury emphasized. Because consumers did not need to add anything but an egg and water, the taste, flavor, and look of the cake was supposedly the same whoever made it—no failure, no personal taste. To personalize, or even humanize, their products, the companies stressed the importance of decorating the cake to present the baker's personality, creativity, and femininity, although they also gave her specific directions on how to decorate cakes.[69]

Other "convenient" foods such as canned goods also helped deskill consumers, thus depersonalizing aesthetic experience. Until the introduction of commercially produced canned foods in the late nineteenth century, the task of canning fruits and vegetables had been one of the American homemaker's most time-consuming chores. By the first few decades of the twentieth century, as canned foods became an everyday staple for many households in the middle and working classes, consumers could enjoy once-perishable produce, such as green peas, peaches, and pineapples, even during winter when only limited fresh fruits and vegetables were available. Flavor science added taste and color to this heavily processed produce. In a way, canned foods and cake mixes democratized aesthetic experience by providing foods of a predictable sensory quality to a broader range of consumers. But these goods also depersonalized what consumers purchased and what they created in their own kitchens. Democratization and depersonalization went hand in hand in the era of mass consumption.

Conclusion

Over the course of the past 150 years, aesthetics became a powerful and pervasive force for driving the capitalist system. By revisiting Böhme's and Reckwitz's conceptualization of aesthetic capitalism, this chapter demonstrated that the rise of aesthetic capitalism originated in the late nineteenth century in a wide range of industries, including those sectors for which sensory appeals were not explicitly the goal or function. Social aestheticization meant not merely the introduction of new design but also the transformation of ways people perceived and understood their surrounding environments.

The development and widespread acceptance of sensory science within industry, particularly the food business, epitomizes how the aesthetic-industrial complex worked under aesthetic capitalism. Beginning in the late nineteenth century, in the era of mass production and mass marketing, sensory science served as a practical, and intellectual, tool to turn what was seemingly subjective taste into "objective" knowledge and perception that can be standardized and depersonalized.

The principles of sensory science, and sensory marketing in general, rested on the long-held Western idea of mind-body duality. Marketers and scientists understood the consumer's body as a mere receptor of sensory stimuli, believing that the mind would simply react to the physical sensation. In their view, the coordination of the body and the mind was a universal given. Hence, their mission was to develop the best marketable taste, flavor, or smell that would, in turn, sell to the largest number of people. This understanding of the relationship between the mind and body also led marketers and scientists to see sensory perception and emotional factors as separate entities, both of which they saw as "irrational" elements in marketing. Sensory scientists commonly focused on one sensory feature, such as smell or taste, in their research and evaluation. The individuation of the senses in scientific research and marketing strategies not only allowed researchers to control and create a desirable sensory profile but also to quantify, commodify, and reproduce the standardized sensation.

So, should we not use perfume to flavor soup? Mixing multiple sensations has created unprecedented variations of sensory stimuli with so many colors, smells, textures, sounds, and tastes. But at the same time, commercial motivations increasingly tamed people's aesthetic sensibility by standardizing, decontextualizing, and deskilling the entire experience of buying and using goods. Consequently, consumer-goods companies constructed a new kind of aesthetics, which became the industry standard in product design and marketing—and the social norm. Certain sensations became acceptable; others, disgusting. Research consultancies like ADL helped raise sensory awareness and enhance aesthetic experience by creating new sensations, but at a cost of diminishing the personal and the local.

We may not be able to get the perfume out of the soup once the fragrance is added to the brew. But it still might be possible to identify the kind of perfume that was added to the soup, and to explain why and when, by historicizing the creation of scientific knowledge and by carefully disentangling the web of social contexts, cultural dynamics, and historical contingencies. In doing so, we can understand the aesthetic experience of historical actors through the entirety of their mind and body. Aesthetics as emotions and sensations are social, economic, and political forces, but after all they are also personal experience.

CHAPTER 2

Chasing Flavor

Sensory Science and the Economy

INGEMAR PETTERSSON

Epistemic Things and Economic Things

In 1937, the American chemists Washington Platt and Ernest C. Crocker wrote an editorial entitled "Food Flavors" in the newly established journal *Food Research*. They argued that a new type of food science was emerging. Cooking knowledge was no longer just an art for the home kitchen; it was becoming an industrial project and there was a need "for the application of science to the flavoring art in order to advance it to a higher status where it will become more exact and more generally useful."[1]

The statement signifies crucial changes in the production and consumption of foods in the twentieth century. Meals became industrial commodities, science expanded within food industries, cooking became engineering. Notably however—and this will be a main theme of this chapter—the words of Crocker and Platt illustrate a shift in the mindset of food quality assessment. "Tasting" became an act of industrial science. The area of food research Crocker and Platt wished to frame in their editorial developed rapidly after the 1930s to become an integrated part of food development. It was later referred to as "sensory analysis," "sensory evaluation," "sensory science," "flavor research," or "food sensory science."

Flavor is, as this chapter illustrates, an example of what the science historian Hans-Jörg Rheinberger calls an "epistemic thing"; an entity tangible enough to be recognized by everyone, elusive enough to avoid clear scientific definitions—"a mixture of hard and soft."[2] This chapter examines how food sensory science employed new methods and how they were elements of an expanding "experimental system," a term Rheinberger uses to describe the ranges of tools and scientific methods involved when scientists attempt to understand the nature of an epistemic thing. The experiental system of sensory science comprised sensory techniques such as evaluation panels, machines measuring texture, odor detectors, and professional flavorists.

There are a number of recent historical studies examining the intriguing methodologies involved in a "science of subjectivity."[3] This chapter is no exception. It highlights the peculiarities of a science attempting to capture the highly individual and phenomenological qualities of food flavor. But the main aim is to reveal the linkages between the work done in laboratories and industrialization at large. Because in these contexts—among corporate labs, consultants, innovators, and managers—epistemic things were capitalistic things. The sniffing and tasting of food samples, the meticulous descriptions of mouthfeel and texture, the odor chemistry—they all connected to an expanding mass market intrinsically dependent on sensory appeal.

The chapter suggests a way of interpreting the economic roles of food sensory science: economization. The concept refers to the theoretical framework associated with the French sociologist Michel Callon. Briefly explained, economization suggests that economic markets do not evolve naturally. Instead, markets are constructed, they are formed through processes that make social entities—objects, behaviors, institutions, people, etc.—"economic."[4] Economization, thus, is the process through which a complex of actors and objects evolves and forms a stable economic structure: a "market."

The overall hypothesis of this chapter is that food sensory science played a key role for the expanding food industry by stabilizing the associations between the sensory appeals of consumers and the way flavors were assembled by the producers. Specifically, the chapter argues that sensory science comprised a set of "market devices," another Callonian term. Market devices are things in economic life that aid and maintain the construction of markets. Financial analysts, consumer tests, and standardization are some examples.[5]

Combining the concepts of market devices and epistemic things, the chapter highlights practices within sensory science that were important for the expansion of the food industry in the twentieth century, such as test panels, methods for quantification and classification of sensory attributes, and technologies for distinguishing flavor compounds. This range of practices converged in the overall purpose of mastering flavor for industrial mass production. In other terms:

fetching the epistemic thing of flavor and making it an economic thing. As a concluding reflection, the chapter suggests that sensory science should have a key position in the historiography of capitalism and the senses. Sensory sciences impelled a "sentitization" through which the economy became more sensorially oriented.

The chapter deals primarily with the United States, and covers the period between the 1930s and the 1960s, a time witnessing an intense mobilization on flavor research. The main empirical source of the study is scientific literature associated with food production, particularly the United States journals *Food Research* (1936–) and *Food Technology* (1947–) but also a number of other journals, monographs, edited volumes, proceedings, and textbooks of the field. This stock of literature has been used to trace a selection of cases illustrating the economic rationales of sensory science.

One could object to this approach due to the nature of the sources. Certainly, sensory scientists were pursuing their careers through these books and papers. For instance, the chemists Crocker and Platt undertook research for the well-known international consulting firm, Arthur D. Little. It is likely that they and other people in the field exaggerated the importance of their profession. But all was not rhetoric. The procedures, methods, and tools described in these publications were in most cases applied in industry. In the end, they had implications for how the economy was arranged. Furthermore, the rhetoric gives important clues to the professional ambitions of sensory science and how it actually gained prevalence in the production of foods in the twentieth century.

Mass-Produced Quality

To understand sensory science, we must start with the nitty gritty of flavor analysis: deciding what is appealing and what is not. In the scientific vocabulary of the twentieth century, this was coined "hedonic" evaluation, but the practice is, of course, as old as humanity. We have always tasted and evaluated food somehow. But evolving economies required more stable forms of judgment. Examples of tradespeople who have long engaged in systematic hedonic assessment include the professional tasters of coffee, tea, and spices in the early modern international shipping trades, the evaluators of cheese, fruit, and vegetables at agricultural fairs in the nineteenth century, and the experts grading export butter in the era of industrialized and globalized dairy production.[6]

Platt and Crocker referred to such professional tasting as an "art" but claimed that by the mid-twentieth century, it was becoming an obsolete way of assessing food.[7] As Platt put it: "one may seriously doubt whether the opinions of the so-called experts really represent the preferences of the general public." And continued: "[i]n the end we have to fall back upon public preference as the ultimate authority."[8] An expansive food industry required, they argued, more general and systematically collected knowledge of flavors and consumers.

This shift was described by Robert K. Hower at a symposium on flavor research arranged by Arthur D. Little in the mid 1950s. Hower was in a good position to speak about sensory experience in the American food industry. He was director of research at the large United States food processer Nabisco (the National Biscuit Company). His first encounter with flavor evaluation at Nabisco was the judging procedure by the laboratory director, who fancied himself an expert on flavor. "He was the 'Laboratory Taste Panel,'" Hower recalled. "He considered his taste buds to be the keenest in the food field and, regardless of anyone else's opinion, he knew exactly which samples merited further consideration and which should be discarded." If the sample would pass the laboratory tests, it was further assessed by the executive committee, a group Hower looked on with even greater skepticism. "The executive committee was comprised of vice presidents, most of whom were heavy cigar smokers," he explained. "When they met to discuss a sample they would lay their wet cigars on a convenient ash tray and proceed to decide the acceptability of a prospective new variety." After a series of reorganizations, Nabisco adopted a more controlled way of evaluating products. They were first tested by a laboratory panel and then forwarded to a larger panel of testers at the general office. If the new product seemed promising the company would arrange a consumer survey to test it in larger scale.[9]

The critique of taste experts corresponded with a demand in industry for more organized and predictable means for measuring subjective responses. Writing for *Food Industries* in 1931, Washington Platt suggested a highly controlled procedure based on a set of principles. Judges should be selected through testing with samples of products known to be popular among consumers; they should be unaware of the origins of the food samples, what they contained and how they were prepared; they should not communicate with one another; and duplicate samples should be used for testing the reliability of judges. He recommended a group of five to ten experienced judges using a "score board" where they could place the different samples in columns. The testing room should be free from distractions and disturbing odors. Judges were to follow a certain procedure where they first judged odor and then taste, continually reporting their impressions.[10] Tasting was becoming laboratory work.

It is a common understanding that the rise of food sensory science was a product of World War II, particularly the problems with soldiers disliking food rations.[11] Experimental practices that involved senses and flavors obviously existed long before the war. There is nevertheless much truth to the assumptions about the importance of the war to the development in the field. Military food was an important factor in the formation of sensory science. One example is William Franklin Dove and his work at the United States Quartermaster Food and Container Institute for the Armed Forces in Chicago during the war. Dove was a biologist, famous for a bizarre yet serious attempt to create a unicorn by fusing the horns of a calf in the 1930s. It could seem distant from food flavors, but his work on livestock was important for his employment at the institute. Dove had studied palatability among animals and could convert that knowledge to human appreciation of food.[12] He made a larger experiment using a method from agricultural science in the early 1940s. These investigations suggested that nutrition alone was a poor measure for the actual value of foodstuffs. Flavor had to be brought into the equation: "Each food must be evaluated not by what it possesses but what it gives to the consumer."[13]

Dove brought these conclusions to the Food and Container Institute and presented them at the Sixth Annual Food Conference in Buffalo in 1946. He talked about it being "easier to dress men alike, even though they come from different regions, with different social, economic, and cultural and racial origins than it is to feed them alike." The United States military faced the same problem as the food industry: What sensory qualities appeal to a vast and diversified group of people? To solve the problem of making food rations widely appealing, taste-wise, to soldiers, Dove launched what he called "Operation Culinary." Like Crocker and Platt before him, Dove placed his project on a higher scientific level and argued that food acceptability had to be attacked from a multidisciplinary approach, by scientists engaged in "the psychology and physiology of appetite and hunger, in taste and flavor tests, in psycho-physics, in psychometrics, in organoleptics, in food habits, in food preparation, and in statistics of populations, to name a few."[14]

Dove, Platt, Crocker, and Hower exemplify some important features in the rise of food sensory sciences and how they differed from earlier assessment practices. One feature was that industrialization caused a widening gap between the consumers and the producers of food. Production was increasingly centralized, and food was distributed to areas and people little understood by manufacturers and their taste experts. Moreover, industrialization implied a change in terms of quality. Who was to judge food innovations such as Rice Krispies cereal, soft serve ice cream, and Spam canned meat? What expert could evaluate the appeal of ethyl butyrate, the synthetic ester that industrial soft drinks and candy a distinctive yet obviously artficial flavor of pineapple?[15] Flavor quality was not simply measured against a given standard in those cases. Developing such foods required grids of actors that put food scientists and engineers in contact with distant consumers and their sensorial liking. Quality became diffused and complex. One can note that Crocker and Platt cited Frederick V. Waugh's 1929 doctoral dissertation, "Quality as Determinant of Vegetable Prices," in their 1937 editorial.[16] Waugh was an agricultural economist who emphasized quality rather than price as a factor for consumer demand, a line of economic reasoning later to be known as the hedonic price model. It is an indication of a shift in the mindset around flavor. There was something beyond "good enough" and traditional standards, and food scientists were beginning to acknowledge it.

Humans as Instruments: Differences and Descriptions

In his list of disciplines, Dove mentioned psychophysics, the science of stimuli and sensations commonly traced to Gustav Fechner and his *Elemente der Psychophysik* published in 1860. As Ana María Ulloa describes in Chapter 5 of this book, psychophysics rests on the assumption that the relation between stimulus and sensation is logarithmic and thus predictable. Briefly put, at the lowest thresholds of sensation, humans will detect small increases of stimuli, but at higher levels of stimulus, the ability to sense changes diminishes at an exponential pace. There are plenty of everyday examples supporting the theoretical backbone of the theory. You will quite easily sense the difference between 0.5 percent and 1.5 percent fat in milk, but you will find it significantly more difficult to detect the difference of 39 percent and 40 percent fat in cream. The relation of objective and subjective is predictable and calculable according to Fechner's law.

Psychophysics is commonly described as a foundational discipline of sensory science.[17] It is unclear however what practical role psychophysics actually played early in the formation of the field. Platt and Crocker did not mention psychophysics in their 1937 editorial in *Food Research*, but it is evident that this disciplinary specialty became a strong tier of food sensory science after World War II. One explanation is that psychophysics was a numerical form of science. Quantitative data has a veil of objectivity that appealed to managers and food engineers. Another key for understanding the adoption of psychophysics in the postwar era was an ongoing reinterpretation of the methodological basis. As Ulloa notes, a "new psychophysics" emerged in the mid-twentieth century. It allowed for numerical estimation based on sensory evaluation. Hence, a sensory panel that was describing, for instance, different concentrations of preservatives or thickening agents could form the basis for psychophysical calculation. Descriptions of flavor became seemingly more deductive and generalizable by adding psychophysics.

Another characteristic of the mid-twentieth-century boom of sensory science was an emphasis on *differences*, which was a central concept for psychophysics. The interest in differences was not new to food sensory science. Platt had recommended duplicate samples in his early work.[18] And according to Rose-Marie Pangborn, one of the most distinguished sensory scientists of the postwar era, the methodological distinction between differences and preferences was introduced by Florence King at the Bureau of Home Economics at the United States Department of Agriculture (USDA) in the 1930s.[19] However, it was not until the 1940s that the breakthrough for more elaborate forms of difference tests on food came about. Dove was a part of this crucial development through his ideas of a "difference-preference" test, which prescribed that all evaluations should first establish what samples the panel could differentiate. When that was established, accurate hedonic evaluation could commence.[20]

One reason for the interest in differences was that food scientists realized that consumers often lacked capabilities to distinguish the flavors of different brands. For instance, two psychologists at the University of Wichita in Wichita, Kansas, made an experiment in the late 1940s in which 168 college students were served four samples of cola drinks for blind testing. Surprisingly, the results showed that few of the subjects could successfully distinguish between Coca-Cola, Pepsi Cola, Royal Crown Cola, and Vess Cola.[21] This research on differences had obvious economic implications. Why bother to make flavor adjustments that are too subtle for the average human sensorium? And who is the average taster, and who is not? Based on such thoughts, a range of models for difference testing was introduced from the 1940s onward: the "triangle test" developed at the Wallerstein Laboratories in New York; the "duo-trio test" and the "dual standard" invented at the Joseph E. Seagram Laboratory; and the "A—not A" developed at Brown University by the psychologist Carl Pfaffmann among others.[22]

The plethora of procedures for difference testing illustrates a growing interest in human sensory perception in food science, not only in terms of the consumers and their palates, but also regarding the capabilities of the professional tasters in industry. The tasters were controlled, surveyed, and trained to become makeshift laboratory instruments.[23] Ernest E. Lockhart, sensory scientist at the Coffee Brewing Institute in New York, pictured the laboratory taster as half man, half machine. Sensory analysts became "experts through rigorous training and in essence form a machine that can be adjusted and calibrated; their precision and reliability can be measured and defined in the same manner and terms that apply to a machine; parts, if not functioning or proven defective, can be replaced; new models can be exchanged for old."[24]

Yet, differences, thresholds, and numbers give little essential knowledge of flavor. To be meaningful and applicable in industry, flavor science needs descriptions and precise terminology. The problem was hardly new to sensory scientists. For instance, Crocker and his colleague Lloyd F. Henderson of Arthur D. Little presented the "Crocker-Henderson system" for classification of odors as early as the 1920s. The system transformed ideas from the Dutch physiologist Hendrik Zwaardemaker and the German psychologist Hans Henning into a code system based on the principle that there are four primary odors: "fragrance," "acidity," "burntness," and "caprylic" (or "goaty"-ness). All smells are composed of different concentrations of the primary odors and are possible to detect sensorially and describe quantitatively through four digits, Crocker and Henderson argued. According to the logics of the system, the scent of rose was 6423, ethyl alcohol 5414, and camphor 5735.[25]

A related, yet more successful, attempt to describe sensory attributes systematically was developed at Arthur D. Little in the 1940s. It was called the Flavor Profile Method. The main inventors, Loren B. Sjöström and Stanley E. Cairncross, argued that flavor evaluation could be taken to a higher level: "The need has been felt for a more objective method of judging products which does not depend upon personal preference."[26] The new method presented by Sjöström and Cairncross was "descriptive" and aimed to yield "a tabular record of the intensity of the detectable character notes of a product in the order of their appearance, including taste, aroma, and feeling." An important novelty of the profile method was its lingual standardization. Panelists were trained to identify "character notes" through a standardized set of references such as "sweet," "metallic-bitter," or "tongue-coating." The "character notes" could also connect to a chemical compound; for instance, the reference for "horsy" was Phenylacetic acid.[27] The profile method, hence, was a standardized procedure that generated "certain generalizations about flavor" to be used in assessment and product design.[28] It was successful. Numerous food companies consulted Arthur D. Little to solve flavor problems using the Flavor Profile Method. Today, it is still a cornerstone of food engineering.[29]

The difference tests, the psychophysics, and the descriptive methods provide keys for understanding the forms of market devices embedded in sensory science. These techniques provided food R&D with quantitative data and precise terminology that supposedly made it easier to innovate, asses, manufacture, and modify food products. Moreover, they had implications for the human body and how it was used commercially. An obvious and essential part of sensory science has been concerned with controlling the human sensorium, a need to "form a machine" as Lockhart from the Coffee Brewing Institute phrased it. Although the objectives were purely scientific in some aspects, the whole enterprise of food sensory evaluation was about developing predictable evaluaters and profitable goods. The methods economized the senses of the sniffing and tasting personnel of the food industries.

Flavor Without Organs: The Gas Chromatographer

Back in the early 1930s, R. B. Dustman, chemist at the Department of Agricultural Chemistry at West Virginia University in Morgantown, West Virginia, made a series of experiments on walnuts. The aim was to find out how different types of storage affected the quality of the nuts. The experiments were based on "organoleptic" valuation where panels tasted and smelled different samples. After the second year, Dustman started to question the results of his experiments. The outcome was far from coherent. Identical samples were often given different ratings, even by the same panelists. Troubled by these inconsistencies, Dustman decided to change his methodology and introduced the so-called Kreis test. This purely chemical test, developed in the early 1900s, measured the level of oxidation in fatty oils by adding hydrochloric acid and phloroglucinol. The reaction was displayed through different colors indicating the level of deterioration in the oils. Dustman correlated the results of the Kreis test with evaluations by a smaller group of panelists.[30]

Clearly, this was an experiment gone wrong. When the organoleptic method did not deliver congruent data, Dustman simply reduced the number of tasters and introduced a purely chemical method. Dustman's trust in the purely chemical means of analysis shows a common thread in the history of food flavor science. When the results are unstable, flavor scientists often retreat to methods free from human sensory reception.

Moreover, Dustman's use of the Kreis test illustrates the privilege of the eye. Ironically, the Kreis test had recently been criticized for not giving stable results, primarily because the reading of different colors was too subjective.[31] Nevertheless, the eye was still the superior sense in the laboratory. In sensory science as in modern science overall, vision implied objectivity whereas smell, hearing, taste, and touch were seen as being subjective. Consequently, food sensory science has been marked by attempts to translate taste and smell into visual representations. The Kreis test is an example of such a method, but the most important technique came after World War II in form of gas chromatography. Chromatography, basically a separation technique, goes back to the Russian botanist Mikhail Tsvet and his work on plant pigments in the early twentieth century. The technique was developed and refined by two British scientists, the chemist Archer Martin and the biochemist Richard Synge, in the 1940s and 1950s, for which they received the Nobel Prize in Chemistry in 1952. Gas-liquid chromatography is a form of vaporization that can identify very small amounts of volatile compounds.[32]

Volatiles are essential for food scientists—they are the chemical compounds we smell—and the introduction of gas chromatography provided flavor scientists with a range of possibilities. There were previous techniques, however. Early attempts to create instruments for detecting odor were made in the late nineteenth century in the Netherlands with Hendrik Zwaardemaker's "Olfactometer," and in the 1910s by V. C. Alison and S. H. Katz at the United States Bureau of Mines with their "Odorimeter" designed to measure odors in mining and industrial processes. Another example from outside the field of food science is the 1930s invention of the "Odor observer and odor meter" (later to be called the "Osmoscope") by the sanitary engineers Gordon M. Fair and William Firth Wells. These instruments used the principle of odor dilution, that the concentration of the compound that carries smell is reduced to a level where it will not chock the olfactory receptors.[33] An artificial smelling device working without human sensory perception was the "Stinkometer" invented in the 1940s by Lionel Farber, biochemist at the Fisheries Research Laboratory at the Hooper Foundation, a disease and hygiene research unit at the University of California, San Francisco. The device was, as Farber's affiliation should hint, used to detect strong odors in fish. Technically, it worked by letting air flow through a solution of alkaline permanganate that changes color depending on the concentration of volatiles.[34]

Gas chromatography was a much more refined technique, and it was adopted quickly by food scientists. A path-breaking flavor experiment was published in *Food Technology* in 1956 by K. P. Dimick and J. Corse. Dimick had previously attempted to isolate flavor compounds in strawberries through distillation but was not impressed by the results. The experiments required large amounts of strawberries but produced very little knowledge on flavor. When the examination was repeated with gas chromatography the machine revealed thirty individual volatile compounds in strawberries. Dimick and Corse saw great possibilities and concluded that "the development of gas chromatography opens the door to the flavor chemist to problems which were heretofore essentially unsolvable."[35]

The gas chromatographer initiated a scramble among food scientists to publish analyses of the flavor of foodstuffs. Many seem to have originated out of pure curiosity, driven to ask: What is the chemical explanation to this specific flavor? Gas chromatography was a powerful tool for answering that question. It produced data in the form of curves with peaks identifying the different compounds. The graphs produced by gas chromatography were called chromatograms and flavor scientists soon started to name the graphs of foodstuff "aromagrams."[36]

Gas chromatography was also a new way of tracing off-flavors, hence creating the possibility to produce more appealing and lucrative foods. For example, a study made by dairy chemist Stuart Patton at the Pennsylvania Agricultural Experiment Station, a research arm of the Pennsylvania State University in Harrisburg, Pennsylvania, gave new hope for the possibility of preserving milk with ionizing radiation. Tests with gas chromatography indicated that the "malty" off-flavor found in irradiated milk was caused by high concentrations of methyl sulfide and acetaldehyde.[37] With such knowledge at hand, food engineers could make precise flavor adjustments.

Yet, the gas chromatographer was a machine, and the data lacked the richness and sensuous refinement of organoleptic methods. Loren B. Sjöström, the inventor of the Flavor Profile Method, was skeptical about the aromagrams. He claimed that while a competent human organoleptic tester could distinguish juice from celery stalks versus celery tops, the gas chromatographer could not. The device failed to interpret the layers and complexes of compounds that constitute flavor. Therefore, he argued, "objective" methods must be paired with "subjective" techniques.[38] Mechanically informed knowledge should correlate with human sensory knowledge.

An important step to bridge man and machine was taken in the 1960s by George H. Fuller, Robert J. Steltenkamp, and G. A. Tisserand of the Colgate-Palmolive company, a large American manufacturer of household chemicals and personal care products. In a 1964 paper, they presented the results of an experiment with a professional flavorist, or "perfumer," using gas chromatography to enhance organoleptic testing. The team built what they called "the bird cage," an odor-safe booth in which the perfumer sat down and smelled the vapors from the exit port of the chromatographer. The notes of the perfumer were then compared with the chromatographic data, allowing the scientists to conclude which chemical compounds that were "true" odors and at how low concentrations compounds were detectable by human olfaction.[39] The apparatus was the first prototype of the technique later to be called gas chromatography-olfactometry.[40]

These machines tell us important things about food sensory science and capitalism. They are indicative of a form of industrialization of science, showing that laboratory work became automatized just like industrial labor did. Gas chromatography appealed to the food industry because it allowed corporate engineers to easily distinguish and envision odor compounds. It made possible the rapid analysis of how different processes produced certain compositions of volatiles. But one thing was certain. Gas chromatography had obvious shortcomings for industries that were first and foremost interested in consumer appeal. Flavor, in the industrial mindset, was holistic and escaped the attempts to reduce it to one or few components. Writing on food science methodology, Loren B. Sjöström summed things up nicely when he wrote that "food aromas are not due to one or two compounds, but are an integrated response to a larger number of compounds."[41] Machines could not deal with the complexity of flavor. But as we shall see in the next section, there was a way to grasp holistic features mechanically: constructing instruments imitating human physiology.

Defining Gooeyness: Texture and Biomimicry

Texture is a key constituent in flavor and a range of tools were developed in the early days of the food industry to measure the physical qualities of products. Some were rather simple constructions, like the Magness pressure tester presented in 1925, a hand tool for measuring ripeness of fruit, and the "pressometer" for juiciness of meat, developed at the Minnesota Agricultural Research Station at the University of Minnesota in the 1930s.[42] A 1938 article in *Food Technology* marks a shift in the understanding of food texture and how it can be measured. It was written by Nikolaus N. Volodkevich at the Institute of Refrigeration at University of Karlsruhe in Germany and showcased an apparatus "for measurements of chewing resistance or tenderness of foodstuffs." The machine had an ability missing from earlier instruments. Volodkevich's device imitated the human mouth and its interactions with food, reproducing the "real chewing resistance of foodstuffs."[43]

The German chewing machine was constructed with two metal wedges, or sometimes artificial teeth, that formed a mechanical jaw. It produced graphs showing the amount of pressure required for the jaw to bite through the meat. Allegedly, these curves gave food scientists valuable data of how eating requires different amounts of pressure in the sequence when the material is chewed. Volodkevich argued that the machine added new knowledge about why some meats are more tender than others. Veal, he argued, was perceived as more tender than beef due to less remaining fibrous tissue when someone bites into the meat.[44]

Volodkevich's conclusion could seem simple, but the significance of his machine was not about the results per se. Rather, it was about the avenues of thought it materialized and brought forth—the very idea that objectivity of flavor could be obtained by copying the human sensory physiology. The German apparatus became an important inspiration for the Strain Gage Denture Tenderometer, developed in the 1950s at the Department of Food Technology at the Massachusetts Institute of Technology (MIT). The machine was constructed by the food scientist Aaron L. Brody as part of his doctoral thesis. Brody's instrument was a striking imitation of the human jaw, with pink gums and a grinning set of dentures (Figure 2.1). To achieve a realistic chewing process, the machine was sometimes equipped with plastic lips. When the machine was started, an electric motor moved the dentures in a physiologically authentic way and took a bite of the food sample. The jaw was attached to electronical gauges registering strain and an oscilloscope targeted by a camera. In this way the instrument produced photographs with signatures of masticatory qualities of food, giving food scientists "objective" data on texture.[45]

Brody's agenda was clearly to make impressions of texture commensurable with industrial logics. The machine "simulated the human system for commercial purposes by averaging the human masticating mechanism, standardizing its nervous system, and then applying a many-brain interpretation to the data obtained." Accordingly, Brody fed the Tenderometer with a range of typical American industrial foods: canned peas and corn from Green Giant, chewing gum by Dentyne, frozen shrimp, and two New England favorites: jelly beans made by Necco in Boston and ice cream from H. P. Hood, a well-known regional dairy.[46]

The idea of an electronic tool mimicking the human jaw was refined by the MIT-trained Polish-American food scientist Alina S. Szczesniak in the 1960s. Szczesniak started working at the General Foods Corporation Research Community in Hoboken, New Jersey, after receiving her doctorate from MIT's Department of Food Technology in 1952. At General Foods, Szczesniak engaged in bakery research focusing on texture. One particular issue was cake mixes with dried egg white. While evaluating different test bakes, she thought that it had to be a better way than using a "trained finger" to measure the tenderness of

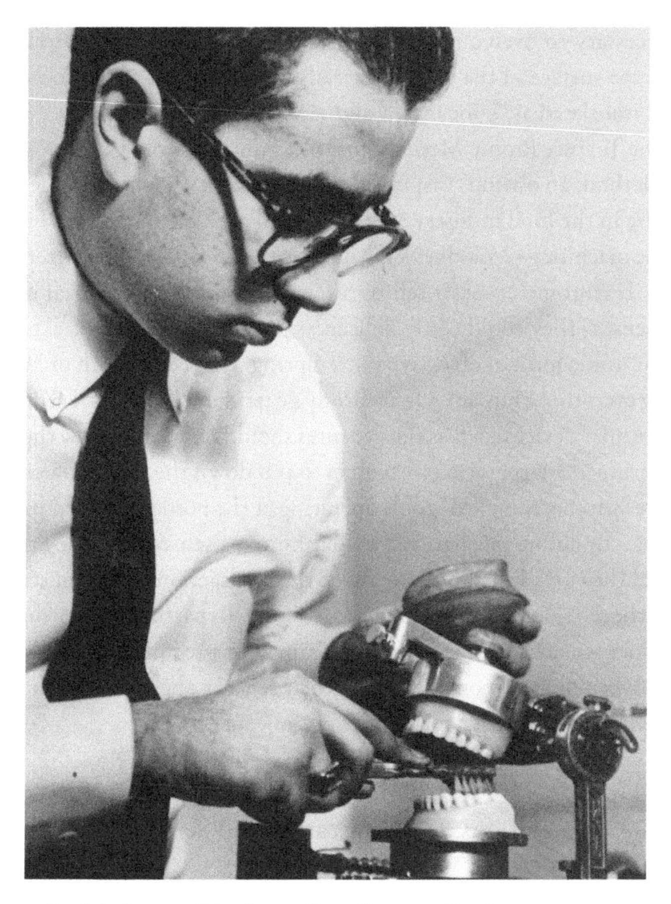

Figure 2.1. Brody's design of the Strain Gage Denture Tenderometer gave it a striking humanoid look. It attracted public attention and the Tenderometer appeared in a 1956 issue of *Life* with pictures showing the instrument eating mozzarella cheese. The image above was taken at MIT, assumedly after an experiment. Courtesy of The MIT Museum, Cambridge, Massachusetts.

the cakes.[47] From observations like that, Szczesniak developed a quantitative methodology and an instrument for texture measurement. Her machine, the "Texturometer," lacked the eye-catching appearance of its predecessor, the device by Brody at MIT, but was based on careful studies of human mastication. Most importantly, Szczesniak developed a system of functions that associated mechanical measurements with popular texture qualities using easily understandable vernacular terms. For instance, what the Texturometer registered as work "necessary to overcome the attractive forces between the surface of the food and the surface of the other materials with which the food comes in contact" was translated as "gooeyness," and vice versa. Using such data, Szczesniak created the Texture Profile Method. Just like Sjöström's and Cairncross's Flavor Profile Method, an obvious inspiration, Szczesniak's system was aimed at commercial use in the food industry, where it is still used regularly.[48]

These machines—Volodkevich's apparatus, Brody's Tenderometer, and Szczesniak's Texturometer—can tell us a few things about industrial capitalism and the senses. They could easily be seen as products of epistemic extremism, a somewhat ironic form of objectivity attempting to discover truth of humans by removing everything human. Or, in Brody's case, some sort of scientific theater. But spectacular devices such as the dentures should not overshadow the fact that these instruments were serious attempts to pin down the nature of food flavor. They were "psychoreological" tools operating at the border between psychology and physics to define mechanically what humans sense when they masticate. Therefore, they give valuable clues about the transactions between sensory science and the development of mass-produced food. In particular, they suggest that food sensory science was translational. It aimed to streamline industry's gathering of knowledge about consumers and their sensory appeals through networks of mechanical instruments, formulas, and concepts.[49]

Conclusions: Economization and Sensitization

All the techniques and methods described above formed a system. Platt's scoreboard, the "bird cage," Brody's Tenderometer, the Crocker-Henderson system, the Osmoscope: they were all related. Although many of the engineers and scientists were distant from one another, perhaps even in conflict, they were united in the same pursuit of making flavor a scientific matter. This endeavor tells us important things about how capitalism was intertwined with the senses in the era of industrialization. Economic advances required different forms of predictability, and sensory science played a significant role in that transition. For food to become industrial commodities their sensory qualities had to be subordinated to market rationalities. It became imperative for visual characteristics, smell, and taste to have a certain level of coherence and standardization.[50] Food sensory science responded to those market demands. It emerged as a node associating the palates of consumers, industrial food R&D, and the sensory attributes of the foodstuffs in an economic network.

What is important, though, is that sensory scientists did not simply react to economic change. They actively reconstructed capitalism by inventing techniques that were scientific devices and market devices simultanuously. This chapter has highlighted a handful of those mechanisms: the ways in which rigorous hedonic testing facilitated new terms of quality when markets expanded; how psychophysics and difference tests defined the sensory capabilities of the average consumer; the numerical methods that made standardization possible; and how elaborate nomenclature mediated knowledge between the realms of food engineering, organoleptic expertise, and the consumers. By doing these things, food sensory science played an important part of capitalism in the era of mass production. In Callonian terms, sensory sciences economized the senses by making them legible for consumer capitalism.

But the historical contribution of sensory science is not only about the "market" as an abstract form of economic life. The development of sensory science had material and corporeal dimensions too. It is, in many ways, a history of expanding joyfulness and sensory bliss. Imagine, for instance, how chemicals such as vanillin, monosodium glutamate (MSG), and esters have added new dimensions to the world of flavors over the course of industrialization. Think of the perfect blandness of a cold filtered lager on a hot day, the refreshing coolness of minty chewing gum, or the gooey crunchiness of cheese-covered nachos. Regardless of how sensory impressions in industrial societies are normatively understood, the second wave of industrialization witnessed a sensory boost, an expansion of the flavor registers of food. Sensory science contributed to all this. So by way of conclusion, let us consider the ways in which sensory sciences affected how commodities were designed, produced, and consumed.

"Hyperesthesia" is sometimes used in sensory studies for describing how bodily appeal was at the heart of consumer capitalism. David Howes speaks of how capitalism "works by generating spectacle and creating consumer desires of all sorts in all people."[51] Hyperesthetization certainly describes the context in which sensory sciences emerged. But what concept can describe the specific roles of sensory scientists and their methods in this change? One way is to talk about "sensitization," a behaviorist term originally meant to describe how biological organisms amplify sensory reactions by responding to certain stimuli. Sensitization is strongly associated with biologist and Nobel Laureate Eric Kandel and his experiments on the giant marine snail Aplysia in the 1960s. Interested in the neurological processes of learning, Kandel examined the gill withdrawal reflex of the snail. He found that repeated tactile stimuli of the siphon did not, as one could expect, result in weaker responses. Instead, the responses of the snail's gills became increasingly intense. Furthermore, the responses were memorized neurologically, as new synaptic connections. The effect was called sensitization.[52]

Obviously, sensitization is not a theory of the human senses in history. It is an analogy, a way of describing and understanding food flavor science and its developments. Sentitization, as a historiographical term, highlights the process through which consumers and producers gained more refined sensibilities to the tastes, tactile qualities, sounds, smells, and looks of industrial goods. The push toward stronger interest in flavor was, by a logic similar to Kandel's theory, reinforced through a dynamic interplay between producers and consumers, reciprocally refining their sensibilities of good flavor. In this analogy, sensory science tickled the collective palate of the economy and made it more responsive to flavor.

The concept of sensitization allows us to acknowledge the historical agency of sensory science and how it shaped the way that food was produced, sold, and consumed. This chapter provides an array of examples of how sensory techniques contributed to an economy in which goods were meticulously designed to please.[53] The pressure testers helping apple farmers pick their fruit at the perfect stage of maturity; the texturometers giving food engineers mechanical definitions of crisp and crunch; gas chromatography providing roasters with knowledge of the volatiles in appealing coffee; and the Stinkometer deodorizing fish markets from the smell of putrid cod—they all indicate that the second wave of industrialization was the era of intense sensory appeal. Flavors mattered increasingly, and sensory scientists contributed to this change not only by developing tools and methods but also by convincing industry that flavor equals benefit.

Thus, food sensory scientists should have a key place in the historiography of the senses and capitalism for their two-fold contribution as economizers of the senses and sensitizisers of the economy. Indeed, scientists and engineers associated with the food industry formed a movement that successfully introduced and expanded the idea that food manufacturers had to adjust the flavors of their products in close contact with the appeals and senses of the consumer. Back in 1937, Washington Platt and Ernest C. Crocker stressed the salience of sensory knowledge for food producers: "attention to flavor becomes increasingly important."[54] And in the same issue of *Food Research*, Bernard H. Smith of the Virginia Dare Extract Company talked about a "modern trend" in food production characterized by "a well-defined effort to produce better flavors, since the public is more flavor conscious now than formerly."[55] In contexts long overlooked by scholars of economic change, we find powerful early testimonies of the sentisizing capitalist economy.

CHAPTER 3

Richer Sounds

Capitalism, Musical Instruments, and the Cold War Sonic Divide

SVEN KUBE

Pop culture constituted a major battleground for the Cold War power struggle between West and East. In both form and content, cultural production in the two hemispheres reflected different social, political, and economic realities; and in popular music, the primary medium of postwar youth culture, this bipolar competition was characterized by a major imbalance in power and influence. While Eastern bloc states never succeeded in creating uniquely communist styles that resonated with their people, North American and Western European countries cultivated the creative and commercial evolution of pop music. This process extended beyond broadening lyrical themes, molding music genres, and launching star performers. Frequent technological advances and consistent economic growth strengthened the material infrastructure for composing, performing, and recording music across the West. Throughout the Cold War era, artists from capitalist countries set the standards for sonic excitement with mass appeal. Western rock, pop, and dance music sounded distinct to listeners on the other side of the Iron Curtain, particularly in comparison with homegrown equivalents. Delayed arrival and permanent scarcity of the latest musical instruments, which were products of decentralized innovation, free competition, and international trade, deepened the divide. Particularly in East Germany, where foreign radio and records enabled millions of listeners to draw comparisons between West and East on a daily basis, this contrast shaped the creation and reception of popular music. Usually the first among bloc dwellers to encounter new styles, East German artists and fans equated Western popular sounds with prosperity, modernity, and liberty.

American and British musical genres gained enormous momentum in Cold War competition as capitalist record industries underwent a long boom period. By the 1970s, recording businesses claimed the largest revenue shares in Western commercial entertainment. With a $2 billion income in 1973, American record labels distanced professional sports ($540 million) and comfortably outperformed Hollywood ($1.3 billion).[1] Adding to record sales the profits from ticket sales and stereo equipment retail, popular music-related businesses earned $7.4 billion in the United States and the equivalent of more than a billion dollars in both Great Britain and West Germany.[2] In these leading marketplaces, record sales generally doubled between the mid-1970s and mid-1980s.[3] Consequently, the West's music industries wielded far more commercial and cultural power than Eastern bloc counterparts. While tens of thousands of new releases arrived in Western stores every year, pop music fans in Eastern Europe could choose from a selection of hundreds at best. Particularly in East Germany, where some 85 percent of people had access to foreign radio stations, this asymmetry led fans who yearned for novelty and variety to turn their heads westward.[4] According to state-commissioned studies, listening and dancing to music represented the favorite leisure activities of East German youths, 88 percent of whom preferred "rock music" (an umbrella term that covered the full range of late-1970s styles from disco to heavy metal), and in the absence of distinctly communist alternatives, fans came to equate popular music with innovation from beyond the Iron Curtain.[5]

The sonic properties of musical instruments underpinned the appeal of music from the capitalist sphere. Unable to grasp this aspect of modern pop music, communist elites striving to define characteristics of acceptable songs routinely focused on lyrical content. Screening committees checked the verses of native artists for objectionable messages prior to approving recording sessions and granting concert permits, and translators scrutinized all lyrics before a foreign release could be imported to circulate commercially.[6] Post–Cold War studies like that of anthropologist Alexei Yurchak, however, have emphasized that to young fans "the literal meaning of these songs was irrelevant. What was important was their Western origin, foreign sound, and unknown references." According to Yurchak, Soviet Russian youths of the 1970s embraced echo, distortion, and other common effects in the period's progressive rock, which they heard as expressions of a futuristic sensibility perfectly in line with communist narratives of space-age progress.[7] More rebellious peers showed a similar fascination for the sonically unknown. "The first time I ever heard punk music, I was listening to a Western station's broadcast of the Sex Pistols on a pocket-sized AM transistor radio," recalled music journalist Steffen Könau, then a nonconformist teenager in the East German city of Halle. "But the bad quality didn't matter. There wasn't even need for decent volume to perceive the loudness of those guitars. From what was coming out of that tiny one-Watt device, I could tell that something literally unheard-of was happening."[8] As rapid electrification, and ultimately digitalization, in music production unlocked a broad swath of possibilities for making noise, Western artists increasingly relied on new instruments and equipment to fascinate audiences. Psychedelic, progressive, and punk rock in particular excited listeners by subverting established sonic aesthetics. "We had no clue what the [Sex] Pistols were singing, but their razor-sharp guitars said it all. What we did know was: if something like this was possible 'over there' [in the West], then that's where we wanted to be," added Könau.[9] To listeners of his generation, audio signals from capitalist countries overseas, much like visual depictions in foreign print media and on Western television, confirmed perceptions of greater freedom and more individualism on the other side.

Exposed to noises unlike any they knew, East Germans heard the *sound* of popular music from the West as an aural marker of originality, modernity, and liberty. While domestic artists could emulate structural elements of American and British music, like rhythm, melody, and harmony, with relative ease, they faced more intricate challenges in adopting Western sound. Since the advent of rock and roll, foreign performers who played on their own equipment when performing in East German venues enjoyed what musicologist Michael Rauhut has called the "unconditional bonus of authenticity" for their ability to meet the "sonic expectations" that audiences had come to form.[10] "It was really not that their musical craftsmanship was superior," recalled Ole Krüger, who was a rock fan and amateur musician in the 1970s. "But they had the instruments, effect devices, and amplifiers to offer sonic variations that were far ahead of ours. Their sound was more powerful and versatile. They could embed vocals in instrumental backdrops that had so much more color, depth, and detail."[11] Many music fans associated the West's expanded sonic palette with better conditions for cultural production in capitalism. Perceptions of sophistication in noise resonated with impressions of high living standards in West German visual media, where depictions of prosperity in everyday life abounded. "The Western sound was just more proof that those living in the capitalist sphere were better off," said Steffen Könau. "At the time, the anti-capitalist stances of punk bands were kinda lost on us. They lived 'over there;' so from where we stood, they were free and rich. They could look and sound any way they wanted. They could even smash their guitars at the end of a show if they felt like it—and then just buy new ones. Unbelievable!"[12] The material situation of Westerners, including those who opposed ideals of capitalist consumption, appeared as a remarkable advantage to bloc youths with musical aspirations.

Throughout the Cold War era, musical instruments ranked among the most sought-after commodities in communist countries. Even in East Germany, one of the materially better equipped Soviet satellites, musicians faced permanent scarcity. This situation originated from state policies that diminished technological and economic competition in sectors like leisure. After World War II, Soviet administrators and East German elites replaced market mechanisms with central-planning coordination to balance supply and demand. The architects of this new economy prioritized heavy industries, leading to continual shortages of domestically produced consumer goods by the 1960s and a reliance on imports from capitalist nations from the 1970s onward. In the realm of entertainment, this trajectory had far-reaching consequences. Goods that Eastern bloc manufacturers could not produce remained largely absent from the commercial sphere, circulating only in limited numbers as state-organized imports or trading at astronomical prices in black markets. The deeper communist countries sank into this cycle, the less they could satisfy demands for nonessential items. Falling out of step with international developments in technology, particularly electronics, East Germany began slipping into a vortex of foreign debt to buy licenses and facilities for core industries by the mid-1970s.[13] To relieve pent-up demand in the realm of entertainment, the state operated a facility on the outskirts of Berlin where technologists reverse engineered imported prototypes of component parts for the state's television network, radio stations, and record industry.[14] The lab, however, did not come close to meeting the technological needs of commercial entertainment sectors. As the government focused on keeping conveyer belts moving and truck wheels turning, musical instruments and recording equipment never approached the top of its priority list.

The permanent problem of instrument shortages created a sonic development gap between West and East. Throughout the Cold War, Eastern bloc countries failed to shut out new genres and, for fear of losing the loyalty of younger generations, tended to find justifications for why they should occupy niches in communist music life. The scarcity of instruments from the West prevented domestic musicians from swiftly naturalizing styles from capitalist countries, a circumstance that limited their appeal to native fans. Particularly in East

Germany, where audiences could constantly compare foreign and domestic offerings, music makers had to improvise and experiment in attempts to reproduce pop's latest sounds. When Beatlemania inspired thousands of teenagers to form rock groups in the early 1960s, a vast majority of those youths had to build their own instruments—converting lutes into acoustic guitars or assembling drum kits from buckets.[15] Yearning to replicate the trendy sounds of Hammond organs in the early 1970s, rock performers waved cardboard panels in front of speakers to imitate the pulsating vibrato effect of Leslie pedals.[16] By the early 1980s, domestic talent needed more sophisticated measures to keep up. "Getting wah-wah pedals that added effects to the sounds of guitars was near impossible," remembered Ole Krüger. But makeshift wiring schemes with component parts enabled tinkerers to construct their own. "In our world," Krüger chuckled, "you had to be a virtuoso with the soldering iron before you could become one with the guitar."[17] The audible consequence was a phase shift in sound aesthetics between West and East. Musical trends from the United States, Great Britain, and other Western European countries inevitably rippled eastward, but the speed at which they reshaped the sound of pop songs in communist countries depended on the pace at which capitalist equipment proliferated.

The most significant instruments to define the sound of Western styles were electric guitars, which evolved for a long time under capitalist conditions. Originally played by African American performers of jazz and blues, these instruments expanded the spectrum of tones and timbres a guitar could generate and enabled players to match the loudness of ensembles and orchestras. Further, as they added a gripping lead voice to musical tracks and encouraged idiosyncratic playing styles, they fueled the rise of solos as the ultimate individualistic statement in Western rock. More than any other instrument, electric guitars accelerated Americans' musical quest for new frontiers beyond the confines of inherited European traditions. Fittingly, these instruments emerged in the Progressive Era, when rapidly commodified scientific inventions opened new business opportunities in the cultural sphere. Innovation particularly in the United States' expanding electrical infrastructure and communication networks inspired countless attempts at generating previously unheard sounds. Component parts that had been developed by telephone manufacturers to transmit the sound of human speech drove early experiments with electric string instruments.[18] During the interwar period, the American market witnessed a race for the most advanced approach to capture and convert the vibrations of steel strings. The first "commercially sold practical" electric guitar originated from a joint venture between inventor-musician George Beauchamp and engineer-businessman Adolph

Rickenbacker.[19] Their 1932 Electro model, which used phonograph-inspired pickups to capture electromagnetic signals directly from the strings, heralded the era of amplified guitar noise that revolutionized Western popular music. Throughout the 1930s, tinkerers and technologists filed hundreds of patents that pertained to electric guitars while entrepreneurs flocked to invest in Gibson, Epiphone, and other early industry leaders. In the postwar years, American and European teenagers, particularly in Great Britain, encountered electric string noise on the jazz and blues records of American troops.[20] Fascinated by unknown sounds that had never been heard in the "Old World's" classical and folkloric music, they embraced electric guitars as modern youth culture's quintessential instrument.

As growing teenage affluence and accelerated circulation of leisure goods in the capitalist sphere connected transatlantic music scenes, electric guitars remade the sound of popular music. During the 1950s, which the United States experienced as a "golden age of capitalism," economic and technological competition made these instruments increasingly affordable and widely available. Particularly influential were the creations of Leo Fender, the owner of a radio repair shop who moonlighted as an inventor. Thanks to its stripped-back mechanics and practical design, Fender's 1950 Telecaster model became the first mass-purchased electric guitar and inspired droves of young talent to venture into pop music.[21] His follow-up, the 1954 Stratocaster, instantly struck a chord with early rock 'n' rollers. Easy to hold and play, with handy tone controls and a vibrato lever, the "Strat" had an edgy and twangy output that pioneers from Buddy Holly to Jimi Hendrix established as one of rock's signature sonic markers. When Great Britain lifted import restrictions on leisure goods such as music equipment in 1959, American electric guitars produced a wave of excitement among musicians and fans.[22] Taking the edge off rock 'n' roll's rowdiness, The Beatles and their peers preferred hollow-body electric guitars that firms like Gibson and Rickenbacker had perfected in the mid-1950s, as these instruments' warmer, gentler, and jangly sound complemented their harmony-centered songs. Meanwhile, after the erection of the Berlin Wall, Eastern European adolescents were finding it harder to stay attuned to Western music, but when they did hear it, they perceived the "unexpected sound" of beat music combos as emblematic of the capitalist sphere's cultural excitements.[23] Eventually, the Eastern bloc witnessed a "British Invasion" that introduced young listeners to noises native talent struggled to reproduce.

During the second half of the Cold War, electric guitars catalyzed the diversification of rock through sound and design. In a period of political turmoil after Watergate and economic downturn in the wake of the 1973 oil crisis, rock music grew angry. As idiosyncratic "guitar gods" worked the strings at furious speeds, specific models came to embody the aural and visual aggressiveness of hard rock and heavy metal, inspiring devoted fans to rely on their heroes' equipment in efforts to acquire technical skills. With its arrow-shaped body, sparkling steel frets, and strings so high above the neck that players needed substantial physical strength to hold them down, Gibson's Flying V became heavy metal's consensus instrument. As genre founders from Black Sabbath and Judas Priest to Scorpions adopted "the V" for its vigorous tone, amateurs hoped to succeed by purchasing the same model. "That guitar held out the promise that you, too, could accomplish what you admired. It was like buying oneself into a club, belonging by way of ownership to a circle of players," recalled Scorpions lead guitarist Michael Schenker.[24] Demand for these instruments prompted American firms including Dean and Jackson as well as Japanese competitors like Ibanez and ESP to launch V models of their own, stimulating market growth by lowering entry-level prices. Gibson, meanwhile, enlisted celebrity players like Schenker and Dave Mustaine of the band Megadeth to pick their preferred hardware setups and choose design finishes for signature models that were marketed as status symbols. Parallel to popular music's commercialization and diversification in the final Cold War decades, guitars became commodities that expressed distinct cultural preferences and lifestyle choices.

Severe lack of technological and economic competition in corresponding markets impeded stylistic innovation through sonic novelty in communist locales like East Germany. Pursuing international recognition as the self-proclaimed preserver of the German nation's classical heritage, the state funded manufacturers of traditional instruments like pianos and violins, but afforded itself only a handful of enterprises that made tools for popular performers. "The Politbüro stipulated production capacities across the entire economy," explained pop record producer Volkmar Andrä, "and rock music had absolutely no priority in their designs."[25] Acoustic guitars were so rare that most children could only practice in schools, and obtaining a professionally built electric guitar was far more difficult. An admirer of Cliff Richard's band The Shadows, music producer Klaus Peter Albrecht had to become an autodidactic instrument maker in the mid-1960s to approximate their sound. "We took a photo showing the top view of a Fender Telecaster, projected the slide against the wall, made a scale drawing, and then we cut out the board and looked for parts to reverse-engineer the electromechanical components." Using magnets from the closing mechanisms of cupboard doors as cores for coils, and spending many hours tightly wrapping delicate wire around them, the band members even built their own pickups. "It was all trial-and-error," Albrecht reminisced, "but we simply didn't have any other shot at sounding like our heroes" (Figure 3.1 and Figure 3.2).[26] Meanwhile, the Musima manufacture, which crafted most of the models that made occasional store appearances, had no resources for development and resorted to copying Western innovation. Musima's Elektra de Luxe from the early 1970s, for instance, was an imitation of Fender's legendary 1950s Stratocaster.[27] By and large, East German-made electric guitars were scarce but also of inferior quality, such as having clunky necks with edgy tie bars and tending to detune quickly.[28] "It was super frustrating to face this development gap," said amateur band member Ole Krüger. "We admired iconic players like Mike Oldfield and Mark Knopfler for how they attuned their techniques to the guitars they used in order to create their very own brand of sound, and at the same time we knew that we'd never have the opportunity to take a page out of their books."[29] This problem pertained to supplemental equipment as well. The absence of distortion devices and a constant shortage in amplification technology represented permanent grievances for ambitious rock musicians.[30] Without adequate technological infrastructure, aspiring talent had no practical means to innovate and, as the evolution of guitars and genres in the West intensified, increasingly struggled to even emulate.

As players scrambled to get their hands on imported models, the national rock circuit stratified into a two-tier system. While a state-supported and well-connected elite with access to import goods was able to acquire instruments from capitalist countries and adopt Western sounds, a broad base of artists had to make do with scarce domestic supplies of inferior quality. After the Berlin Wall went up, a black market flourished through which professional bootleggers and holders of diplomatic passports sold equipment to aspiring musicians at staggering prices.[31] A more problematic trend set in during the 1970s, when authorities permitted successful groups to perform in capitalist countries and earn hard currencies for the state. Not only did privileged artists take every opportunity to procure up-to-date instruments for themselves, which opened up an internal sonic gap between loyalists with travel permits and commoners who remained grounded, but some high-profile representatives of the former accumulated fortunes from reselling their private imports to the latter.[32] This officially tolerated gray market increased the availability of guitars and amplifiers overall, but it also spawned a sonic arms race that let prices for imported instruments explode. "The only way to approximate the sound of [progressive rock bands] Yes or Genesis was to gain access to their kind of equipment," remembered Ole Krüger. "If you knew where to go, you could buy pretty much anything, even a brand-new Gibson—but such a guitar would trade for 10,000 marks. Mortals, like

Figure 3.1. Klaus Peter Albrecht reverse-engineered a Fender Telecaster electric guitar from catalog images in the late 1960s. He played the instrument for several years, performing songs by The Shadows and other British bands with his group EC Combo. Private photograph, 1969. Courtesy of Klaus Peter Albrecht, Berlin, Germany.

apprentices and students, didn't have that kind of money."[33] Yet as bad as this situation was, it may have been worse in other bloc countries. Because of their close proximity to the capitalist enclave of West Berlin, East German artists stood better odds at staying connected to international sonic trends than their peers further east. The famous Polish band Czerwone Gitary chose its name, The Red Guitars, not in reference to communism but rather in homage to the only guitar model then available from Warsaw stores, a Czechoslovakian import that happened to come in bright red.[34]

Figure 3.2. As a fan of American Western and country music in East Germany, Klaus Peter Albrecht had to become an instrument builder to have appropriate equipment at his disposal. In the early 1980s, he constructed his own pedal steel guitars from scratch. One model, assembled from more than 170 individual parts, is on display at the Berlin Musical Instrument Museum. Private photograph, 2020. Courtesy of Klaus Peter Albrecht, Berlin, Germany.

In the late 1970s, stylistic innovation began to shift from rock stages to dance clubs. Decentralized technological development, free enterprise, and international trade underpinned dancing music's expanding sonic palette. In American metropolises like New York, Chicago, and Detroit, clubs and parties drew multiracial and multiethnic crowds that embraced diverse influences. Disk jockeys, meanwhile, circulated meticulously crafted mixtapes, commissioned their own vinyl pressings, and infused chart hits with complex beats generated by drum machines.[35] Originally designed for keyboard players and bands lacking a complete rhythm section, drum machines aspired to imitate the sound of a live drummer, but falling short of their original purpose, they opened avenues for sonic experimentation.[36] The breakthrough device, Roland TR-808, originated in the workshop of Ikutaro Kakehashi, a Japanese music aficionado and inventor-entrepreneur who had launched his first business at age sixteen. Realizing that the market for standard keyboard instruments left start-ups like his little space to flourish next to Yamaha, Kawai, and other giants, Kakehashi sensed growth potential in the niche for supplemental equipment. At a time when Japanese companies expanded their shares in international markets for automobiles and home electronics, he founded the Roland Corporation to make rhythm devices that helped organists keep time.[37] Some models included programmable microprocessors, and more than that, the TR-808 from 1980 synthesized drum sounds in real time instead of playing previously sampled patterns. Sourcing parts under the dictate of cost efficiency, Kakehashi obtained from transistor manufacturers defective units that had been disposed for the flaw of producing a sizzle noise and incorporated them in his constructions. The resulting unit's output resembled drumbeats but also had a sterile, simplistic, and synthetic sheen that sounded flashy and futuristic to contemporary music makers.[38] While the apparatus failed to impress organists, it unexpectedly changed the sonic aesthetics of dance music, hip hop, and eventually mainstream pop.

Roland's TR-808 began its rise to influence in the dance subcultures of American metropolises. Disk jockeys like Kool Herc and Afrika Bambaataa released club tracks that introduced dance floor crowds to its curious noises. Tinkerers like New York's Beastie Boys expanded its range of applications, for instance by reversing its output and using backward-played beats as backdrop for their raps. Pioneers of Detroit Techno and Miami Bass adopted it as a signature instrument to distinguish their instrumental tracks from the output of other regional scenes.[39] Soon, its unique sounds crossed from the musical periphery over into the mainstream. Contrasting warm and soulful vocals with its coolly percolating rhythms, Marvin Gaye's iconic 1982 single "Sexual Healing" became first in a long series of top hits that credited the TR-808.[40] Even professional drummers like Phil Collins of the band Genesis, who used it as the centerpiece in the instrumentation of "One More Night," "In the Air Tonight," and other early hit singles, embraced the machine. Chart toppers of the past three decades, from the American boy group New Kids on the Block to contemporary star performer Kanye West, have substantiated the TR-808's sonic relevance in popular music.[41] By empowering amateurs, elevating subcultures, and energizing the musical mainstream, drum machines like Roland's epitomized the close links between technological inventiveness and cultural innovation in the capitalist hemisphere.[42]

A success story like the TR-808's was most improbable in a country like East Germany, where centralized cultural policymaking eliminated room for subcultural experimentation. Drum machine beats remained permanently absent from domestic music because neither the recording nor broadcasting sectors had sufficient hard-currency budgets to stay on the heels of capitalist industries. Officially, the sonic lag signaled resistance. "Addiction to technological innovation for the ultimate purpose of pursuing profits, a common feature of capitalist countries, is alien to us," summarized veteran sound engineer Klaus Siebholz of the unity party's stance.[43] Fans and artists, by contrast, shared a vivid attraction to novelty in noise. "Regardless of genre, Western artists had at their disposal sonic canvases that no-one [in the Eastern bloc] could dream of," recalled music journalist Steffen Könau. "Dedicated fans like us were unable to tell what instruments the likes of Queen collected and how they used them. Once the Westerners had moved beyond the basic rock setup of drums, bass, and guitars, many of the things they did became mysterious to us" (Figure 3.3).[44]

For East German music professionals, meanwhile, tackling those conundrums became an aspect of daily work. Volkmar Andrä, who produced albums by the country's rock avant-garde after the mid-1970s, frequently encountered challenges in reconstructing cutting-edge noise. "It was the ultimate test for our engineers to figure out how Westerners had created their distinct soundscapes," he reminisced. Andrä recalled an episode from the sessions with Klaus Renft Combo, an iconic group on the East German rock circuit. Fascinated by the very deep tone in the final minute of Simon & Garfunkel's 1970 album cut "The Boxer," Renft requested that same kind of bass layer. "We tried so many things, like playing deep notes on a trombone and then rolling that tape at half-speed—but we simply couldn't decode how they'd done that drone. Later on, we learned that they'd used an early Moog synthesizer, but at the time none of us had ever heard of that machine."[45] His former colleague Klaus Peter Albrecht found himself in a similar dilemma when producing a 1980 cover hits album with East

Figure 3.3. An adolescent in the late 1970s, Steffen Könau teamed up with his grandfather, a carpenter, to build his first acoustic guitar. Freehand-drawn, made from heavy wood, and with somewhat arbitrarily placed frets, the four-string model enabled young Könau to jam along with recordings by his beloved Sex Pistols. Private photograph, 2022. Courtesy of Steffen Könau, Halle/Saale, Germany.

Germany's heartthrob singer Frank Schöbel, who wanted to include the Beach Boys' "Good Vibrations." The 1966 original, which had cost the Californians a large five-digit dollar sum to record, features the high-pitched vibrato of an Electro-Theremin, an instrument that listeners may have recognized from science-fiction film soundtracks of the period.[46] "We pursued several routes, like bringing in a cellist to let him play staccatos that we'd then filter over and over. But it was a tough lock to pick," recalled Albrecht. "Getting that sound right was too hard without electric instruments, which we simply didn't have at our disposal."[47] The aesthetic gap between West and East widened when capitalist music production embraced electronic instrumentation and moved toward digitally contoured soundscapes.

No other devices shaped popular music of the 1980s in more audibly distinct ways than keyboard synthesizers. Instruments that generated sounds with the aid of electric current had been in development for decades, but became influential only when the American engineer Robert Moog pioneered his portable and user-friendly prototypes in the mid-1960s. With the aid of voltage-controlled oscillators to regulate pitch and an assortment of filters, Moog's analogue models emitted warm synthetic noise that expanded the tonal palette.[48] Inspired by the success of his 1970 Minimoog, other companies like ARP in the United States and Electronic Music Studios in Great Britain began catering to growing demand in capitalist markets. Simultaneously, a transatlantic avant-garde of electronic musicians that featured American composer Walter/Wendy Carlos, the West German group Kraftwerk, and France's Jean Michel Jarre pursued sonic experimentation with an emphasis on popular appeal.[49] By the early 1980s, the comparatively organic output of analogue synthesizers gave way to the rather artificial noises of digital models. As incessant innovation in microelectronics and data processing heralded the computer age in North America and Western Europe, artists and audiences began to equate digital aesthetics with sonic modernity. Young and tech-savvy bands like Orchestral Manoeuvres in the Dark, Depeche Mode, and Soft Cell made Britain the world's epicenter of mass-appealing "synth pop."[50] Continental European audiences, meanwhile, appreciated digitally enhanced dance music genres like sultry Italo Disco and Teutonically thumping Techno Pop. In North America, digital keyboard synthesizers reshaped mainstream pop music when star performers like Madonna and Michael Jackson adopted their crisp and crystalline sound.[51] Across the West, the digitalization of popular music unfolded at a rapid pace.

The synthesizer that epitomized the Cold War era's ultimate sound gap developed as a joint venture between an American private university and one of

Japan's leading businesses. Stanford professor John Chowning, a trained musician and mathematical physicist, invented a computerized process to frequency modulation that generated output signals with a stable pitch analogue apparatuses could not provide.[52] Chowning's breakthrough caught the attention of the Yamaha Corporation, which intended to introduce the first affordable digital instruments. In 1974, the company bought the license from Stanford and recruited Chowning's team to accelerate its development of easy-to-operate devices. By the early 1980s, Yamaha hardware came to represent the gold standard in electronic instrumentation. The success of the American-Japanese endeavor rewarded Stanford with its second-most profitable patent (behind the Google search engine) and cemented Yamaha's position as undisputed leader in the world market for keyboard synthesizers.[53] Combining compact design with affordable pricing, the 1983 model DX7 became the first to sell in the hundreds of thousands.[54] While its programming still required significant expertise, the unit boasted a wide range of preset modulations that enabled players to sculpt the distinct sound of the period's synthesizer-driven and radio-friendly chart pop. Artists from across the Western hemisphere instantly embraced the DX7 for its shiny, spikey, and stringent signals. In the years that followed its introduction, the machine featured in "West End Girls" by the British pop duo Pet Shop Boys, "Take On Me" by the Norwegian act a-ha, "Fresh" by the American disco group Kool & The Gang, and a multitude of other international super hits.[55] The first mass-produced musical instrument of the digital era, Yamaha's keyboard synthesizer redefined the sound of Western pop songs during the final Cold War years.

As they became mass commodities in capitalist countries, demand for these new instruments eclipsed supply behind the Berlin Wall. East German musicians wanting to adopt the latest sounds of their Western role models during the 1970s could only resort to makeshift solutions, such as using the amplified one-tone noises of telecommunication signal generators to substitute for early synth noise.[56] Then, in the 1980s, the United States led Western countries in embargoes against exports of microelectronic components to Eastern bloc countries. This move curtailed the ability of the East German government to compensate for the shortage of domestic know-how with imported devices.[57] Its inability to develop digital technologies widened the West-East divide, as the case of the Vermona synthesizer underscored. Technologically inspired by the 1970 Minimoog but arriving at the same time as Yamaha's digital DX7, the monophonic and analogue Vermona went on sale in 1983 as the only commercially available item of its kind. Despite its steep price of 4,350 marks, the equivalent of half of an average worker's yearly income, the Vermona remained notoriously hard to find in stores since most units were exported to the Soviet Union.[58] East German musicians dismissed the boxy apparatus as hopelessly outdated, but the only domestic alternatives were even less sophisticated units assembled by hobbyist engineers. Supporting do-it-yourself approaches to help people navigate scarcity, magazines for the technically skilled published circuit diagrams and guidelines on "How to Build a Musical Synthesizer."[59] "I received offers from tinkerers who sold self-made devices that had a one-tone output but still cost horrendous sums," remembered record producer Klaus Peter Albrecht.[60] Competitive synths never materialized in the Eastern bloc for as long as the Iron Curtain remained in place.

The explosive impact of digital synthesizers amplified musicians' dependency on Western equipment and expanded the class divide within East Germany's music scene. Only established artists with state support and travel permits found means to stay loosely connected to international trends in sound, most commonly by performing abroad and spending their salaries in equipment stores prior to retuning. In 1982, Puhdys, the country's most commercially successful group, recorded an album titled *Computer-Karriere* (*Computer Career*) that showcased the "novel, computerized keyboards" that band members had procured on trips abroad.[61] Karat, runners-up in the hierarchy of super groups, put similar equipment on display on their concurrent release *Der Blaue Planet* (*The Blue Planet*). Boasting unmatched production values by domestic standards, the title track featured synthetic bass patterns of an American-made ARP Odyssey synth, flute-like adornments courtesy of a Japanese Korg Micro Preset M500-SP unit, and artificial harmonies supplied by the String Performer of Hohner, a West German instrument manufacturer.[62] With such resources, elite performers retained their advantage over native competition and increased their chances of appealing to audiences in capitalist countries. But established artists had another economic motive for showing off Western technology. As quasi-monopolists, the owners of modern equipment could loan their prized possessions to newcomers. "Facing a domestic audience with Westernized sonic expectations in this environment of scarcity, aspiring talent needed such instruments to make a splash," said producer Volkmar Andrä. "So it became common practice for them to rent the synths for studio sessions from those who were lucky enough to have them."[63] The ironic consequence was the emergence of a capitalistic cycle enabling the private owners of production means to accumulate money and power under the conditions of East Germany's "actually existing socialism." Only artists who enjoyed access to hard currencies or commanded extraordinary budgets in domestic funds were able to acquire equipment with which they could bridge the sonic gap between West and East. Imported synths made by Moog, Roland, Korg, and

Yamaha traded for sums of up to 16,000 marks, the equivalent of twice an average worker's annual salary.[64] Consequently, the vast majority of amateur musicians stood no realistic chance of ever touching such keyboards. These circumstances rendered sonic experimentation at the grassroots level, which had been the engine of Western musical innovation since the days of rock and roll, unfeasible.

To the ears of Eastern bloc music fans, Western pop music sounded different. Across decades and genres, the production values of songs from the capitalist sphere were audible markers of progress and prosperity. Profiting from competition-driven technological innovation, dynamic markets that commodified inventions, and largely unregulated space for cultural expression, artists from capitalist countries served as sonic trendsetters on either side of the Iron Curtain. Operating in the tension field between the illiberal policies of state architects and the unrealistic expectations of listening audiences, East German talent resorted to emulating Western styles early on. Yet the scarcity of advanced instruments and, by consequence, the limited palette of available musical noises rendered their offerings sonically tame and dated. Even the most privileged domestic performers had no access to production techniques to rival their role models. By the time Eastern groups had naturalized the sound of The Beatles and their fellow British invaders, Western artists with fully electrified equipment were exploring the adventurous soundscapes of psychedelic, progressive, and hard rock. And just as bloc musicians had managed to go electric, players of digital instruments on the other side were already revolutionizing the sound of pop once again. In a period when sonic characteristics tended to determine the appeal of popular songs at least to the same extent as lyrics and melodies, the aesthetic divide between West and East deepened. From the rowdy twang of Fender's electric guitars to the cool chirp of Yamaha's digital synthesizers, Eastern bloc dwellers understood that novel and exciting sounds came from instruments that originated in the capitalist sphere. Years after the sensation of reunification, as East Germans began looking back with a sense of nostalgia, the rather sedate and oftentimes improvised pop songs of their Cold War decades gained appreciation as sonic artifacts from a bygone world.

[illegible] reached five times of [illegible] the equivalent of [illegible] average working woman's salary.[illegible] Consequently, the vast majority of [illegible] [illegible] the chance of ever [illegible] [illegible]. These [illegible] [illegible] Western [illegible] [illegible] [illegible]ssible.

In the case of [illegible] blog [illegible] [illegible] values were [illegible] markers of progress and prosperity. [illegible] competition-driven technological innovation, dynamic markets that connect[illegible] [illegible] and larger, [illegible] [illegible]

[illegible]

[illegible] British [illegible] Western [illegible]

[illegible]

PART II

Resisting Rationalization

CHAPTER 4

Altered States and Gustatory Taste

The Sensory Synergies of Whiskey Marketing in the Mid-Twentieth-Century United States

LISA JACOBSON

Capitalism thrives simultaneously on novelty and predictability. It produces novel goods and experiences to create new wants and desires, but it also seeks reassuring predictability to guarantee demand for its output. These dynamics explain why business has invested so heavily in managing sensory perceptions since the late nineteenth century. Tapping the expertise of flavor scientists, color specialists, and sound designers, business developed new technologies and techniques to stimulate and standardize consumers' sensory perceptions. Despite its army of sensory engineers, however, business never achieved full control of sensory perceptions. Even as entire industries endeavored to "create alternate realities and new worlds of sight, taste, sound, smell, and tactility," Ai Hisano has written, "the senses proved more challenging to control than manufacturing processes."[1]

This chapter explores this conundrum, among several others. Why did consumers' tastes and sensory perceptions resist standardization? How do goods with psychoactive properties, such as alcoholic beverages, complicate the process of standardizing tastes and perceptions? How do social and cultural factors—factors that businesses might bend to their favor or struggle to undercut—influence the construction of sensory knowledge? Rather than viewing knowledge creation as a top-down process guided by flavor engineers and color specialists, my chapter examines how ordinary consumers, motivational researchers, and advertisers created, translated, and spread knowledge about the senses.[2] This process takes on particularly fascinating contours when the commodities in question—in this case, alcoholic beverages—have intoxicating effects. While many activities, including eating and drinking, engage multiple senses, the psychoactive properties of alcohol add yet another dimension to such multisensory experiences. Under alcohol's influence, consumers process sensory inputs and their surroundings in ways that can be both pleasurable and painful, predictable and unpredictable, socially beneficial and socially disruptive.

In the mid-twentieth-century United States, consumers and purveyors of alcoholic beverages developed a language that further muddied the boundaries between the senses. As market researchers and advertisers came to understand, when consumers (usually men) expressed a preference for mild, smooth, and light whiskey, they were not just describing taste. They were also describing the type of intoxicating experience they preferred—one that enabled those men to manage the demands of liquor-fueled sociability and business networking and still meet their workplace obligations the next day. In learning how to sell alcoholic beverages, mid-century market researchers and advertisers became ever more inventive in the ways they blended messages about the pleasures of gustatory taste with more covert messages about the pleasures of altered states.

To analyze how consumers, market researchers, and advertisers created, disseminated, and sometimes deliberately muddied knowledge about the senses, I examined dozens of marketing research studies for whiskey firms between the late 1940s and the early 1960s completed under the auspices of Ernest Dichter, one of the pioneers of motivational research. Dichter and his team at the Institute for Motivational Research, a consulting firm with offices in Croton-on-Hudson, just forty miles north of midtown Manhattan, included passages from the in-depth interviews they conducted with consumers in their client reports. These detailed reports provide a fascinating glimpse into the ways Dichter and his subjects thought about the senses and the boundaries between them. Dichter's reports sought to explain a central paradox revealed in the interviews: even though mid-century American consumers often failed to distinguish between brands in taste tests, they nevertheless relied heavily on the language of gustatory taste to describe their preferences. Such inconsistencies convinced Dichter that consumers were merely parroting advertising claims when they praised whiskeys that were mild, smooth, and light. Yet, the vague language of taste and flavor retained some utility within particular communities of drinkers who used alcoholic beverages to make statements about their class and racial respectability, their masculine fortitude, and their sophistication or lack of pretension. Dichter's motivational research studies revealed that past experiences and historical memories of deceptive industry practices also conditioned consumers' expectations of flavor and influenced what consumers actually tasted when they ate and drank. The construction of knowledge about the senses was thus a multifaceted process—one that relied on consumers' sensory memories, the exchange of knowledge and alcohol folklore within particular taste communities, and market researchers' expert translations of consumers' sensory perceptions into marketable messages. This process went beyond creating knowledge about the physiology of the senses; it also entailed creating identities and knowledge about the self.

Ernest Dichter and Memory's Role in the Creation of Sensory Knowledge

When Ernest Dichter launched the Institute for Motivational Research in 1946, he offered clients a service few other market researchers then performed: a deep probe of the consumer psyche that promised to uncover the real but often hidden reasons that determined consumers' likes and dislikes. Dichter's qualitative assessments of consumer behavior departed significantly from the statistics-driven studies that had dominated market research in the 1930s and 1940s. Leading market researchers and pollsters such as A. C. Nielsen, George Gallup, and Elmo Roper conducted surveys to determine the products shoppers purchased, the brands and styles they preferred, and the frequency of their purchases. Sorted by occupation and income and sometimes by gender and region, such data gave firms a better sense of their target audience but little insight into why consumers preferred some brands to others.[3] By identifying the unconscious motives overlooked by traditional market research, Dichter promised to help firms target consumers with unmatched psychological precision. Companies who wanted to redeem unpopular brands or elevate their brand in a product category marked by little real differentiation came to view motivational research as the "magic bullet" that would give them a competitive advantage.[4]

By temperament and professional training, Dichter was especially well equipped to interpret the irrational behavior, social anxieties, and unconscious drives that shaped consumers' desires. Growing up poor in early twentieth-century Vienna, Dichter developed something of an inferiority complex from his outsider status as both a Jew and a redheaded boy. "This deep-rooted, lifelong insecurity," historian Lawrence Samuel astutely observes, "afforded him a special ability to see it in others." As a teenager, Dichter became aware of consumer culture's seductive power when he worked as a window decorator in his uncle's Viennese department store. Years later, he mastered the theoretical frameworks at the University of Vienna that would help him penetrate consumer psyches. There he studied Freudian theory and became a star pupil of psychologist Paul Lazarsfeld, an early practitioner of motivational research. After earning his doctorate in psychology in 1934, Dichter left Vienna to escape the Nazis and took a job in Paris selling fake labels from expensive clothes that buyers sewed into cheap garments—an experience that yielded valuable insights for his future career in motivational research. "Dichter could not have received a better education," Samuel surmises, "in how the perceived value of a product was more important than its quality—an idea he, perhaps more than anyone else, would bring to American business."[5] The clients Dichter acquired after he immigrated to the United States in 1938 would only enhance his appreciation of the symbolic power of goods.

North American distillers began seeking Dichter's services in the late 1940s, when, for the first time in nearly a decade, consumer demand for whiskey, especially blended whiskey, began to fall. As the economy's reconversion to a civilian footing gathered steam, discretionary spending on small luxuries took a back seat to purchases of homes, second cars, and appliances. Whiskey still claimed about 80 percent of the distilled spirits market in the United States and still outranked both wine and beer in popularity and prestige, but the easy-selling days of wartime had clearly passed.[6] Consumer surveys delivered other, potentially ominous news. A 1953 survey of 7,167 adults, including men and women of varied races, incomes, and occupations, found that 55 percent disliked the taste of hard liquors (other than the relatively tasteless vodka). The survey also warned that consumers who disliked the taste of liquor had a penchant for "switching rapidly from one drink to another."[7]

North American whiskey reinforced Dichter's conviction that a commodity's perceived value outweighed objective measures of its quality. Dichter's whiskey studies found that many consumers imagined themselves to be a good judge of whiskey quality, but the vast majority—75 percent by Dichter's estimation in a 1951 study—did not fully understand the terms they used to characterize whiskey quality and lacked sufficient knowledge to select or reject a brand on that basis.[8] A twenty-eight-year-old taxi driver, for example, admitted not knowing enough about whiskey to explain what "proof means" (the measure of a whiskey's alcohol content), but he did "know that proof means it's a better type of whiskey than the ordinary type that is just cooked."[9] More than half of the respondents who identified themselves as well-informed bourbon drinkers could not accurately define proof. Some associated the term with strength, others with mildness—evidence, in Dichter's view, that drinkers assigned the quality they most valued to their favorite drink, "regardless of whether, in reality, the drink possesses that quality."[10] In another study, Dichter's respondents clearly understood that the process of aging mellowed whiskey but only 15 percent knew how many years their favored brand had been aged.[11] Although whiskey aficionados could judge quality with considerably more sophistication than novices, Dichter observed a consistent pattern in the way *all* whiskey drinkers talked about and assessed quality. No matter their degree of whiskey knowledge, consumers unfailingly identified taste, smoothness, and the "absence of after effects" (in that order) as the most important attributes of quality whiskey. Instead of viewing such criteria as evidence of consumers' discernment, Dichter concluded that respondents were simply echoing oft-repeated advertising claims.[12] New York City liquor dealers similarly portrayed whiskey buyers as an undiscerning lot, noting that shoppers selected the most widely advertised brands (Calvert, Schenley, and Four Roses) and rarely spontaneously requested brands not backed by big advertising budgets.[13]

Dichter and New York City's liquor dealers had a point. Advertising's power of repeated suggestion undoubtedly bolstered sales of highly advertised brands, and advertising's repeated emphasis on taste, smoothness, and freedom from hangovers undoubtedly influenced how consumers talked about whiskey. Other considerations, however, also shaped the remarkably uniform (and sometimes uninformed) ways consumers thought about quality. For one, the bland uniformity of many blended whiskies, which mixed aged whiskey with neutral grain spirits, militated against the development of a discerning whiskey palette. Composed of 75 percent to 85 percent neutral grain spirits, blended whiskies got most of their flavor from the aged whiskey that filled the remainder of the bottle. Liquor dealers readily admitted that they, like their customers, thought all blended whiskies tasted the same.[14] In addition, Americans could likely pinpoint better what they disliked in a whiskey than what they liked. Even drinkers of straight bourbon, who often prided themselves on their sophisticated palates, could more easily characterize the qualities a good bourbon lacked. One such drinker explained that he liked bourbon's "pleasant" aroma because it didn't "smell like gasoline or medicine" or taste "too sharp."[15]

Consumers' reliance on negative taste descriptors to explain their whiskey preferences underscored postwar distillers' limited ability to shape consumers' sensory knowledge and manage their sensory perceptions. By 1949 and 1950, when Dichter conducted his first round of whiskey motivational research studies, many American consumers had accumulated considerable experience drinking bad whiskey, thanks to the limited stocks of aged whiskey after the repeal of Prohibition in 1933 and the deteriorating quality of whiskey during World War II. Dichter's respondents were rarely at a loss for adjectives to describe the harsh-tasting, throat-burning, and headache-inducing brands they avoided. When consumers prioritized taste, smoothness, and the absence of aftereffects, they implicitly highlighted the very qualities bad whiskies were most sorely missing. Simply put, drinkers assessed whiskey more by what it lacked and how it made them feel than by any pleasing flavor characteristics.

One way out for distillers was to downplay gustatory taste and highlight the other pleasing sensations whiskey could deliver. When some distillers attempted to educate consumers how to discern the difference between a good whiskey and a mediocre one, they implicitly taught drinkers more about the sensations that whiskey produced rather than its distinctive flavor characteristics. Seeking to boost its market share in 1953, the Kentucky distiller who made Calvert blended whiskey invited consumers to conduct their own comparisons using Calvert's Taste Test Kit. The kit arrived in a small cardboard box, just big enough to hold a short guidebook, two shot glasses (one marked A, the other marked B), and four cards certifying anyone who took the sixty-second blind "showdown" taste test as a "fully accredited Whiskey Expert." After the buildup of writing away for the kit and then waiting for the delivery, it would be easy to imagine the consumer disappointment that set in after reading the guidelines for judging whiskey. The instructions merely advised the taster "to sniff one brand for *aroma* . . . taste it critically for *smoothness* . . . roll it over his tongue and carry it up to the roof of his mouth" and then "swallow slowly to judge its freedom from bite, burn or sting." That was the sum total of consumer education Calvert provided to become a "fully accredited Whiskey Expert" (Figure 4.1).[16] Since richness of flavor was not a major selling point of blended whiskey, the failure of Calvert's Taste Test Kit to identify distinctive aromas and flavor characteristics that consumers could use to analyze the taste experience is not especially surprising. Why not stress instead the absence of unpleasant sensations?

Consumer resentment of bad wartime whiskey also limited the ability of postwar distillers to manage consumers' sensory perceptions. For nearly a decade after World War II, sensory memories of degraded wartime whiskey quality fueled consumer skepticism of blended whiskey and its manufacturers. One of North America's largest liquor makers, Schenley Distillers Company (known as Schenley Industries after 1949) paid a heavy reputational price for using inferior

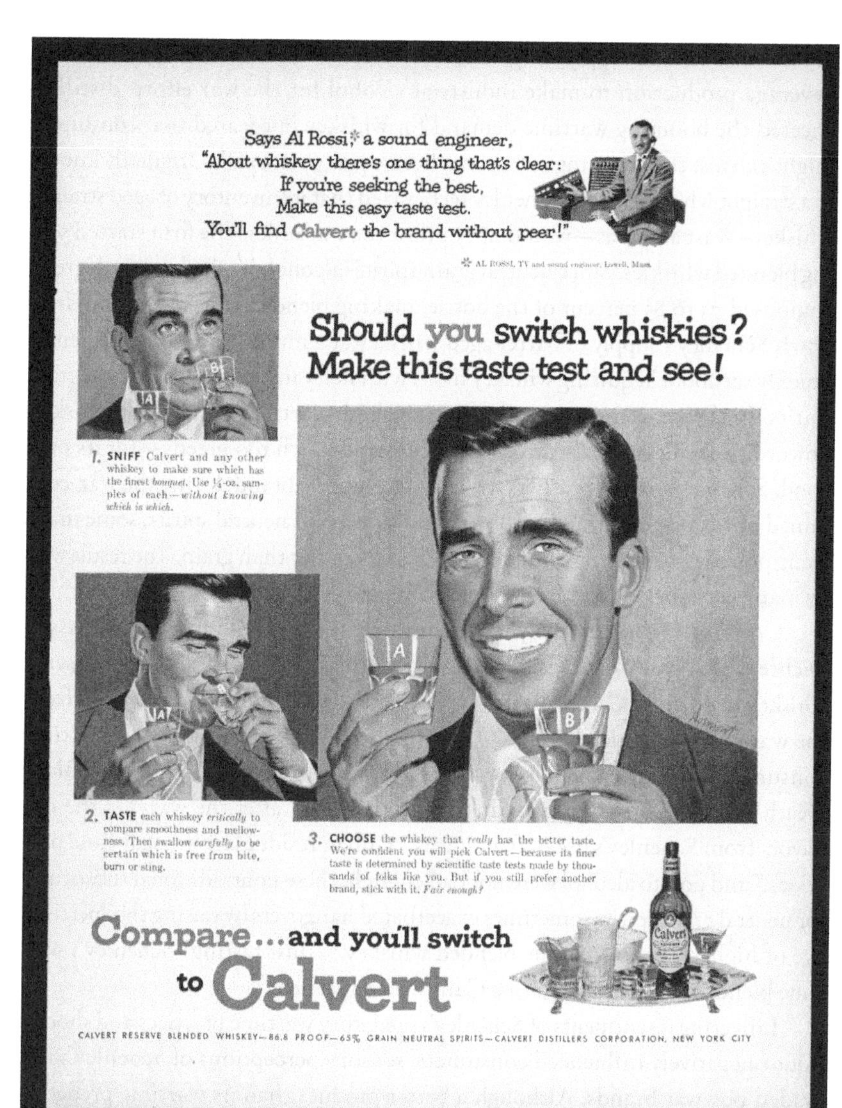

Figure 4.1. Seagram's advertising taught consumers to judge whiskey quality by the sensations it produced rather than by its distinctive flavor characteristics. Calvert Reserve Advertisement, 1953. Collection of the author. Reproduced with permission of Luxco.

spirits to stretch its supply of aged whiskey during the war. Having abandoned beverage production to make industrial alcohol for the war effort, distillers cheered the booming wartime demand for whiskey but feared that consumers might exhaust their existing inventories before peace returned. Originally known as a straight whiskey house, Schenley recognized that its inventory of aged straight whiskey—vast as it was—would not outlast the war unless the firm started selling blended whiskies. Since neutral grain spirits (alcohol distilled to 190 degrees) composed 75 to 85 percent of the bottle, making blended whiskies would draw down Schenley's supply of barrel-aged whiskey at a much slower pace. Schenley quickly set about acquiring whiskey firms with hefty inventories of neutral grain spirits. In their eagerness to profit from the high wartime demand for whiskey, however, Schenley got a little too creative—and much too greedy—for its own good. Schenley's Three Feathers whiskey, the biggest brand during the war, contained only 5 percent straight whiskey and 95 percent neutral spirits, some made using potatoes, cane sugar, or redistilled brandy rather than grain. The result was, by many accounts, odd tasting, unpleasant, and physically punishing.[17]

Consumers did not easily forgive or forget Schenley's wartime trespasses. Dichter's 1953 study on the sales and advertising problems of Schenley Reserve whiskey in postwar California uncovered a deep reservoir of ill will leftover from the war years. Schenley Reserve's "Black Label" blended whiskey gave wartime consumers such "terrible hangovers" that some dubbed the brand the "Black Death" and "sw[ore] they wouldn't drink the stuff" after the war.[18] If the off-flavors from Schenley's use of fruit juices, "Cuban residues from sugar cane processes," and potato alcohol were not bad enough, these nontraditional substitutes for neutral grain spirits sometimes exacerbated hangovers by raising the "percentage of higher alcohols" in the blended whiskey.[19] "Just tasting" Schenley's wartime blends "made you sick," one Californian recalled.[20]

Lingering resentments of Schenley's predatory wartime practices and shoddy liquor negatively influenced consumers' sensory perceptions of Schenley's upgraded postwar brands. Although a better product than its wartime predecessor, Schenley Reserve found few takers in postwar California. As a first step toward rehabilitating the brand, Dichter advised Schenley to abandon the "Black Label," which condemned the brand to recurring mockery as the "Black Death." Schenley Reserve's prospects for postwar redemption, Dichter discovered, also hinged on rebuilding trust with California liquor dealers, who blamed Schenley's use of inferior ingredients in their war whiskey for bringing ill repute to the entire industry. In retaliation, liquor dealers refused to recommend Schenley

Reserve to customers—a move that simultaneously reinforced existing consumer prejudices and protected the dealers' reputation with customers predisposed to distrust the brand. The taste of Schenley that lingered in consumers' sensory memory was the taste of deception.[21]

Consumers' distaste for Schenley's Black Label illustrates how conversations about taste preferences could extend well beyond the sensory experience of the palate to the sensory dimensions of digestion, intoxication, and their aftereffects. Anthropologist Melissa Caldwell uses the concept of "digestive politics" to illuminate how citizens in post-Soviet Russia interpreted bouts of indigestion through a political lens. Instead of blaming their gastric troubles on mayonnaise left out in hot weather (one possible culprit), the Russians Caldwell had dined with attributed their "apparent bout of food poisoning" to Russia's new capitalist economy, which had increasingly replaced safe, high-quality domestic products with low-quality, foreign foods. Viewing sensory experiences "as expressions of political engagement and critique," Caldwell argues that sensory perceptions and taste preferences become "powerful precisely because they transform the personal body into a civic body."[22] California consumers similarly used their taste preferences to communicate moral values and political sensibilities. By linking their memories of Schenley's ill effects to a critique of deceptive wartime marketing and corporate greed, they too were practicing a form of "digestive politics."

In casting Schenley Reserve as a "scapegoat brand," Dichter may have been looking for a face-saving way to deliver devastating news to his client. It could not have been easy for Schenley executives to read that California consumers risked ridicule if they served Schenley Reserve to guests or that Schenley and Three Feathers (another blended whiskey in the company's portfolio) not only "taste lousy," as one respondent observed, but "have connotations of being down at the heels."[23] Dichter's assessment that Schenley haters needed a "scapegoat brand" because they were "overwhelmed with guilt after drinking" may have softened the blow.[24] Dichter's evidence, however, also revealed how historical memory and "digestive politics" impinged on consumers' sensory perceptions. As anthropologists have recognized, the evocative power of smells and tastes—their ability to cue memories of places and social experiences—also enables memory to overwhelm objective assessments of taste. Rather than dissipating over time, "a powerful (positive or negative) first experience" of a food's taste or smell, David Sutton writes, "may color all subsequent sensory experiences of that food."[25] Consumer's potent memories of drinking Schenley's "Black Death" made Schenley's postwar assurances and its Black Label Reserve simply too hard to swallow.

Creating and Disseminating Sensory Knowledge Within Consumer Taste Communities

Alcoholic beverage producers' efforts to manage sensory perceptions collided with other social and cultural factors that shaped sensory perceptions of taste. As scholars have long understood, our perceptions of taste are not solely determined by the way our taste buds and olfactory system process various stimuli. Culture and the imagination also come into play. The sway of group affiliations, shifting norms about moderation and excess, memories of past taste experiences, and the social contexts in which drinking and eating occur all influenced sensory perceptions of taste.[26] Because taste and smell can be difficult to describe, they may even hold more symbolic meaning and evocative power than other senses.[27] In their interviews with Dichter's research team, respondents often conflated their evaluation of a whiskey's gustatory taste with their evaluation of its intoxicating effects. In so doing, white, male (and mostly white-collar) whiskey drinkers participated in a project of self-definition and boundary construction—one that sorted the reputable from the disreputable, the moderate drinkers from the problem drinkers, and the savvy consumers from the dupes of mass advertising and industry deception. These conversations suggested that middle- and upper-middle-class men's mastery of the cultural scripts that defined white masculine success and respectability often exceeded their ability to describe whiskey's taste.

The cultural scripts that guided white, middle-class men's pursuit of success implicitly associated class respectability with whiteness. Although Dichter's mostly male and white respondents never explicitly invoked race when describing their whiskey preferences, whiskey itself was fraught with racial symbolism. During the period of Black enslavement, and even more so after emancipation, white Southerners aggressively patrolled Blacks' access to whiskey, a beverage many whites viewed as either too prestigious or too potent for Black men.[28] The practice of protecting whiskey as "a white man's drink" continued during World War II, when some white military officers took steps to bar Black soldiers' access to whiskey during their rest and recreation.[29] In the 1950s and 1960s, white male consumers acquired whiskey knowledge not just from advertisements and colleagues but from magazines like *Esquire* and *Gourmet* that envisioned liquor connoisseurship as the exclusive domain of white men.[30] Although Dichter's analysis privileged social class as a demarcation of taste, in the minds of his white, middle-class respondents (and perhaps in Dichter's as well) whiteness and class respectability usually went hand in hand, especially when it came to consumers' whiskey preferences.

As Dichter's motivational research studies demonstrated, middle- and upper-middle-class white men formed themselves into distinctive communities of taste by virtue of their preference for different types of whiskey, among other consumer goods. In the social pecking order of liquor drinkers, drinkers of straight bourbon, bonded bourbon, and Scotch invariably placed themselves above drinkers of blended whiskey. Although blended whiskey outsold all other spirits in the 1950s, its share of the market fell from 85 percent to 65 percent in 1951 and then dropped to 47 percent in 1955 as consumers upgraded to Scotch and bourbon or switched to less expensive vodka and gin.[31] Unlike blends, straight bourbons contained only bourbon and a small amount of water to lower the proof to ninety-one or eighty-six. To qualify as an American bourbon, the mash had to be distilled from at least 51 percent corn, and the whiskey had to age at least four years in *new* charred white oak barrels. Bonded bourbon (sometimes called bottled-in-bond) had the same minimum aging requirements and grain composition as straight bourbon, but by law, it could hold only whiskey made by one distiller in the same distillation season. Additionally, whiskey bearing the bottle-in-bond stamp had to be stored continuously in a federally bonded and supervised warehouse before being bottled at 100 proof, making it the strongest whiskey on the market. At eighty-six proof, imported Scotch would have been less alcoholic than most straights and bonded bourbons. Differences in production and grain composition lent Scotch its lighter color and distinctive peaty aromas.

Although many whiskey drinkers ranked straights, bonded bourbons, and Scotch above blended whiskey, the image of bourbon drinkers varied widely by region. Dichter's research revealed that East Coasters considered bourbon a "prestige drink"—not quite as prestigious as Scotch but suitable for discriminating, affluent professionals. By contrast, Midwesterners saw bourbon as "a highly popular but run-of-the-mill drink." West Coasters viewed bourbon even more dimly as a lower-class beverage for the non-discriminating "heavy drinker." As one Californian observed, "Scotch is for gentlemen, Bourbon is for the yahoos." Bartenders perpetuated such regional perceptions by serving blended whiskies to Midwestern and West Coast customers who tended to use the term "bourbon" indiscriminately. Unless the customer ordered by brand name, bartenders served them a cheaper blend.[32] Bourbon drinkers, of course, saw themselves much differently. They belonged to a "knowing minority of mature drinkers" who appreciated the undiluted flavors and aromas of bourbon and preferred its "unadulterated" purity to blended whiskey.[33]

Dichter's studies abound with examples of drinkers who touted their superior palate as evidence of their class respectability and commitment to responsible drinking. Straight bourbon drinkers saw themselves as responsible hedonists who drank for sensual pleasure and conviviality—"not just to get drunk." Ideas of what constituted responsible drinking varied widely, however. As one respondent (possibly in denial) relayed, "I can drink as many half jiggers of Early Times [bourbon] with a tall glass of soda as I want and still get up in the morning and take care of my children and not feel I had lost two or three days."[34] Despite (or perhaps because of) such elastic views of intoxication, straight bourbon drinkers denigrated blended whiskey drinkers who ostensibly drank for effect. Many straight bourbon drinkers were, in fact, former blended whiskey drinkers whose tastes had evolved with their rising income or who had abandoned blends after experiencing headaches and ill-tasting spirits. In their view, blends were the beverage for people looking to "skimp on cost" and "get tight"—a group that included immature college students, workingmen, and alcoholics.[35]

Whiskey became such a potent signifier of class in postwar America that some inferred a whole complement of consumer goods and experiences that would likely accompany the purchase of blended whiskey.[36] In the assessment of one snobbish straight bourbon drinker, the blended whiskey consumer would choose "beer stew instead of Hungarian goulash or . . . a fried steak [over] a perfectly broiled one." Lacking "gourmet" sensibilities, blended whiskey drinkers were content to "get their taste," he continued, from their "7-Up or Coca-Cola" mixer rather than from the rich aromas and flavors of straight whiskey.[37] The professionals and business executives who exclusively drank bonded bourbon and Scotch were even more status-conscious. Bonded bourbon drinkers, in Dichter's estimation, liked to see themselves as people of "ability, intelligence, and drive," with discerning tastes and an appetite for gracious living, while Scotch drinkers took pride in having what one respondent called a "palate with a college degree."[38]

Dichter's psychological portraits of bourbon and Scotch drinkers invariably presumed the drinker to be a *white* professional or *white* business executive, even though prestige whiskies attracted racially diverse buyers. Although Dichter sampled a small number of African Americans, his reports rarely quoted Black consumers or acknowledged their potential to shape whiskey markets. Operating in a deeply racist society that devalued Black workers and consumers, Dichter recognized that race and racism might structure the unconscious motivations and sensory perceptions of both white and Black consumers. Dichter hinted to one client that whiskey brands known to be popular among African Americans risked losing their cachet with white consumers, and he suggested to another that status-oriented branding might especially appeal to Black consumers. Neither client took Dichter up on his proposal to investigate further.[39] Although the large Canadian-based Seagram distillery company appointed "special markets" salesmen to court Black consumers in urban neighborhoods—perhaps explaining Black consumers' affection for Lord Calvert blended whiskey (a Seagram label)—other whiskey manufacturers seem to have concluded that whiskey's public face—in advertising and packaging—needed to remain white.[40]

Regardless of their preferred whiskey style, most of Dichter's respondents viewed the mildness or harshness of whiskey's intoxicating *effects* as a component of its taste. The whiskey that tasted best was the whiskey that produced the most ideal altered state. Consumers struggled to separate their evaluations of taste from the sensory experience of intoxication partly because they cultivated whiskey knowledge synesthetically, blending experiences from the sensory registers of taste, smell, and intoxication.[41] When discussing the pleasures of drink, Dichter's respondents often betrayed their own anxieties about excess. Consider the reflections of a salesman from Oak Park, an overwhelmingly white, Republican suburb near Chicago, on the pleasures of bonded bourbon: "Some people drink to forget and others drink for taste. If you drink to forget, any old drink will do. If you drink for taste and quality you would have to drink Bonded."[42] Scotch drinkers expressed similar disdain for those who drank "to escape from life." In Dichter's view, the Scotch drinker resembled the cigar smoker who sought "a pleasant climax to an enjoyable meal," while the undiscerning liquor drinker was more like the smoker who used cigarettes "to relieve tension."[43] For the former, drinking was a sensual pleasure; for the latter drinking, like cigarette smoking, was a compulsive vice.

Dichter's white respondents repeatedly drew contrasts between those who drank for pleasure and those who drank for effect in part because the stakes of losing control were so high. As one respondent noted, "A man in my position can't afford to have hangovers" and suffer the lost productivity and social prestige.[44] Yet, despite their self-avowed commitment to moderation, drinkers convinced themselves that the supposed purity of Scotch, bonded bourbons, and straights also made it possible to drink more rather than less. Drinking eighty-six-proof light Scotch eased some drinkers' anxieties about losing self-control and suffering the consequences. Lower-proof drinks, however, also allowed for maximum self-delusion. Consider the respondent who enjoyed "drinking bouts with friends" in which they "emptied a bottle of Scotch together. We were discussing who could drink the most and the fastest without feeling any bad effects. . . . My friends said Scotch was the only drink if you don't want to get a hangover."[45] This example hints at the ways white, upper-middle-class men worked to reconcile the demands of masculinity with the demands of respectability. The Scotch itself conferred prestige and respectability, while men's ability to drink voluminously without consequences demonstrated their drinking prowess.

Such stories reveal the subtle yet significant ways in which postwar Americans wrestled with shifting norms of masculinity and white racial respectability. Drinking had long been a turbulent proving ground on which men both risked and affirmed their masculinity. In the mid-eighteenth-century Chesapeake, historian Sarah Meacham writes, the planter elite "delighted in bragging about their own drinking exploits" and "drank toasts on any pretext" in their private social clubs, even as they disapproved of excessive drinking by enslaved Blacks and lower-class whites.[46] A sense of camaraderie and competition also pervaded the nineteenth-century saloon, where working-class men compared the size of their arm muscles and "bragged about how much alcohol they could drink without effect." Yet, saloon goers also understood that the inability to hold their liquor could cast doubt on their manhood and their commitment to breadwinning.[47] Drinking remained a masculine proving ground in the postwar period. As one respondent informed Dichter, "I have to drink a certain amount to keep up my prestige—all the boys consider themselves real hellers."[48] Men had to reconcile such performances of masculinity, however, with competing cultural trends that sanctioned liquor-fueled sociability but eschewed overindulgence. Confirming a trend that had already been underway for several years, *Business Week* reported in 1963 that "while drinking today is much more socially acceptable, intemperance is correspondingly less acceptable."[49]

It is not clear how much the culture of moderation restrained actual drinking practices. The 1950s, after all, were the heyday of the three-martini lunch and the domestic cocktail hour, or at least this is how popular culture has characterized the era, both at the time and since. Moderation had acquired enough cultural authority, however, to shape how Americans assessed their own drinking practices and the drinking habits of peers and strangers. At once permissive and restrictive, the new culture of moderate drinking that reporters and motivational researchers documented in the 1950s and early 1960s required virtuous drinkers to either know their limits or learn to mask and manage overt signs of drunkenness. As alcoholic beverages became an integral—and even expected—dimension of home life, hospitality, and business negotiations, hosts and guests alike altered their drinking practices to promote conviviality but avoid overindulgence. Like two other key components of the suburban sensory landscape—the shopping mall and the supermarket—the midcentury domestic cocktail party created an enticing yet reassuringly controlled environment in which guests could experience pleasure.[50] Lower-proof blended whiskies and bourbons likely retained their postwar popularity because many Americans viewed them as a "more permissive drink"—one that enabled partygoers to drink freely, as the conventions of sociability demanded, but not lose control. Hosts served guests lower-proof spirits, knowing that "for an evening of drinking," both the host and guests would "want something milder."[51]

The concept of a "milder" drink, of course, was open to interpretation. Vintners and brewers had long promoted beer and wine as beverages of moderation, but distillers could not easily make the same claim owing to the greater potency of their product. Though they might point to a lower proof—eighty-six instead of ninety-one or 100—as evidence of a brand's gentler psychoactive effects, advertising copy used terms like "mild" to describe whiskey's taste and the sensations it produced going down, hoping to leave consumers with the impression that the mild taste would also produce gentler aftereffects. In short, mass marketers coopted the language of sensory taste to convey vital information about alcohol's psychoactive effects. Consumers also drew upon personal experience, superstition, and the word-of-mouth folklore that circulated among friends and colleagues to create their own interpretation of what constituted a mild spirits-based drink. Conceding that he could possibly get drunk on Scotch, one man told the Dichter team that he diluted Scotch with soda so that he could drink "seven or eight highballs at a party" and leave with his respectability intact.[52] Another respondent, however, thought soda spoiled the Scotch and produced the effects of "a mixed drink," virtually guaranteeing a hangover.[53]

As philosopher Carolyn Korsemeyer has observed, the "aesthetic qualities" of food and drink "take on their fullest meanings" when their consumption is embedded in particular social occasions. "The taste sensation alone is just a sensation," Korsemeyer writes, but the social contexts in which people drink and eat give meaning "to that taste experience."[54] Social contexts similarly shaped how people experienced the psychoactive effects of particular alcoholic beverages.[55] Many men and women tended to view cocktails as relatively benign because they associated cocktails with home entertaining and refined social gatherings. More than the spirits a cocktail contained, the quiet heterosocial setting mellowed the cocktail's psychoactive effects. "Drinking cocktails is a more refined way of drinking," a man from Chicago confided to Dichter, and "you can enjoy the taste of the liquor more because it isn't going down in one big gulp."[56] Such examples illustrate how "set and setting"—the consumer's mindset and the setting in which they consume alcohol—can either intensify or moderate its psychoactive effects.[57] They also suggest why so many American drinkers struggled to disentangle the sensory synergies of gustatory taste and altered states.

Motivational Researchers as Creators of Sensory Knowledge

Motivational researchers played essential roles in the process of creating knowledge about the senses. As cultural intermediaries between consumers and alcohol producers, they helped to translate consumers' sensory perceptions into marketable messages. During the decade and a half that Dichter spent conducting motivational research studies for the North American whiskey industry, he diverged little from his initial conclusion: consumers' stated reasons for preferring certain whiskey brands were really rationalizations that masked deeper emotional needs and status anxieties. In this, whiskey drinkers were little different from consumers of other types of commodities. Convinced that the complexities of consumer behavior necessitated an interdisciplinary approach, Dichter kept more than twenty-five specialists in psychology, sociology, and anthropology on staff at the Institute for Motivational Research in upstate New York.[58] Like other motivational researchers, Dichter drew more heavily on sociology when devising marketing strategies for cars and clothing, as these publicly consumed products, Lawrence Samuel writes, "were more about status than anything else . . . in postwar America."[59] Dichter leaned more heavily on psychoanalytical insights when it came to "tobacco, soft drinks, liquor, candy"—the sorts of indulgences that might arouse feelings of guilt.[60] He recommended that advertising provide "absolution" for having a good time by presenting whiskey drinking as a well-deserved reward.[61]

As both a sensual pleasure and a marker of status, whiskey demanded a marketing approach that blended the sociological with the psychoanalytical. In his early 1950s whiskey motivational research studies, Dichter drew upon his psychoanalytical tool kit to explain the paradox of consumers' intense focus on whiskey quality and their fuzzy understanding of the terms they used to measure quality. He informed blended whiskey makers that consumers' preoccupation with quality criteria provided the "psychological camouflage" they needed to convince themselves and others that they were not "indiscriminate drunkards."[62] In Dichter's view, the qualities people most valued in whiskey—smoothness, mildness, gentleness on throat, absence of aftereffects—represented psychological needs rather than hard material criteria. Though consumers wanted whiskey to partially intoxicate, they also wanted a whiskey that would "be kind" to them and "at all times serve as a protector and guardian."[63]

Not all whiskey consumers—especially not the ones Dichter classified as "whiskey secure"—were awash in puritanical guilt. Internally driven and less sensitive to the opinions of others, the self-assured whiskey consumer in Dichter's model possessed the confidence to drink alone and embraced whiskey's therapeutic benefits. In their depth interviews, these types of drinkers informed Dichter, "I don't require company when I drink" or "I usually rapidly reduce any supply of whiskey that I have at home by drinking my midnight snack or deliberately drinking to put myself to sleep." Indeed, the secure whiskey consumer turned to whiskey in all manner of circumstances: "I use liquor . . . to forget, to remember, to loosen my tongue in business, pleasure or social situations."[64] Curiously, Dichter's model of the whiskey secure drinker exhibited the behaviors that postwar addiction scientists would have classified as those of an alcoholic: drinking alone, drinking to self-medicate, and drinking heavily on any and every occasion.[65] Dichter practically flipped the existing psychological models of the problem drinker on their head. The drinkers who in Dichter's view suffered from the most delusions about their drinking were not the so-called whiskey secure individuals who drank alone but the moderate social drinkers—those Dichter dubbed the whiskey insecure. The whiskey insecure personality fit the profile of the commuting suburbanite who usually drank at home and only after work and when hosting guests. In depth interviews, whiskey insecure consumers stressed that they did not "drink for the kick of whiskey—just for smoothness" or "just for taste."[66] Not unlike the whiskey connoisseur who intellectualized and aestheticized drinking, Dichter's "whiskey insecure" drinkers affirmed their own refinement by distancing the sense of taste from the baser bodily pleasures afforded by inebriation—a move that perhaps also affirmed their white racial respectability.

Dichter's somewhat bizarre departure from the reigning orthodoxies of addiction science raises the possibility that his psychoanalytical theory served a dual purpose. On the one hand, it informed whiskey marketers that the standard talking points about taste, smoothness, and mildness were failing to connect with the deeper emotional needs of consumers. Dichter's theories, however, also exonerated whiskey distillers' aggressive efforts to boost alcohol consumption.

In an age when Alfred Adler's theories of the well-adjusted personality and his concept of the "inferiority complex" circulated widely in popular culture, what was not to like about a theory that cast heavy drinkers as "whiskey secure" and restrained drinkers as insecure, maladjusted individuals who needed the "moral permission" of whiskey advertisers to indulge? Dichter's clients may have seen the "whiskey secure" drinker as a version of the "inner-directed" personality that sociologist David Riesman cast as a dying breed in his 1950 best seller *The Lonely Crowd.* Steered by his own moral compass, Riesman's inner-directed personality, as popularized in Westerns, Ayn Rand novels, and cultural commentary, garnered more admiration than the "other-directed" organization men who bent their own values and tastes to please others and get ahead.[67]

In the mid-1950s, Dichter abandoned his theories of the whiskey secure and whiskey insecure and focused instead on broader cultural trends that shaped consumer tastes and anxieties. Observing American drinkers' eagerness to sample "new, exotic, and foreign liquors," Dichter believed Americans were abandoning "the old puritanical principles."[68] Middle-class culture, however, still encouraged limits on self-indulgence and many attempted to manage liquor-fueled sociability by turning to less potent spirits.[69] Dichter informed clients that the growing consumer preference for vodka, gin, mild Scotches, and lower-proof whiskies amplified a broader rejection of "ruggedness, strength, heaviness, darkness"—traits previously valued in food, cigarettes, cigars, and strong liquor. Much like the trend to "calorie avoidance," lighter spirits, Dichter's team argued, enabled Americans to "indulge and still feel virtuous."[70] Indeed, the rising popularity of lower-proof spirits coincided with the publication of a spate of commercial diet books for men and a growing market for new artificial sweeteners and low-calorie "diet foods."[71] In the face of mounting postwar concerns that consumer abundance and sedentary desk jobs had sapped men's resolve to discipline their appetites, Dichter urged whiskey makers to capitalize on the male desire for a whiskey that could help them achieve self-mastery.

Advertising Makeovers for Brown Whiskey

Advertising both initiated and concluded a circular process of creating sensory knowledge. Whiskey advertisement makers provided consumers with a language for talking and thinking about gustatory taste and altered states, but they also constructed new appeals and adjusted old ones in response to feedback from motivational researchers and changing consumer tastes. In the late 1950s and early

1960s, thanks in good measure to the more versatile tastes of women and younger drinkers, a wide array of distilled spirits began eroding the market share of whiskies produced in the United States. Though North American-made whiskies still represented more than half of the liquor market in the United States, the increasing popularity of home entertaining prompted consumers to stock their private household bars with an array of spirits to satisfy the varied tastes of guests. The common denominator uniting North American whiskey's most significant competitors—Scotch, Canadian Whiskey, and the so-called white liquors (gin and vodka)—was their lower proof and claim to "lightness"—a marketing buzzword that reflected the growing cultural salience of moderate drinking.[72]

Seeking to exploit these trends, Seagram debuted Calvert Extra, an eighty-six-proof blended whiskey, in 1962. Magazine advertisements presented Calvert Extra as a "soft whiskey that does everything 'hard' liquor can do. But does it softer." The advertisements' closing lines claimed that those who try the drink "may never touch a drop of 'hard' liquor again" (Figure 4.2).[73] At a press conference, Seagram's chief blender explained that the distiller wanted to offer a drink "with a light, delicate, soft flavor" that would have broad appeal. "We think that the day when a man demanded a drink that would shake his back teeth is nearing an end."[74] In referencing Calvert Extra's "soft flavor," Seagram's advertising deployed the language of sensory taste to convey ambiguous messages about Calvert Extra's psychoactive effects.[75] Launched three years after the Distilled Spirits Institute, a trade association for the American liquor industry, lifted its self-imposed ban on representing women in liquor advertisements, Calvert Extra directly appealed to women consumers, who increasingly did the bulk of the household liquor shopping.[76] One full-page magazine advertisement, dominated by a photograph of a glamorous, high fashion model preparing to sip Calvert Extra, acknowledged that many women found whiskey "hard to take" but promised that Calvert Extra treated its drinkers "so tenderly" that "A lady can even drink Soft Whiskey straight. Without batting an eyelash."[77]

Calvert Extra masqueraded as a woman's drink—one that might appeal to the expanding market of women and younger drinkers who enjoyed drinking but disliked whiskey's taste.[78] Seagram's advertisements made Calvert Extra the whiskey for those who wanted potency but did not want to taste that potency or feel its burn. The real genius of the campaign, however, lay in the copy's subtext—the way it struck an ambiguously androgynous pose and addressed an array of contemporary cultural anxieties. As Dichter's studies had revealed, what corporate-climbing, white-collar men most desired was a whiskey that could foster masculine conviviality and ease the day's tensions while protecting them

Even a lady could learn to like Soft Whiskey. It's not hard.
Many women don't find whiskey very likeable.
In fact, they find it hard to take.
So you usually find them with gin or vodka, or one of those lady drinks.
But we've changed all that. We've given whiskey more appeal.
A lady can even drink Soft Whiskey straight. Without batting an eyelash. Soft Whiskey swallows nice and easy, treating her ever so tenderly.
But don't get the wrong idea. Soft Whiskey is no softie. It's 86 proof. And does exactly what any 86 proof does. It just does it softer. So lady, be discreet.
Now, about the softening process. All we can tell you is, some of Calvert Extra is distilled in small batches instead of huge ones. Forgive our being so closemouthed. But we fell flat on our faces in year after year of experiments before we found the formula.
After all that, we're not going to make it easy for anyone to steal our women.
THE SOFT WHISKEY
CALVERT
EXTRA
BLENDED WHISKEY · 86 PROOF · 65% GRAIN NEUTRAL SPIRITS ©1965 CALVERT DIST. CO., N.Y.C.

Figure 4.2. Seagram's advertising used the language of sensory taste to convey ambiguous messages about whiskey's psychoactive effects. Calvert Extra Advertisement in *Life*, May 21, 1965. Courtesy of the Hagley Museum & Library, Wilmington, DE. Reproduced with permission of Luxco.

from the physiological and reputational hazards of overindulgence. Calvert Extra promised to deliver not the gustatory pleasures of a richly flavored brown whiskey, but the spritely delights of the taste of success.

The trend toward lightness in distilled spirits—and the elevation of white liquors over traditional brown whiskey—encapsulated something of the zeitgeist of the postwar moment. It satisfied a thirst for commodities of consistent quality that delivered consistent results and consistent sensations, even if that consistency came at the price of bland uniformity. Lightness satisfied yearnings for sensory experiences that delivered pleasure without the punishment. If nothing else, the trend toward lightness reflected consumers' willingness—and eagerness—to collude with mass marketers in perpetuating the illusion of consequence-free drinking. As cocreators of sensory knowledge, advertisers, consumers, and motivational researchers helped to consolidate a sensual revolution that normalized pleasures previously regarded as *vices*.

* * *

Historians say that the changing descriptive and evaluative vocabularies consumers use to talk about gustatory taste tell us much about the particular temporal and cultural moments in which they came into use. Early modern European texts, for example, identified only four tastes of wine (sweet, acute, austere, and mild) and, in keeping with Galenic medicine, judged wines "pleasant" and "agreeable" based on how well those wines complemented the temperament and bodily needs of the taster. The twentieth-century chemistry of flavor components produced a more elaborate taste vocabulary.[79] Since the mid-1970s, when enologists at University of California, Davis formulated the Wine Aroma Wheel, consumers have learned to talk about the jammy, peppery flavors in Zinfandel, or the notes of pear and passion fruit in Sauvignon Blanc. Following the wine industry's lead, the coffee, bourbon, and beer industries developed their own, equally complex flavor wheels. Had those flavor or aroma wheels existed in the 1950s and 1960s, Dichter's respondents might have used descriptors like vanilla, caramel, and burnt sugar to talk about their favorite bourbon. But consumers did not have such taste vocabularies at their disposal. Nor were as many consumers invested in the culture of connoisseurship that gave those highly specific, seemingly objective descriptors meaning. In the postwar era, serving the right brand and style of whiskey was a sufficient demonstration of connoisseurship or good taste.

Despite the limited taste vocabularies of postwar consumers, the descriptors that Dichter's respondents used to characterize good and bad whiskey give us some insight into the values, preoccupations, and aesthetic sensibilities that shaped middle-class life and white, middle-class masculinities in the postwar era. Was Dichter correct that consumers were merely parroting advertising claims when they praised whiskeys that were mild, smooth, and light? To some extent, yes. But as advertisers understood all too well, words like mild and smooth also functioned as code for the type of intoxicating experience consumers might anticipate. They offered reassurance that men could manage the demands of liquor-fueled sociability and business networking and still meet their workplace obligations the next day. Mild and smooth were also meaningful because they contrasted with consumers' sensory memories of the harsh, biting, raw whiskey many encountered after Prohibition, during World War II, and through the late 1940s when stocks of four-year-old aged whiskey were still low. The negative descriptors reveal how past experiences and historical memories of deceptive industry practices could condition expectations of flavor and influence what consumers actually tasted. Even though Schenley's postwar version of its Black Label blended whiskey bore little resemblance to its wartime predecessor, the taste of deception still lingered on the palate. Above all, postwar gustatory vocabularies underscored the subjectivity of taste: how what we taste "derives less from our physiological selves than from our social, cultural, and political selves." These social and cultural selves, of course, also include our gendered selves.[80] In the postwar United States, gustatory taste, subjective though it was, proved a particularly potent sense through which white men could affirm their masculine fortitude and racial respectability and mark their place within the increasingly varied gradations of the middle class.

CHAPTER 5

The Psychophysics of Taste and Smell

From Experimental Science to Commercial Tool

ANA MARÍA ULLOA

An experimental science of sense experience—that is psychophysics. Defined conventionally as the scientific study of the relation between the intensity of a stimulus and its perceived magnitude, psychophysics might sound to our contemporary ears too narrow and too specialized a place to begin. Yet, if today it is a specialized field largely hidden from view, with few active practitioners, and scarcely funded,[1] for pioneer psychophysicists of the second half of the nineteenth century, their object of study held big epistemological promise. To Gustav Fechner, physicist and philosopher and author of *Elemente der Psychophysik*, published in 1860, experimental efforts to bind material and mental phenomena could demonstrate a universal relation between body and mind, and furthermore constitute a paradigm for translating the material into the spiritual.[2] With such concerns and moving between physics and philosophy, psychophysics became an early ancestor of experimental psychology. But its scope and influence did not end there. It took half a century more for psychophysics to find its commercial destiny, with profitable potential in producing objective knowledge about subjective sensations, feelings, and likings.

This chapter focuses on the psychophysics of taste and smell, a field with tremendous consequences for the business of food. While these so-called lower senses have been the object of measure since the last decades of the nineteenth century, their measurement was only further developed since the 1930s with the advent of sensory science and a marketplace increasingly designed to stimulate the senses.[3] Psychophysical thinking, with its early attempts to bridge mind and body, inner and outer experience, the mental and the material, morphed into a suitable enterprise for measuring and reproducing new and controlled sensory qualities essential for the selling of commodities such as food, clothing, and media devices in late-modern industrialized societies.[4]

Exploring psychophysics as a precursor of food sensory science, this chapter analyzes the continuities between psychophysics as epistemic undertaking and psychophysics as commercial technology. It is based on historical accounts of psychophysics, psychophysicists, and ethnographic fieldwork carried out in 2014 in taste and smell laboratories and flavor companies in the United States. It also builds on Steven Shapin's 2012 call for "ethnographies—contemporary and historical—of how taste judgments come to be formed, discussed, and sometimes shared" and the scholarship that has come in its wake.[5]

How do early psychophysical thinking and its metaphysical promises bear on its contemporary industrial applications? What features of psychophysics make it a suitable and profitable enterprise to account for sensations, feelings, and likes? In reconstructing some of its history and giving some ethnographic examples of psychophysical methods in practice, the purpose of this chapter is twofold. First, it shows the tensions intrinsic to the measurement of phenomena as fleeting, unstable, and subjective as are smells, tastes, and flavors. Quantification, in this case, involves more than numbers and units of measurement. Rather, it depends on "communicative infrastructures" and other robust qualitative strategies for meaningful experience sharing. Tastes, smells, and flavors resist straight quantification and capitalist rationalization because of how they are bound to human subjectivity.

Second, this chapter challenges traditional notions of the relationship between science and industry, which are often perceived to be at odds or espousing different and irreconcilable values. Instead, it offers psychophysical research on taste and smell as a clear example of the science-industry complex at work. The story that unfolds here is not one in which science is equated with reductionism and industry with commoditization. Nor is this a story of disenchantment in which human experience is filtered through science and reduced to the factual. For when it comes down to tastes, smells, and flavors, which pertain to both objects and subjects, nature and culture, experimentation and manufacture, standardization and artisanship, such compartmentalization and assumptions are of little help.

On Tastes, Smells, and Flavors

That which cannot be universally measured and tested is considered unfit for science, and for a long time, smells, tastes, and flavors—matters of individual perception and preference—were ignored and treated as too fickle, idiosyncratic, and tied to pleasure to be considered scientific objects. From Plato to Kant, philosophers agreed on the low status of the senses of taste and smell, understood as bodily, intimate, proximal, subjective, and closer to our animal nature. These conceptions influenced the fate of scientific research on what later became known as the chemical senses—those sensitive to the chemical composition of the environment, mainly smell and taste.[6]

For the purposes of measurement, taste, smell, and flavor cannot be more than the result of the impact of chemical stimuli on our tongues, noses, and throat, and the psychophysical responses that follow. The technical conception of flavor starts by divorcing itself from taste—a sensory modality accessible to all human beings and other animals that exclusively registers the sensations of sweet, sour, bitter, salty, and umami. Likewise, technical conceptions of flavor discount the matter of "taste"—a social category with a complex history that speaks of an inclination toward refinement, socially promoted and favored by a few. From one technical point of view, the *taste* of a pineapple is not the same as the *flavor* of a pineapple. Its taste, as captured by receptors located in our tongues and perceived by our brains, would be a combination of sweet and sour. Its flavor would be a multisensory experience created by our brains from all the sensory stimuli it receives while we eat the pineapple. While flavor taps into all sensory systems (taste, smell, vision, hearing, and touch), smell is the most significant component of it.

From another scientific point of view, flavor can also be thought of as the sensory attributes of the pineapple that come from a mixture of hundreds or even thousands of volatiles. This is the approach of flavor chemists and the flavor industry, left with the difficult task of controlling volatile chemicals and using them to recreate an aesthetic experience. It is in this double nature of flavor—flavor as *experience* that is interpreted and deciphered by the brain and as part of the chemical *makeup* of foods that may be isolated and mastered—that attempts at quantification lie. Usually, this duality of flavor has called for dualistic research strategies: some approaches concentrate on the object, others on the subject. In trying to bridge subject and object, psychophysical methods have been used as a tool to address persistent challenges in measuring flavor, thereby filling the gap between chemistry, physiology and psychology, molecules and perception, and ultimately qualities of objects and subjective judgments.

The Measurement of Sensation: Between Experiment and Experience

At the center of the enterprise of measuring perception and the stimuli responsible for it we find the work of psychophysics, a "speculative science" that, according to literary scholar Erica Fretwell in *Sensory Experiments*, "tested people's subjective responses to auditory, gustatory, olfactory, tactile, and visual stimulation" and was developed in the second half of the nineteen century.[7] It built on the progressive division of the body into separate systems and functions, including the senses of sight, hearing, taste, smell, and touch, and the earlier science of sense perception that increasingly paid more attention to the physiological makeup of the human subject than the mechanics of the stimuli.[8]

Psychophysics occupied the minds of many who were equally attracted to physics, physiology, and philosophy, and even mysticism, as was the case with the German physicist and philosopher Gustav Fechner—a key figure in the founding of psychophysics.[9] The idea that there is nothing in the mind that has not come through the senses was a good platform for the development of a scientific approach to epistemology, and also for understanding sensations as related to the stimuli that caused them. The ways in which light was transformed into a perception of brightness or sound into a perception of loudness were for the most part the focus of this emerging science—a focus that was thought essential to a scientific understanding of how the human mind works. The problem for psychophysics was not necessarily (or at least not yet) how to communicate private experience, but how to measure it: how to find a number that could represent the feeling of hearing a louder sound, or of entering a brighter room, or eating a sweeter apple.

This was happening at a time when measurement and precision were highly prized, though elusive, scientific goals. Throughout the nineteenth century, in science, industry, and government, matters of measurement, calibration, and standardization increasingly became a central concern.[10] Metrology, a new branch of physics in charge of researching, producing, and disseminating standard values, came out of this environment, and the new subdiscipline proved useful in unifying and regulating scientific activity.[11] Practices that had previously been evaluated qualitatively were now seen as a suitable for experimentation and capitalistic rationalization. As the historian David Singerman argues in his work on how sucrose was made the sole standard of sugar, the power carried by laboratory science and metrology had a direct impact on the establishment of economic value attached to labor and things.[12]

But not only was psychophysics aligned with processes of standardization. It was also employed in support of evolutionary theories of the nineteenth century. Physical anthropologists of the 1890s, very much influenced by psychophysics, introduced measurement of natives' vision, olfaction, audition, and taste into their studies of "racial differences." The 1898 Cambridge expedition to the Torres Straits led by the zoologist-turned-ethnologist Alfred C. Haddon was one of the first experimental grounds outside of the laboratory that employed psychophysical techniques as developed by Fechner and others. In their expedition, a battery of tests and instruments was used to measure the sensory acuity of the "Other" and corroborate an alleged "primitive superiority."[13]

As for the nascent psychophysicists, the coupling of the body or the physical with the mind or the psychological became something that could be analyzed and even predicted through the measurement of the limits of human sensitivity.[14] Fechner, rescuing the observations of the physiologist Ernst Heinrich Weber—who noticed that the greater the intensity of a stimulus is, the more you need in order to detect a change in sensation—proposed that in fact this relationship obeyed a logarithmic principle.[15] That is, at low levels of intensity of a stimulus, humans can easily detect a small increase, but at higher levels of intensity of the same stimulus, this ability for detecting a change diminishes proportionally. The conclusions of Fechner and Weber were much debated in the late nineteenth century and their laws were long seen as the most important achievement of psychophysics. The practical implications of having an equation (sensation increases as the logarithmic of stimulus intensity) for measuring the sensations produced by lights or sounds were not minor. Whether the stimulus was applied to the eye, ear, skin, nose, or tongue, the belief that there was a pattern in the relationship between perception and the level of stimulus intensity provided much hope for the measurement of sensation and its amenability to experimental manipulation.

For over a century, Fechner's equation was accepted as the paradigmatic measure in psychology, and his work, as that of Wilhelm Wundt, became crucial in forming the foundations of psychology as experimental science.[16] But the mere fact that a science measures, counts, and calculates does not make it an exact, irrefutable science. Psychophysics grew from a method for measuring thresholds of sensation indirectly to a scientific basis for scaling sensations and perceptions directly. For a wider application of psychophysics to occur, a lot of work was devoted to as much observation of sensory phenomena as to getting around methodological limitations and devising new ways of measuring sensations.

Out of this later work, and carrying a different conception of measurement, came what the American psychologist S. S. Stevens labeled the "new psychophysics."[17] S. S. Stevens is a prominent figure in mid-twentieth-century experimental psychology, contributing greatly to studies of sound and hearing through work carried out in his Psycho-Acoustic Laboratory at Harvard. He studied under experimental psychologist Edwin Boring, a fierce proponent of the separation of philosophy and psychology at Harvard and a committed experimentalist for the study of sensation and perception. Stevens defined measurement simply as "the assignment of numerals to events or objects according to rule."[18] As Howard Moskowitz, a practicing psychophysicist and market researcher, explained, "It was Stevens's abiding view that the human subject could assign numbers validly to reflect the perceived intensity of stimuli, and that the numbers themselves had ratio-scale properties."[19] For Stevens, if sensations have measurable magnitudes, it is possible to establish the distance between them and leave individuals free to use any number they wish. The numbers would reflect ratios of perceptual magnitude, their nominal quantities being irrelevant.

What is the big difference here? With the new psychophysics paradigm that is used today, scientists can conveniently just ask somebody to rate a sensation on a scale—something, as we will later see, that is quite useful for market and consumer research. Stevens's direct method of magnitude estimation did not conform to Fechner's law, but he was still interested in a law that could help elucidate how sensory systems operate. In Stevens's words: "Despite the variability of human reaction, despite the lack of high precision with which a given sensory effect can be gauged, and despite the inevitable fact of individual difference, it grows increasingly clear that there is a simple and pervasive law that controls the overall dynamics of sensory intensity."[20] What was for Fechner a logarithmic relation was for Stevens a power relation—that is, the magnitude of the sensation increases in a proportional and predictable manner relative to the strength of the stimulus.

Beyond measurement and experimentation, there is another side to psychophysics that we have yet to explore: the role of experience. Measurement of sensations depended not only on agreement on formal definition of units or instruments, but also on introspection. For over half a century of classical psychophysics, this meant the practice of training subjects to carefully observe and describe their mental states and sensations to obtain experimentally relevant and truthful data as it was first promoted by "the father of experimental psychology," Wilhelm Wundt. For instance, a subject could require as long as twenty minutes to report on an experience that could have lasted less than two seconds. Much responsibility was then placed on the subject, who if trained, could be genuinely trusted.

The point is that for psychophysics there is no way of sidestepping the mind, as its purpose defies such an approach. Psychophysical measures of experience always need in some way or another to confront the fact that subjective perceptions cannot be directly shared but are nevertheless understood as measurable. Because of this, classic psychophysicists considered that much could be gained by introspection, even of one's own sensory experience. This phenomenology of sense experience could even be found around the turn of the century in America, where disciplined self-observation was trusted by figures like Edward B. Titchener, a prominent psychophysicist at Cornell University who studied under Wilhelm Wundt for several years and elaborated methods of experimental introspection with the aid of laboratory tools and standardized stimuli for the measurement of sensation.[21]

As Erica Fretwell has recently argued in her study of psychophysics and the cultural-aesthetic environment of nineteenth-century America, and contrary to what one would expect from an experimental and analytic science, early psychophysicists such as Weber, Fechner, and Hermann von Helmholtz considered that "sense experience is material but not strictly so—it is shaped, but not entirely governed, by nerve structure."[22] By investigating individual variations of sense experience, and focusing on more *how* people perceive than *what* they perceive, psychophysics came with a phenomenological inclination, stimulating the revaluation of sensation as lived experience. The quest for quantitatively measuring sensorial differences, which depended on all sorts of conditions to be scientifically rigorous, came with a qualitative approach toward sensations as objects of knowledge. Moreover, the same perceptual sensitivity that psychophysicists studied was interpreted in nineteenth-century culture as the basis of finer feelings, aesthetic judgement, and a marker of civilization. The ability of registering slight sensory changes acquired social meanings outside of the laboratory. Something similar would occur in the twentieth century with the incursion of psychophysics into sensory science and the food industry, where slight sensory changes acquired commercial value and the cultivation of the senses was at the service of the economy and the market.

But the trust in introspection did not last long, especially among American psychologists. With the rise of animal psychology, many researchers paid less attention to the study of sensation and adopted a more behaviorist approach. Fearing the language of introspection as imprecise, unreliable, cumbersome, and unstable, discrimination tasks—for example, choosing which of two options was sweeter—became the norm. This is why most psychophysicists favor measurements based on performance, such as thresholds, in taste and smell research. Since they appear to be less subjective than other measures based on self-reporting, threshold measures are still a common tool kit in psychophysics found in many different applications like clinical assessments, sensory evaluations, and flavor analyses. These measures are useful for comparisons as they are considered to sidestep language and to avoid complicated semantics and idiosyncratic judgments.

At first sight, thresholds appear to be straightforward measures that establish the weakest stimulus an organism can perceive (*absolute threshold*) or recognize as a distinctive quality (*recognition threshold*) or the smallest increase in stimulus that can be detected (*difference threshold*). But in taste and smell research, where adaptation and fatigue affect reporting, such measures present more technical challenges. Thresholds also have the negative effect of not taking into account one of the basic features of the chemical senses—odors and tastes are evanescent and frequently change—which renders single and static measurements problematic.[23]

Given the limitation of thresholds, psychophysicists such as S. S. Stevens began in the late 1950s looking at the possibility of incorporating direct assessment, that is, directly asking people what they felt and estimating a measure of magnitude.[24] This made modern psychophysicists turn their attention to subjective measures, transforming the subject from its previous role as a tool for learning about private experience into a measuring instrument for estimating the magnitude of sensations. After Stevens, the ability of untrained individuals to act as true measuring instruments was not only recognized and accepted but also increasingly promoted.[25] With these more subjective measures and direct scaling procedures, taste and smell psychophysics gained importance for commercially oriented practices. Research and development departments across corporations (particularly those manufacturing sensory products where aesthetic considerations play an important role, like perfumes, foods, cleaning products, etc.) recognized the value of psychophysics as an area of knowledge whose application could eventually provide a desired technological advantage.[26]

What for basic science might look like an otherwise stagnant field, for applied science served as an important tool to master and further develop. It was precisely through sensory science, an explicitly commercial practice, that psychophysics experienced a reawakening and gained a new identity. No longer concerned with intractable metaphysical problems, psychophysics became a tool equally serving academic and applied sensory research in which experimentation and reporting on sensory experience were called for. As experimental psychologist Edwin Boring wrote, "The lesson to be learned from psychophysics is, therefore, that, in respect of the observation of sensory experience, introspection has thrived for a hundred years and is still in style."[27]

Measuring Sensory Differences in the Laboratory

Today, practitioners hold a wide range of opinions about the most appropriate methods for sensory measurement. Despite the theoretical transition described in the previous section and the widespread adoption of introspection in industrial settings, not all scientists who research the chemical senses favor subjective measures. One trained psychophysicist I talked to during my ethnographic research at the Monell Chemical Senses Center, a leading institution located in Philadelphia dedicated to basic research on the senses of taste and smell, admitted his behavioral bias. He finds the more objective data more satisfying and has always tended toward experiments that involve performance tests.

I participated in one of his experiments, which was intended to investigate the "off" sensation of potassium chloride, a compound whose taste lies between bitter and salty. The task was to sort numerous taste solutions into two different categories. On the day of the experiment, I was taken into a barren-looking test room and sat in one of the six separated booths where a small sink and a table were at hand. I was given a complete set of taste solutions in plastic medicine cups placed on a tray, and had to sip each sample with a nose clip pinching my nostrils, hold it in my mouth for five seconds, and then spit it out. The samples looked the same but tasted slightly different, though all were between bitter and salty. They seemed odorless to me, but the nose clip was necessary, I was told, to prevent any normal taste-smell interactions. After tasting each sample, I had to assign it to one of several categories I devised. One would expect that the differences would be obvious and hence the task simple. But as is the case with most sensory experiments, the differences between stimuli are not significant.

Unless one is testing for taste malfunction, there is no point in making some discriminate, for instance, between sweet and sour.

This experiment, in particular, was particularly challenging because the bitter/salty range in its pure compound form is highly unpleasant, and I had to compare the bitter or salty or bitter/salty samples to one another. At one point, for instance, I thought I needed three categories instead of two, as there was a sample that I could not fit in my criteria. But this is precisely the point of a performance-based test. I was not being asked if I found the sample bitter or salty, but was simply being given a task to perform: sorting. This task, the scientist told me, could be thought of as objective because it was tied to physical criteria, and even if the test subject could use different criteria to make her judgments, the experimenter had objective criteria to decide whether the subject was right or wrong.

Because having people understand and perform a task correctly is often difficult, researchers routinely conduct training sessions before carrying out the actual experiment. Before going into the sorting task, I was given prior training that sought to familiarize me first with basic taste sensations abstracted from the olfactory, tactile, and temperature sensations that usually go with them in the foods we eat; that is, taste abstracted from flavor. The tastes were the currently recognized basic tastes (bitter, sweet, sour, umami, and salty), plus the sensations of astringency and metallic. These last two, which combine taste and touch, usually go with our experiences of bitter and salty, and are not easily recognized as separate sensations. Given that there are different chemical compounds that elicit a single taste quality, the scientist needed to choose which compound to use to represent each taste sensation.

As another sensory scientist told me, "Nothing sensory is truly objective, instead it moves in a spectrum that can be made more or less objective." Thanks to training, people in experimental conditions can get better at evaluating the same stimulus, and this can be considered an objective measure. And it is considered even more objective to have people rate how similar or different two smells are rather than asking them if something smells grassy, for instance. However, what are considered to be subjective measures have been also judged, in certain conditions, reliable. In our different conversations over the issue of objectivity in sensory studies, the same sensory scientist insisted that in her studies she found that, time and again, people were more consistent in their reports of liking than in their intensity judgments. Yet intensity rating and the use of scales are often seen as more objective and scientific. Studies of likes and dislikes, what is referred in the literature as hedonics—a branch of psychology that deals with the study of pleasurable and nonpleasurable states—has usually been left to industry. However, over the years, it has also gained some ground in scientific research as a subjective measure.

The question for this later scientist, who is interested in understanding food preferences, is how to measure an experience that has much to do with education and culture. Behavioral end points, while useful, fall short for her in this regard, so instead of using forced-choice methods that circumvent justification through language, she would make the case for trusting and encouraging studies that treat verbal reporting, that is introspection, as valuable data. According to her and other scientists, humans reflecting about their inner states provide important information, *because* and not despite their linguistic ability. And as it was previously pointed out, these more subjective measures found a place in studies of use to the food industry.

But as smell and taste researchers repeatedly told me, there are very few scientists who can make a career out of psychophysics alone. Funding for this type of research basically only comes from industry and is not necessarily highly regarded as hard-core science. Psychophysical methods in the chemical senses, compared to molecular biology, have not made great breakthroughs. Or as a smell scientist explained to me: "psychophysics is not likely to produce major breakthroughs because it is not driven by technology or data. There are limiting factors in humans sniffing even if we make an amazing machine for delivering odors. There always has to be someone sniffing at the other end, doing something in response to it."

Discussing Sensory Differences in a Sensory Panel

During my fieldwork at a middle-size American flavor company, I got to sit in a sensory panel meeting with trained experts from different departments. Sensory or taste panels are one method among others (such as flavor profiles, consumer preference tests, quality controls, and other descriptive analyses) that have become standard tools for flavor characterization, measurement, and sensory design.[28] These panels are based on consensus established among participants (experts or novices) who serve as measuring instruments under controlled conditions, that is, making sure samples are presented uniformly and judged equally. They are part of what Christy Spackman and Jacob Lahne have named "sensory labor"—practices of tasting and smelling capable of producing a valuable fact about collective experience.[29] How this occurs and what is at stake in turning humans into measuring instruments for science and industry by repeated exposure to odorants and tastants has been the subject of recent scholarship in the social sciences.[30] Complementing this work, ethnographic observation of what happens inside taste panels has provoked different questions about consumer culture; expertise and sensory attunement; and critiques about processes of standardization of the senses and food marketization.[31] Here, the ethnographic vignette serves as an illustration of how much and in what way the measurement of sensory experience, as tool for the food industry, begets communicative and corporeal practices. As Sarah Besky has found in the case of the establishment of prices at tea auctions, however important numbers are, they "can never be insulated from the embodied experience of the tea they represent."[32]

In the case of the sensory panel I participated in, the only trained sensory scientist at the company led the meeting. The group needed to help characterize different vanilla yogurts sold in the United States and Canada. According to the flavor experts working for this company, vanilla flavor and Greek yogurt are not exactly a perfect match, but the combination has gained popularity in the United States and elsewhere, due to the Greek yogurt explosion on supermarket shelves in the last decade. Emphasizing its health benefits, many competing brands today have transformed Greek yogurt into a variety of products with numerous flavors. Vanilla Greek yogurt is one variation. Greek yogurt is known for its thicker consistency and tangy flavor; vanilla for accompanying many sweet goods. Their combination is challenging to sensory evaluators. For the flavor industry, this raises questions about how to describe it and, more importantly, on what basis can different formulations of the same profile be compared?

The panel had already come up with a series of descriptors in previous meetings, but they now needed to decide which were working and which were not. Instead of coming up with new terms, the sensory scientist urged participants to stick to the list of descriptors provided. People in the room took turns voicing their concerns and apprehensions regarding some of the terms that they were using. One person said, "I'm having trouble with the cheese reference, because to me there is a good (pleasant) reference: say, ricotta, cottage, or mozzarella, and a bad (unpleasant) reference: what we refer to as stinky cheese." Immediately another person continued, "Yes, it is like spoiled milk, but we don't have it as a term, but in some yogurts, there is that note." The sensory scientist paused to think and then added, "And then, again the 'dirty note' is different from an 'earthy note.' So how about goaty?" Someone then replied, "Well, but there is an overlap between sweaty and goaty." "Okay," she conceded, "I want us then to differentiate between cheese (let's pretend it's good cheese) and sweaty/goaty."

The discussion did not end there. A different objection came up: "I think the fruit cocktail reference is causing trouble," someone else announced. "How about canned pear?" the panel leader proposed. Trying one more time a sample of one of the products, J.—the head research chef at the company—spontaneously voiced her opinion about Greek yogurt: "It's very sour. It's just such an unpleasant product. I say take it back to Greece." She continued, "Besides, yogurt is a live product; you leave it two days in the fridge and it changes. So how do we account for that in our description?" There was no immediate response, but the participants were familiar with such problems. Despite having to try two more samples of vanilla Greek yogurt, the meeting ended on a humorous note.

The sensory scientist explained to me that the idea for those meetings is to *collectively* understand the flavor qualities found in vanilla Greek yogurt and be able to quantify them in order to provide a visual rendering of the tested products' sensory characteristics and an indication of where each product stands in relation to the others. The final outcomes of these sensory panels, after statistical analyses, are product maps and spider charts—graphical visualization methods to represent multivariate data and to help the client visualize the relationship among products according to their sensory qualities.

"The ideal scenario for these expert panels," said the company's sensory scientist, "is to leave judgments about liking behind, but it is often irresistible. You saw it with J. [the head research chef]. Also, for instance, it is hard not to say that a particular brand is yucky, over-flavored, or over the top. If the reaction is extreme disgust, it is hard to do a judgment test." However, these are commentaries that stay within the meetings and are not necessarily shared or tabulated in any form for later presentations about the products' flavor profile. Yet to say that they are not part of the evaluation would be a misrepresentation. Flavor profiling is possible not only because of the discriminative capacities of experts, but also because their judgment is intrinsic to the experience.

The resulting flavor map or chart is an instrument of sensory measurement to aid qualitative interpretation. Or better yet, both are instruments of *qualitative measurement*, an oxymoron that the industry has learned to define and refine. "At the end," said the sensory scientist, "we know that individuals tend to be consistent with their ratings, particularly if trained, so the most important thing is that they can *differentiate* the attributes of different products." While sensory panels put much labor into minimizing the effects of time, temperature, color, and other factors that can affect flavor judgment, the success of the panel is based on whether participants can exercise their olfactory and taste judgment to the best of their ability, so it is possible to point out what makes one product different from another. Because this is not about testing consumers' flavor preferences but providing flavor profiles to understand sensory differences, the sensory scientist pointed out, "We rather need to be on the 'oversensitive' side than on the consumer side. Sensory measurement is not like a machine but you do expect to get input from it."

However, at the time of analysis, it was clear that differences among the products did not stand out as self-evident. After running a principal component analysis for choosing which variables could explain variance, the sensory scientist said she wished to make the differences more apparent, so it was necessary to play around with the data, change the terminology in some cases, create new categories, and separate measures. If there is no discrimination, the information is not helpful or easy to market. In the end, she came up with four quadrants and four representative yogurt samples according to their levels of sweetness, citric acid, lactic acid, and fruity notes. The dominant characteristics of quadrant one were base notes (cheesy notes, chalky, etc.), quadrant two was also dominant in base notes but also sweet, and quadrant four was found dominant in aromatic fruity components. She had trouble defining the dominant attribute of the third quadrant, but after repeated tastings and thought, she came to the conclusion that while the base notes of the first quadrant were "fresh dairy," those of the third were "dirtier dairy"—an observation also present during the discussion among panelists.

Unsurprisingly, when the flavor profile map was given to clients the categories didn't turn out to be self-evident. Representatives from different food companies were asked to try four yogurts and to situate each yogurt in one of the quadrants. Many people confused the samples and were surprised to hear about a citric note they did not perceive. The power of the panel's explanation of the yogurt's flavor lost clarity when taken out of its controlled environment. The issue of developing a common vocabulary kept coming up. The expert's flavor profile could be debated on subjective grounds. Thus, the objective communication of sensory and chemical qualities of foods remains an elusive goal and is rarely an indisputable matter. It is only through multiple iterations of different tests that something as ephemeral and subjective as flavor gets quantified and visualized, and even then with the knowledge that limitations in experimental control will persist. What is studied under controlled conditions quickly acquires a life of its own outside those conditions, and capturing this constantly moving target is a never-ending challenge.

Conclusion

So, what do early psychophysical thinking and its metaphysical promises have in common with their contemporary industrial applications? While psychophysics has not remained a fixed set of approaches and laws for the measurement of sensation, there are some continuities and commonalities between past and present. As both scientific enterprise and commercial tool, psychophysics has placed great value on experimental control, acknowledging that sensory measurement is not a straightforward affair. Rather, as the preceding ethnographic accounts show, it is difficult to reach firm conclusions about olfaction, taste, or flavor under the constraints imposed by the laboratory. While flavor companies might not pursue precision the way science does, there is still much labor put into making stable conditions to judge and quantify sensory attributes and reach consensus. In both the lab and in businesses, scientists are attentive to the ways slight sensory changes (things that otherwise pass unnoticed by others) come to matter—as with the conversation about sweaty/goaty descriptors. This level of awareness or sensory attunement is as much a part of experimental control as a product of the cultivation of the senses put to work in psychophysical experimentation. The differences between science and industry in this respect are manifest in the ways in which sensory differences are signaled and come to matter. For basic research on taste and smell, differences in perception matter as long as they can be biologically accounted for and contribute to the understanding of underlying mechanisms. For sensory scientists, differences in perception matter as long as they can be related to the assumptions, expectations, and goals of the food industry.[33]

Contrary to the early belief that sensorial judgments were subjective measures not to be trusted, modern psychophysics picked up its classical counterpart's interest in sense experience and perceptual sensitivity and turned experimental subjects (both panel experts and consumers) into measuring instruments that inform others about subjective experiences through scales, reference samples, and technical lexicons. Since its mid-twentieth-century resurgence, psychophysics has occupied an important place in the study of the chemical senses, despite being the field least funded by nonindustry agencies. Simultaneously, it has also become a tool to study commercial products and our reaction to them (as part of the canon of sensory science) and a method to study individual sensory differences.

Within this new role assumed by sensory science and marketing research in the flavor and fragrance industry, measurement of sensory attributes has moved away from quantification of what there *is* in flavors to a focus on what flavors *do*, particularly as "drivers of liking." In this shift, psychophysics, a minor discipline with few trained experts, has played an important role in turning flavor into an object of commerce which responds to scientific and technical developments and to the commercial imperative of recognizing that consumers' opinions are the determining factor of product success. It has also depended on the increasing convergence of words and numbers and the fact that objective (descriptive and discriminative) and subjective measures (affective) are no longer understood as antagonistic and independent of each other.

In the end, this paring of history and ethnography hopes to contribute to a more comprehensive vision of psychophysics—a science that is often portrayed as reductionist by its standard definition as the measurement of the relationship between stimuli and sensation. Building on Erica Fretwell's notion of speculative science, the image of psychophysics presented here maintains that a quantitative measure of a sensation relies on a broader conceptualization, encompassing both language and embodied responses and defying the notion of a simple correspondence between physical stimuli and experience. The ups and downs of psychophysics show how while our subjective experience cannot be reduced to objective measures, neither is our experience alien to them. Psychophysical measures in the lab and in industry have been used, sometimes reductively and other times expansively, as tools of sense-making and, later, product design. Descriptive and analytical tools remain intertwined. Neither subjective nor objective measures exhaust what there is in a taste, a smell, or a flavor; rather, both serve as means for communicating, discussing, agreeing, and disagreeing with others about what sense perceptions are, how they change, and what they do to us, depending on context and its needs.

CHAPTER 6

Sky's the Limit

Capitalism, the Senses, and the Failure of Commercial Supersonic Aviation in the United States

DAVID SUISMAN

Early in the 1960s, President John F. Kennedy set two aerospace priorities for the United States. The first was that by the decade's end Americans would walk on the moon. The second was that the nation would develop a supersonic transport (SST) plane—a commercial aircraft that would whisk passengers across the skies faster than the speed of sound. The first project culminated in July 1969 when astronauts Neil Armstrong and Buzz Aldrin famously strode across the lunar landscape, some 240,000 miles from the earth's surface. The second ambition was never realized, and the promise that the American aerospace industry would lead an age of supersonic travel fizzled. Some of the reasons for this were complex and distant from the day-to-day lives of Americans, but one—the Achilles heel of the SST program—was neither abstruse nor remote. Unlike the moon landing, which was essentially a onetime spectacle which Americans experienced on television screens and through the front page of newspapers, the supersonic transport would have profoundly affected people's daily lives, invading their homes and assaulting their senses on an ongoing basis. Relatively few travelers would have flown on supersonic planes, yet on the ground, each passage overhead would have produced a jarring, ear-splitting roar. That is, had the supersonic transport program "succeeded" (in the eyes of its proponents), sonic booms would have become the sounds of daily life.[1]

For those who have never heard a sonic boom, it is difficult to conjure its effect. For one thing, it is not merely sound but a powerful shock wave, an explosive release of compressed energy caused by an object traveling in space faster than the sound waves its movement creates. The result is a blast not merely heard in the ear but also felt in the body, experienced instantaneously, like an explosion, without buildup or warning to the brain. More than simply loud, sonic booms are forceful, disruptive, and often frightening. They jolt people, interrupt the flow of their lives, make babies cry, and wake children and adults from their slumber. Under the right circumstances, they also can shatter windows, send objects perched on shelves crashing to the floor, and cause cracks in plaster walls and ceilings. In January 1967, newspapers reported that sonic booms from American military aircraft damaged prehistoric cliff dwellings and geological formations at two national parks. Seven months later, accounts circulated that three people were killed when booms triggered by the French Air Force caused a Breton farmhouse to collapse.[2] Although sonic booms are often described as "startling," this familiar word does little to capture the effect of their suddenness. In 2009, when sonic booms caused by military aircraft rocked Seattle, local residents tweeted their reactions soon after the fact: "Scare [*sic*] the fuck out of me!"; "Freaked me out: I thought we were getting nuked"; "I thought I had lived through my first . . . bombing!" and "Nearly Crapped Myself! . . . terrifying."[3] To be sure, no answer was needed to the rhetorical question posed by a letter writer to the *New York Times* in 1967, "Who will want to be under the surgeon's knife when a sonic boom jars his hand?"[4]

In the end, this sensory onslaught is not the only reason that widespread supersonic air travel did not materialize. Rather, the American SST program was scuttled by a combination of economic and environmental factors.[5] Numerous other essays in this book detail how capitalist forces sought to coopt, absorb, or exploit sensory experience in the twentieth century. This chapter explores what can happen when capitalism and the senses are in tension and cannot be reconciled. Born in some of the most intense years of the Cold War, the SST program was propelled by powerful rhetoric, and vast resources were marshaled to ensure its success. The fact that the program failed, therefore, is both notable and surprising, given the political and economic support it had enjoyed. Yet by the early 1970s, many citizens had lost faith in the inherent and invariable benignity of American science and engineering, and a growing number were sounding alarms about unchecked technological "progress." In this context, critics questioned the power that industry and government had over people's bodies, and the human sensorium became a site of intense contestation. The result was that the unwanted corporeal effects of the SST program ignited an opposition movement that rendered the program as a whole untenable. The sensory impact of sonic booms cannot alone explain why the program ended, but it stood shoulder to shoulder with other considerations and reveals how the expansion of markets may stall when they have widespread sensory consequences.

Why SST?

Sound does not occur in a vacuum, acoustically or politically. The sonic booms that undermined the SST program must be heard in the context of the Cold War, which was not merely the setting for the SST program in the 1960s; it was its raison d'être. Kennedy and other SST proponents envisioned that these supersonic aircraft would symbolize the United States' standing as the preeminent leader in global aviation, a position it secured in the years after World War II. Moreover, sales of the new planes to airlines worldwide would enhance the United States' industrial power and strengthen the country's balance of trade. Producing such planes would not come cheap: in 1969, the development costs of the SST were projected to rival those of the Manhattan Project. Yet these expenditures were seen as warranted in the tense political environment of the Cold War. American officials knew that the Soviet Union had also undertaken to build a supersonic transport, and many early proponents believed that if the United States failed to develop such a plane first, the result would be "another Sputnik"—a great international embarrassment and blow to the country's stature on the global stage.[6]

At the same time, the United States had another competitor in the race to build an SST as well. In 1962, the governments of France and Great Britain entered into an agreement to build their own supersonic passenger plane, later named the Concorde in honor of their harmonious cooperation. It was this rivalry as much the one with the Soviet Union that forced the United States' hand. In his speech launching the program, which came immediately after Pan American World Airways, one of the country's leading airlines, announced an order for six supersonic aircraft from the French-British group, Kennedy did not mention the latter effort by name but called on the government "in partnership with private industry to develop . . . a commercially successful supersonic transport superior to that being built in any other country in the world." In short, Kennedy asserted, "neither the economics nor the politics of international air competition permit us to stand still in this area."[7]

When a battle over booms erupted in the years that followed, it grew directly out of this Cold War setting. More specifically, the way people reacted to sonic booms in the 1960s was prefigured by conflicts over military jets flying at supersonic speeds beginning in the 1950s. Relatively few people experienced flyovers by these planes directly, but those who did certainly knew it and often lodged complaints. Consequently, as early as 1959, the navy and air force sought to stanch the grievances that often followed supersonic airborne exercises with a public relations film titled *Mission: Sonic Boom*. In a tone that bordered on boastful, the film's narrator warned viewers that a single aircraft flying at 1,200 mph "could create a boom that would startle the tens of millions [of people] along the eastern seaboard in a mere ten minutes." But rather than protest, urged the voiceover, Americans would do better to think of sonic booms as the "sound of security."[8] In the following years, however, this suggestion did little to mollify disgruntled civilians, leading the military to refer to sonic booms as the "sound of freedom" instead.[9] Still, as news reports of the effects of sonic booms mounted, many citizens resented being told they should be grateful for these disturbances. As one Wisconsin resident wrote to Senator William Proxmire, "I know they will give you the old saw that they are doing this to protect the country. BUNK!"[10]

The boom battle sparked by the SST, therefore, resonated with political meaning, as it embodied the "danger that public policy [had become] captive of a scientific-technological elite" and of the militarized fusion of the public and private sector which President Dwight Eisenhower warned of in his farewell address in 1961.[11] When the SST program was formally launched in 1963, it was understood that the aerospace industry on its own would never develop a supersonic transport because of the enormous expense and risk, so the government committed to covering 75 (later 90) percent of the aerospace industry's development and design costs. "This is the land of private enterprise," the chairman of American Airlines wrote in a letter sent to every U.S. senator in 1967, but without a "very substantial" infusion of government funds, the nation's SST would never get off the ground.[12] At stake was what a vice president of the Boeing Company, which won the competition to build the SST, characterized as the biggest program in aviation history in terms of potential sales.[13]

Less often mentioned was that Boeing and other leading aerospace manufacturers were also major military contractors with a clear interest in cooperating in any program urged on them by their most valuable customer. In this way, the SST program epitomized what Eisenhower had called the "military-industrial complex," a convergence of the most powerful forces in government and business. By 1964, for example, President Lyndon Johnson's advisory committee on the supersonic transport was chaired by Robert McNamara, the secretary of defense, and its other members included Luther Hodges and C. Douglas Dillon, the secretaries of commerce and the treasury; the head of the National Aeronautics and Space Administration (NASA), James Webb; the head of the Federal Aviation Agency (FAA, renamed the Federal Aviation Administration in 1967), Najeeb Halaby; the director of the Central Intelligence Agency, John McCone; Stanley Osborne, a former airline executive who was chairman of the board of the Olin Mathieson Chemical Company, a major producer of ammunition; and Eugene R. Black, former head of the World Bank and a board member of the Chase Manhattan Bank, the International Telephone and Telegraph Company, and other companies and financial institutions.[14] This was not a group to be taken lightly.

From the outset, officials guiding the development of the SST program recognized that sonic booms might pose a threat to its implementation. To address this concern, they sought to gauge and shape public response. First, they presided over numerous community impact studies of sonic booms, essentially blasting a test area with sonic booms and then conducting public opinion polls to see how residents felt about them. The most extraordinary of these was the study carried out in Oklahoma City in 1964, bombarding Oklahoma's capital city with eight sonic booms a day, every day for six months. The results were a Rorschach test. Nearly three quarters of respondents said they *could* live with such booms, a finding trumpeted by the program's boosters. Conversely, more than one quarter responded they could *not*, a figure seized on by critics and opponents. A subsequent report by an elite committee of the National Academy of Sciences called for more testing and better public relations.[15]

Recommendations for more data notwithstanding, no major community-oriented studies followed. In fact, in 1967 William "Bozo" McKee, the four-star general who was head of the FAA, actively blocked subsequent community impact studies for fear of the political fallout they could have.[16] Instead, the leaders of the SST program pushed for more studies on how to control and limit the intensity of the booms and tried to influence popular opinion through more aggressive public relations. In 1969, for example, the Department of Transportation issued a booklet for schoolchildren, titled *SST-T-T (Sound, Sense, Today, Tomorrow, Thereafter)*, a seventy-three-page primer that sought to normalize sonic booms and the disruptions caused by supersonic aviation. Its cast of characters included Marita the Supersonic Pussycat, the first feline to fly to Paris on the SST, and a "smooth chick with good looks" named Deci Belle (a play on "decibel"), who was "attracted to noise—the louder the better," as well as

The House That Had to Move ("Now the airport has room to grow"). The teacher's guide outlined a role-playing exercise in which students imagined themselves as the head of the Federal Aviation Administration who must confront a group of citizens concerned about sonic booms and convince them of the importance of continuing the SST program. More than 50,000 copies were distributed to educators and remained in use in some classrooms for years.[17]

A year later, as the debate over the SST program grew toward a crescendo, the charm offensive continued. In April 1970, President Richard Nixon appointed William Magruder, a charismatic, forty-five-year-old crew-cut-sporting aeronautical engineer to head the national SST program. A former test pilot for the air force and designer for Douglas Aircraft, Magruder was, as the SST program's most exhaustive historian put it, "a true believer in aviation generally, and in the SST in particular." Even Magruder's political opponents conceded he was "an excellent salesman" who gave a "hell of a presentation" and was extremely effective in congressional hearings, in day-to-day lobbying in the U.S. Capitol, and when he appeared on television programs like the *Dick Cavett Show*.[18]

By this time, the Cold War notwithstanding, the arguments in favor of the SST focused almost exclusively on economics. Typical was a promotional film made by Boeing, *You and Me . . . and the SST*, which presented supersonic transportation as an inevitability with broad implications for trade, jobs, and consumer goods. "The airlines of the world *will* buy [SSTs]," asserted the film's narrator, journalist Bob Considine, but what remained an open question was whether or not the aircraft would be American made. "If [American airlines] buy an American model," he explained, "the money stays in the family, so to speak. If they buy a foreign model, the money goes abroad, and so does leadership in aviation." Support for the SST, then, amounted to an "investment story" whose moral was that an American SST would produce 150,000 jobs, "bolster the domestic economy," and "keep balance of trade in *our* favor." He drove home these points by translating them into terms consumers could easily appreciate: "One American SST sold abroad will pay for 20,000 small foreign cars; 400,000 silk suits; 10,000,000 transistor radios."[19]

Why Not SST?

Despite the powerful forces propelling the SST program forward, by the end of 1960s its political support was much less solid than in the heady years when President Kennedy had first set the nation's sights on supersonic air travel. The

American war in Vietnam reached an inflection point with the Tet Offensive in early 1968, and the dynamics of the Cold War were changing as President Nixon moved toward détente with the Soviet Union and China. Denunciations of the military-industrial complex were then appearing with greater and greater frequency, and a growing range of critics assailed the SST program as bad politics, bad business, and bad for people's bodies and peace of mind. Then, in April 1970, Earth Day triggered an awakening of environmental consciousness resulting in a David-versus-Goliath showdown over a congressional bill to extend funding for the SST program, in the midst of which an entirely new issue emerged—the possibility that regular SST flights would pollute the upper atmosphere, triggering serious effects on the planet's climate. By a narrow margin, opponents of the SST defeated the extension of funding, effectively bringing the program to an end in the spring of 1971.[20]

In retrospect, the SST program can be said to have collapsed under pressure from two directions, external and internal, with some of the forces acting on it apparent and others not. On the ground in 1970–71, it was evident that the defeat of SST was the outcome of organizing by a group called the Coalition Against the SST launched in Washington, D.C., in spring 1970 by a clutch of scrappy but savvy young activists. Together, they marshaled the political support of dozens of other organizations, lobbied members of Congress from both parties, and mobilized thousands of citizens to press their elected officials to oppose the extension of SST funding. Less obvious to the public but clear to insiders was the fact that the work of the coalition built on years of agitation by two extraordinary gadflies, the Swedish aeronautical engineer Bo Lundberg, who had begun speaking out against sonic booms and the SST as early as 1961, and a tireless Harvard physicist named William Shurcliff, who in 1967 founded the Citizens League Against the Sonic Boom with his Harvard colleague John T. Edsall. As I have detailed elsewhere, these activists persisted against overwhelming odds and ultimately delivered a victory that shapes what planes are in our skies to this day.[21]

Seen in retrospect, however, we can appreciate the degree to which the opposition to sonic booms and the SST belonged not just to the initiative of a few activists but to a specific historical moment as well. That is, as disruptive, invasive, and frightening as the booms often were, activism against the sensory impact of sonic booms and the SST was neither natural nor automatic. It grew out of specific circumstances.

Although noise had vexed city dwellers for centuries, not until the Progressive Era did reformers, often middle-class women, start noise abatement societies to police and quell what was deemed "unnecessary" noise. Their organizations, however, tended to be hyperlocal and short-lived, and despite American metropolises growing even noisier, political mobilization against unwanted sound essentially disappeared after the 1920s.[22] In the postwar period, noise concerns returned with the dawn of the jet age, as jet engines were substantially louder than those of the older propeller planes. Organized opposition, though, sprang up primarily in communities around airports and tended to be limited in scope in the 1950s and early 1960s. Challenging the SST, therefore, was far from preordained.[23]

Part of what made opposition to sonic booms different was the unprecedented scale of the issue. Noise concerns are generally local, but the sonic boom problem threatened people almost everywhere.[24] At the same time, agitation against the SST was also deeply contextual, belonging to what cultural theorist Stuart Hall would characterize as a historical "conjuncture." Such periods, in Hall's terms, are shaped by social, political, economic, and ideological contradictions. They are both moments of danger and of possibility and present a distinct opportunity for intellectual, social, cultural, and political action.[25] The traction that opposition to sonic booms got in the 1960s and early 1970s was not only a function of the suddenness, volume, and force of the booms themselves. It also grew out of a cultural and political moment particularly sensitive and responsive to these effects.

Timing

The way people reacted to the clear proximate issues—the sensory impact that commercial supersonic aviation would have on people's daily lives and the government's assertion that the SST was crucial to the Cold War—was informed by numerous exogenous concerns at the same time. Most obvious was the war in southeast Asia, primarily in Vietnam but by 1969 recognized to involve Cambodia and Laos as well. Although activism against the SST had no connection to the antiwar movement and in many ways was quite distinct from it, the growing distrust of government in relation to the war helped the challenge to the SST, a major government initiative, to take root. Meanwhile, so too did shifts in the ways that people thought about three other subjects: privacy, bodies, and sound.

First, the SST emerged at a time of heightened anxiety about, and debate over, privacy—and especially protection against violations of privacy by the government. As historian Sarah Igo has shown, privacy has long been a contested concept in American society, both shaping and shaped by what it meant to be a citizen. One form in which this appeared in the 1960s was intense debate over the privacy that individuals were entitled to from intrusion by government officials. Today, the U.S. Supreme Court's landmark decision *Griswold v. Connecticut* (1965) is best known for opening the door to legal access to contraceptives. This ruling, however, rested on an argument with far-reaching implications, namely that Americans enjoyed a constitutional "right to privacy" which was not identified in the specific guarantees of the Bill of Rights but existed in what Justice William O. Douglas, writing for the majority, referred to as the "penumbras" of the protections afforded by the First, Third, Fifth, and Ninth Amendments (the amendments concerning free speech, prohibition against forced quartering of troops, freedom from self-incrimination, and other rights, respectively). The "spirit" of these amendments suggested there existed "zones of privacy," Douglas wrote, where the state did not belong and could not legally penetrate.[26]

This understanding of privacy from government intrusion had implications far beyond access to contraception. In another landmark decision two years later, *Katz v. United States* (1967), the Supreme Court expanded the right to privacy in a case concerning the legality of wiretapping a public telephone booth (which was in this instance done to record the calls of a man who regularly used one specific payphone to place illegal bets). In 1890, in a famous article in the *Harvard Law Review*, Louis Brandeis and Samuel D. Warren had pondered whether Americans had a "right to be left alone" and warned against invasions of privacy by "mechanical devices," namely, surveillance technologies. When the issue came before the Supreme Court almost four decades later, a majority held in *Olmstead v. United States* (1928) that wiretapping did not violate an individual's protection against illegal search and seizure, as guaranteed by the Fourth Amendment. By the 1960s, however, the landscape changed. Electronic miniaturization opened up new possibilities for listening in on people's private conversations, and popular magazines like *Life* were running sensational cover stories about bugging devices that could be hidden in telephone mouthpieces, the handles of briefcases, and even in the olive of a martini.[27] Then, in light of the "right to privacy" established in *Griswold*, the *Katz* decision in 1967 overturned *Olmstead*, finding that the Constitution afforded American citizens "reasonable expectations of privacy" both in their homes and on their persons. The Fourth Amendment, wrote Justice Potter Stewart in what would become the decision's most famous phrase, "protects people, not places."[28]

The sonic boom debates resonated in this climate of heightened concern about sound and privacy. Of course, in one respect, supersonic aviation represented a qualitatively different kind of threat than surveillance did, in that the SST involved the state *making* sound, not listening to it, but the conflicts over supersonic jets and surreptitious wiretaps both involved people's right to seclusion and how people experienced the intimacy of aurality. Moreover, although *Griswold* and *Katz* concerned *government* intrusion in private life and the sonic booms of the SST represented a threat posed by *commercial* aviation, the two spheres were inextricably interconnected. The impetus and most of the funding for the SST program came from the federal government, and it was the military whose supersonic planes were used to conduct community impact studies of reactions to sonic booms. When it came to privacy, the menace of the government could not be disentangled from the threat posed by the aerospace industry. Because of its sensory impact, the SST marked a kind of home invasion by the military-industrial complex.

The second factor informing the reaction against sonic booms was a shift in how people thought about bodies in relation to the environment. In the 1960s, what historian Christopher Sellers has called a new "environmental imaginary" emerged in the then-incipient environmental movement, recentering the older concerns of conservationists around the human body (and, to a lesser extent, the bodies of nonhuman animals as well).[29] Exemplified by (though not limited to) Rachel Carson's *Silent Spring* (1962), this discursive framing posited bodies as vulnerable and under threat.[30] Not in one specific locale or region but essentially everywhere in the contemporary world, humans and other animals were now living in a state of corporeal danger, menaced particularly by the predations of private industry. The work of Carson and others pierced a naïve belief in the ethical infallibility of science, the result of which was that bodies were now increasingly understood as subject to a wide range of environmental hazards, some visible, others invisible, some slow moving or incremental, others affecting people precipitously and with no warning. This body-centered imaginary enabled the growth of the environmental movement, Sellers argued, because it made sense and appealed to people across lines of region, class, gender, race, and ethnicity, and in turn, the movement reinscribed and amplified the notion of the body in environmental danger. Linked as it was both to critique and activism, this idea of the body at risk underlay the way that many people reacted to the sensory impact of the sonic booms.

Finally, the anti-noise discourse reflected a heightened awareness of sound and noise in the arts, science, and politics, when sonic subjects were receiving unprecedented critical and creative attention. The international community of avant-garde artists known as Fluxus, for example, took shape in the early 1960s in the shadow of composer John Cage, many of whose members worked extensively with the materiality and experience of sound, including Dick Higgins, Al Hansen, Nam June Paik, Alison Knowles, Yoko Ono, and others, and became important figures in the proliferation and legitimization of sound in (and as) art. Meanwhile, composers Alvin Lucier and R. Murray Schafer also pushed audiences to think about sound in new ways. Lucier's pathbreaking work *I Am Sitting in a Room* (1969) focused listeners' attention not on a sequence of musical notes but on the ambient acoustics of an enclosed room.[31] Around the same time, Schafer fused artistic and environmentalist conceptualizations of sound, condemning how the clamor of modern, industrialized society corrupted what he called the "soundscape."[32]

While it would take several decades before the term "soundscape" came into more general use, by the time the SST debate reached its climax, many people had become acutely aware that sound was an important factor in shaping the environment in everyday life. Indeed, another index of the growing significance of sound in the 1960s was the revival of the grassroots noise abatement movement and the emergence of a new term for the degradation of the aural environment—*noise pollution*. In New York, a Broadway theater manager named Robert Alex Baron founded a noise abatement group, Citizens for a Quieter City (CQC), in 1966 to fight against the urban cacophony of jackhammers, metal garbage cans, car horns, and screeching subways but soon expanded the group's remit to battle noise pollution at large, including both sonic booms and aircraft noise generally.[33] He and likeminded reformers in New York and elsewhere drew on a growing body of scientific and social-scientific literature showing the psychological and physiological effects of noise. By 1969, the *New York Times* was reporting on a symposium of the National Council on Noise Abatement which found noise pollution caused both hearing loss and a dangerous constriction of blood vessels, as well as a congress by the American Medical Association decrying excessive noise as a danger not just to the body but to mental health as well.[34] A year later, in the wake of Earth Day, the *Times* and the *Wall Street Journal* both published reviews of three separate books on noise and the aural environment, two by science writers and one by Robert Alex Baron of Citizens for a Quieter City.[35]

This broad concern about noise was evident at the national level as well. Asserting that tranquility was "a national resource," Lyndon Johnson's secretary of the interior, Stewart Udall, announced in December 1967 that he was assembling a panel of distinguished scientists to study the impact of sonic booms and noise abatement more broadly.[36] In the next few years, the federal government took numerous steps to limit airplane noise, workplace noise exposure, and the din of automotive traffic on federal highways. More and more, people were calling on the FAA to set limits on airplane and airport noise, and in 1968 the House of Representatives voted 312 to zero for a bill mandating that the secretary of transportation establish measurement standards for aircraft noise and sonic booms.[37] In 1969, the Department of Labor set a maximum constant sound level for workers of companies having contracts with the federal government, and a year later, these standards were applied to all workers under the new Occupational Safety and Health Act of 1970, a shift hailed by organized labor.[38] The National Environmental Policy Act of 1969 included noise among the considerations of environmental impact studies henceforth required for all major activities of the federal government affecting the environment.[39] In 1970, Congress mandated that the Federal Highway Administration develop standards for mitigating the noise of highway traffic and federally funded transportation-related construction projects.[40]

This groundswell of regulation peaked over the next two years, even after the defeat of the SST. In March 1971, a government-sponsored panel found that noise in the United States was "on the verge of reaching a serious level" and recommended new federal and state standards to protect against hearing damage and annoyance.[41] In October, the Department of Transportation and NASA formed a joint office of noise abatement, and in 1972, Congress passed the Noise Control Act, allocating funds for a new federal Office of Noise Abatement and Control, which had been authorized by the Environmental Protection Act of 1970.[42] By that time, moreover, the fight against noise was evident not only on the level of municipal, state, and federal governments but also in formal declarations by the United Nations and the World Health Organization.[43] "Noise pollution" was now a widely recognized concept, marking a clear shift from only a few years earlier when a congressman from New York had needed to explain this term on Capitol Hill when he fought (unsuccessfully) for the establishment of a federal noise control agency.[44] Thus, without minimizing the crucial work done by anti-SST activists like Bo Lundberg, William Shurcliff, and the Coalition Against the SST, we can acknowledge that opposition to sonic booms in the late 1960s and early 1970s also fit into a bigger phenomenon: an expanding, heterogeneous discourse about sound and noise.

Internal Weakness

The flip side of the pressure applied by activists and critics from the outside was the instability of support from within the movement promoting the SST. On the one hand, the SST did enjoy a great deal of strong and consistent backing from the government and the aerospace industry. Not only did three consecutive presidents—Kennedy, Johnson, and Nixon—push the program forward, but Nixon actively suppressed a report which he himself commissioned that recommended the program be terminated.[45] In Congress, the two leading backers of the program were the senators from Washington state, Warren Magnuson and Henry "Scoop" Jackson, both of whom had been in the chamber for decades and wielded much political influence. Although they were both known as solid environmentalists on many issues, the two fought indefatigably for SST funding—much of which went to the Seattle-based Boeing Company—until the bitter end.[46]

On the other hand, neither the government nor the aerospace industry was monolithic, and at the same time that activists were attacking the program publicly, the forces advancing the SST were increasingly compromised from within as well. As early as 1964, Wisconsin representative Henry Reuss raised doubts about the government's rationale, arguing that the SST was uneconomical, unnecessary, and a giveaway to the aerospace industry. Admittedly, Reuss commanded far less power in the nation's capital than the senators from Washington state, but by the late 1960s, he was well known as a persistent congressional critic of the program.[47] Another important antagonist was William Proxmire, the senior senator from Wisconsin and a relentless crusader against superfluous and excessive government spending. In 1970, for example, Proxmire published *Report from Wasteland: America's Military-Industrial Complex*, which condemned the dependence of the major aerospace manufacturers, including Boeing and General Electric, on lavish military contracts. It characterized the SST program as yet another example of government profligacy. As he put it, the very proposition of supersonic travel was undermined by "the destructive sonic boom," which made flights over heavily populated areas impracticable (or at best impractical). And realistically, he added, the amount of time the SST would save travelers was greatly exaggerated if the inconvenience and distance of airports from city centers were factored in.[48] Eventually, the arguments against the SST program undermined its formerly solid political support. By the time the Senate voted down the extension of SST funding in December 1970, eighteen members who had previously supported the program, including twelve Republicans, had been persuaded to switch their votes. Some were moved by political arguments; others, like John Pastore of Rhode Island, flipped after receiving thousands of letters from constituents and a petition with the signatures of 1,600 schoolchildren.[49]

Moreover, by the time of the high-profile showdown in Congress over the extension of SST funding in 1970, it was evident that the private sector had a more fraught and complex relationship with the program than was publicly acknowledged. In practice, the aerospace industry was not a unified, undifferentiated entity, nor was it unqualified or unanimous in its support for SST. Airports, for example, were liable for violations of local noise ordinances, and in July 1970 the Airport Operators Council International urged the Senate not to fund the SST if the planes could not meet noise regulations. (Two years earlier, the same group had broken with the industry-wide National Aircraft Noise Abatement Council, which it felt was not taking meaningful steps toward reducing noise, and shortly thereafter, two other industry groups, the American Association of Airport Executives and the Air Line Pilots Association, left as well.)[50] In contrast to the airports, the airlines generally supported the SST program, although some carriers, especially American, Delta, and Braniff, which flew primarily domestic routes, had expressed concern about the supersonic plane's design and its noise problem, and after Congress defunded the program, one of the heads of the airlines' trade group, the Air Transport Association, expressed doubts about the airlines' political effectiveness. Unsurprisingly, the strongest push by the private sector for renewal of congressional funding came from the manufacturing sector, yet later, when the dust settled, some observers faulted Boeing, General Electric, and the Aerospace Industries Association for not lobbying harder and in concert with one another. Indeed, some scholars have suggested Boeing executives had conflicted feelings about the SST and were relieved when the program was ended.[51]

Even more telling was the opposition burbling beneath the surface. The official support by the major aerospace manufacturers notwithstanding, some of their employees had doubts about the SST and a few tried actively to undermine it. In Seattle, many Boeing workers belonged to the local chapter of the Sierra Club, one of the country's leading environmentalist organizations, and this became a back channel through which they could express their disapproval. As the group's Pacific Northwest representative, Brock Evans, recounted in 1982, "I can't begin to remember how many members of Boeing came up to me and said, 'I don't like this [SST] thing either. This is a dumb thing. I work for them. I may even have a job in the project, but I still think it is a dumb thing.'" More consequentially, such people often leaked unfavorable information about the SST program to Evans, who redirected it to activists lobbying in Washington. "[I remember] meeting people in parking lots in the dark of the night and getting little documents and stuff like that and shipping them back [East]," he said. "We got a lot of material that way."[52]

Likewise, Gary Soucie, chair of the Coalition Against the SST, also received valuable leaked information. In one instance, a former Boeing engineer came to his office in Washington and discussed with him how "shaky some of [Boeing's] studies were." Other times, he got intelligence from deep within the airline industry, as when internal engineering studies and other reports from TWA, United, and SwissAir (where he himself had worked in the public relations department) arrived in anonymous packages with no return address. For fear of exposing his sources, he could not publish the documents themselves, he remembered, but they furnished the anti-SST opposition with a great amount of helpful data.[53] The seeds of the SST's demise were sown, therefore, in multiple locations by a variety of dissenters, some of whom even depended on the aerospace industry for their paychecks.

Reverberations

Congress voted to terminate the SST program conclusively in March 1971, an outcome President Richard Nixon called "distressing and disappointing" and a "severe blow" both to the aerospace industry and to the leadership of the United States in the Cold War.[54] By the time lawmakers delivered the coup de grâce, though, the government had already spent more than a billion dollars to design and develop a supersonic aircraft, and the aerospace industry had not yet even built a prototype.[55] For the United States, commercial supersonic aviation was an unequivocal failure.

Did it matter? The Soviet Union's version of the SST, the Tupolev Tu-144, had taken to the skies at the end of 1968, but its maiden voyage proved not to be "another Sputnik" as the Americans feared. Rather, the Soviet achievement was soon upstaged by the American moon landing eight months later, and in 1973, a Tu-144 suffered a spectacular crash at the Paris Air Show, the world's premier trade event, which all but doomed its commercial potential.[56] Meanwhile, the now-iconic Concorde, the plane produced jointly by France and Great Britain, took its inaugural flight in 1969 and entered regular service in 1976. Its commercial operations, however, were far more limited than originally envisioned—flying only routes from New York and Washington to London and Paris and restricted to subsonic speeds when flying over land. This service continued for twenty-seven years, and most experts judged it a mixed success. The planes were glamorous, sleek, and fast, but only fourteen were ever built and were only ever operated by two heavily subsidized national airlines, Air France and British Airways. Because of safety and maintenance issues, they were withdrawn from commercial service in 2003.[57]

Given this bigger picture, what might the failure of the American SST teach us? For one thing, it stands as an object lesson in accountability and limits in large-scale technological innovation and, raising these issues, it shows what can happen when prevailing ideological assumptions are revealed and challenged. In the 1960s, an unprecedented number of citizens started to question two precepts that had long been part of the nation's creed: first, the inherent beneficence of American science and engineering, and second, the certainty of frictionless, limitless technological progress. Debates over these two ideas—beneficence and progress—confronted a range of issues, from nuclear weapons to pesticides, and the battles over the SST contributed to the moment in postwar history when these shibboleths began to appear untenable to a growing number of Americans. To be sure, they did not disappear altogether and have survived in multiple forms down to today, but scrutinizing and contesting the SST added momentum to a wave of skepticism about this dogma that broke over the United States in the 1960s and 1970s.

For another thing, the fall of the SST program brings attention to the possibility of sensory assault as an unwanted byproduct of economic development (what economists would call a "negative externality") and this can help us think about how capitalism and the senses are bound. Neither the abstract economic arguments nor the material, corporeal considerations alone brought about the SST's defeat, but rather it was the fact that these concerns were twinned and complementary that proved politically decisive. On the economic side, boosters notwithstanding, a general consensus emerged across the ideological spectrum that the numbers did not add up. This was driven home in September 1970 when the Coalition Against the SST circulated statements it collected about the economics of the supersonic transport program by seventeen of the country's leading economists—including Milton Friedman, John Kenneth Galbraith, Paul Samuelson, James Tobin, and others—all but one of whom stood against it. Indeed, so emphatically was Friedman opposed that he invited the coalition to pass his private telephone number on to any member of Congress who harbored doubts about the economic arguments.[58]

Meanwhile, those who were concerned about booms and bodies scored a major victory in November 1970 when none other than Warren Magnuson, one of the SST's staunchest, most influential backers in Washington, proposed legislation that would ban commercial planes from triggering sonic booms over populated areas. This concession was a calculated gambit intended to undercut the environmentalists' arguments against the SST. Ironically, though, restricting these aircraft to subsonic speeds would also have increased the airlines' net costs, making the SST even *less* economical to operate than it would have been already.[59] That is, minimizing human exposure to sonic booms and maximizing aerospace profitability pulled in opposite directions. Ultimately, Magnuson's bill failed and the SST was defeated, but this flashpoint exemplified the congeries of political, economic, and environmental issues that the SST program could not resolve.

In the end, then, the SST proved more difficult to realize than sending astronauts to the moon. Unlike lunar exploration, the obstacles were not essentially technological; American engineers were fully capable of designing airplanes that flew faster than the speed of sound. They lay instead in the elusiveness of an acceptable balance between economic and political goals on the one hand and the material realities of sonic booms and other effects of supersonic flight on the other. The priorities of the government and the aviation industry could not be reconciled with the right of citizens not to be assaulted by the sound and force of sonic booms and the obligation of government to protect that right. The American SST program threatened to transform the sensory experience of everyday life for countless people around the country and throughout the world. At this particular moment of conjuncture, however, it was undone by the tensions and contradictions in the nation's competing agendas. The economic and political issues could not be quelled, the sonic booms could not be silenced.

Since the defeat of the SST in the early 1970s, initiatives to revive commercial supersonic aviation have returned, zombie-like, every few years. Currently, several companies have resumed intensive work to develop supersonic passenger planes, promising design modifications that would reduce the sonic boom to a thud no louder than the slamming of a car door.[60] Like the highly publicized 2021 space tourism initiatives of technology billionaires Jeff Bezos and Elon Musk, these programs have been funded by private capital and, like their predecessors, the new planes would consume immense amounts of fuel for the benefit of only a small number of elite travelers. Whether or not these companies can resolve the sonic boom problem remains to be seen, but what is evident is that flying in the face of today's climate crisis, such aircraft raise familiar questions about ephemeral versus long-term rewards and the gains for the few versus the costs borne by the many. The idea that aerospace technology can have unwanted consequences remains today as relevant as ever.

CHAPTER 7

Sounding Maritime Metal

On Weathering Steel and Listening to Capitalism at Sea

NICHOLAS ANDERMAN

What does capitalism sound like? And what might we learn about it through listening?

I recently tuned in from the deck of the French containership *Cendrillon*, moving through the northern Pacific Ocean at twenty knots. Here, standing amid the container stacks, the air is filled with the rhythmic, resonant noises of maritime metal—mostly steel and steel alloys—twisting and flexing against oceanic forces.[1] Like a tall building lying on its side, the segmented steel skeleton of the ship is designed to torque and bend in rough weather and heavy seas. This flexibility enables the vessel to absorb enough of the energy generated by the wind, waves, and currents to avoid breaking apart. For the seafarers who live and work on board the *Cendrillon*, the ship's structural elasticity is experienced in two ways: first, as motion, with the potential to induce seasickness; and second, as noise.[2] These effects are not unrelated. As the ethnomusicologist David Novak notes, "the Latin root of the word noise is *nausea*, from the Greek root *naus*," which means ship.[3] Noise, nausea, and ships go together etymologically and phenomenologically.

But the rolling and pitching motion of the *Cendrillon* is not the most immediate source of the sound on the ship's deck. During my time on board, the vessel was fully loaded, carrying around 9,000 shipping containers from ports in China and Korea to the West Coast of North America. Most of the noise on the deck is generated not by the medium-carbon and high-strength structural steel of the ship itself, but by weathering steel—the alloy used in the manufacture of shipping containers—groaning, cracking, and shrieking as the containers flex against one another and against the ship's hulking mass. What to make of this metallic din? What, if anything, can the sounds of maritime metal tell us about the ship and its cargo, or about the global logistical ensemble of which the *Cendrillon* is a key component? More broadly still, what might these sounds reveal about the global flows of capital that have given rise to the movement of the ship in the first place? Is sound a kind of evidence, and if so, of what exactly?

This chapter probes the sonic life of capitalism. As the term "life" suggests, the aim is to explore the relationship between sensing bodies, ensounded commodities, and sound as such. The term "ensounded" comes from the anthropologist Tim Ingold, who deploys it as a critique of the commonplace notion that sound exists or lives *in* the body, or in a contained, discrete corporeal space. Rather, for Ingold, the body is always in actuality penetrated by or immersed in sound—it is ensounded.[4] Let me straightaway point out that theorizing sound is a notoriously slippery undertaking. Research centered in the transdisciplinary field of sound studies suggests that to take sound seriously, to seek to understand sound on its own terms, one cannot simply recombine and redeploy the various moves to critique that have for more than half a century fallen under the heading "theory."[5] The problem, first, is down to etymology. Both "theory" and the closely related term "speculation" invoke vision and seeing clearly: the Greek term *theoria*, like the Latin term *specere*, means "to look." To theorize thus entails, first and foremost, meticulous looking. But how does one look at sound? There is literally nothing to see here.[6]

Second, sound has a tendency to destabilize the conventional epistemological frameworks routinely deployed by Western academics to order, organize, and interpret the world. Sound blurs the classical Aristotelian hylomorphic division between form and matter, for instance, and it muddles Descartes's strong distinction between subject and object.[7] Moreover, as James A. Steintrager and Rey Chow have recently pointed out, "you cannot theorize sound without thinking the engagement of interior and exterior, of perceiver and environment."[8] Ironically, then, sound would appear to *demand* scrupulous theorizing, even as it dissolves through sheer sonic excess most attempts to think about it.[9]

My solution to this paradox—we might call it the problem of sonic ambiguity—is to approach sound circuitously, specifically through and as reverberating matter. To wit, the first part of this chapter consists of a historical account of the development of weathering steel, a highly resonant compound material that has been vitally important to capitalist operations since at least the 1970s, when containerized cargo first became a global logistical norm. Despite (or perhaps because of) its ubiquity, weathering steel has been mostly overlooked by scholars, save various technical studies in metallurgy, engineering, and chemistry journals. The account I provide here begins to fill this gap. The historical analysis of the development of weathering steel in the first part of the chapter leads, in the second part, to a discussion of the symbolic significance of metals to the development and maintenance of capitalism. This section situates weathering steel in relation to broader narratives about metallurgy's relationship to capitalism, and seeks to deepen arguments that correlate, in a relatively simplistic manner, metal and capital. This section concludes with an account of what is almost certainly the most influential metallurgical metaphor in the social sciences, the so-called iron cage, in which, according to Max Weber, all of us who live under capitalism are confined.

In part three, I return to the noise on the deck of the *Cendrillon* in order to probe the methodological possibilities of listening as political-economic research and political practice. Working with the sounds of weathering steel containers in motion, I develop what amounts to an imaginative theorization of listening. Presented schematically, the argument proceeds as follows: by speculatively tracing sonic reverberations across disparate material thresholds, it may be possible for an astute listener to begin to sense capitalism otherwise, beyond and beneath its false appearance as an impenetrable totality. Listening to capitalism in this speculative manner, I propose, destabilizes not only capital's capacity to represent a world, but specifically its ability to represent itself as *the* world *in toto*.

Sound thus opens up space for thinking the everyday existence of capitalism beyond capitalist totality, though it must be said that this opening up does not happen automatically or "naturally." Rather, the kind of listening I am proposing here requires the listener to make creative inferences about sound and, based on those inferences, to actively construct vibratory sequences across space, time, and matter. The primary basis for this sonic play—and it is an extremely playful method—cannot be anything but prior knowledge of the reverberating materials in question. Listening, in the imaginative manner I lay out here, is thus historical and materialist in at least two senses, in that the listener approaches sound both concretely and speculatively through materials.

On Weathering Steel

The invention of the first successful shipping container in the mid-1950s, its subsequent international standardization, and its outsized impact on political-economic organization and social life at the scale of the planet has been well documented by scholars and in popular media alike. "Containers have been more important for globalisation than freer trade," asserted *The Economist* magazine in 2013, summing up an argument advanced by a raft of publications in the first decade and a half of the 2000s.[10] As described by the historian Marc Levinson in his classic 2006 account, the box reduced the cost of commodity transport to nil, relieving manufacturers of the need to locate production facilities near consumer markets.[11] As such, the container set the scene for outsourcing at a global scale, for the rise of China, for the emergence of post-Fordist precarity and income inequality in the West, and so on. "Everything else was secondary to organisation—to the equations of speed, weight and money. Everything else would fall into line," wrote the scholar of organization studies Martin Parker in 2006, glossing the influence of containerization on, well, everything.[12] Despite all this, even in Levinson's book—which still provides the most detailed account available of the container's development—the key material used in the construction of the box is referred to simply as steel. We can and should be more specific.

Upwards of 90 percent of the estimated twenty to twenty-five million shipping containers currently in circulation are made of Cor-Ten weathering steel, an alloy infused with a copper, chromium, and nickel compound invented in the early 1930s by the United States Steel Corporation (USS). "Cor-Ten" refers to the material's corrosion resistance and tensile strength. The fully capitalized designation COR-TEN remains a registered trademark of USS, though today the variant term Cor-Ten is used generically to describe weathering steel produced by any manufacturer. As such, I will use the terms weathering steel and Cor-Ten interchangeably here. Today most of the world's Cor-Ten is manufactured in China, which produces more steel of any kind than any other country in the world by a factor of ten. China's Cor-Ten manufacturing industry supports, in a vertically integrated fashion, the country's container manufacturing industry, which has been the world's largest since the early 1990s, when targeted government incentives resulted in the migration of global container production from South Korea to China. By 2020, according to industry data, Chinese manufacturers produced upwards of 96 percent of the global supply of new standard dry containers and 100 percent of new refrigerated containers ("reefers" in industry lingo). In the same period, just three Chinese state-owned enterprises were responsible for 82 percent of global container production, together churning out roughly 2.5 million new twenty-foot equivalent units in total.[13]

Cor-Ten is four to eight times more resistant to atmospheric corrosion (rust) than common steel.[14] This resistance manifests as a self-healing capability. When unpainted weathering steel is exposed to repeated wet-dry cycles, it begins to oxidize like any other iron alloy. Soon, however, given the right conditions, a thin surface layer of extremely fine-textured rust forms, slowing the corrosion rate and safeguarding the structural integrity of the base metal. This shell of rust, called the patina, makes weathering steel uniquely well-suited for use in maritime shipping, where rust is a constant and existential problem. In the steel industry and among materials scientists, the formation of the patina is often described metaphorically in organic or biological terms, whereby the metal is said to grow a kind of protective skin. According to one Cor-Ten distributor, for instance, the alloying elements in the steel "produce compounds that clog the pores at the rust/steel interface."[15] Cor-Ten is generative of a unique set of risks. The protective layer of rust will only form properly if the unpainted metal surface is subjected to repeated wet-dry atmospheric cycles. Furthermore, early in the oxidation process, Cor-Ten tends to produce iron-rich runoff, which can discolor and contaminate surrounding areas, presenting problems for architects working with the material, for instance. In the case of shipping containers, this latter issue is counteracted by painting the box with a primer rich in zinc, which reacts with the copper and other infusions to further protect against rust.

Steel, which is today among the most common manufactured products on earth, has probably been supplemented with various additional elements going back to ancient African and Chinese bloomery smelting. In the early 1820s, Michael Faraday and James Stodart published a series of influential papers on steel alloys, marking the beginning in the West of an intensive period of metallurgical experimentation.[16] This culminated in Henry Bessemer's 1856 patent for the so-called Bessemer process, an inexpensive method for mass-producing steel at relatively high speeds. Meanwhile, alloying experiments continued in England and the United States.

In 1913, D. M. Buck, a research metallurgist at USS (established 1901), conducted a preliminary exposure test of steel infused with 0.3 percent copper by mass, which indicated that copper steel, as Buck called his test product, was able to withstand atmospheric corrosion considerably longer than conventional steel.[17] Buck's discovery led USS to carry out a series of large-scale exposure tests—notably in 1916, 1926, and 1929—in a range of diverse atmospheric environments across the United States, which showed that a minimum infusion of 0.2 percent copper by mass extended the lifespan of mild steel by at least 50 percent. The tests also indicated that a series of localized variables probably played an important role in the success or failure of a given piece of steel—things like the angle of installation relative to the sun, the season in which the steel was installed, and even the amount of pollution in the air. Indeed, the protective capacity of the copper on the integrity of the base metal was discovered to be significantly more effective in heavily industrialized Pittsburgh than in rural areas, leading USS scientists to surmise (correctly) that industrial pollutants were eating away at conventional steels at a rapid rate.[18]

By 1920, at least one American railroad had adopted copper steel as the standard material for its freight and passenger rolling stock, with others soon to follow. In 1933, USS launched Cor-Ten commercially as part of a slate of newly developed steel alloys aimed specifically at the railroad industry. A year later, the company sent two research metallurgists, George Schramm and R. F. Johnston, to the November 22, 1934, meeting of the Railway Club of Pittsburgh, to present a paper on the technical and economic benefits of Cor-Ten to the railway industry. The paper is equal parts metallurgical analysis and sales pitch.[19] "It may be of some interest to know," wrote Schramm and Johnston, "that more than 30,000 samples have been tested [by USS] in the last six years. This number comprises about 850 different steels and protective coatings in about 145 laboratory and field tests."[20] The result of all this testing was Cor-Ten itself, the paper argued, "pointing the way to substantial operating economies" for railway operators.[21] Schramm and Johnston made much of weathering steel's corrosion resistance, but they also repeatedly emphasized how light the material was compared to its precursors. Weathering steel's weight—or, rather, its relative lack thereof—would go on to become a major selling point, as evidenced by a 1945 advertisement for Cor-Ten in *Railway Mechanical Engineer*: "Stop using half of your power to pull deadweight."[22] Cor-Ten proved to be a hit among "railroadmen" through the 1930s and 1940s, in particular. "180,000 freight cars have been built better with USS COR-TEN steel since 1933," reads advertising copy from a 1954 issue of the trade journal *Railway Locomotives and Cars*.[23]

By 1967, Cor-Ten had become so central to USS's brand identity that the company conspicuously built its new, sixty-four-story corporate headquarters out of weathering steel. The building is the tallest structure in Pittsburgh today. Over the past half century its patina has darkened to a murky auburn, approaching matte black. By the 1960s, the color and texture of Cor-Ten had become one of the material's key selling points. USS marketed Cor-Ten directly to architects and artists, stating in a 1970 advertisement: "with age, it only grows more handsome."[24] Sculptors, in particular, favored Cor-Ten for its "rich, natural tonalities."[25] Richard Serra, Anish Kapoor, and the late Donald Judd, among others, produced a series of works in weathering steel, many on explicitly maritime themes. Serra, whose father was a pipe fitter in a San Francisco shipyard, has emphasized in interviews and in his own writing the continuities between ships and his large-scale sculptures. He describes a memory from childhood of an enormous steel tanker being moved from dry dock to the sea as an almost mystical experience of bulky heaviness becoming, in an instant, buoyant lightness. As he later put it, "all the raw material that I needed is contained in the reserve of this memory, which has become a reoccurring dream."[26]

In 1961, the International Standards Organization (ISO) established a technical committee to develop standards for freight containers, which at the time were built not of Cor-Ten but of other steel alloys.[27] As Levinson's book shows in detail, the debates around standardization were exceedingly fraught, playing out over many years and drawing in hundreds of stakeholders from across the global transport industry. In 1972, the Customs Co-Operation Council, an intergovernmental body operating under the auspices of the United Nations and the International Maritime Organization, introduced the Customs Convention on Containers, the result of more than a decade of deliberation among public sector trade bureaucrats from almost every nation on earth.[28] The first round of ISO international standards was published in 1979, nearly two decades after the formation of the ISO's technical committee. These early frameworks did not specify which materials container manufacturers should use, nor do more recent iterations of the ISO's international standard 668, which continues to define global specifications for freight containers today.[29] However, by the late 1970s, many cargo transport firms had spent decades experimenting with various container materials, and it was becoming clear that weathering steel was the cheapest way to meet the strength and weight requirements set out by various container-focused standards organizations. By the early 1980s, most of the world's newly constructed containers were built of Cor-Ten.

Metal and Capitalism

I have described Cor-Ten's early history and material features in some detail because in the context of container shipping, weathering steel functions as a key interface—perhaps *the* key interface—between capital and sound. Containers are noisy things; Cor-Ten, I want to suggest, is a crucial medium through which capital becomes ensounded at sea. The political stakes of this sonification require further explanation.

My analysis is motivated in part by a desire to come to terms with the emergence today of a new capitalist subject, one dedicated not to the manic rituals of self-improvement demanded by neoliberal market logics, but aligned instead with the ostensibly smooth, transparent operations of automated systems. Karl Marx's figure of the "automatic subject"—capitalist value itself—anticipated this contemporary transformation of subjectivity more than 150 years ago. Marx writes:

> [Capital] is constantly changing from one form into the other, without becoming lost in this movement; it thus becomes transformed into an automatic subject. If we pin down the specific forms of appearance assumed in turn by self-valorizing value in the course of its life, we reach the following elucidation: capital is money, capital is commodities. In truth, however, value is here the subject (i.e. the independently acting agent) of a process in which, while constantly assuming the form in turn of money and commodities, it changes its own magnitude, throws off surplus-value from itself considered as original value, and thus valorizes itself independently. For the movement in the course of which it adds surplus-value is its own movement, its valorization is therefore self-valorization. By virtue of being value, it has acquired the occult ability to add value to itself. It brings forth living offspring, or at least lays golden eggs.[30]

The automatic subject infinitely self-perpetuates; it reproduces itself endlessly, through the everyday lives and corporeal existence of capitalists and laborers alike, both of which personify it, albeit in differentiated ways. We might say that capitalist value is an intrinsically inert substance which has nonetheless acquired material agency to act on society and in society—it is an abstraction that has attained a concrete reality in the world.[31] And in the process of reproducing itself, the automatic subject "changes its own magnitude," that is, it adds surplus-value, which from its own delimited perspective appears simply as *new* capital. In this way, additional value seems to have been created out of thin air.

Transposing Marx's figure of the automatic subject to the contemporary era, the cultural theorists Stefano Harney and Fred Moten conceptualize a *logistical* subject, which might not actually be a subject at all, but rather a "porous object that still talks like a subject," and which is dedicated to "hollowing itself precisely by expelling the negativity of labor."[32] This blurring of subject/object (which is simultaneously a blurring of person/thing) is exemplified, for Harney and Moten, by the capitalist science/logic of logistics—hence this new subject's logisticality. It is in this specific context, with reference to ongoing debates around logisticality and logistical capitalism, that I deploy the Cor-Ten container metonymically for the movement of capital as such.

I am by no means the first person to connect metal to economic development. Indeed, across the European historical disciplines, metals of diverse sorts are frequently deployed as symbols of progress and power in general and of capitalist modernity in particular. Consider, for instance, the so-called Iron and Bronze Ages: eras defined by the discovery, production, and use of specific metals, never mind the historical validity of these designations.[33] Or think of the Roman stoic philosopher Seneca, who described iron as an instrument of murder, and gold and silver its reward. In the late nineteenth century, the city of San Francisco—a metropolis that was self-consciously modeled on Imperial Rome—took Seneca's words as its city motto: "Gold in Peace, Iron in War." The geographer Gray Brechin points out that at least in practice, the social effects and meanings of metals are rarely so neat as this maxim suggests, "for gold . . . has long served as one of the chief stimulants and objectives of war."[34] But the overarching point stands: metals are *significant*—they do signifying work, both for scholars and in a more general sense. Furthermore, metals are more often deployed to represent powerful, dominant actors as opposed to minoritarian or subaltern groups. Metallurgy, writes Brechin, has "operated from the appearance of the first cities down to the present to give humanity its growing dominion over nature, and a few control of the many."[35]

A comprehensive account of capitalism's material/symbolic relationship to metal is beyond the scope of this chapter, but I want to engage briefly with two pieces of scholarship that move beyond simply identifying capital with metal in an undifferentiated manner.[36] First, starting from the premise that "metals are extraordinarily fluid—full of local sources of transformation and instability—actually more fluid than fluids," the geographer Andrew Barry argues that what makes metals politically significant is their basic *irreducibility* to ideological structuration or economic control.[37] Barry's contention is not that metals are politically null—precisely the opposite—but rather that despite routinely being caught up in dynamic, information-rich assemblages with broad social and political-economic significance, metals have a general tendency to resist representational capture. They are deeply meaningful, but their meaningfulness always exceeds our ability, and also that of the metallurgist, to grasp it. We can begin to glimpse here, I think, a correspondence or shared resonance between metal and sound.

Barry's notions of irreducibility and fluidity also help us to think more concretely about Cor-Ten. Despite its ability to heal itself, weathering steel, like all materials, is constantly in the process of failing. Cor-Ten struggles against the corrosive effects of oxygen longer than ordinary carbon steel, but even rust-resistant metal eventually rusts out. We can think of Cor-Ten, then, as a particularly vivid example of a material that is, in more than one sense, active or agential. It changes and flows over time, both in reaction to external events and as a result of the dynamism of its own internal chemical structures and physical properties. Cor-Ten's resilience—to corrosion, to fractures and cracks, to the passage of time itself—and also the inevitability of its eventual failure can be construed as evidence of a certain material unruliness, which overlaps, albeit in complicated ways, with Barry's notion of irreducibility.

Cor-Ten's relationship to capitalism is further complicated by Peter Baehr's influential account of the translation history of Max Weber's famous metallurgical metaphor the "iron cage," from the final pages of *The Protestant Ethic and the Spirit of Capitalism* (1905). Detailing the alienating effects of the unholy alliance between religious asceticism and the capitalist world order, Weber writes: "In [the seventeenth-century English Puritan theologian Richard] Baxter's view, the care for external goods should only lie on the shoulders of the 'saint like a light cloak, which can be thrown aside at any moment.' But fate decreed that the cloak should become an iron cage."[38] The metaphor of the iron cage represents "the care for external goods," or what today we might call the bottomless desire for commodities, a yearning which capitalism seeks continually to reproduce in individuals and which can indeed feel like a prison cell.

Baehr suggests that the image of the iron cage is not Weber's metaphor at all, but the work of Weber's English-language translator, the Harvard sociologist Talcott Parsons. Furthermore, Baehr shows that Parsons probably pinched the image of the iron cage from John Bunyan's seventeenth-century Christian allegory *The Pilgrim's Progress*. In Parsons's deployment of the phrase, then, metal reverberates not only at the same frequency as capital but in the same key as Christian morality and manifest destiny. According to Baehr, a more precise English translation of Weber's original German phrase, "*stahlhartes Gehäuse*," would be "a shell made of steel." This steel shell turns out to be a more complex and ultimately a richer metaphor for capitalism than the iron cage. To wit, steel is a result of industrial-era invention and fabrication, unlike iron, which is an element found in nature. Steel is both rigid and flexible; its malleability varies along a continuum of mild, medium, and high, depending on how much carbon is added to the base iron. "Just as steel involves the transformation of iron by the mixing of carbon and other elements," points out Baehr, "so capitalism involves the transformation of labor power into commodities."[39] It is thus fitting, as Baehr points out, that Frederick Winslow Taylor's influential ideas about the rationalization of labor, codified in his system of scientific management, were initially developed and tested in the context of Taylor's long career in the steel industry. Driving home the point, Baehr quotes the historian Siegfried Giedion: "the stretching of human capacities and the stretching of the properties of steel derive from the same roots."[40]

Baehr's adroit analysis suggests at least two additional points relevant to our investigation here. First, and at the risk of stating the obvious, a Cor-Ten shipping container literally is "a shell made of steel." It is as if Malcolm McLean, who is credited with developing the container in the 1950s, read Weber's metaphor as a draughtsman would read an engineering blueprint. Second, we might add to Baehr's catalogue of the similarities between steel and capitalism the observation that Cor-Ten's capacity for self-healing has much in common with post-Fordist capitalism's capacity for incorporating into itself (and thus eradicating) anti-capitalist critique. Working out how contemporary capitalism nullifies critique—often by commodifying it and selling it back to the masses as counterculture—has been a major thrust of Marxist theory in recent decades.[41] The explicit aim of much of this work is to develop new critiques of capitalism that can deflect, resist, or sidestep capitalist assimilation. The imaginative or speculative mode of listening discussed in the next section might just be capable of this.

One other obvious but important feature of Cor-Ten shipping containers is that they hide their contents, a key selling point in the early years of containerization. After all, if longshoreman and seafarers do not know what they are transporting, they are less inclined to help themselves to the cargo than otherwise. Here, then, is another correspondence between the shipping container and capitalism: both project a false image of imperviousness, of uniformity, of opacity, and of permanence. The container, like Marx's commodity, "conceals the social character of private labour and the social relations between the individual workers, by making those relations appear as relations between material objects, instead of revealing them plainly."[42] At the beginning of *The Society of the Spectacle*, the French Marxist Guy Debord describes how the commodity fetish reifies visual perception at the expense of all the other senses: "The whole life of those societies in which modern conditions of production prevail presents itself as an immense accumulation of spectacle. All that once was directly lived has become mere representation."[43] The shipping container conceals the labor time that is the real source of all capitalist value in a doubly fetishistic fashion, obscuring not only the social relations of production but also the social relations of circulation. Put simply: you can stare at a stack of containers for as long as you like, but you will not be able to see what they carry, where they came from, where they are going, or who moves them.[44]

Listening

Returning now to the noise on the deck of the *Cendrillon*, I will first describe how imaginative or speculative listening might work, then discuss some of its features and limitations. In a lovely evocation of the tone produced by acoustic instruments, the anthropologist Kathryn Marie Dudley succinctly captures the affective complexity of the processual form of listening I want to describe here: "A stringed instrument's tone is not simply 'built into' it by the luthier or 'heard' in more or less sophisticated ways by the listener; it is also the 'structure of feeling' that organizes the encounter and invests it with a force and intensity that is hard to put into words. Reducible to neither the properties of artifacts nor the sensibilities of individuals, tone demarcates an affective field of interaction between people and things that materializes the general mood or feeling of that relationship."[45] It is precisely this "affective field of interaction"—the dialogic flux that mediates the sound/listener relationship—that imaginative listening seeks to operationalize. The approach works, basically, through a kind of speculative transduction, whereby the listener tracks the real and imagined reverberations of a given material across as many material interfaces as they care to think up, all the while proliferating the possible historical causes of the sound under investigation. The stringing together of contiguous materials and histories in this manner is a necessarily creative process, open to endless interpretation.[46] For instance, there is no rule or external metric that says it is any *better* to move analytically from, on the one hand, the vibrations of weathering steel to the reverberations of the common steel of the ship to the movements of the seawater below; versus, on the other hand, moving from weathering steel to the history of USS's alloys research, to a 1934 Railway Club of Pittsburgh meeting, and so on. Both approaches are valid instances of imaginative listening to the extent that they focus attention on the processes of composition and mediation that produced the sound under investigation.

Combining these two approaches, a possible sequence might proceed as follows. First, we can say quite a lot about the noise aboard the *Cendrillon* based solely on the immediate reverberations of Cor-Ten itself. After all, this sound, like all sound, is not the result of any single or simple cause. Rather, it is the outcome, first, of the whole history of weathering steel. Listening imaginatively, then, we might hear in the noise on board the *Cendrillon* Buck's 1913 exposure test and USS's subsequent laboratory and field tests; the Railway Club of Pittsburgh's bourgeois pomposity, and so on. Then, moving from the sound of the Cor-Ten containers to the closely related reverberations of the carbon and high-strength structural steel of the *Cendrillon*, we might hear the broader history and significance of steel to capitalist development in general (as detailed in part two, above). Next, we might move from the carbon steel deployed in the construction of the ship into the oceanic space on which the *Cendrillon* floats. This would require, first, an account of the composition and movement of seawater in this particular part of the northern Pacific, and perhaps a further explication of the history of this part of the ocean. Has its chemical makeup or current pattern changed, for instance, due to ocean acidification, warming, etc.? The idea here is that these oceanic forces—currents, water pressure, salinity, temperature, wind, etc.—are sonically present in the sound of containers on board the *Cendrillon* because these forces are materially continuous with the container stacks, mediated by the ship. From here the analysis could move almost anywhere, so long as we continue to attend closely to the history of materials. One approach would be to move to the nearby Aleutian Islands, thus opening up the imperial history of American and Russian colonization efforts in Alaska. Alternately, a listener might choose to stay on board the *Cendrillon*, in order to grapple with the sounds of maritime labor. Another might carry out a sort of autocritique, moving from reverberating Cor-Ten to the vibrating cartilage in the listener's outer and inner ear, as a means of bringing the body of the listener into a discussion of capitalist processes. The point is that all these things, together, are contained in the sounds emitted by the containers stacked up on the ship's deck.

This approach to sound probably does not qualify as a method proper, insofar as a method is meant to guarantee a specific analytic or political outcome. Rather, I think of imaginative listening as an orientation toward sound, or, more concretely, as a sort of guide to analyzing sound in the world. It is an intentionally underdetermined and open-ended approach, but it does have a few specific goals. Its primary aim is simply to draw the listener's attention away from appearances and toward ensounded materials and their histories. It thus turns the problem of sound's intrinsic ambiguity into an analytic asset, opening up manifold lines of potential interpretation. Moreover, due to sound's blurring of the clear distinction between perceivers and environments, imaginative listening implicates the listener in the process of analysis, highlighting the provisional, constructed nature not only of knowledge about sonic phenomena, but also of knowledge production in general. Given its conditional, imaginative mechanism, there is of course no guarantee that a specified resonant material will yield analytically valuable or politically useful results. Unlike more prescriptive methods, imaginative listening does not promise explanatory certainty. Rather, the primary aim of the approach is to establish the conditions for what the Marxist sociologist Stuart Hall might call an open horizon of historical-materialist theorizing.[47]

One convenient way to conceptualize this manner of listening is as a slightly more directed and self-conscious mode of the routine kind of listening most of us do all the time anyway. Listening in even the most banal situations is always an intrinsically inferential practice—we can only ever listen *to* or listen *for*. Which is to say that listening is fundamentally about trying to "hear what is not there," as the musicologist Cornelia Fales puts it.[48] Imaginative listening simply proliferates the possible *not theres*, and makes explicit what is generally left implicit, namely the ambiguity of sound.

More than this, however, the practice of imaginative listening also makes clear right from the jump how difficult it is to grasp sound "as such" or "in itself." Even in the absence of a concrete source, sounds always direct their listeners to potential sources, which is to say that listeners draw on their previous sensory experiences in order to try to make sense of what they are hearing. Listening, like all the senses, is embedded firmly in history. "The meaning of any sound . . . is inseparable from its historical moment, site of production, or reception," writes the musicologist Brian Kane. "Rather, sounds need to be recognized as sedimentation of historical and social forces."[49] History is not all sound is, though. When we listen, we do not just tune in to a preexisting sonic world that exists independently of our hearing it. Rather, we are ourselves implicated at every turn in what we hear. Sound hails each of us as individualized listeners. We might say that sound gives form to our wandering ears, in the process interpellating us as subjects, and so lending fleeting stability to the chaotic churn of everyday sensory experience.[50] Imaginative listening is meant to encourage potential listeners to engage with this subjectivizing aspect of sound as well.

Finally, I want to argue that this approach has the potential to produce analyses of capitalism that undermine capital's power, in at least two ways. First, by focusing attention on material history and on the boundary zones between different kinds of materials, listening, as it has been described here, may help to subvert the routine assumption that capitalist economies operate efficiently and autonomously. Like studies of infrastructure, sound calls attention to the joints and friction between things, rather than to the things themselves. By disclosing chains of poorly joined material interfaces and weaker or stronger acoustic signals, as opposed to the smooth, uninterrupted surfaces of capital-in-motion, the mode of listening I propose here has the potential to reveal sites that may be susceptible to interference, rupture, or refusal. Second, imaginative listening entails an extension of the listener's concern to encompass a broad set of material relations that are often otherwise obscured. It thus has the potential to generate a sort of sensory reckoning with one's own role in the continued development of capitalism. Maybe what we hear in the sound of maritime metal is our own, ongoing involvement in the capitalist mode of production, thrown back at us in muddled, low-fi, sonic attire. In which case it seems likely that all of our sensing is always already political, and that politics precedes and lends structure to phenomenological experience. To practice directing and redirecting our ears toward the sounds that produce us as particular kinds of subjects is, at least potentially, a liberatory act. If sound is capable of these things, I propose that attuning to the noise of weathering steel at sea is a meaningful step in the right direction.

PART III

Production

CHAPTER 8

Making Human Trash Tasty

A History of Sweet Cattle Feed in the Progressive Era

NICOLE WELK-JOERGER

Introduction

Taste has powerful qualities that connect sustenance with sensation and physiology with feeling. Historians and anthropologists have illustrated the importance of the taste—sweetness, in particular—in human society, and have used it to explain the building of economic infrastructures and accompanying social developments. Sugar and its sweetness influenced the global distribution of wealth and power, the justification of empire and enslavement, and the violent consequences of racism and ecological degradation.[1] However, sweetness is not just a sense that has enticed, corrupted, or persuaded humans. Nonhuman animals also gravitate toward sweetness and participate in its sensation.

Today's farmers, veterinarians, feed salesmen, and food scientists understand this reality, and use their knowledge of animal taste preferences in livestock management. From my ethnographic research with cattle farmers, I have seen how a dairy farmer can take simple pleasure from breathing the aroma of newly cut hay, appreciating that his cows will also respond to its freshness, saltiness, and sweetness. I have helped pour diluted molasses from watering cans to bring sweetness to sour feed, and I have placed salt blocks in troughs to lengthen the time cows spend standing next to their meals. The senses are crucial in the contemporary dairy and meat industries, but in the United States, the role of taste and smell as tools in agricultural practice have a long history that dates back to the nineteenth century; a history that gave rise to agribusiness in the Progressive Era.

This chapter proposes that a nonhuman history of sweetness can tell important stories about the development of Progressive Era food systems in the United States, particularly food systems that relied on animal proteins. The chapter is divided into three major sections that consider how agricultural businesses learned to justify sweet feeds and feeding. The first section focuses on the origins of the sweet feeds industry alongside examples of both acceptance of and resistance to feeding sweetness to cattle, particularly in the dairying industry. The second section discusses Progressive Era debates about sweet feed as an adulterant in the context of United States pure food legislation for cattle. The third and final part of the chapter highlights instances of sweet feed advertising, providing a glimpse into how farmers read about, navigated, and embraced sweetness on their farms as a viable economic benefit.

Philosophically, following nonhuman experiences with sweetness can help highlight moments when humans and animals have been seen as inherently connected, and when they have been made distinct from one another in scientific and social contexts. The examples in this chapter will show that, although we seem to share a sense of pleasure in seeking out sweetness, humans describe sweetness as operating differently in agricultural animals. Practitioners and businesses craft different purposes for this taste in cattle from when it is targeted toward human consumers. Some scholars have illustrated that sweetness enabled unpalatable foods to become more palatable for animals, which funneled undesirable materials into our food systems and even inadvertently changed our metabolic landscapes.[2] But these practices emerged in the context of concerns about the purity, "naturalness," and healthfulness of sweetness—concerns anchored in products meant for humans but extended to livestock companions.

Using sweetness to make undesirable industrial trash tasty for animals required quite a bit of work, and the embrace of these feeding techniques by scientists, legislators, and farmers took time and trust. The development of the early twentieth-century sweet feed industry demonstrates these intricacies—intricacies which informed the later adoption of other kinds of "impure" or "unnatural" feeds, including antimicrobial residues and growth hormones.[3] Feed businesses of this earlier time pursued three major avenues for legitimizing sweet feed for cattle: professionalization of the trade, pure food legislation, and evidence-based marketing. Those familiar with the history of Progressive Era food industries will recognize these strategies. However, the intermediary role of farmers challenged businesses, experts, and legislators in all these developments. Although human farmers bought and human businesses capitalized on these materials, it was ultimately the cattle that ate them. In this arrangement, the "consumer" protected by specific laws and labels was not always clear. Was it the farmer-buyer, the animal-eater, or the human who ultimately ate the animal proteins reared by that farmer? Sweet feeds crosscut this "great chain of eating," and the history of the sweet feed industry brings some of these philosophical and legislative dilemmas across species into higher relief.

Scholars have traced the importance of various kinds of human sensory experiences in the development and success of late nineteenth and early twentieth-century businesses. Using the latest medical science, businesses addressed the smell and appearance of cleanliness in the transition from sanitary science to germ theory.[4] Food companies harnessed and standardized the taste and color of fruits and vegetables to evoke freshness, flavor, and nutritional value.[5] Nonhuman animals occupy a unique sensory space in this history since they exist as both commodity and consumer simultaneously. As urbanization and technological developments changed interactions with animals, humans valued their labor less than their bodies (for food) or being (for companionship). In the case of livestock, the more milk and meat they could produce, the more valuable they were considered. Thus, humans sought to control animal productivity through various means, including through appetites by manipulating senses—using texture, smell, and taste to reproduce and reengineer livestock bodies.[6]

In these efforts, studying nonhuman sensation has taken on different forms. Anthropologists such as Katy Overstreet have shown that one way to study nonhuman sensation—particularly in cattle—comes out of embracing shared and similar sensory experiences: a recognition of the rich intersubjectivity that exists within animal agriculture.[7] In addition to these and other multispecies ethnographic findings,[8] scientists have long documented, behaviorally, the draw animals have toward tastes like sweetness.[9] Physiologically, however, the idea of shared sensory expression is more complicated. Scientists have theorized how taste buds in cattle may increase or decrease sensations of flavor, but in attempts to compare the 9,000-bud count in humans with the 35,000-count in bovines.[10] Historically, humans have relied on their own senses to inform their understanding of bovines' experiences with flavor, which, taken to its extreme, challenges the human-animal boundaries that keep industrial livestock farming intact. Acceptance that farm animals sense in the same, or at least in very similar, ways as humans presents an ethical dilemma about the obligations we have to our nonhuman compatriots, rendering livestock operations as inequitable and violent spaces.[11] The human-livestock observations and interactions detailed below demonstrate just a small segment of these long-standing complexities in animal agriculture, with the sensorial similarities and differences between humans and their cattle negotiated through food research, legislation, and marketing.

The focus on cattle in this story acknowledges that agricultural animals do not experience sweetness in the same way. Bovines occupy a unique place in this history of flavor, especially considering that their "natural" diets (defined by scientists as the substances cattle would eat in nature) are wholly plant-based. They are herbivores in comparison to their omnivorous chicken and hog compatriots, and, as such, scientists have come to understand cattle palates as different from these monogastric animals.[12] In my ethnographic fieldwork, farmers voiced how steers had different palates from cows, who had different palates from calves. Specificities in animal age, breed, and type (dairy versus beef cattle, in this case) often get lost in stories about agricultural animals, but this speaks to the agency and change animals undergo in their lifespan as they express their desires. In eating and refusing their meals, cattle have long participated in a dance with their owners and with the companies who marketed feed products to their owners. If cattle refused to eat the feed bought for them, recalibrations had to be made.

Making sweet feed a common product for cattle consumption in the twentieth century took a series of academic, regulatory, and technological developments, all interconnected through an intricate network of people watching and thinking about animal senses. Feed mixes with molasses not only needed to be justified scientifically in the laboratory, but they also needed to be marketable for the feed company and ultimately *work* for farmers aiming to expand and profit off their beef and dairy operations. In order to understand these realities, we need to examine earlier agricultural practices and trace how they evolved into the systems still used in industrial livestock farming today.

The Origins of Sweet Feed

In the United States, farmers have long pointed out the significance of sweetness in "natural" cattle feeds. During the early republic, white settler farmers competed with one another to transform animals of European descent into specifically "American" breeds. They fed their cattle sweet plants and grasses that were unique to the United States with the goal to create "American" cows.[13] Some observers argued the one major advantage of draining the marshes of the southeast would be to expose the indigenous sugar cane that could be used as "sweet and nutritious feed for cattle." The clearings also helped to mitigate swamp diseases such as yellow fever and cholera, but the quest for sweet-tasting cattle food was a major imperative.[14] European farmers new to areas of the North American landmass (along with transplanted mill feed companies) frequently called these pastures sources of "sweet feeds."[15]

Mid-nineteenth-century developments in cattle feeding led to debates on the role of different kinds of feed in producing (and potentially affecting the taste and quality of) milk. With limited pasture, farmers running urban cattle operations sought out different feeding materials to sustain their businesses, often attaching to mills, breweries, or distilleries so cattle could consume processing waste. Swill dairies gained special notoriety from an exposé in *Frank Leslie's Illustrated Newspaper* in 1858, which cited that cows fed "swill," or distiller's mash, produced thin, foul-tasting, poisonous milk.[16] Early state-level pure food laws from the 1880s cited swill milk as a justification for limiting the feeding of cattle rations from distillers and brewers' grains, despite protests from organizations like the United States Brewer's Association that these byproducts were a nutrient-rich cattle feed.[17]

Around this same period, farmers and researchers began to experiment with ensilage, or "silage," as a feed product in the late 1870s. This fermented corn or hay (known as haylage) produced a stronger, often sweeter, odor that enticed cows and encouraged robust eating which resulted in robust production gains. Early reports about silage feeding, however, also raised concerns about altering the taste of milk, as raw milk products of the time were susceptible to feed flavors—from brewing grains to garlic. Such reports were authored by chemists who relied on their own experiences with taste and odor to inform their research and gauge the value of products in cattle feeding recommendations. This fact cannot be understated. Scientists inhaled smells and placed feed samples on their tongues to assess feed and food products. In these efforts, they attempted to make clear distinctions between sour and sweet silage. Sweet silage, they found, formed better in stacks than in silos, sour silage was the result of quick (rather than slow) fermentation, and the line between them seemed thin and dependent on whether the crop was cut too early or too late in the season.[18]

In its novelty at the time, the taste of silage was challenging for agriculturalists to pinpoint, and even the distinction between "sweet" and "sour" flavors was considered by some to be a misnomer. Scientists who were committed to an idea of a standardized, desirable, and natural "sweetness" found describing the flavor of silage difficult. As animal scientist and cattle breeder W. W. Crane of Dayton, Ohio, wrote, "The taste of sweet ensilage is very attractive, but it is not sweet as the title implies. I call it sub-acid; while it has not the saccharine flavor of sugar it has none of the acrid taste of vinegar; a medium, not unlike some pleasant fruit, which the palate pronounces [as] neither sweet nor sour."[19] These efforts to classify the taste of silage illustrate how the struggle to create technoscientific flavor profiles extended beyond concerns for products meant for humans. Just as pure food legislation wholly involved nonhuman consumers, efforts to standardize the taste of foods for humans also encompassed the taste profiles of livestock who ate fancier feeds.

Silage sweetness had particular significance in the production of milk, which flowed as a commodity to different kinds of consumers. For milk that was meant to be consumed by calves, agricultural stations emphasized how cows fed "palatable and nutritious" food like silage produced similarly palatable and nutritious milk.[20] But palatability meant something potentially different outside bovine sensibilities. Milk meant for humans needed to be tested and tasted carefully, not only in hope of a "standard" milk flavor, but also to ensure uniform coloration and consistency in the transformation of fluid milk into solid products like cheese.[21] Cross-referencing what both calves and humans would experience in tasting "silage milk," chemists organized milk-tasting exercises with the secretaries and students in the scientists' laboratories, which later evolved into milk-tasting competitions hosted by 4-H clubs and Future Farmers of America meetings.[22]

Sweet feeds did not just come from pasture or fermented fodder. By the late nineteenth century, agricultural writers made recommendations for farmers to sprinkle water-diluted molasses on top of feed to add nutritional value and desirable flavors on a case-by-case basis.[23] However, molasses was not the only basis for sweetness in cattle feeds. Carob bean was also an important sweet source and served as the major ingredient for mixes in calf meal. The calf meal industry is credited by historians as forming the foundation for the beginning of the "pre-mixed" or "ready-made" animal feed industry in the United States. Historian Larry Wherry identified Blatchford's Calf Meal Company, owned and operated by John Barwell, as one of the first American feed companies (Figure 8.1). As their name suggested, Blatchford's Calf Meal Company was best known for its calf meal product, made from a mixture of carob beans and valued for its sweetness that enticed young animals.[24] Barwell brought his family's century-old manufacturing methods to America from Leicester, England, in 1875, building his plant in Waukegan, Illinois, with the intention that it would be solely an animal feed operation.[25] Barwell's company produced feed that was then sold outside the factory's immediate Midwest geographic region, distinguishing it from other contemporary operations. Products like Blatchford's Calf Meal became widely available across the United States by the early 1890s, and other companies promoted its utility for directing more fluid milk from cows into the human consumer market (rather than saving and using it for young animals).[26]

Blatchford's Calf Meal

BLATCHFORD'S CALF MEAL is now recognized as one of the best substitutes for new milk for raising calves ever placed before the farmer, and its use has in thousands of cases satisfactorily solved the problem "How to Raise Calves Cheaply and Successfully Without Milk."

A Calf can now be taken off new milk when three or four days old, a porridge made of Blatchford's Calf Meal and skim milk, substituted for the new milk diet, and the skim milk can gradnally be dispensed with altogether until the calf is feeding on the Calf Meal Porridge alone with no milk whatever. A reference to the weighty testimonials appended herewith covering this speeial feature, will show how easily, economically and satisfactorily this is done.

ANALYSIS OF BLATCHFORD'S CALF MEAL

Protein . . . . 33.44 per cent
Fat. . . . . 5.23 per cent

Figure 8.1. Blatchford's Calf Meal Company advertisement from the late nineteenth century. Courtesy of the National Museum of American History Warshaw Collection of Business Americana.

Agricultural colleges and manufacturing organizations studied the efficacy of feeding cattle substances like carob bean and molasses with promising results. In the 1890s, for example, experiment stations in Texas and Maryland found that sugar led to "profitable consumption of a larger amount of food," with molasses feeds recommended particularly for milking cows because their use correlated to increased milk sugar.[27] The Sugar Planters' Association took note of the United States molasses exports for European cattle feed and completed a number of studies on feeding sugar to livestock, suggesting to planters, processors, and researchers that a more robust regional and national market for sweet feeds would benefit producers of both sugar and cattle.[28]

Federal scientists supported the literature, popular and professional, that highlighted the usefulness of sweet feeding, which eventually led to the codification and regulation of the sale of such animal feeds. During the 1902 hearings for federal pure food legislation, Harvey Washington Wiley, chief chemist of the United Stated Department of Agriculture and champion of the proposed Pure Food and Drug Act, which became law in 1906, repeatedly cited the efficacy of feeding manufacturing byproducts to cattle, from cottonseed to corn. He specifically emphasized the profitability of the sweetness—the glucose—that came from these and other materials in sugar manufacturing, noting how sweet byproducts made "valuable" feed for cattle.[29] This value could not be underestimated, since the waste fodder produced by these various industries could be made commodities regardless of the quality of a crop in a given year. Producers, particularly the South, would have something to sell, even if it was not for human consumption. "It is a pure gift from the Creator," Wiley professed, as he pointed to the feed industry's ability to repurpose waste through animals.[30]

Wiley saw the cattle industry as wholly integrated into the United States' sugar and sweet additive processing, which included the then-controversial but still-sweet substitutes of glucose, sucrose, and dextrose. Historians have credited Wiley's recognition of the "cattle connection" to his work as a consulting chemist for the Marsden Company of Philadelphia. Wiley worked with this company to process cornstalks and molasses into pressed brick cakes to be used as a protective lining for war ships.[31] When this lining was no longer needed, given developments in warfare, materials made through this application, known as the Marsden process, were fed to animals. By 1898, big early players in the sweet feed industry, including the American Milling Company which manufactured "Sucrene Oil Meal," adopted the process to make commercial sweet feeds.

As intriguing as the warship story may be, Wiley had been preoccupied with the many kinds and uses of sugar for over a decade before his Marsden appointment, with experience and research that earned him recognition as the "sugar expert" in the pure food debates. The government funded his earlier work with sorghum and sugar beets in efforts to make the United States self-sufficient in sugar production.[32] Based on this experience, during the federal pure food hearings, Wiley was committed to making a case for glucose (derived from grapes, beets, etc.) and dextrose (from corn) as legitimate sweeteners alongside, not adulterants of, sucrose (from sugar cane).[33] Wiley's efforts to legitimize glucose and dextrose included highlighting how producers could capitalize on cattle consuming sugary waste products. His fight for these feeds aligned with numerous scientific and commercial publications of the time, including many that cited him. Lewis Sharpe Ware's 1902 publication on the topic even opened with a dedication to Wiley, mentioning their friendship and Wiley's work on the significance of sugar and sweetness for American commerce.[34]

Wiley's interest in sugar thus informed how the Pure Food and Drug Act of 1906 conceptualized industry byproducts for livestock feeding. Their use was rendered an entirely acceptable practice, if not one encouraged by experts as both economically valuable and enticing to bovine palates. At the time, the national infrastructure for processing, shipping, and feeding sweet products to cattle was still in its infancy, with shipping and mixing often left to the farmers as feed companies continued to troubleshoot the best ways to mix and process rations. Through the legislative hearings, Wiley laid the groundwork for the future of the commercial animal feed industry and the use of sweet byproducts in, particularly, cattle feed rations.

Sweetness as Adulterant

To anchor this legitimacy conferred by the newly established Food and Drug Administration, feed companies aimed to better standardize their products and their operations on a national level. At the same time, they worked hard to form professional organizations that would convey trustworthiness to the public in part by aligning their efforts with the latest science and contemporaneous scientific organizations.

The first years of the twentieth century proved tumultuous for feed companies in the wake of new feed regulations. As more companies adopted the interstate model, they found it difficult to navigate both idiosyncratic state feed laws and the overgeneralized language of the nationally enforced Pure Food and Drug Act. There was, they realized, need for a professional group that dedicated its time to legislative matters—advocating on behalf of feed manufacturing groups to policy makers. Although one group, the National Association of Feed Dealers, had been formed in early 1908,[35] its members saw the purpose of that group as largely a social one, with annual "pleasant affairs" giving fellow feed dealers a chance to get to know others in the business.[36]

On March 26, 1909, thirty-five feed manufacturers from across the country met in Chicago to discuss the prospects of forming a legislatively focused feed organization. That day, they founded the American Feed Manufacturers Association (AFMA), whose main goals included obtaining more uniform feed laws across the country and "carry[ing] out such other plans as are for the benefit of the members collectively and individually and for the uplifting of the feed manufacturing business in general."[37] The formation of AFMA mirrored contemporaneous efforts made by other American professional groups, including doctors, to burnish their reputations before the public and distance themselves from unsanctioned practitioners. Proper licensure, registration procedures, and labeling procedures in compliance with state laws were important elements of this overarching professional structure adopted by feed companies.[38]

After the establishment of the AFMA, a group of men leading in the sweet feeds industry decided to establish an offshoot organization in 1917: the Sweet Feed Manufacturers Association. They did so despite doubts on the part of the general feed companies that such a group was necessary. By this time, molasses was an accepted, if not desired, ingredient used across different companies, and many believed that the problems facing producers of sweet feed affected all livestock feeding businesses. However, some challenges in public relations fell more specifically on sweet feeding practices and warranted closer attention by a smaller organization.

One reason sweet feed manufacturers felt they needed their own group was to further standardize their products in the face of renewed public scrutiny. Through dedicated sections in publications like *Flour and Feed*, AFMA refuted "baseless charges" with advice from veterinarians and agricultural scientists. Many of these sections focused on "attacks" against the sweet feed industry, including the belief that molasses feed caused kidney problems in livestock.[39] Public media targeted sweet feeds with such force that AFMA leaders joked they were no more than "disreputable molasses dopesters" in publications of their meeting minutes.[40]

Although some experts praised the use of molasses in dairying and cattle rearing, others remained skeptical because of the variability of sweet tastes on the market and the inconsistency of individualized responses cattle had toward sweetness. Despite efforts to embrace cattle as standardizable, controllable commodities for human consumption, their behaviors reminded scientists and farmers that sensory experiences can be uncontrollable, with experimental cases throwing doubt on the efficacy of sweet feeds. When Maryland state nutritionists fed a group of cows a ration of "sugar feed" in 1908, only one of the animals "relished" the sweetness while the rest seemed nauseated by it. As detailed in the report, the "unsatisfactory nature of the ration appeared from the fact that the cows attempted to eat their straw bedding and seemed nervous and hungry."[41] Other studies found that beet molasses acted as a diarrhetic when compared to cane molasses, which posed some concerns about the overall healthiness of sweet feeds in cattle.[42] Still, the laxative qualities of materials like beet molasses had some advantages when used as a supplement to subpar rations. The molasses not only allowed undesirable feed materials and low-grade roughage to be transformed into a more palatable meal for cows, it also lowered the risk of animals getting sick from these trashy materials. In these cases, the "molasses, being mildly laxative, may [have been] beneficial in preventing impaction when large quantities of poor quality course roughage [were] fed."[43]

These inconsistencies contrasted with the blustery corporate feed advertisements that entered as evidence in the Adulteration of Mixed Feeds hearings, held before the Committees on Agriculture and Forestry in September 1918, and would inform proposed changes in the Food Production Act of 1919. The foundation of the debates in these hearings focused on the use and value of certain byproducts in any commercial animal feed: products dubbed the worst of the worst in "low-grade" feeds which could be hidden through molasses mixing. A proposed amendment to a section of the Food Production Act by Oklahoma senator Thomas P. Gore banned the use of certain byproducts, including peanut hulls, cocoa shells, "clipped oat byproduct," flax-plant refuse, or sorghum pulp.[44] As such, scientists, feed company owners, and legislators debated fiercely about the use of molasses to "cover up" what were considered "worthless" feed products during these meetings.[45]

The debate demonstrated that molasses could be interpreted in feed products in one of two ways: (1) as an ingredient that had nutritional significance and added to the quality and content of feed, and (2) as a flavoring agent with sole purpose of masking unnatural or subpar ingredients. The distinction depended on how experts defined and understood the ultimate consumer of these products. For the farmer buying the product, the molasses masked smells and qualities difficult to identify under a microscope, as described by Whitman H. Jordan, a scientist with the New York Agricultural Experiment Station at the hearing. For the bovine eating it, molasses transformed trash into desirable dishes, but this trash could potentially harm their bodies in this process if fed these items too regularly.

Present at the congressional hearings, the president of a business known as Chapin and Company from Hammond, Indiana, urged the group to reconsider their question of molasses adulterants. R. W. Chapin noted, "We do not want to be understood as basing this appeal on the present exigent food conditions. It is an appeal against a waste of food, an appeal which we have violated at no time."[46] Molasses played many roles for feed manufacturers. It made waste feeds more desirable, but it also helped bind nutritious material together in transport. S. C. Cropley of Virginia Feed and Milling Corporation, of Alexandria, Virginia, emphasized this point with an analogy between wheat for bread-making and alfalfa for feed-making: "Why do we put water into flour? To be able to knead it, to keep down the dust, and to produce a bread . . . When you take alfalfa and grind it as we do . . . it contains 14 per cent of protein. The dust contains 24 per cent . . . [The molasses] is used to bind the flour of the grain and the ground hay and it is the most important ingredient in the feeds."[47]

The arguments of these and other feed manufacturers at the 1918 adulteration hearings triggered the first successful lobbying effort of the AFMA and its offshoot, the Sweet Feed Manufacturers' Association, resulting in the amendment being tabled. In response to the criticisms laid out in the hearings, the Sweet Feed Manufacturers' Association was transformed into the Pilot Wheel Manufacturers' Association, which would distinguish high-grade mixes from feeds that used molasses and low-grade products with a seal featuring a sea captain's wheel and the slogan "good feed steers you right." This was intended to help farmers recognize "efficient" feeds which "[got] the most out of the least."[48] However, of the thirty-eight members in the organization, only fifteen companies secured the right to use the emblem for their feed bags and advertisements.[49] Mass resignation of the members led to the dissolution of the professional sweet feed group by the end of 1919. Despite the disbandment of the professional group, sweet feed specialists continued to act as members of AFMA, which later became today's American Feed Industry Association (AFIA).

Marketing Sweetness and Service

The sweet feed industry operated within the previously established networks of sugar production. These legacies informed how facilities initially processed sweet feed, and how they evolved and played into marketing campaigns that would target the flavor profiles of cattle. Crucial to popular sweet feed adoption, newspaper campaigns set the stage for how early twentieth-century farmers would view these companies and their products. However, farmers present at the 1918 mixed feed hearings demonstrated clear community distrust of feed manufacturers at this time. E. C. Lasater, a Texas dairy farmer, pled to the committee to ban all interstate mixed feeds, which signaled a clear disconnect between industry advertising and popular adoption.[50] In selling sweet feed, manufacturers often aligned themselves with the well-established brands and businesses, such as The American Sugar Refining Company, when advertising their sweet by-products. Leveraging national brand recognition and even using popular slogans attached to them (such as "Sweeten it with Domino") helped companies establish legitimacy.[51] However, the hearings made it clear that it was also important for companies to commit to bolstering interpersonal relationships between feed salesman and farmer (while recognizing farmer concerns for cattle) when building successful early twentieth-century feeding relationships.

Advertising campaigns marketed sweet feed products to farmers at local, regional, and national levels, using third-party data, consumer testimonials, and allusions to current events to gain readers' trust. Third-party data aided in the creation of an informational model of advertising, and often used results from scientific publications to identify and highlight the physiological efficacy and economic efficiency of a certain feed. Purina Mills, a major animal feed company based in St. Louis, Missouri, cited publications from agricultural colleges as well as its own laboratory facilities to emphasize the uniform quality of its feed mixes.[52] Other kinds of advertisements relied on the use of consumer testimonials, sometimes appearing as reproductions of handwritten or typed letters to the company thanking them for their products. Entertaining or emotive imagery also worked well to link products to current events, with Purina Mills and Arcady Farms Milling Company of Chicago, Illinois alluding to ammunition, patriotism, and even supply chain delays during the Great War.[53] Often, companies used all three advertising techniques, but added to these, sweet feeds companies also created unique publicity campaigns geared toward human and nonhuman senses.

Evoking senses alongside the inherent paternalism of livestock farm work, Tarkio Champion Molasses Feed Company of Kansas City, Missouri ran a series of two-page newspaper advertisements with the tagline "Cattle are just like children." The text continued, "They love sweets. Sweet is fattening. Sweets make them thirsty. Feed them Tarkio Champion Molasses Feed and they eat, drink and put on fat." Tarkio Company further played on the human-animal mirroring with the imagery in the advertisement. While three oval portraits of the president, general manager, and vice president of the company sat on the left-hand page, a scene of cattle in a feed lot took up the right-hand page. This configuration changed from publication to publication, but in each, the bottom of the wordy advertisement identified where readers could find the pictured cattle, owned by one of the most successful feeders in the business and fed the Tarkio Champion brand feed.

Beyond their published advertisements, feed companies also used on-the-ground salesmen and local storefronts to build relationships with farmer clientele. After the Great War, companies encouraged their local dealers to make on-farm visits to their customers. This strategy, called "service-merchandising," was heavily promoted by Purina Mills' G. F. McMillen, who believed that promoting prices alone was the worst way to sell feed products, including sweet feeds. In a 1924 article in the industry journal *Feedstuffs*, he emphasized that feed companies were in the "business of animal nutrition" and needed not only to educate themselves in the intricacies of the science but also to advise individual farmers on "how to get the most economical results" from mixed feed rations.[54] McMillen suggested to fellow feed sellers that "[we] take off our sales clothes . . . and put on our service clothes, develop an honest, sincere desire to help and serve [the farmer]."[55]

Washburn-Crosby Company, the millers of Minneapolis, Minnesota of Gold Medal Flour fame, promoted the service-merchandising strategy in *Feedstuffs* for their Gold Medal feed products. Encouraging feed stores to carry its merchandise, Gold Medal ran a campaign between 1922 and 1924 that emphasized the role of service to farmers and animals. The striking imagery of one advertisement, titled "The Man Depends on You," featured a white male farmer smiling with his arm around a Holstein dairy cow (Figure 8.2). The text below read, "This man whether he be farmer, dairyman or poultry raiser is depending upon you for the best feeds for his requirements."[56] The drawing of the farmer and his cow recalled the proximity and connection in the Tarkio Champion advertisements that tapped into shared human-animal sensations of sweetness. Although Gold Medal only highlighted sweetness in the names of its sweet and molasses-based feeds, their advertisement suggested that sweet feed promotion could be considered an act of service for both the farmer and his cow. Decades later, studies by Ernest Dichter would show that feed companies that committed to service-merchandising techniques—promoting feed through both advertising and advising—garnered more trust and respect from farmers than companies that neglected to conduct regular visit farms.[57] Unique to the feed industry,

This Man
Depends on you
Eventually
GOLD
MEDAL
FEEDS
WASHBURN CROSBY COMPANY
THIS man whether he be farmer, dairyman or poultry raiser is depending upon you for the best feeds for his requirements.

Figure 8.2. Gold Medal advertisement featured in *Feedstuffs* (September 1923): 23. Source: Google Books.

service-merchandising led to sweet feeding, as well as other farming practices, being embraced on farms across the United States.

Conclusion

Sweetness connected human farmers with their cattle, but it also served an important purpose in the industrialization of animal agriculture, which arguably resulted in a wider chasm between the two creatures. As far back as 1884, some agriculturalists explained that sweetness enabled farmers to create the "basis of a new economy," by "inducing the cows to thoroughly clear out every particle of food from the manger." Sweet feeding also "improve[d] the flavor of the milk and . . . increase[d] the percentage of cream," aiding in both the quantity and quality of cattle products.[58] Feed businesses latched onto this concept when advertising and advising farmers on their sweet feeds, with their merchandise posing to help farmers maximize their businesses by producing more human food for market with less animal feed.

As such, it is important to note that feed companies played an important role in the spread of industrial farming, characterized by practices that included careful bookkeeping, attention to the efficiency of inputs and outputs, and a goal for high production and profits through specialization.[59] In this system, sweet feeds not only allowed cattle to eat *anything*, including previously wasted industrial products, they also insured those cattle would eat *everything* that sat in front of them. Sweet feeds worked best away from uncontrollable outdoor pastures, and such products encouraged farmers to contain and observe what their animals ate through confinement with fences, tie-stalls, and mangers. These arrangements relied on feed businesses, and feed companies, in turn, flourished with this intensification of livestock farming.

Sweet feeds continue to signal both industrialized and profitable livestock operations. Returning to my experiences in the field, smelling sweetness upon entering a cattle barn can signal the prosperity of the business, and some farms even have the means to invest in animal flavoring products that create unique sensations for cattle, including blueberry, raspberry, persimmon, peanut butter, and even candy apple flavors.[60] The "animal feed flavors and sweeteners industry" alone is considered $1.2 billion business, and it is estimated to continue to grow along with "global demands" for cheap pork, poultry, dairy, and beef.[61]

Alongside this synthetic livestock flavoring industry, an outgrowth of early twentieth-century human olfactory research,[62] both human food products and the sweet things fed to our beef and dairy cattle have changed in the United States. In 2017, for example, red Skittles made international headlines as a "secret" American feed additive and alternative to certain livestock grains.[63] These stories tend to capture the public's imagination and can even provoke disgust when we reflect on how we feed or do not feed the animals we eat *naturally*. This is due, in part, to how sweetness has gone on to cause a mix of anxiety and hope in our animal food systems.

For much of this history, the goal of feeding sweetness was to enable ever increased meat and milk yields with the fewest of materials. Sweet feeds presumed the gluttony of bovines, that they would eat their fill and more when persuaded through flavor. Such reengineering remains an important task at hand for many beef and dairy farmers today as they attempt to maintain their cattle operations in the context of the climate crisis. Molasses helps mask the fishy, bitter, and musky flavors of additives that could potentially aid in mitigating methane production in bovine guts, including green tea extract and seaweed.[64] However, this model also presumes humans' gluttonous appetite for beef and milk, which have shown health and ecological consequences that may not be fixable by new kinds of cattle feed. If we are truly what we eat, we must also be made up of what the animals that nourish us eat. Considering these metabolic relationships, sweetness connects us humans with our nonhuman compatriots, from the tips of our tongues to the pits of our stomachs. It may be our doom, as we assess the health and labor consequences of sweetness across the food chain, or it may be our salvation, as we reassess how we might better feed our companion species with our shared futures in mind.

CHAPTER 9

Getting a Handle on It

Thomas Lamb, Mass Production, and Touch in Design History

GRACE LEES-MAFFEI

Introduction: Handles, Theory and Design Practice

A hundred years ago, sociologist and philosopher Georg Simmel published an aesthetic study of handles. Industrialization and capitalism have produced a material world of applied arts objects, such as handles, serving functional needs for many people, Simmel contended, and that "each one is only the random example of a universal."[1] For Simmel, the relationship between handle and bowl, utility and beauty, is a microcosm of the relationship between the individual and society. An uncomfortable handle is symptomatic of an unjust society, while an aesthetically appealing and ergonomically successful handle can be socially beneficial. This chapter responds to Simmel's proposition that a handle can represent a society by examining the work of designer Thomas Lamb (1896–1988) as a rich example of the value of studying capitalism in ways attentive to the senses. Lamb was known as "the handle man" for his focused work designing handles. He is best known for the Wedge-Lock handle which followed his Lim-Rest Crutch.

Design is a creative and pragmatic process which engages the senses. The history of design can provide a focus for understanding the sensory experiences of people within capitalist societies. Yet historians have yet to address adequately the role of the senses in design and have tended to focus on the outcomes of the design process more than the process itself. While the field of sensory studies has begun to engage with design,[2] a disjuncture exists between the literatures of design history, on the one hand, and business and capitalism, on the other. This chapter extends the influential, but now rather neglected work of Eugene S. Ferguson. Ferguson (1916–2004) was an engineer, historian of technology, history professor at the University of Delaware, and curator of technology at the Hagley Museum and Library. His ideas about nonverbal knowledge in engineering inform the analysis here of the relationship between the theory and practice of design and the importance of touch and embodied research in the history of design and design history respectively. Bringing a range of literatures together, this chapter seeks to understand Lamb's outputs as evidence of his practice—a sensory, tactile process of embodied research. Embodied research in the form of direct handling is used here as a way of engaging with the design of the past that illuminates the design process and showcases the role of touch in design practice. This account of Lamb's work also interrogates "Universal Design" and considers how it may be understood differently through object handling. The research raises provocative questions about a normative pattern in which male designers create objects for mass production, which are sold around the world for mass consumption by female as well as male consumers.

In Theory: Capitalism, Hands, Machines, and Tools

Capitalism is theorized both as an economic model, underpinning globalization, practiced at scale by big business and the state, and as a world view. The mass production, exchange, and mass consumption of designed goods and services rely on migration and population increases to create concentrated labor in industrial towns and cities. This occurred initially in the West, where large numbers of workers operated capital-intensive machines to produce the commercial goods exchanged in modern economies. Hands and machines are commonly used as metonymic symbols for polarized positions in debates about the economics, politics, and ethics of mass production. In practice, mass production combines hand and machine techniques, and very few production tasks are wholly mechanized. Yet, the individual phenomenology of people operating within capitalism and their sensory experiences have not been overlooked: Charles Fourier and Karl Marx each attended to the sensory engagement of laborers within capitalism, with Fourier believing that "societies could be judged according to how well they gratified and developed the senses of their members" and Marx laying "the blame for the alienation of the senses in capitalist society on the dehumanizing regime of private property."[3]

An 1899 United States government report on *Hand and Machine Labor* proceeded from the premise that while "hand methods are going out of use," there is much evidence of "obsolescent processes."[4] The purpose of the report was to inform managerial decisions about capital investment in machinery based on the time saved in specific manufacturing tasks and the relative cost of wages in hand and machine processes.[5] It was "designed to bring into comparison the operations necessary in producing an article by the old-fashioned hand process and by the most modern machine methods, showing the time consumed by the workmen and the cost of their labor for each operation under the two systems." The author notes, "The words 'hand' and 'machine' have not been used in the strict sense of their meaning, but have been adopted, for want of better terms, to express the two methods of production."[6] The main body of the report comprises quantitative data on the time taken to fulfil tasks in a variety of trades, from glove making and baking to pitchfork manufacturing, all of which used both hand and machine methods. Over more than 120 years since the report was published, few areas of production remained untouched by mass production. Even in the luxury trades, such as bespoke tailoring and haute couture, manufacturing can incorporate elements of machine sewing.[7] At the same time, most apparently mechanized or automated processes rely on some level of handiwork.

Not all researchers have drawn the same conclusion. Curator and writer Glenn Adamson has contended that "industrial weaving," for instance, has left "the domain of direct craftsmanship behind" before nuancing his position: "This doesn't mean the material intelligence is any less important, however—as you might well reflect if you were about to hit the start button on a machine that can produce miles of cloth without stopping."[8] The hands which operated the machinery of capitalism were not merely units of power; rather, they were sentient and individuated and, as such, worthy of historical attention.

As a leading twentieth-century theorist of relationships between people and technology, Lewis Mumford conceptualized the latter as just one part of a large matrix of "technics." His *Technics and Civilization* (1934) is a history of the machine as a "technological complex" over one thousand years.[9] Mumford distinguishes between machines and tools on the basis of their autonomy. Tools are manipulated by their operators, while machines have the capacity for automatic action. People using tools are like machines: "using the tool, the human hand and eye perform complicated actions which are the equivalent, in function, of a well developed machine." Most important, "the skilled tool-user becomes more accurate and more automatic, in short, more mechanical, as his originally voluntary motions settle down into reflexes." And "even in the most completely automatic machine," Mumford argues, humans consciously participate "in the original design" and intervene with refinements and repairs. While tools are relatively flexible, the machine emphasizes specialization, and by speeding up production, it services an acquisitive capitalism. Mumford critiqued technics using the philosophical yardstick of what he later termed "organic humanism."[10] Nevertheless, he remained optimistic about the potential of machines as subordinated to humanity: "We can now see plainly that power, work, regularity, are adequate principles of action only when they cooperate with a humane scheme of living: that any mechanical order we can project must fit into the larger order of life itself."[11]

While Mumford's project was to write a thousand-year history of the machine, his contemporary, Siegfried Giedion, aimed in *Mechanization Takes Command* (1948) to provide what his publishers billed as "a study of the evolution of mechanization in the last century and a half." Both Mumford and Giedion examine the social effects of the machine and mechanization, but Giedion's book is sufficiently distinctive—with its focus on "anonymous history," its detailed empirical case studies, and its typological approach[12]—for Mumford to praise it as novel: "Even in the realm of technics itself, far more attention has been paid to machines, particularly to those that converted energy into motion, than to the utensils, the apparatus, and the utilities that have modified the character of building."[13] Giedion's only omissions, as Mumford saw it, were the Morris chair, the so-called Craftsman handicraft movement in the United States, the importance of personality, and the origins of mechanization.

In promoting anonymous history, Giedion intended to explore the ways in which "mechanization penetrates the intimate spheres of life"[14] to reveal the impacts and influences of overlooked things such as abattoirs, Yale locks, and breadmaking techniques on human perception and cognition. In writing about the movement of the hand, Giedion notes that "vital to all this integrated work is the mind that governs and the feelings that lend it life." The hand was both a marvel and a mystery, both an adjunct to mechanization and an unwitting agent of resistance: "For all the complicated tasks to which this organic tool may rise, to one thing it is poorly suited: automatization. In its very way of performing movement, the hand is ill-fitted to work with mathematical precision and without pause. . . . It wholly contradicts the organic, based on growth and change, to suffer automatization."[15] Mumford and Giedion each argued that technology should be kept in check through subordination to nature and the human: "Being less easily controlled than natural forces," Giedion wrote, "mechanization reacts on the senses and on the mind of its creator."[16] He wished for the "time that we become human again and let the human scale rule over all our ventures."[17]

Mumford's and Giedion's calls for the march of technology to be circumscribed by the human differed from the vision of a technological future popularized by another contemporary leading theorist of technology, Marshall McLuhan. McLuhan was strongly influenced by Giedion's conceptualization of technological modes of cognition and by his interdisciplinarity,[18] and like Mumford, he wrote a glowing review of *Mechanization Takes Command*.[19] For our purposes of exploring Simmel's contention that a handle is a microcosm of the society in which it was produced, McLuhan's theory of tools is his most salient contribution. He elaborated in *Understanding Media*: "The tool extends the fist, the nails, the teeth, the arm. The wheel extends the feet in rotation or sequential movement. Printing, the first complete mechanization of a handicraft, breaks up the movement of the hand into a series of discrete steps that are as repeatable as the wheel is rotary. From this analytical sequence came the assembly-line principle."[20] Notwithstanding his critique that "technology needs not people or minds, but hands,"[21] rather than seeing technology as something which threatens humankind, as needing to be circumscribed or held in check by the human, McLuhan presents technology as enabling people's interactions with the world.

Mumford, Giedion, and McLuhan each theorize the ways in which people, tools, and machines interact in ways that change human cognition. Their writings illuminate the symbolic and communicative dimension of modes of production. Because tools are utilitarian first and foremost, their symbolic dimensions are often overlooked. In tracing *A History of the World in 100 Objects*, the British art historian Neil MacGregor begins with a stone chopping tool from Olduvai Gorge, Tanzania. This ancient object, which is 1.8 to two million years old, is a basic tool such as "other animals might use." MacGregor contrasts it with a representational bird-shaped pestle from Papua, New Guinea, dating from 6,000 B.C. to 2,000 B.C. He identifies the second object as art and associates it with an expression of meaning, perhaps spiritual.[22] MacGregor's discussion recalls Ferguson's description of a disregarded dimension of technological design: "Technologists, converting their nonverbal knowledge into objects directly (as when an artisan fashioned an American ax) or into drawings that have enabled others to build what was in their minds, have chosen the shape and many of the qualities of our man-made surroundings. This intellectual component of technology, which is nonliterary and nonscientific, has been generally unnoticed because its origins lie in art and not in science."[23] Handles share with Ferguson's axes their utilitarian affordances; they assist human hands in carrying and holding objects from suitcases to knives. They rarely take on representational qualities such as those of a carved or painted bird. However, that does not mean that the appearance or aesthetic qualities of a handle lack meaning. MacGregor's distinction between utilitarian artifacts and fancifully decorated utilitarian artifacts, and Ferguson's call for attention to nonverbal knowledge as demonstrated in the work of technologists or engineers, are both applicable to the work of product designers such as Thomas Lamb. When Lamb's Wedge-Lock handle was exhibited at the Museum of Modern Art in New York in 1948, the press release admitted that "at first glance" Lamb's handle "resembles a piece of abstract sculpture" before going on to enumerate its ergonomic and utilitarian qualities.[24]

This brief survey of some key twentieth-century ideas about technology, craft, and design process contextualizes the histories of technology, engineering, and design practice, among other fields of endeavor at the time Lamb was active. The chapter will now move to consider hands in practice.

In Practice: Touch and Hands in Design and Making

With few exceptions, existing theoretical discussions of the relative roles of hand and machine have not adequately recognized the experiences of makers. One exception is found in craft practice. The potter Julian Stair has participated in a multidisciplinary Victoria and Albert Museum research project, "Encounters on the Shop Floor." Stair was filmed at his wheel demonstrating and describing how he creates a firm triangular form with his left elbow on his left thigh, and his right elbow on his right thigh, leaning forward to brace for steadiness, supporting his hands.[25] Sharing techniques with ceramic artists, ceramic modelers create prototypes for plates, cups, and teapots in mass production contexts but the intellectual, material, or bodily processes involved in their work remain largely undescribed in the relevant literatures. Automotive designers, too, have traditionally created models in clay, although this practice is now either wholly replaced by, or combined with, Computer-Aided Design (CAD). Images of the design staff at General Motors modelling automobile prototypes under the auspices of Harley Earl in the 1950s have been obscured in historical accounts in favor of an emphasis on design management and the resultant vehicles.[26] This chapter responds to this relative absence by examining the work of another designer who used clay modelling, Thomas Lamb.

Thomas Lamb represents an unusual example of a successful designer who focused the majority of his working life on creating one type of object (or, rather, one component part of lots of different objects): handles. His apparently diverse formative experiences converged in this activity. From early childhood, Lamb wanted to become a doctor. He was studying anatomy informally by the age of eight and, at eleven, according to a 1948 press release, he "assisted in an emergency operation for the removal of the fifth finger" of a patient.[27] Later, Lamb's medical aspirations were curtailed by financial circumstances, so he began to design patterns for household textiles and took night classes in drawing, painting, and anatomy. He established his own textile design studio serving New York City's department stores in 1919,[28] and then worked in children's illustration from 1924 onward. His Kiddyland serial cartoon was published in *Good Housekeeping*, a popular American women's magazine, and led to spin-off merchandise lines.[29] When Lamb's attention was caught by the problem of improving handle design to increase the stability of crutches used by veterans, he changed direction.[30] Along the way, Lamb developed a philosophy that he called "manuskinetics," informed by, but irreducible to, "art, engineering, anatomy or physics." Manuskinetics was promoted in grand terms as the first time "design has created a new science."[31] He did not pursue mass production of one promising design, the Lim-Rest crutch, partly because, as a 1954 profile put it, Lamb "always felt kind of funny about going into crutches to make money."[32] But, its handle formed the basis of his commercially successful Wedge-Lock handles, which he spent the rest of his career refining across many applications. Lamb began working on the Wedge-Lock in 1941. It was made public in 1946 and was featured the following year in *Home Furnishings Review*. Edgar Kaufmann, Jr. invited Lamb to stage an exhibition at the Museum of Modern Art in New York City which took place in 1948. Contracts with Wear-Ever Aluminum (a division of the Pittsburgh-based Aluminum Company of America, or ALCOA) and its upstate New York knife-making unit, Cutco (short for the Cooking Utensil Company) followed.[33]

One way to understand Lamb's contribution is to focus on his working methods. Because he wanted his products to feel good in the hand, to have "feel appeal" as the advertisements for his Cutco handles put it, Lamb made touch and handling crucial parts of his research and design methodology (Figure 9.1).[34] He built up an extensive study collection of handles from other products. Through handling these samples, Lamb sought to understand user experiences of grasping, carrying, and using handles. He created hundreds of prototype handles which, like the complete objects in his study collection, he evaluated using his hands and modified accordingly.[35] In 1954, design journalist Deborah Allen visited Lamb in his workshop and witnessed his working processes. In her profile in the inaugural issue of *Industrial Design* magazine, Allen described watching Lamb, "pink-cheeked, besmocked, and exuberant, filing away at his latest handle.... His

Figure 9.1. Thomas Lamb is demonstrating his working method in this photograph showing the designer wearing a protective jacket over his shirt and tie, and seated at a desktop wrapped in paper. Lamb measures a prototype handle while surrounded by parts, tools, drawings, and books. Courtesy of the Hagley Museum and Library.

work is timeless, he explains as he whittles." Lamb attributed his practical concern for tactile experience to his mother's New England roots, quoting an imagined Yankee as commenting on his work, "'That's nice, Mr. Lamb; how do she feel in the hand?'" Lamb was more than a rosy-cheeked whittler, however. He pursued the need for objects that feel good in the hand by combining his training in drawing, painting, and anatomy with measurement, "manuskinetics," hand making, and machine making. One academic researcher, Rachel Elizabeth Delphia, summarizes Lamb's methods: "He cut profiles of handles on the band saw, turned them on the lathe, and carved elements without radial symmetry by hand. Throughout the process he used calipers and dividers to check his dimensions and to maintain bilateral symmetry. Carefully transcribed contour lines, which often matched the ones on his scale drawings, helped him visualize the high and low points of complex, intersecting curves as he carved."[36] Delphia notes that Lamb worked diligently with a careful eye for detail: "If he accidentally removed too much material, he would add Chavant clay, a hard, oil-based clay capable of being sanded and painted. Once he had refined a design, he often made a plaster mold so that he could easily cast duplicates in plaster, lead, plastic, or aluminum."[37]

In addition to the "volumes of notes and meticulous sketches comprising the three hundred and sixty studies of handles he has already made toward some 15,000 or so potential applications for the Lamb Wedge-lock Handle," Allen encountered "tray upon tray of oddly curved and twisted sculptures in glass, plastic, aluminum, steel, clay, wood and plastic wood. They look like the bones and shards of a civilization; in fact, they are the record of Mr. Lamb's extraordinary life work designing handles to 'make full use of the forces of the hand for better and safer manipulation of objects'" (Figure 9.2).[38] This example of hand-whittled objects serving as models for mass-produced handles provides a telling instance of the role of the hand in machine production. Lamb licensed his handle designs to selected manufacturers in a range of product categories. The resulting products were touted as having Lamb's Wedge-Lock handle, and Lamb received a royalty for each one sold (or compensatory payments if sales fell short of expectations). Each of his handles, Allen continued, was "protected under his patents describing a scientific mechanism for exploiting the hand," and manufacturers were required to "accept his Lamb Handles without modification, which means using Mr. Lamb's hand-sculptured models to make the molds without intervention of engineering drawings."[39] Lamb's motives in protecting the form and application of his handles were not purely altruistic, in preserving their superior functioning for users. The brand value of the Wedge-Lock handle, and Lamb's own branded persona, were enhanced when they were prominently applied to products.

Lamb's working practices exemplify Ferguson's "nonverbal thought."[40] Ferguson's now-classic defense of nonverbal learning in design is based on his insight that a good deal "of the creative thought of the designers of our technological world is . . . not easily reducible to words; its language is an object or a picture or a visual image in the mind." Ferguson elaborates: "As the designer draws lines on paper, he translates a picture held in his mind into a drawing that will produce a similar picture in another mind and will eventually become a three-dimensional engine in metal. Some decisions, such as wall thickness, pin diameter, and passage area may depend upon scientific calculations, but the nonscientific component of design remains primary."[41] One of Ferguson's many examples is Peter Cooper Hewitt, the early twentieth-century inventor of the

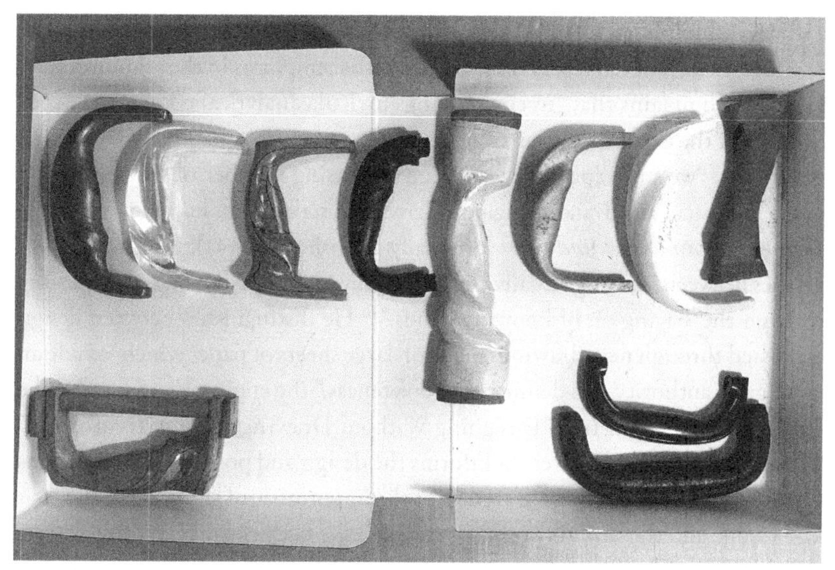

Figure 9.2. Open this archival box, held at the Hagley Museum and Library, to reveal eleven handles made from a variety of materials including wood, metal, plaster, clay, and acrylic. Most of the handles appear to be working models, part of Lamb's iterative development process, but two may be from Lamb's reference collection. Photograph by Grace Lees-Maffei. Courtesy of the Hagley Museum and Library.

mercury-vapor lamp. Quoting Hewitt's friend Michael Pupin, Ferguson writes, "'Those who knew him . . . watching him at work, felt that a part, at least, of Hewitt's thinking apparatus was in his hands.'"[42] Lamb asserted something similar: a "man's hand is a supreme evolutionary achievement, almost another brain."[43] Lamb did preliminary research by touching objects and making drawings of what he saw in front of him and in his mind's eye. He drew handles, and hands using them, and modelled his prototypes in clay. Lamb's hand-crafted handles were passed to manufacturers as patterns for molds, rather than being translated into technical drawings in the way Ferguson describes. Ferguson's concept of nonverbal thought is, therefore, arguably even more applicable to Lamb's way of working.

Ferguson's focus is the role of images in learning about technology and design. He says little in his 1977 article about what engineers learned through engagement with objects, other than making brief references to the failure of Norman A. Calkins's *Object Lessons* (1861) to gain long-term traction in education and to Rudolph Arnheim's complaint that "beyond kindergarten . . . the senses lose educational status" in favor of a verbal emphasis in the schoolroom.[44] Ferguson complains that "in engineering curricula analytical courses have proliferated at the expense of courses attempting to teach design," and when the latter are cut, "we can expect to witness an increasing number of silly but costly errors that occur in advanced engineering systems today."[45] In his follow-up book, *Engineering and the Mind's Eye* (originally published in 1992), Ferguson distinguishes between learning visually, for instance by copying a drawing, and learning through the "laying on of knowing hands."[46] He distinguishes between design expressed through neat drawings made on large sheets of paper which "exude an air of great authority and definitive completeness," the engineer's way, and, as he puts in in his chapter title "Designing Without Drawings: The Artisan's Way," wherein working with materials informs the design and post-hoc modifications can more easily be made.[47] He argues for the importance of the latter: "The tacit knowledge and the skills of workers may not have been the determining factors in Britain's leading role in the Industrial Revolution, but they were essential components of it. Today, similarly, the knowledge and skills of workers—sensual non-verbal knowledge and subtle acts of judgement—are crucial to successful industrial production."[48] This chapter adds to Ferguson's call for attention to nonverbal learning and practice in design an analysis of embodied research as both a design practice and a historical research method for understanding design. Ferguson claims that the "opportunities for a designer to impress his particular way of nonverbal thinking upon a machine or a structure are literally innumerable."[49] And yet, impressing "his particular way of nonverbal thinking" into his designs can lead to unanticipated consequences that are, in fact, contrary to the design philosophy and aims of that very designer, as we shall see.

Embodied Research: Handling the Handles

Designer John Christopher Jones wrote about the Lamb handle for the United Kingdom's *Design* magazine in 1954, the same year that Allen's *Industrial Design* article appeared. Unlike Allen, Jones could not travel to meet with Lamb, visit his workshop, or even handle his handles. However, just the sight of the Wedge-Lock assured Jones of its use and function. "It can . . . be seen that the curved shapes have the visual purpose of indicating the manner of gripping and the direction of movement," Jones writes, "and this is a truly ergonomic virtue."[50] More recently, Rachel Elizabeth Delphia has used this as evidence that the "value of Lamb's work, both during the time period that he created it, and from a historical perspective, is that he made the invisible apparent. We can both see and feel the ergonomic impulse at work in his handles; the Wedge-lock exposes what more nuanced designers integrated seamlessly into their designs."[51] The implication here is that the very appearance of the Wedge-Lock handle communicates the experience of using it (Figure 9.3).[52] If this were true, then direct object handling and embodied research methods would have no value for research on objects that are seen, by some, to communicate their tactile experience visually. But is it true? What do we learn from handling Lamb's handles?

Because Lamb's design process incorporated embodied research, it is appropriate and instructive for researchers to use embodied research to understand his work. Like Jones, albeit for different reasons, today's researchers are unable to follow in Deborah Allen's footsteps and visit Lamb's workshop to watch him work. However, unlike Jones and Allen, we have access to the comprehensive Thomas Lamb design archive at the Hagley Museum and Library in Wilmington, Delaware, which preserves Lamb's working methods in both artifacts and documents. At Hagley, researchers can touch and examine both the handle specimens Lamb collected for reference and the prototype handles that he made. Researching Lamb's work using the Hagley collection therefore becomes necessarily embodied, whether or not that is the researcher's intention. Embodied research is a method, or group of methods, that acknowledges and employs the researcher's own physical experiences in relation to the research material as well as those of the research subject(s).[53] It can recover information lost to a history focused on documentary evidence; for instance, just as culinary historians recreate historical recipes, so historians of sciences can participate in historical making workshops.[54] Embodied research is suitable for a study which seeks to better understand the role of the senses in the history of capitalism, and the sense of touch in particular.

Handling is a well-established method in education—learning through doing, experiential learning—and in museology, where it is an effective tool of audience engagement. However, embodied research is not much used as a method by historians. Innumerable historical objects and images survive, yet the fact that some historians need encouragement and training in how to engage directly with them is exemplified by the steady stream of books which promote the use of material culture for historical research.[55] Even design historians, whom we might suppose to be in the vanguard of object-centered research methodology, do not typically handle the objects they study. While object analysis entails "close first-hand examination of individual objects and groups of objects, and the

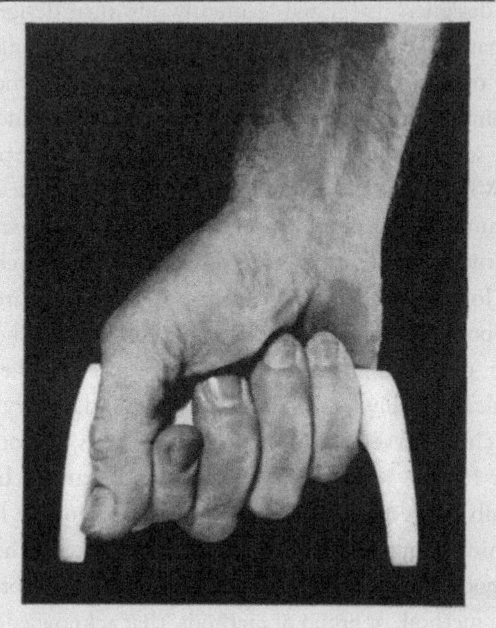

LAMB WEDGE-LOCK HANDLE
Pat. No. 2390544
STANDARD
HANDLE CO.
48 WEST 37th STREET
NEW YORK 18, N. Y.

Figure 9.3. This promotional leaflet for the Standard Handle Co. features a studio photograph of a male hand grasping a handle to show how the fingers, in different positions, are accommodated by the grooves of Lamb's Wedge-Lock Handle. Photographs such as this one are designed to communicate visually the physical experience of holding the Wedge-Lock Handle. Courtesy of the Hagley Museum and Library.

placement of the object as the central focus through examination of its design, manufacture and use," a researcher's firsthand examination is more likely to be visual than tactile.[56] In practice, it is not always possible for researchers to touch artifacts held in archives and museums, and even when it is possible, it is usually forbidden to handle objects in the way that they were intended to be used, for instance, by placing a ring on a finger.

Jeffrey L. Meikle has reflected on the shortcomings of document-driven research, which informs his classic work, *Twentieth Century Limited*. "I rarely saw, touched, used or otherwise physically interacted with the material objects and environments I purported to describe, analyze and interpret," he recalled. Working from photographs, Meikle approached his research "as a literary historian" rather than "with the object-oriented expertise of an art historian or curator" grounded in visual and material evidence.[57] Meikle's call for direct handling in design historical research is part of an effort to address the marginalization of nonverbal knowledge, discussed above. Tracing his account back to the Renaissance, Ferguson lamented the fact that for designers and engineers, "as the scientific component of knowledge in technology has increased markedly in the 19th and 20th centuries, the tendency has been to lose sight of the crucial part played by nonverbal knowledge in making the 'big' decisions of form, arrangement, and texture that determine the parameters within which a system will operate."[58] Design historians, designers, and engineers alike have much to gain from direct manual engagement with materials, models, prototypes, and objects.

As noted, researchers undertaking archival research in the Thomas Lamb archive at Hagley are, in some ways, engaging in a research process similar to that of Allen during her visit to Lamb's workshop in the early 1950s. Allen's interest in Lamb's handles opened her series, in the early issues of *Industrial Design*, "on what Americans then called 'human engineering' (only the British called it 'ergonomics')" as design consultant Ralph Caplan put it.[59] Lamb described the Wedge-Lock as fitting "the average hand."[60] But whose hand served as the prototype for average? Embodied research in the archive helps to answer this question. As a researcher opens box after box of handles made by Lamb, the difference in size between his hand and her hand becomes readily apparent.[61] Lamb asserts that his handle fits all hands, and this universality is an important principle of his design practice. Yet when handling Lamb's handles, this researcher felt that while an attempt had been made to shape the handles to suit the grip of many sized fingers, unless the grooves were the same size and distance apart as her own fingers, they would become irksome ridges that would exacerbate the discomfort of a heavy tool or load. Delphia recorded a similarly mixed response to the

Lamb handles in the archive at Hagley: "hands-on experience with extant models suggests that the handle worked better in some applications and orientations than in others."[62] Delphia concludes that a "Wedge-lock handle that fits the hand feels amazing, but if the scale is too large or small or the angle of a groove does not quite match the hand, it feels incredibly awkward."[63] Lamb's universalizing aspirations are countered by other designers who have recognized that "certain users will prefer certain handles," as one study of handle shapes in the specific context of train drivers pointed out. "This matters for comfort in everyday life just as it matters for optimal performance in professional contexts."[64]

While direct handling of the handles Lamb collected for reference purposes and the handles he fabricated as part of his design process engages a researcher's sense of touch, it cannot replicate Lamb's own tactile experience. Clues to his experience exist in his notes and the choices we see preserved in the archives, but despite the proliferation of objects and documents, the record is sometimes silent. Delphia laments the shortcomings of the archives: "Parts of Lamb's process are more transparent to a researcher than others. Some of his notebooks and sketches are dated and easy to interpret, but others lack labels and render parts of the process a mystery."[65] The information gleaned through direct object handling offers a more direct mode of accessing Lamb's working processes, albeit a suggestive rather than complete one.

Universal(izing) Design?

Lamb made great claims for his work. The foreword of Lamb's draft memoir claims that his "handle will transcend and cross all barriers between peoples of every race, creed and color, and all levels of intelligence, for all of mankind has the sense of touch, and all human beings seek personal comforts, a sense of cooperation, and aid is transferred to the hand that touches a Lamb handle."[66] In a handwritten editorial plan for the memoir, dating from 1948, he notes, "You have got to learn to sell a principle not *a Handle*."[67] The principle Lamb was selling is indicated in another document from his archive: "The objective of the designer was not only to create beauty in form, but to make the handle forms render human service" and to "create for the manufacturer merchandise which would not be measured in dollar value alone, but would also be measured in terms of service and safety, greater use of human facility, better and more precise work."[68] Lamb's determination that his designs be evaluated by yardsticks other than that of profitability should not be taken as evidence that he was a poor businessman. On the contrary, Lamb excelled at promoting his handles under his own name and the Wedge-Lock brand in ways which made clear their universal utility. His inclusivity is seen in marketing materials published by some of Lamb's clients such as the Cutco Division of Wear-Ever Aluminum, which claimed in the March 1960 issue of its newsletter that the Wedge-Lock handle is "not just another handle but actually A WAY OF LIFE. Many people who are crippled by paralyzing arthritis or rheumatism and people with only one hand have praised Lamb handle Cutco because it distributes the tension in their hand evenly and gives them a safe grip."[69]

Delphia has described Lamb as "an evangelical crusader, hoping to save the world one handle at a time. His pioneering use of anthropometric design methods provided a model for other designers and foreshadowed a significant shift in twentieth-century design practice" toward ergonomic design.[70] Hagley's online exhibit on Universal Design explained that Lamb "wanted his handles to be used comfortably by as many people as possible. His attention to anatomy, people's varying body sizes and abilities, and universal functionality formed the foundation of the Universal Design movement."[71] Recognizing that "the vast majority of consumer products are not designed with disability in mind, meaning that handles are too delicate, buttons too stiff, and graphics too small for certain users," the historian Bess Williamson has cautiously welcomed Universal Design as a "deliberate effort on the part of designers to address the ways things can go wrong for hand, eye, and body."[72]

Universal Design is certainly well-intentioned, but achieving universal applicability is extremely difficult. Williamson and Aimi Hamraie, another historian, have critiqued Universal Design for failing to accommodate disabled people. Williamson points out that Lamb's design for war veterans with leg injuries, the Lim-Rest crutch, was not successfully mass produced, unlike his ubiquitous Wedge-Lock handle which drew on the innovations of the Lim-Rest. The Lim-Rest remained a benevolent failure. In Henry Dreyfuss's *The Measure of Man*, an influential resource for designers, "people with disabilities were literally off the charts" and confined to special side projects, Williamson observes.[73] Williamson shows as evidence Dreyfuss's "Hand Positions—Average Man," in which maximum reach, finger grip, and hand grasp are illustrated with a "semi-statistical approach to design."[74] While Dreyfuss's Humanscale did recognize disability, it demonstrated the difficulty of achieving truly Universal Design. Hamraie concludes that Universal Design must be combined with disability justice in order to function more equitably.[75]

Williamson notes that Lamb's handles are not formed merely by Lamb clasping pieces of clay in his hand, rather they are based on his study of anatomy and

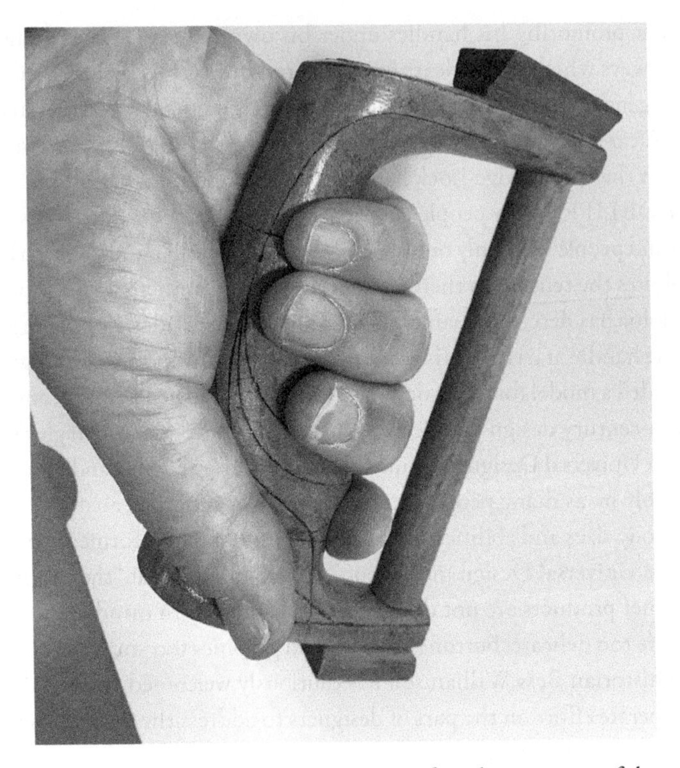

Figure 9.4. This photograph shows the disparity of size between one of the author's hands and one of Lamb's model handles. There is a gap to the right side of the thumb and fingers. Compare this with Figure 9.3 to see the impact of size associated with the sex of the user. Photograph by Grace Lees-Maffei. Courtesy of the Hagley Museum and Library.

on many measurements, and their finger grooves have cutaways to help them accommodate different sized fingers and grips.[76] But the experiences of female and nonbinary researchers handling the Wedge-Lock handle suggest that it is only partly successful in accommodating difference, a reality that has implications for Lamb's bold ambitions for universality and for Universal Design more broadly (Figure 9.4). The British feminist and activist Caroline Criado-Perez exposes two injustices in the design of the contemporary world. First, a gender data gap—a basic lack of information about women's bodies, expectations, customs, and activities—results in, second, products and services designed for a male norm, which Criado-Perez calls "reference male." This echoes Aimi Hamraie's critique of the "normate template."[77] These twin injustices affect every area of life from medical diagnoses and treatments to safety equipment.

Criado-Perez refers to data showing that "women have, on average, smaller hands than men, and yet we continue to design equipment around the average male. . . . This one-size-fits-men approach to supposedly gender-neutral products is disadvantaging women."[78] For instance, increasingly large smartphone screens become difficult for women to hold and to tap single-handedly, which negatively affects women's hand and arm health as well as our safety.[79] In United States agriculture, where there were nearly a million female farm operators in 2007, almost all equipment and tools "have been designed either for men or for some average user whose size, weight, strength, etc. were heavily influenced by the average man" even though "women's hands are on average 0.8 inches shorter than men's."[80] Hand tools such as wrenches "tend to be too large for women's hands to grip tightly."[81] Women have about half of the grip strength of men throughout their lives. Even an older male will have a stronger handgrip than a young woman.[82] Female athletes have only half the manual strength of untrained males, and in general, 90 percent of women have a weaker grip than 95 percent of men.[83] So the fact that tools are designed with reference to male bodies limits the competence of women using those tools, which ultimately has a negative impact on women's health, safety, and well-being. Research is needed to fill the gender data gap and to develop standards and measurements sensitive not only to relative size and strength but also to diverse ways of making.[84]

The technological advances that underpin mass production and globalization have enabled manufacturers to drive down costs and offer consumers more goods at more accessible prices. The right tool combined with manual skill enhances dexterity. Historically, dexterity has been gendered, with textile processes such as crocheting, needleworking, and lacemaking all associated with women while activities such as watchmaking, model making, and whittling have been associated with men, whether professional or hobbyist. These persistent stereotypes underpin contemporary globalization. For instance, clothing production and electronics manufacture both rely on a cheap off-shore labor force of female workers. Among the apparent benefits resulting from economies of scale and efficiencies of distribution and logistics is a broad product range. But rather than offering consumers a wider choice, mass production relies not only on labor inequities, but also on industry standards centered on a normative male end-user. The majority of consumers, who are not best represented by reference male, pay other costs in addition to those on price tags, including reduced suitability and utility.

Conclusion

This chapter began with Georg Simmel's assertion that a handle could be read as a microcosm of the society in which it was produced. It has contributed to an understanding of capitalism through attention to the senses, using an archival study of Thomas Lamb, the twentieth-century's self-appointed, preeminent designer of handles to analyze both the role of design as a building block for the material world of capitalism and of the role of touch in the design process. In so doing, it has shown that making things by hand is not insurance against normativity. This chapter extends Eugene Ferguson's work on "knowing hands" as crucial carriers of tacit, nonverbal knowledge in engineering into a novel discussion of embodied knowledge in design practice and design historical research. By placing handcrafting at the center of his embodied design practice, Lamb attempted to universalize his own experiences at the expense of the needs of consumers with differently sized or shaped hands or different tactile propensities. Embodied research in the Lamb collection has demonstrated that while Lamb's Wedge-Lock handle may have been designed to serve as many users as possible, the *average* user he designed for resembled himself more than anyone else. When the designer's own hands, and their sense of touch, are key determinants of their designs, the suitability of the resultant products for a variety of consumers should be assured via complementary methods. Overarching philosophies of design can be understood differently through embodied archival research. For instance, even in the case of Universal Design, the pattern of male design and female use, and male production and female consumption, serves women poorly. Embodied research as a method for design history, as exemplified by the author's tactile work in the Thomas Lamb archive, has highlighted both the shortcomings of embodied research as a tool for design practice and the need to avoid these pitfalls through blended research methods using a wider data set which overcomes the gender data gap.

Skilled manual work has not yet been mechanized out of manufacturing. Twenty-first century manufacturing processes make extensive use of the dexterity of hired hands to operate and maintain digitized, robotic, and mechanized processes, to assemble miniaturized electronic goods, to complete finishing and packaging, and to ensure quality control, among a variety of tasks. As long as hands are used in the manufacturing which drives capitalism, embodied research using direct handling will be important for understanding design and the role of the senses within the capitalist system.

PART IV

Marketplace

CHAPTER 10

Fragrance and Fair Women

Perfumers and Consumers in Modern London

JESSICA P. CLARK

In January 1911, retailers in London's elite West End developed a new scheme to entice consumers to buy local. The "All-British Shopping Week," launched that spring, brought together retailers from a range of trades to encourage the purchase of goods from Britain and its colonies. The initiative also invoked the senses, as some retailers designed sensory experiences to enhance the desirability of—and consumers' affective connections to—national goods. Nowhere was this more evident than at Harrods, the neighborhood department store dominating London's up-and-coming Knightsbridge district. In their contribution to the "All-British" scheme, Harrods transformed its perfumery department into "The Salon of Fragrance and Fair Women." From March 27 through April 1, fifty glamorous actors from the Edwardian stage including Maud Allan and Phyllis Dare acted as perfumery shopgirls, signed autographs in the official "Souvenir of the Salon of Fragrance and Fair Women," and offered a spritz of Luce's British-made eau de cologne. All proceeds went to the Middlesex Hospital Prince Francis of Teck Memorial Fund.[1]

A case study of the All-British Shopping Week of 1911 allows us to interrogate the relationship between commercial modernity, smell, and visual culture in early twentieth-century London. It also frames this chapter, which explores three attempts to develop distinct "smellscapes," the olfactory counterpoint to visual "landscapes":[2] in the department store and its urban environs, at the national level, and across an imagined empire via commercial space, scented goods, and visual marketing campaigns. This approach suggests that modern Britain's commercial smellscapes were ambiguous, ill-defined, and relatively underutilized in perfumery marketing, defying definition in a similar manner to urban, national, or colonial smellscapes more generally. As we will see, retailers and commercial perfumers struggled to establish stable smellscapes on which to market their brands. Instead, broader sociocultural contexts—including urban conditions and imagined national and imperial geographies—shaped popular understandings of smell and space. They also animated consumer responses—or lack thereof—to perfumery wares and publicity campaigns. Commercial attempts to promote perfumery subsequently remained ambiguous and at times contradictory, furthering retailers' dependency on visual forms to sell olfactory experiences and commodities.

The heavy reliance on visual experience in the 1911 Harrods's "Salon" is one example of the ways that, in early twentieth-century London, the senses shaped the design of commercial and spatial experiences. Historians have devoted attention to these experiential schemes, pointing out how, from the early modern period, sensory elements were central to new consumer practices.[3] This included the role of the senses in the development of fixed shops, bazaars, and arcades, which functioned as commercial but also sensory "pleasure zones" for new cohorts of shoppers. In the West, this dated back to the "consumer revolutions" of the eighteenth and nineteenth centuries, when shopping became an increasingly accessible activity for an emerging middling sort. These upwardly mobile shoppers relied on consumer goods and activities, concentrated in sites of visual spectacle and commercial extravagance like London's West End, to communicate their enhanced social standing.[4] However, shopping was not an isolated activity separated from broader sensory experiences that shaped the city and its inhabitants, not to mention ideas about nation or empire. This chapter addresses relationships between retailers' manipulation of the senses and existing understandings of smell already operating across London as an imperial metropolis. In doing so, it roots commercial spaces and marketing campaigns within broader urban and cultural contexts to think about how retailers aligned with or departed from dominant sensory trends to promote their wares. This is especially clear in the case of Britain's commercial perfumers, who, as we will see, struggled to define cohesive olfactory messages for consumers and ultimately resorted to visual forms to communicate their brands' stories.[5]

A focus on smell is especially significant in relation to processes and perceptions of Western modernity and in particular its privileging of visuality. The turn of the twentieth century was arguably a highpoint of the modern, with the expansion of colonialism, complex consumer and exhibition cultures, advertising, transportation, urban mobility, and the anomie that allegedly accompanied it. Because these developments both relied on and generated new visual regimes, modernity is often construed, in both historical and scholarly sources, as an ocularcentric phenomenon.[6] However, modern life entailed a range of sensory experiences. This included the existence of smellscapes, which, in the case of London, ordered and periodically regulated the modern city.[7] They also extended—both deliberately and inadvertently—into modern London's commercial settings, where retailers worked to create distinct olfactory environments conducive to elite, refined consumption. This included Harrods in the spring of 1911, where consumers found themselves immersed in "The Salon." There, organizers invoked yet another spatial element in the design of their smellscape—that of the nation—in the event's explicit support of the British economy. This raised implicit questions of an even larger, all-encompassing smellscape: that of empire, whose raw materials and colonized labor supported the creation of British perfumery and buttressed the nation's international standing. Yet these three smellscapes remained ephemeral and fleeting. Inconsistencies in these commercial, spatial, and sensory schemes foreground struggles among retailers and perfumers to develop effective marketing schemes that extended beyond the visual, not to mention stable understandings of "national" versus "foreign" smells.

The All-British Shopping Week and the Importance of Fragrance

The idea for an All-British Shopping Week originated in a nationalistic British trade association called the Union Jack Industries League, in conjunction with leading West End retailers, the Drapers' Chamber of Trade, and commercial associations in more provincial locales like Exeter. According to League founder and honorary secretary F. Mountjoy Humphrey Davy, the themed event sought "to secure the display of home and colonial and Indian goods with a view to the pushing of such British-made articles. If tradesmen would enter into the movement heartily he felt sure that they would reach the purchasing public."[8] Davy initially generated support among principal retailers in London's West End, including Marshall and Snelgrove and Liberty and Co., but also attracted firms in the burgeoning districts of Bayswater, to the northwest, and Knightsbridge, just south of Hyde Park: W. Whiteley, Harrods, Harvey Nichols.[9] This broad support suggests firms' attempts to move beyond the deep localism of their operations, as London's department stores strove to establish themselves as national and international powers on the global retailing scene. Harrods and other commercial providers took up these national imperatives, designing window and counter displays to explicitly highlight British commodities. Meanwhile, organizers issued 100,000 free shopping guides to the public "with maps of local areas and exhaustive information for shoppers"; took out full-page advertisements in London's leading print periodicals; and posted elaborate signs featuring Britannia and a "'British Lion'" at key railway stops across England and Wales to "bring large numbers of people to London."[10]

In their planning and execution of the All-British Shopping Week, organizers and commercial providers depended on the visual modes of marketing and advertising that dominated London's early twentieth-century commercial scene. This reflected modern developments more generally; from the late nineteenth century, London's commercial providers distinguished themselves via vibrant print campaigns that touted the alleged superiority of Britain's consumer goods.[11] Advertisements, handbills, and other visual spectacles became central features of fin de siècle Western modernity, as vivified in the sights of London's leading shopping district, the West End.[12] Commentators and commercial figures emphasized the centrality of visual culture in this urban milieu, creating and contributing to dominant messages about the civilizing influences of sight over other, base senses like touch and smell.[13]

Cultural emphasis on visuality extended to coverage of the All-British Week, which primarily focused on visual elements of the scheme. "Kensington High-street is a great sight this week," touted the woman's page in the *Daily Mirror* on March 28 "and the windows of these shops alone enable us to understand the stupendous importance of Britain as a manufacturing land." Reports for the following day further foregrounded visual spectacle, detailing a shopping district bedecked with Union Jacks and themed window displays. Live demonstrations complemented the spectacles, as skilled artisans working at looms demonstrated processes of production for curious passersby.[14] This extended to Harrods, notes the theater historian Catherine Hindson, "where lace-making, embroidery and hand weaving were 'executed by pretty Irish colleens [or single young women] in their national costumes,' echoing the living displays of national cultures and empire that permeated London's exhibition culture."[15] To help visitors navigate these sights, organizers designed and precirculated a map in leading print publications that sketched out the spatial parameters of the Shopping Week. While invoking the lived environment, the map provided a visual representation of the

West End, Bayswater, and Knightsbridge to patrons of the All-British spectacle, organizing and providing order to the sights on offer.

In addition to performances of labor, Harrods also organized elaborate experiences of sensorial luxury and commerce via a charity drive featuring London's preeminent stage actors. "The Salon" took place in a donated space at the fashionable department store, stocked with donated fragrance from Luce's of Jersey and donated time from some of the West End's leading actors, singers, and dancers. The charity workers took rotating shifts during the week to sell Luce's "British-Made" eau de cologne, as well as autographs, postcards, and in-person interactions (Figure 10.1). By creating the opportunity for customers to interact with theatrical celebrities, scheme organizers positioned shopping as an embodied experience, which engaged a range of sensory faculties. Consumers not only smelled the fragrance on offer, as was standard practice at contemporary perfumery counters. They also had the chance to sensorially engage with the actors themselves: the sound of their voices, the feel of their gloved hands, the scent of their skin. The scheme thus enlivened the already sensorial experience of shopping via the added dimension of theater performers brought to life. In this way, it transcended divides between on and offstage, adding yet another embodied experience to the overloaded sensorium of London's western shopping districts.[16]

The central role of vision in the consumer culture of this period nonetheless made for limitations—and tensions—in representations of these embodied experiences. Modern dependencies on visual forms infused the Harrods event in its promise of "Fair Women," despite its additional organization around space ("Salon") and scent ("Fragrance"). In this instance, "Fair" meant the dominant version of beauty as white and Anglo-Saxon. While there were some differences in the actors' ages (ranging from eleven to thirty-eight), all fifty women were of British or settler-colonial descent, representing Canada, South Africa, Australia, and the United States. Meanwhile, the event's official souvenir—a pamphlet called "Souvenir of the Salon of Fragrance and Fair Women"—was a piece of visual rather than olfactory memorabilia designed to be preserved and cherished as a memento. The attractive booklet featured studio portraits of forty-two celebrity participants, who signed their likeness for a charitable donation. The keepsake allowed consumers to "capture" their encounters with leading actors, transforming it into a visual reminder of the lived experience. Finally, the emphasis on the visual extended to the behavior of Salon visitors themselves. Some shoppers seemed limited in their interactions with performers, finding themselves unable to engage with the women as embodied subjects. Instead, actors

ACTRESSES SELL ALL-BRITISH SCENT.

Miss May. Miss Augarde. Miss More. Miss Cowie. Miss Chase.

Miss Pauline Chase, Miss Laura Cowie, Miss Nancy More, Miss Adrienne Augarde and Miss Olive May were among the charming actresses who assisted the funds of the Middlesex Hospital by selling British Eau de Cologne at Messrs. Harrod's yesterday. They will continue to do so each day during the "All-British Shopping Week."—("Daily Mirror" photograph.)

Figure 10.1. Leading actresses, singers, and dancers from London's West End volunteered as "shopgirls" during the All-British Shopping Week. Article in the *Daily Mirror*, March 28, 1911. Courtesy © British Library Board (Shelfmark NEWS.REG1544/17).

reported the presence of "curiosity-hunters," who preferred to gawk rather than participate. Indeed, the noted English actress Lilian Braithwaite observed that "[s]ome of the women [shoppers] were quite candid in the admission that they had come to *see* the actresses and not to buy. . . ."[17]

The sensorial tensions that underpinned "The Salon" reflected broader challenges facing retailers in their marshalling of smellscapes across London's West End, the nation, and its colonies. As a class of commercial provider, British perfumers also struggled to hone the effects of smells when selling their wares, relying instead on the dominance of visual spectacle to promote their goods.[18] This is especially evident in the role of perfumery in London's early department stores.

As the city's leading commercial institutions, these retailers proposed to transform the urban smellscape for shoppers who crossed their thresholds.

Commercial Space and London Smellscapes

That "The Salon of Fragrance and Fair Women" took place at Harrods reflected the centrality of department stores to London's modern consumer culture. This dated from the 1860s, when London's commercial leaders attempted to redefine consumers' movements—and sensory experiences—via the careful design of elaborate, new shopping experiences. As the historian Erika Rappaport has shown, enhanced transportation systems meant the opening up of new areas beyond London's West End to greater levels of commercial and pedestrian traffic. After the initial establishment of William Whiteley's store in Westbourne Grove in 1863, additional businesses sprung up across Bayswater and Knightsbridge. Institutions such as Harrods (expanded in 1905) and Selfridges (opened in 1909) further enlarged the reach of London's department store district and the visual spectacles that defined it. Elaborate commercial practices turned in large part on visual displays in shop windows, colorful advertising, extravagant interiors, and ornate architecture that communicated the grandeur of an elaborated Western consumer culture. Visuality dominated sensory experiences in London's spectacular new commercial spaces.[19]

Yet, despite the privileging of visual culture as a key element of British modernity—and city-dwellers' alleged indifference to external stimuli—shopping never ceased to be a complex, multisensory experience.[20] Shopping in early twentieth-century London demanded engagement with the full range of senses, as shoppers navigated the tumult of the modern city. Upon exiting the purported sensorial "refuges" that were West End department stores, consumers descended into London's mixed commercial topographies, which defined and delineated some of the city's multiple smellscapes. Wholesale food markets were historically a source of some of the metropolis's most distinguishable odors, a trend that continued well into the twentieth century, and the smell of meat, poultry, and offal at Smithfield Market long characterized its neighboring rooks and alleys.[21] Meanwhile, mobile traders not bounded by the market stall spread commercial (and periodically nuisance) smells across the city. Plebian street victuallers, fruit and vegetable vendors, lavender sellers, and manure collectors did steady business, functioning as peripatetic elements of the capital's interrelated commercial, socioeconomic, and sensory topographies.[22] This extended to London's

West End, and an afternoon of shopping down Regent Street along the borders of Soho, west on Piccadilly, past Hyde Park Corner, or into the burgeoning Knightsbridge and Bayswater districts exposed ramblers to an array of smells, as mixed constituencies of hawkers, peddlers, and shopkeepers proffered their wares across the metropolis.

By the early twentieth century, these multisensory experiences—avoiding pungent horse droppings or being bombarded with the calls of more humble street sellers—became increasingly disruptive in the ways they undermined the controlled, sanitized sensory refuges of the West End. On crossing the threshold of a leading department store, shoppers ostensibly traversed a classed boundary that controlled and refined their sensory experiences. "It was a dramatic change," argues the cultural historian Constance Classen, "from the often muddy, rainy, dingy, and malodorous conditions of traditional marketplaces and shopping streets."[23] But even the shiny new department stores were not fully free of sensory assaults, and the mixing of rank and pleasurable odors occurred despite the best efforts of many high-end retailers. For example, floorplans from the early twentieth century reveal that, when entering Harrods from Brompton Road, shoppers navigated a virtual microcosm of London's broader commercial smellscapes, crisscrossing multiple and periodically disparate scents of urban commercial modernity: through the Wine and Tobacco Department to Produce and Foodstuffs, before reaching Meats and Fish with a final foray into the Florist's shop.[24] In this way, the metropolitan assault on consumer senses did not end once a shopper entered a West End retail establishment, as multisensory experiences continued to define movement through even the most rarefied spaces.

One notable exception to this lack of olfactory control was department stores' perfumery counters. Here was one of the only realms in which commercial providers could effectively curate the smellscapes that welcomed their consumers. The American entrepreneur Gordon Selfridge, founder of the eponymous Oxford Street department store, acknowledged the power of this sensory experience by moving the perfumery and beauty department to the front entrance of his emporium. Customers' first experience upon entering Selfridge's store was a wall of manufactured commercial scents, which was no doubt a powerful juxtaposition against the more common smells just beyond the front doors.[25] In this department and others, consumers were invited to sample the perfumery wares on offer.[26] Harrods had adopted these same sales strategies in "The Salon," as visitors received the attention of famous "shopgirls" and their bottles of Luce's cologne. In this way, experiences in smell—and particularly the transition from street to store, from sight to scent—became a principal means to encourage sales among discerning customers.

And yet, as was the case in "The Salon," perfumery counters continued to depend in large part on the visual appeal of their displays to attract consumers. Department stores, and not individual perfumery firms, most likely managed fragrance counters, in contrast to the concession system that operates today. Perfumers' trade publications and publicity photographs nonetheless emphasized the importance of lighting, display, and product arrangement as key means to sell perfumery wares—rather than smell alone. Writing in the *Bulletin of Pharmacy* in 1914, an American author explained the importance of attractive shelving on which to display eye-catching perfumery bottles. He compared and contrasted the benefits of center shelving versus wall cases, advising the use of glass, mirrors, and electric lighting to highlight the contents of glass bottles. Concluded the columnist, "no matter what fixtures perfumes are displayed in, it is important to keep the bottles in orderly array, and to keep both the bottles and the glass shelves, as well as the case itself, always polished to the shining point."[27] This focus on visual extravagance—and specifically the brilliance of perfumery bottles—is also clear in photographs of Harrods's and Selfridges's perfumery counters circa 1912 and 1910, respectively (Figures 10.2 and 10.3). Glass and crystal decanters contain myriad varieties of perfumery representing distinct brands. A Harrods's catalog from 1913 reveals that the department stocked goods from some sixty-two firms: Harrods's own brand, as well as Luce, Gosnell & Co., Grossmith, Piesse & Lubin, among others.[28] While some bottles feature visible yet discreet branding via labels, neither photograph betrays signs of large-scale visual marketing schemes. Those moving through the spaces with more ready access to the counters would nonetheless be able to recognize the various scents on offer, given the goods' organization by brand and maker.

Notably, neither trade articles nor photographs suggest the ways that a scent itself could feature in perfumery marketing and sales. To be sure, the arrangement at Harrods suggests that consumers *could* smell and sample the wares given the presence of carefully arranged chairs flanking rows of display cases. While absent from the images, shop assistants would have served as product experts who guided customers through the olfactory sales experience. Nonetheless, the extravagance of perfumery departments as spectacularized commercial space suggests the enduring power of the visual in attracting customers. Perfumery counters ostensibly functioned as respites from London's more heterogeneous smellscapes with their carefully curated offerings. But to initially attract a buyer

Figure 10.2. The perfumery counter at Harrods c. 1912 was a spectacularized commercial space, suggesting the enduring power of the visual in attracting perfumery customers. Courtesy of Harrods Company Archive, London.

Figure 10.3. Like their competitors, Selfridges also relied on visual spectacle to sell scented goods. Selfridges's Perfumery Department, c. 1910. Courtesy Chronicle/Alamy Stock Photo.

in a bustling urban department store, visual sale tactics prevailed in courting a shopper's eye before their nose.

Perfumed Commodities and National Smellscapes

If perfumers attracted London consumers with attractive visual and spatial displays, how did this extend to those living outside the metropolis who had limited access to the West End's spectacular offerings? In this case, visual advertising and marketing campaigns appeared in Britain's expansive periodical press, communicating the appealing qualities of scented wares from Luce, Gosnell & Co., Grossmith, and other leading perfumers. Some of the advertisements featured nationalist themes that communicated the alleged superiority of Britain and its manufactures; other perfumers took this a step further by invoking a "national" smellscape via the goods themselves, which allegedly captured the olfactory essence of a unified British people. In doing so, perfumers echoed numerable marketing schemes dominating the Victorian and Edwardian periods, when nationalistic imagery of Britannia, the British lion, or the monarch promoted goods ranging from mustard to bouillon.[29] In the case of British perfumers, nationalist marketing included attempts to harness a distinctly British smell or scented commodity that engendered in its wearer connections to the nation, all while signaling to others the wearer's patriotism and belonging. This was a challenging feat as smellscapes are, by definition, deeply localized, ephemeral, and often time sensitive. Perfumers and their commercial retailers subsequently struggled to create a stable "national" scent in a decidedly heterogeneous commercial market.

By invoking the nation—as a symbol and a smellscape—perfumers attempted to harness major trends in early twentieth-century advertising systems, an area in which they were reportedly faltering. Writing in *The Perfumery and Essential Oil Record* in April 1911, an anonymous expert argued that perfumers' efforts did not compare to those of soap makers and other leading industry advertisers. They complained that perfumery marketing lacked the creativity of other industries and suggested tradesmen develop "selling points" that included new ways to use traditional scents.[30] Notably, this meant mobilizing advertising copy—and *not* smells themselves—to explain perfumery's various uses: to improve the complexion, revive the weary, scent the sickroom. This absence of olfactory qualities in their marketing reflected specific difficulties facing perfumers, given the challenges of relying on language to describe smells. Researcher

Tom Zelman observes that perfumers struggle to "find an adequate means of using discursive symbols to define and distinguish individual fragrances" or "describe and promote their indescribable products."[31] This challenge manifested in historical perfume marketing and eventually engendered a transformation in messaging, argues Classen, "from origin or cause to effect." Specifically, nineteenth-century perfumery campaigns focused on sites of production and ingredients (origin or cause) before shifting, in the twentieth century, to the alleged effects of wearing perfumes: sexual attractiveness, affluence, taste.[32]

The observations of Classen and other scholars of the senses align with the early twentieth-century British case, when leading perfumery companies attempted to define national smells by emphasizing perfumery ingredients, mode, and place of production—that is, the "origin" or "cause" of these scents. These firms included Luce, whose "British-made" eau de cologne was the sole brand available for sale at the Harrods's "Salon" in 1911. Luce was just one of many British perfumery firms that, in the late nineteenth and early twentieth centuries, marketed deliberately "British"-scented commodities. Those most frequently positioned as "British" dated back to the earliest days of London's commercial perfumery industry, in the eighteenth century. Single-note perfumes dominated the industry in ensuing years, allegedly turning on natural resources available in Britain.[33] This included English lavender, harvested in Mitcham in Surrey and Hitchin in Hertfordshire, as well as violets from Devon. Advertisements touted the local origins of perfumes' raw materials, as well as their production in London, Jersey, and other locations across the British Isles. Following suit with other commercial and industrial firms, some advertisements featured attractive ink renderings of modern sites of production, from Gosnell & Co.'s manufactory on Blackfriars Road, London, to Luce's humbler but definitively English operations on the southern coast in Southampton.

It can also be argued that British perfumers mobilized "effect," the third mode of advertising discussed by Classen, by invoking the symbolic consequences of using their products. It was not only the "origins" of these British-made perfumes that made them a national commodity. These manufactured scents allegedly allowed consumers to *embody* Britishness, and through their wearing, British consumers could contribute to a shared national smellscape. Advertisers engaged patriotic imagery to communicate this sense of British authenticity and the shared British values that underpinned their perfumed commodities. In doing so, perfumers sought to compete with leading advertisers in fin de siècle Britain, many of which circulated romanticized and inaccurate images of empire, monarchy, and military power.[34] This manifested in a variety of nationalist themes across early twentieth-century perfumery ads. Advertisements for Gosnell & Co. included the British lion to symbolize the "British Superiority" of their goods, supported by "generation after generation of the British race."[35] Gosnell and others also mobilized images of royalty to promote their wares, including a very young Victoria whose profile adorned their Cherry Blossom line. Some campaigns featured bucolic scenes of an idealized English countryside. Others, such as Gosnell & Co.'s "Society Cologne," relied on depictions of eighteenth-century courtiers to signal the alleged timelessness of British perfumery. Despite relying on very contemporary understandings of nationalism, these latter ads harkened back to shared understandings of what was in fact a fictionalized English past.

Perfumers' promotion of British ingredients, production, and collective values belied more complicated processes in establishing stable national smellscapes. In reality, most of the raw materials for British perfumery came from Europe, most often France.[36] Little publicized was the fact that much of the perfume industry's renowned English lavender went to market in its raw state, garnering high prices among urban consumers at sites like Covent Garden. Less often was English lavender distilled for the less-profitable purpose of perfumery production.[37] In reality, French distilleries in Grasse, in the south of France, along with Spanish spike lavender producers, provided most of Britain's distilled lavender oil.[38] It was not just lavender that derived from alternate locales, as musk, civet, and attar of roses came to Britain via East and South Asia and regions of the Ottoman Empire.[39] Belying their dependency on raw materials sourced from other nations, British perfumers' marketing of "English" perfumery obfuscated the deeply global origins of its ingredients, not to mention British producers' relationship to an international community of distillers and essential oil producers.[40]

The alleged Britishness of perfumes contradicted the international sourcing of ingredients, just as it obscured perfumery's rich continental history and design. This includes eau de cologne, a scent that many national firms touted as "British made." Despite competing origin stories, eau de cologne is typically attributed to Johann Maria Farina (1685–1766), an Italian emigrant who, it is alleged, first produced the fragrance in a workshop in Cologne.[41] Farina's recipe was highly guarded, but typically included a blend of essential oils such as neroli and bergamot. The Cologne-based firm dominated production for the next 200 years, with the authentic German fragrance in high demand across Europe. This included Britain, where shoppers purchased original Farina eau de cologne at neighborhood London retailers like Whiteley's.[42]

British advertising schemes promoting nationalist versions of eau de cologne obfuscated the scent's international ingredients and its German history. In this way, firms like Luce revised the sensorial realities of the item and instead promoted messages about a singularly national scent that was exclusively British. The contradictions defining the creation of "national" scents reflected the ambiguities and ephemerality of smellscapes more generally, as they operated across London, the nation, and beyond. Despite commercial efforts, there was no definitive "London" or "British" smell. This did not stop some perfumers from promoting their wares via understandings of shared "British" smellscapes that were allegedly simple, stable, and consumable.

Advertising and Imagined Imperial Smellscapes

The impossibility of defining—and subsequently promoting—a stable national smellscape reflected broader challenges in attempting to forge a singular "British" consumer identity more generally, especially in a commercial milieu as heterogeneous as that of modern London. Schemes like the West End's All-British Week reflected circulating anxieties among commercial retailers about the public desire for foreign wares over British manufactures. The scheme was meant to stoke the patriotic instincts of local consumers via multisensory experiences and encourage the consumption of nationally produced goods for the benefit of local industry. Yet, this limited focus did not account for the broader cosmopolitanism that defined London in this period, not to mention the internationalism of many of its major industries, including perfumery. What is more, the scheme only minimally invoked Britain's imperial pursuits as a colonizing force and particularly its deep dependency on raw materials, colonized labor, and consumption to buoy its national economy—and its national identity.

Other promotional schemes in British perfumery did invoke the industry's colonial undergirding, but in imagined rather than accurate forms. While firms like Luce centered the "Britishness" of their commodities, other commercial perfumers mobilized Britain's global standing to profitable effect. They actively engaged with the cosmopolitanism that defined twentieth-century London as a world city by attempting to harness global "exoticism" in the form of marketable scents. This meant that, despite the best efforts of Luce and other firms, some of London's leading perfumes were not the old standbys lavender and eau de cologne, but a cadre of new, exoticized smells allegedly invoking "Eastern" qualities. With their strong musk accents, these "Oriental" perfumes came to dominate the fin de siècle market.[43] Some of the most popular new fragrances were created by Grossmith, which in 1891 launched "Phul Nana," purportedly named for the

Hindi word for "lovely flower." Phul Nana was just one of a series of Grossmith commodities that Anandi Ramamurthy, a media and culture critic, observes were racialized in their very design; others included "Hasu-No-Hana" (1888) and "Shem-al-Nessim" (1906).[44] Given their focus on mixed geographies, these "Oriental" perfumes did not explicitly feature in coverage of the All-British Shopping Week of 1911. Visitors to "The Salon" found these Orientalist scents as standard offerings at Harrods's perfumery counters.[45]

The rise of Oriental perfumes on the British market reflected broader transformations in perfumery production. At the fin de siècle, the popularity of traditional fragrances like lavender was challenged by a growing sophistication in perfume design, as advanced by continental European tastemakers in Paris and beyond. By some accounts, Phul Nana ushered in a new generation of London-made perfumes that were on par with the complex creations dominating European markets, where it became less common to discern any one olfactory note in leading perfumes. This shift was enhanced not only by continental influences, but also the widespread adoption of synthetic essences and oils, particularly by German distillers, which increased the diversity of ingredients available to even modest perfumers.[46] Alongside the rise of synthetics, perfumers across Europe continued to depend on raw materials from places like Northern India and China, as they had since the nineteenth century.[47] From these international locations, producers procured important ingredients like civet and musk.[48] In the early twentieth century, British distillers continued to rely on materials from foreign nations and colonized locales to buoy their commercial perfumery production. For Britain's commercial perfumers, global, often-colonized labor forces and raw materials were central to their success.[49]

Realist depictions of colonial resource extraction in service of British perfumery did not feature in marketing and advertising for these new, cosmopolitan scents. Instead, visual campaigns presented elaborate, Orientalist images of "far-off" lands populated by exoticized subjects catering to the needs and desires of white, British women like those who attended "The Salon" in 1911. Advertisements reflected fin de siècle Orientalist and Japonisme trends more generally,[50] which were in many ways constitutive of modern British consumer culture. As the historians Sonya Rose and Catherine Hall compellingly argue, from the nineteenth century, many Britons developed key elements of "national identity and race-consciousness" via imaginings of and interactions with empire, often through emerging forms of mass consumer culture.[51] Representations of imperial "Others," in widespread enactments of commodity racism, circulated via marketing campaigns, consumer goods, novels, newspapers, and music hall songs.[52]

Advertisements in particular, functioning as a "capitalist form of representation," advanced "cultural representation[s] of empire."[53] In the case of perfumery, elaborate advertising campaigns communicated the centrality of Oriental smellscapes in this moment, thereby contributing to broader fictions of Britain's relationship to empire.

Like other British perfumery firms, London-based Grossmith depended on visual rather than olfactory means to communicate the cosmopolitanism of their scented products to metropolitan consumers. Visual marketing campaigns amplified the purported exoticism of these complex new scents, which included spatial elements in their invoking of "far-off" lands. But, in their invocation of international geographies, the advertisements were not entirely free from other sensory elements beyond the visual. According to advertising campaigns in high-end society and ladies' journals, exoticized foreign lands had their own distinct smellscapes, which would prove desirable to London's discerning elites. For each of the Grossmith perfumes, ads featured stylized landscapes and stylish women from distinct locations: "Araby" or Arabia for Shem-El-Nessim, Japan for Hasu-No-Hana, and India for Phul Nana. Meanwhile, advertising copy elaborated on the smellscapes of these discrete locales, touting the "distinctiveness" of "spice-laden breezes . . . of Ceylon" or the "perfumed incense of a garden of Araby."[54] Unsurprisingly, such smellscapes represented Western imaginings of exoticized settings rather than any lived experiences in Britain's colonized territories. They also did not invoke allegedly malodorous "foreign" smells frequently criticized in popular travel accounts and ethnographies, as white, British traveler-authors conflated unfamiliar smellscapes with otherness and outsiderness.[55] Instead, when adorned by the white, metropolitan consumer, Oriental smells indicated refinement, individuality, and culture rather than danger and difference.[56] Any reference to foreign "danger" or olfactory pollution was sanitized in the advertising campaigns through visual and textual descriptions of fantastical gardens, flora, and fauna.

Grossmith's visual configurations transported viewers to far-off imperial smellscapes while signaling the accessibility of empire to urban female consumers. In doing so, the advertisements obscured London shoppers' access to more immediate cosmopolitan smellscapes: those of the metropolis' "ethnic" neighborhoods, often populated by first- and second-generation Londoners who were subject to spatial othering based on class and perceived racial and cultural differences.[57] The establishment of London's cosmopolitan modernity, starting in the late nineteenth century, meant that shoppers experienced a range of sensory experiences moving through the city, including the elite but heterogeneous West End.[58] Instead of acknowledging this diversity, print ads invited women to be whisked away from a dreary, *un*cosmopolitan London to distant colonial settings like India and "Arabia." According to the copy in one 1912 advertisement, Oriental scents introduced "a suggestion of the mingled sweetness and mystery of the East to the boudoirs and drawing-rooms of the West" via scented sachets, bath crystals, and soaps.[59] In one of numerous examples, Grossmith advertisements and commodities juxtaposed "home" and "away," definitively situating the consumer in an imagined, white Britain, but with ready to access to colonized overseas luxury. Empire was conceptualized in a geographically distant mode that placed Britain's "internal others" outside of London in a deferential colonized state, rather than, as the historian Sadiah Qureshi argues, a constitutive part of the modern city.[60] By contrast, Grossmith ads depicted imperial geographies, subjects, and their smellscapes in removed "outsider" forms, thereby reifying alleged spatial and sensory distinctions between "home" and "empire" for its white female audience. In this configuration, multiethnic encounters—with their attendant smellscapes—did not happen in London itself, but rather in imagined colonial geographies many miles away from the metropolis.

The imaginary conditions portrayed in Grossmith advertisements were not limited to local and "foreign" smellscapes but also extended to conditions of labor. Ads for Grossman's Oriental scents did not feature realist depictions of industrial production in the firm's manufactory on 29 Newgate Street, in the heart of the bustling commercial district adjacent to St. Paul's Cathedral in the City of London. Instead, racialized workers laboring in idealized "away" settings populated the perfume manufacturer's advertisements. This aligns with other examples of late nineteenth and early twentieth-century product advertising, observes Ramamurthy, which frequently represented production as labor undertaken by workers of color. "Within this, racism plays an important role," she argues, as people of color "were naturalized as laborers for the white man"; thus, such depictions were "not seen as a symbol of exploitation since [labor] 'appeared' to be their 'natural' place."[61] This dynamic is most evident in a 1912 series in the *Illustrated London News* for the scent Shem-El-Nessim, which featured "Arabian" women collecting flowers and other raw materials for perfumery production.[62] Adorned in attractive, flowing outfits and featuring long, covered hair, the women smile and gesture as they complete their work for the benefit of the white, British customer. As the respectable consumer takes a whiff from a distinctive Grossmith bottle, she envisions the contented workers at their productive tasks, collecting "the perfumed incense of a garden of Araby, redolent with the mingled odours of a thousand flowers, and breathing to the stars the sweet enchantments of the Eastern night . . ." (Figure 10.4).[63] In this visual and imperial fantasy, colonized women of exoticized beauty hold the secrets of Eastern smellscapes and are willing to impart them onto white English consumers. These images obscured more accurate dynamics of imperial power, in which Western colonizers extracted knowledge, resources, and labor, often through violence and coercion.[64] Meanwhile, visual marketing schemes substantiated racialized and classed distinctions between the perfume's wearers and those allegedly involved in its "Oriental" cultivation. While ostensibly signaling the superior smellscapes of imagined imperial geographies, such messages instead underscored sensory distinctions between an allegedly backward East and civilized West.[65] Even while celebrating foreign smellscapes in advertising copy, marketing schemes reinforced the alleged differences between white Britons and British colonized subjects and accentuated the latter's connections to the "base" sense of smell versus superior forms of Western ocularcentricity.

Figure 10.4. J. Grossmith and Son marketed their "Shem El-Nessim" via Orientalist images of colonial laborers. Advertisement in *Illustrated London News*, September 14, 1912. Courtesy © British Library Board (Shelfmark P.P.761/402).

Visual campaigns for Oriental scents communicated messages about white consumer power over the alleged mysteries—and the smells—of an exoticized "East." But what of the Oriental scents themselves, once worn or embodied by white, British customers as they exited the West End department store and moved through London's heterogeneous smellscapes? In the case of Phul Nana, its socioeconomic associations could not be contained or regulated by perfumers, and this manufactured scent took on a life of its own life beyond production and sale. Indeed, the fragrance had a decidedly ambiguous reputation on the streets of London, being primarily worn by working-class consumers, including "fast" women.[66] In *Miss Million's Maid*, a 1919 novel by Berta Ruck, for example, a character describes the smell of perfumes in a late-night ballroom "of which you catch a whiff if you pass down the Burlington Arcade—oppoponax, lilac, Russian violet, Phul-Nana—all blended together into one tepid, overpowering whole."[67] While London's Burlington Arcade, a short distance from Piccadilly Circus, was certainly home to retail perfumers, readers in the know would also recognize this commercial corridor's associations with solicitation and sexual commerce.[68] In its sensory form, then, Phul-Nana had connections to otherness beyond that of imperial envisionings designed by commercial perfumers. These others were less reputable, London-based figures: the actress, the socialite, the commercial sex worker. Perfumers and retailers had little control over these olfactory associations once their wares moved beyond the controlled spectacle of the visual realm, outside the frame of the department store perfumery counter or a printed advertisement. On the streets of London, commercial scents took on lives of their own, recalibrating the lived smellscapes of the early twentieth-century imperial city.

Conclusions

If associations between perfumed actresses and debauched femininity circulated in Britain's twentieth-century cultural imaginary, the West End theater celebrities who participated in "The Salon of Fragrance and Fair Women" in the spring of 1911 actively worked to dispel such connections. Their very purpose for being at Harrods represented efforts to revise and upgrade the theater's reputation; as Hindson argues, charitable campaigns were central to recasting—and enhancing—the social standing of those laboring in London's theater industry.[69] The symbolic messaging and reputation of the scents on offer also helped the actors' cause. Luce's eau de cologne did not carry the potentially illicit undertones of more cosmopolitan scents available elsewhere in Harrods's perfumery department. Rather than signal a wearer's "dangerousness"—within London's social topographies or across imagined imperial smellscapes—British-made, British-smelling goods were definitively situated within a realm of respectability, timelessness, and patriotism.

Yet the fact that these various associations coexisted in the space of "The Salon of Fragrance and Fair Women" speaks to the complex nature of retailing, commercial perfumery, and symbolic smellscapes operating in early twentieth-century London. Multiple, often disparate ideas about smells—as they functioned across the department store, city, nation, and empire—informed the public's engagement with "The Salon" in March 1911. It was, in many regards, preexisting heterogeneous smellscapes that contributed to the tensions defining this event and in particular the complicated role of the senses in contemporary British perfumery marketing. Those who designed the event—the organizers, retailers, and perfumers—attempted to foreground the strength of British commercial culture and industry in the face of consumer demand for foreign goods. To do so, they developed a uniquely sensorial experience, in which consumers interacted with "shopgirls" whose embodied presence helped promote an explicitly British scent for an explicitly British market. And yet, contradictions defined the experience, with many of these tensions related to the deployment of the senses for marketing purposes. First, organizers' reliance on printed souvenirs, photographs, and maps meant the enduring privileging of visual forms—rather than smell, as promoted—to market the event and attract consumers. Second, despite organizers' promotion of their British eau de cologne, the commodity itself defied classification as a singularly national scent, laying bare the challenges in defining any type of stable, purchasable "British" smell. Finally, the event obscured British perfumers' deep reliance on raw materials from a range of global and colonized sources, not to mention their exploitation of colonial labor. This was instead replaced by the donated "labor" of fifty white women of settler-colonial descent, further obscuring the profound imperial dependencies of the nation's perfumery industry. Ultimately, "The Salon" illuminated the challenges in creating an "All-British" olfactory experience for consumers, as such smellscapes proved impossible to marshal as a singularly patriotic shopping experience.

CHAPTER 11

Sold on Softness

DuPont Synthetics and Sensory Experience

REGINA LEE BLASZCZYK

In September of 1945, the American chemical giant E. I. du Pont de Nemours and Company published a new series of advertisements in *Women's Wear Daily*, the major national newspaper for fashion retailers, to promote its three textile fibers: rayon, acetate, and nylon. The DuPont Company was a large corporation headquartered in Wilmington, Delaware, with offices and plants around the United States. The firm was no stranger to national advertising, its ads familiar to *Women's Wear Daily* readers. DuPont had long spent hefty sums on print promotions in trade journals, popular magazines, and newspapers, using Batten, Barton, Durstine & Osborn (BBDO) of Madison Avenue as its advertising agency.

Let's look at one of DuPont's advertisements in *Women's Wear Daily* to see what it tells us about the chemical industry, consumer marketing, and sensory awareness at the end of World War II. The DuPont ad published on September 11, 1945, had the taglines, "I believe it's better" and "It's labeled Du Pont Rayon" (Figure 11.1).[1] The focal point of the ad is a sketch of an elegant young woman wearing a flirty little hat and clutching a bolt of fabric printed with a heart design. The imagined consumer holds the bolt up against her left cheek, while her chest, right shoulder, and upper arm are draped with loose yardage. With her head coquettishly tilted, the woman gazes at the audience with pursed lips and big bunny eyes. She has just found a lovely bolt of fabric while out shopping, and she conveys her pleasure with a highly personal gesture: a hug. Her body and the commodity become one, fused together in tribute to sensual pleasure.

Figure 11.1. This DuPont Company advertisement, showing the imagined consumer in a sensual embrace with a bolt of rayon fabric, was published in the major daily newspaper for fashion retailers and ready-to-wear manufacturers. Source: *Women's Wear Daily*, September 11, 1945. Courtesy of the Hagley Museum and Library. Image published with permission of ProQuest LLC. Further reproduction is prohibited without permission.

The powerful visual image was accompanied by a short message that explained DuPont's philosophy on textile promotion. "There are two angles to keeping topside in fashion," the text explained. The term "angle" was contemporary sales jargon familiar to the retailers who read *Women's Wear Daily*; they were always angling for more customers. The first angle was "style," the hook, or "stopper," that caught the consumer's eye as she browsed around the store. The second angle was "quality confidence," the secret sauce that made the "style story stick and grow famous." Style was perceived by the eye, quality by the hand. In DuPont's view, it was sight and touch that mattered, the eyes and the hands that determined if the fabric would meet favor with the female consumer. The burden rested on fiber makers, fabric designers, fashion creators, and retailers to acknowledge this reality and to devise ways for managing what the consumer saw with her eyes and felt with her fingers.

Beyond Ruin Porn

Historians of American enterprise have studied the arts of persuasion developed by manufacturers, retailers, and advertising agencies to expand sales and enlarge the consumer culture. Advertising campaigns and industrial designs of the early to mid-twentieth century have been considered in depth, particularly as they relate to big-ticket consumer goods like automobiles and disposable consumer goods like processed foods.[2] With a few exceptions, however, historians of American business and consumer culture have not examined marketing practices for fabrics, fashion, and fashion accessories.[3]

Historically, this type of merchandise—cloth, ribbons, readymade apparel, millinery, and accessories—fell under the rubric of "textiles," a broad category of soft goods that included the fabric for ladies' dresses and men's suits; knitwear; upholstery; household linens; tire cords; and industrial filters. Today in popular culture, few people think twice about fabrics, and they often associate fashion with extremes, high and low. At the top of the pyramid sit the custom-made couture gowns worn by celebrities at the annual Met Gala, and on the lower end is the fast fashion sold by global retailers like Zara. Haute couture outfits are objects of status display, with the very best designs given special treatment by art museums who preserve select items for future ogling. Fast fashion is worn for a few Instagram photos and discarded. Whether upmarket or downscale, no one knows who made the cloth, where, how, why, and when. In our global postmodern world, the fabric has no prestige. Its status has been usurped by the brand, the celebrity endorsement, and the identity statement.

When DuPont advertised rayon in 1945, the cultural and economic landscape was very different. For much of the twentieth century, female consumers knew something about fabrics, sewing, and clothing care, having gained this knowledge at home, in school, and in the stores. American ready-to-wear and make-do homemade fashions were the staple of every woman's wardrobe. The booming American clothing industry produced keepsake fashion that was worn from year to year. There was no fast fashion, no throwaway apparel. The American garment industry had grown substantially in the interwar years, in part by taking advantage of the new, inexpensive man-made textiles. The imaginary consumer depicted in the DuPont advertisement hugs her bolt of printed rayon fabric for good reason. From her school sewing classes, she had learned to value fabrics for their inherent qualities and to treasure the half-dozen outfits in her closet. She appreciated the bright colors, the eye-catching patterns, the soft touch, and the sensuous nature of a cloth that draped gently around the body. She knew the differences between velvet and satin, matelassé and crepe. To her, fashion wasn't something designed in faraway Paris—or produced somewhere in China and shipped to America on a box boat. The American woman created her own style, her own sensual experience, by making some outfits on her family sewing machine and buying some ready-to-wear in the local shops (Figure 11.2).

Few researchers outside fashion and costume studies know this story, and few historians understand its importance. Today, "textiles" is a dirty word in American historiography. The feminized nature of fashion, and the concomitant marginalization of fashion studies as an academic discipline, are in part responsible for this sorry state of affairs. Further, trade policies that fostered the global movement to offshore manufacturing have, inadvertently, played a role in shaping historical indifference. We now have two or three generations of historians who have never worked in a mill over their summer break, with many never ever having set foot in a factory. All around the United States, the industrial past is represented by crumbling manufacturing plants whose hulking, cavernous interiors are appreciated mainly by "ruin porn" afficionados. The end result is a blissful ignorance of industrial history as a lever to prying open broader trends, from race relations to cultural meaning. Many historians looking at our DuPont advertisement would think it frivolous, without understanding that DuPont was the Apple of midcentury America and that the fiber industry was its Silicon Valley.

Figure 11.2. American women combined ready-to-wear, dressmaker-sewn garments, and homemade articles to create outfits that were comfortable and fashionable. This page of candid snapshots from a photo album compiled by an unidentified woman shows the range of easygoing, soft styles that were popular in the 1920s. Author's collection.

The story of DuPont fibers opens the doors onto the hidden history of sensory research in twentieth-century American capitalism. This chapter focuses on the most important firm in one of the most important industries in the world's most important economy. Previous generations of historians examined DuPont as an innovator in three major areas: chemistry, engineering, and management.[4] Here we look at the fourth leg of the stool: marketing.

My analysis is built around two case studies. The first, longer example is drawn from DuPont's role in the man-made fiber industry between 1920 and 1945, an understudied era in the company's textile history. DuPont was the second largest rayon producer in America, and in this capacity, the firm assumed a leadership role in sensory research as related to textiles. In the interwar years, practitioners in marketing, a new business specialty, envisioned the typical American woman as white, married, and middle class, adopting the shorthand term "Mrs. Consumer" to describe this imagined person.[5] DuPont's interest in female sensory experience was driven by the imperative to improve the performance of cellulose fibers and expand rayon sales among the textile mills serving the burgeoning ladies' ready-to-wear industry. The second, supporting example turns to DuPont from 1945 to 1970, when the firm was the dominant player in the American synthetic fibers industry and when ready-to-wear was a mature business. In this period, DuPont dominated the market for "test-tube" fibers—fibers synthetized in the laboratory from materials in the mineral kingdom—through technological innovation augmented by extensive market research and aggressive promotions. Postwar marketers moved away from the monolithic concept of "Mrs. Consumer" and tried to develop a more nuanced understanding of American shoppers.[6] In keeping with this shift, DuPont expanded its market research efforts and explored men's sensory experiences with textiles. Together, the two case studies consider how DuPont embraced sensory market analysis, first as a pioneer in the study of textiles and the senses and then as a major customer for the services of motivational research consultants.

The Aesthetics of Rayon

During the interwar years, the major player in DuPont rayon marketing was Alexis Sommaripa (1900–1945), a textile expert who found his way to the chemical company via Harvard University. Born in Odessa, Russia (now Odesa, Ukraine), Sommaripa, the son of a judge, was educated at the Imperial Law School, a prestigious boys' academy in St. Petersburg that prepared the elite for government service. He fled his homeland in 1918 as the Russian Civil War (1918–1920) created turmoil, using his foreign language skills to support himself as a translator in Europe before immigrating from England to the United States in 1920. In Boston, he attended the Graduate School of Business Administration at Harvard (now the Harvard Business School, or HBS), receiving his MBA in 1922. He then spent a year studying cotton production at the Lowell Textile School, one of many now-forgotten vocational institutes that trained people for skilled jobs in American industry. In tandem with the cotton industry's flight from New England, Sommaripa moved to the South for a position at the Indian Head Mills in Cordova, Alabama, a subsidiary of the Nashua Manufacturing Company of Nashua, New Hampshire.[7] Within a year, he was back at the HBS, helping his former professor, Melvin T. Copeland, a marketing pioneer, with a study of cotton prices. In the fall of 1925, one of the deans recommended him for a job at a DuPont subsidiary in Buffalo, New York. The young

Russian joined the Bureau of Business Research, the statistics office of the DuPont Rayon Company, in November of 1925.[8]

In this era, the discipline of marketing and the practice of market research were in their infancies. Before World War I, the Curtis Publishing Company in Philadelphia undertook some of the world's first consumer surveys to better understand who subscribed to its mass-circulation magazines, notably the *Saturday Evening Post* and the *Ladies' Home Journal*. After the war, advertising agencies like J. Walter Thompson (JWT) on Madison Avenue in New York developed more sophisticated methods for putting the consumer under the microscope, expressly focusing on white, middle-class women. JWT's approach combined quantitative door-to-door surveys on the purchasing patterns of female consumers with the psychological analysis of their product choices. When Sommaripa arrived at DuPont, marketers were only just finding their way with the mythical Mrs. Consumer and sensory experience was not on their radar screens.[9]

Over the course of his DuPont career, Sommaripa laid the foundation for the firm's interdisciplinary approach to textile marketing, bringing together the insights of laboratory science, engineering practice, empirical observations, fabric design, and psychological research on the senses.[10] The sensory marketing pioneer died prematurely on the Western Front in March of 1945, while serving as a noncombatant civilian with the United States Army. He was celebrated in death at DuPont as the mastermind of fabric development in the American rayon business.[11] He earned this accolade for his work at the Bureau of Business Research in the 1920s and, more importantly, for his directorship of the Fabric Development Service in the 1930s. Operating out of DuPont's sales offices in midtown Manhattan, the Fabric Development Service connected the firm's rayon plants to the apparel supply chain—to converters, weavers, knitters, garment makers, and retailers—as a means for gathering trend data that could be used to create better textiles. Sommaripa and his staff developed close business relationships with designers, engineers, and salesmen from the weaving mills, gathering feedback that would be used both by DuPont laboratory scientists to improve rayon fibers and by DuPont designers to create "idea fabrics" to be shared with customers in the textile industry. The senses and sensory experience figured into these activities.

DuPont started producing man-made fibers back in 1920, when it opened the Buffalo plant to make viscose rayon from wood pulp. This venture was part of a DuPont plan to shift away from explosives and gunpowder to a broader range of products that included plastics, paints, and dyes. The man-made fiber industry traced its roots to late nineteenth-century Europe, where chemists first created cellulose filaments to compete with silk, the world's most luxurious material for textiles. Europe was the locus of the artificial silk industry until 1910, when the British textile giant, Courtaulds, established a factory to make viscose in Marcus Hook, Pennsylvania, just north of DuPont headquarters in Wilmington. Starting in the 1920s, numerous American and European firms established fiber factories in the United States. Between 1924 and 1926, a collective effort in rebranding, led by American dry-goods merchants, resulted in the adoption of the generic term "rayon" as a synonym for all types of artificial silk.[12]

In his job at the Bureau of Business Research, Sommaripa served as the principal investigator for a series of research projects that connected the DuPont Rayon Company to the National Retail Dry Goods Association (NRDGA), the major trade group for American textile retailers. In the mid-1920s, there were no national department store chains comparable to Macys today and no global apparel brands like H&M. Fashion chains like Lerner Shops, predecessor to New York & Company, and Lane Bryant, specialists in maternity wear and stout sizes, were just gaining a toehold nationally. Most of the stores that sold textile products were one-of-a-kind, family-operated dry-goods emporiums, mainly stocking fabrics for professional dressmakers and home seamstresses along with smaller selections of millinery, knitwear, and apparel. The NRDGA market surveys gathered quantitative data from hundreds of stores around the country to learn about women's preferences for various types of textiles, including knitted lingerie and dress fabrics. These projects benefitted from Sommaripa's expertise in statistical analysis and textile engineering, while exposing him to the mysteries of sensual experience and consumer motivation.

The NRDGA surveys provided DuPont with insight into how the senses figured into women's choices as consumers. Writing in 1938, Sommaripa recalled some of challenges faced by rayon makers in the mid- to late 1920s. The original viscose rayon, known as continuous filament yarn, was smooth and shiny. It was mainly used in knitted goods like imitation silk stockings and, to a much lesser extent, in the woven textiles used in ready-to-wear. Some rayon advertisements for woven rayon fabrics boasted about the "shimmering sheen" of the material, but the glossiness proved to be a liability. The NRDGA surveys discovered that female shoppers "thought woven rayon fabrics were coarse in appearance, harsh to the touch, stiff in drape and excessively shiny." The gloss looked cheap, and the glassy stiffness of the fabrics sounded "raspy."[13] Sommaripa's market research suggested that rayon textiles offended the senses of sight, touch, and hearing.

Technicians at the DuPont Rayon Company's plant in Buffalo looked to alleviate some of these aesthetic liabilities, starting with the yarns used in knitwear.

The roughness of rayon textiles was rooted in the nature of the material itself. To improve the consumer's sensual experience, it was necessary to modify the fiber. One major problem was the diameter, or denier, of the rayon filament, which was extruded from a machine. This material was three times thicker than cotton fiber and many times wider than silk filament. When these thick rayon filaments were spun together, the result was a yarn that was coarse to the hand. In turn, any knitwear made from these yarns was scraggy to the touch. DuPont chemists and engineers in Buffalo adjusted the manufacturing processes to extrude narrower filaments and to spin finer yarns which, when knitted into garments, would have a smooth hand. The new yarn, DuPont Super-Extra, resulted in knitwear with, in Sommaripa's words, considerable "softness and strength."[14]

The knitted lingerie industry was the major customer for rayon in the 1920s, and the introduction of finer yarns allowed DuPont to wrest market share away from its major competitor, The Viscose Company, the Courtaulds subsidiary at Marcus Hook. Writing in *DuPont Magazine*, a monthly publication for stockholders, Sommaripa noted the rising popularity of knitted rayon lingerie, which in 1926 accounted for 36 percent of all ladies' underwear sales, surpassing silk and cotton merchandise. Among "the advantages of rayon," Sommaripa wrote, "one of the most important to women . . . is softness." DuPont Super-Extra rayon yarn was used by major knitwear manufacturers such as Munsingwear, in Minneapolis, Minnesota, to produce the sensuous, soft form-fitting onesies that were popular under the loose-fitting frocks of the 1920s.[15]

DuPont Super-Extra rayon yarn was ideal for knitted lingerie, where a tad of sheen introduced a bit of naughty glamour to the ladies' boudoir. But shininess was a liability in the woven fabrics used to sew up women's dresses. In 1926, one trade journal contrasted the "richness of sheen and bloom" of real silk to the "harsh brilliance" of rayon, equating silk "to a well-dressed woman, and rayon to an over-dressed woman."[16] In response, DuPont scientists in Buffalo puzzled over how to reduce the "ray" in the rayon. The trick was not to eliminate the gloss—some luster was required if rayon fabrics were to resemble silk—but to control the reflection of light, and hence, the sheen. This was achieved in filament production initially by incorporating into the spinning solution pigments or oils that deflected the light. Bit by bit, the effort to "de-luster" rayon fibers by manipulating optics achieved some degree of success. By the mid-1930s, DuPont had the ability to fine-tune the degree of luster in the fiber, producing a range of gloss from bright to dull.[17]

Another aesthetic challenge with woven rayon textiles, revealed by Sommaripa's research for the NRDGA, was the stiffness of the fabric and the harsh noise that was generated when a consumer rubbed the material. These characteristics were not an issue in the pioneer days of viscose, when the main applications were braids, trimmings, and upholstery. But the weaving mills that made broadcloth for the burgeoning ladies' readymade clothing industry needed yarns with the subtle sheen, warmth, fuzziness, and softness of wool. One way to create fabrics that were dull, soft, and lightweight was to weave rayon yarns together with silk or cotton yarns. These blended, or mixed, fabrics looked refined and were pleasant to the hand and ear. By 1927, major textile companies like Pacific Mills, which operated mammoth factories in Lawrence, Massachusetts, were weaving blended rayon fabrics for sale to dress manufacturers.[18]

These improvements in rayon technology—narrowing the denier, delustering, and blending materials—were steps in the right direction, but more assertive action was required if rayon was to gain a toehold in the booming ready-to-wear market. Ultimately, DuPont promoted a new type of yarn, "spun rayon," as a means for increasing its presence in the New York apparel industry. While continuous filament yarns were silky, smooth, and suited to knitted underwear, spun rayon yarns were intentionally engineered to be lumpy and bumpy in emulation of the wool and cotton used to weave cloth for ladies' dresses. Spun rayon yarns were produced in two stages. First, the DuPont rayon plant took extruded viscose filaments and chopped these long strands into short lengths, creating a material called "cut staple" or "rayon staple fiber." Second, DuPont sold the cut staple to the textile trade, where spinning specialists or vertically integrated mills turned it into yarn using the standard equipment for cotton and wool. These spun rayon yarns had the many of the characteristics of the natural fibers.

Spun rayon presented endless design possibilities and attracted the attention of the apparel industry. Textiles woven from the new yarns had little luster, no rustling, and a good hand. Between 1931 and 1934, most spun rayon yarns were used to weave the crepe dress fabrics relished by the garment cutters in New York's Seventh Avenue garment district, the apparel manufacturing center of the United States. These developments occurred during the darkest days of the Great Depression, and the rollout was slow. But as the economic situation improved, so too did consumers' ability to update their wardrobes. By 1936, Sommaripa had his satisfaction, noting the rising popularity of spun rayon in suiting fabrics and in wool-rayon blends for women's dresses, among other applications that required the cloth to fall, or drape, softly and elegantly across the body.[19]

The Important Basis of Touch

The Great Depression was a challenging moment for American business on several fronts. Between 1934 and 1936, the DuPont Company was subjected to intense public scrutiny for its role as a munitions manufacturer during World War I. The firm countered a brutal journalistic exposé and a harsh congressional investigation on this matter with a major public relations campaign. As part of this effort to rehabilitate DuPont's reputation, in 1935 the BBDO advertising agency introduced *The Cavalcade of America*, a weekly radio show with stories of American heroism, and the now-famous advertising slogan, "Better Things for Better Living . . . through Chemistry."[20]

In 1930, Alexis Sommaripa assumed the directorship of DuPont's Fabric Development Service in New York. This section of the sales department mainly worked to connect DuPont to the textile marketplace. One of the unit's principal jobs was to design woven fabrics that showcased the versatility of DuPont's artificial fibers. Along these lines, Sommaripa and his staff routinely collaborated with mills to weave "idea fabrics" that were shared with DuPont textile customers. Because the DuPont manufacturing plants were constantly improving on the raw materials, the samples showed weavers how to use the latest viscose or acetate yarns to create stylish fabric designs suited to the moment. In 1937, *Women's Wear Daily* announced that a selection of wool-like dress fabrics, styled by Sommaripa, was on display for customers to study at the DuPont offices in the Empire State Building. The collection showed how DuPont yarns could be woven together with natural fibers to create blended fabrics that had distinctive attributes in performance, appearance, and touch.[21]

With his insatiable curiosity, Sommaripa began looking for novel ways to decipher consumer taste to aid his efforts in textile design. The DuPont offices in the Empire State Building sat squarely in the New York textile district, a bustling commercial neighborhood thick with wholesale showrooms that sold cloth to trade customers. The nation's largest cluster of ready-to-wear manufacturers were just a few blocks west, in the garment center on Seventh Avenue. Dozens of upscale retail stores lined Fifth Avenue from Thirty-Fourth Street up to Central Park, while midmarket retailers huddled around Herald Square. The DuPont staff was frequently on the streets sizing up how people dressed, in the shops looking at the latest styles, and in the textile showrooms studying fabrics. Much could be learned from firsthand observation, but Sommaripa yearned for scientific precision. In this context, he turned to a promising new psychological approach that sought to crack open the puzzle of human behavior for commercial gain. Motivational research, with its objective to pry open the consumer mind, seemed to hold the key to sensory perception.

The growth of American consumer society and the concentration of corporate power in Manhattan had spawned a new type of business expert, the specialist in applied psychology. Some Madison Avenue advertising agencies had these social scientists on their payrolls, as did JWT who had elevated the behavioral expert John B. Watson to the executive suite. Some psychologists and sociologists worked as business consultants, advising corporate clients on problems for a fee. Back in 1921, the psychologist James McKeen Cattell, the founder of *Scientific American* magazine, set up a consultancy to bring social science insights to the wider world. His firm, the Psychological Corporation, was run by a small New York staff who hired academic psychologists to work on projects for the clients, from private individuals to industrial companies. The nonprofit's services included consumer surveys, personnel analysis, and advice on sales and public relations.[22]

Sometime in the mid-1930s, the Fabric Development Service asked the Psychological Corporation to undertake a major study on touch and textiles.[23] The objective was to determine how sensory experience shaped women's preferences for different types of fabrics. The sense of touch was one mechanism by which consumers experienced aesthetic pleasure and formed their ideas on what constituted beautiful, desirable products. Since the mid-1920s, major American companies had harnessed "beauty" as a "new business tool" for stimulating desire and increasing sales.[24] The General Motors Corporation (GM) brandished beauty by offering polychrome paint jobs, unique body designs, and colorful upholstery fabrics as it wrested the automobile market away from the Ford Motor Company.[25] During the Depression, some durable-goods manufacturers, including GM, invested in body streamlining as a strategy for stimulating consumption, but there appears to have been no systematic, scientific analysis of the relationships among aesthetics, style goods, and the senses—until DuPont tried to determine what made textiles pleasing to the consumer.

As DuPont learned in the 1920s, the fashion business was highly dependent on consumers' experiences with three of the five senses: sight, touch, and sound. Veteran textile salesmen and old-time garment cutters frequently referred to the "hand," or the feel, of the fabric. But no one knew how the act of touching a soft, luxurious fabric translated into pleasure in the brain or how the sensuality of a silky cloth influenced the consumer's decision to buy the dress. In Sommaripa's view, the time had come for DuPont to demystify the sense of touch and to determine how tactile pleasure influenced aesthetic tastes. Solving this riddle was no matter of idle curiosity. A deeper knowledge of sensory experience was essential to improving DuPont fibers and, in turn, to augmenting the reputation of the DuPont textile brand within the fashion system.

The DuPont project on the sense of touch, undertaken by the Psychological Corporation under Sommaripa's auspices, engaged with a new scientific field called "hedonic psychophysics," a later iteration of which was discussed by Ana María Ulloa in Chapter 5. Paul F. Lazarsfeld, a Viennese émigré who directed a social science institute at the University of Newark (now part of Rutgers, The State University of New Jersey), was a principal investigator along with Rowena Ripin of the Psychological Corporation. Using a controlled laboratory setting, the research team gathered verbal evidence about sensations associated with the touching of textiles from female consumers who were blindfolded, given fabric samples, and asked to describe their tactile experiences as they handled different types of cloth. The test eliminated the "visual stimuli of color, weave and drape" and focused solely on the consumer's response to texture. In April of 1937, the *Journal of Applied Psychology* published the results.[26]

As the corporate adviser, Sommaripa explained the rationale: "There is no question that among the buying motives for textiles, the pleasantness to the touch plays a very important role. No man or woman, probably, would buy a garment without first putting a hand on it. Yet, notwithstanding the magnitude of the textile business or the importance of touch, there is practically no concrete information on the subject."[27] The blindfolded tests found that velvet was the consumer's favorite cloth due to its soft hand, while the least favorite fabric was taffeta, which was stiff and felt rough against the skin.[28] "Particularly interesting," Sommaripa told the Delaware members of the American Chemical Society, a professional association, in 1938, "has been a careful study conducted in cooperation with a psychological corporation among 100 selected consumers, which indicated that there was a definite agreement as to preference of the fabrics on the important basis of touch."[29]

Sommaripa used the tactile study as a clarion call, advocating for greater exploration of the senses by rayon makers. In his speech to the Delaware chapter of the American Chemical Society, he made an impassioned plea for scientists to acknowledge that a deeper understanding of consumer psychology and tactile aesthetics was the key to rayon's future. In his view, the scientific analysis of consumers' sensory experiences could be put to practical use. The research findings could be used to improve the fibers, design more appealing fabrics, and generate trend forecasts that predicted a textile's likely reception in retail stores.[30]

Style forecasting was a relatively new field, mainly practiced by color experts in the automobile, appliance, and fashion industries.[31] Perhaps inspired by this work, Sommaripa came to envision sensory knowledge as essential to the Fabric Development Service. The better DuPont designers understood consumer psychology, the better "idea fabrics" they could produce for DuPont customers. Using inspiration fabrics informed by sensory research, textile mills could weave better cloth and Seventh Avenue could make better fashions.[32] Here we see DuPont's leading marketer of the interwar period giving his take on "Better Things for Better Living . . . through Chemistry."

The Psychological Corporation's study of the sense of touch testified to DuPont's growing interest in the scientific analysis of textile markets, an effort that originated with the NRDGA surveys. In contrast to those statistical reports, the sensory study by the Psychological Corporation was truly touchy-feely, dealing with personal impressions of how the fabric felt to the hands. From the late 1920s onward, popular culture exerted ever more sway over the attitudes and expectations of American consumers. Store displays, magazine advertisements, school sewing classes, and Hollywood films played no small role in teaching the female consumer to appreciate fabrics that were colorful, washable, sensuous, and soft. By the late 1930s, DuPont and other rayon makers were providing the textile mills and garment cutters with something more than raw materials—cellulose fibers were the building blocks for the democratization of women's fashion. Incremental technological innovations by the fiber plants helped to reduce rayon prices, encouraging textile mills to specify man-made materials over natural fibers. But to focus on falling prices alone would miss the point. "Rayon fabrics," Sommaripa told the National Association of Cotton Manufacturers in October of 1937, "have awakened the masses to the joy of a smooth, new touch."[33]

By the time World War II broke out in Europe on September 1, 1939, the textile and fashion industries thought favorably of man-made fibers. Rayon was the preferred fabric for stylish ladies' dresses, whether the frocks were sewn at home, ordered from a Montgomery Ward catalog, or purchased from a J. C. Penney store on Main Street. Rayon's popularity increased during the war, replacing cotton and wool in everyday apparel. Hollywood films put rayon in the public eye, with an endless stream of starlets dressed in man-made fashions. The *Rayon Textile Monthly* estimated that 1.5 billion yards of rayon or rayon-blend fabrics were bleached, dyed, or printed in 1944.[34] The War Production Board controlled the amount of fabric available to the civilian economy, but with a full Allied victory looming in mid-1945, the federal agency predicted greater consumer availability in short order.[35] The *Women's Wear Daily* advertisement of September 11, 1945, pointed to a bright, sensual future. Rayon dresses were remarkable for their affordability—and for their drape, sensuality, and softness. It was not just low prices, but low prices and the promise of sensory pleasure that sold rayon fabrics and fashion—and contributed to their widespread acceptance.

The Complicated Science of Marketing

In the postwar years, DuPont came to dominate the synthetic fiber business due to its first-mover advantages in nylon, which included a strong patent position.[36] Nylon became the company's most profitable product, and seeking to repeat this success, DuPont invested heavily in synthetic fiber development. The firm obtained the United States rights for Terylene from the British patent holders, marketing this polyester fiber under the tradename Dacron. The company also pressed ahead with the scientific research that generated Orlon acrylic, a washable, moth-proof synthetic wool, and Lycra spandex, the ultimate stretch fiber. Back in 1936, DuPont dissolved all of its subsidiaries for tax purposes, and in the process, created an internal department to oversee the rayon business. In the postwar years, this unit became the Textile Fibers Department. The name change pointed to the declining relevance of cellulose fibers in the test-tube era. In a 1949 talk to a textile group, Andrew E. Buchanan Jr., a fiber manager, spoke of DuPont's unwavering commitment to science, exemplified by the belief that "a man ought to be able to make a better fiber by design than a sheep produces inadvertently."[37]

But science alone could not guarantee success in the competitive postwar business environment. The economic and social context of the synthetics age was dramatically different from that of the rayon era. Postwar Americans enjoyed a rising standard of living that was not experienced elsewhere in the world. With this affluence came a greater awareness of individuality in everything from politics to personal style. Stereotypes of cookie-cutter suburbs aside, postwar America was the incubator of multiculturalism and diversity. Businesses cast aside the monolithic concept of Mrs. Consumer and acknowledged that postwar society was divided into many different market segments: teenagers with spending money, African Americans who read *Ebony*, men who loved muscle cars, and others. Marketers became more adept at dissecting consumption patterns with due credence to variables such as age, climate, ethnicity, gender, locale, race, and social class.

The job of managing the DuPont textile business became ever more complex. The Textile Fibers Department built on some of the practices initiated by Sommaripa and the Fabric Development Service in the interwar years. Insights from consumer surveys were combined with feedback from textile mills, apparel manufacturers, and retailers to improve fiber performance, to design "idea fabrics," and to plan advertising campaigns. The marketing research function was greatly expanded, and massive amounts of data on consumers were accumulated. Consumer surveys were undertaken by several different entities: an internal corporate marketing unit, the Textile Fibers Department, advertising agencies and media experts, and motivational research consultants. In 1959 alone, the DuPont market research division produced nearly seventy reports analyzing the attitudes of retailers and consumers on a range of textiles, from suits to carpets.[38] In 1962, one textile fibers manager, Arthur M. Saunders, described DuPont's approach. Put succinctly, the company had transformed the "relatively simple 'art' of selling fabric" into the "complicated 'science' of marketing."[39]

The Peacock Revolution

In any given year, internal reports by DuPont were supplemented with external surveys from consultants such as Ernest Dichter, who we met in Chapter 4 by Lisa Jacobson. One of the pioneers of applied business psychology, Dichter ran the Institute for Motivational Research (IMR), a New York consulting firm that catered to many types of business clients, from automakers to toy manufacturers. In the postwar years, Dichter's consultancy did studies for DuPont on topics such as nylon sheets, men's socks, and ladies' girdles. Having worked at his uncle's department store as a young man in Vienna, Dichter understood that clothing was a highly personal item that evoked emotions, memories, and sensory responses. Consumers often shared intimate details about their wardrobes in face-to-face meetings. In one such interview, a woman explained why she treasured an old article of clothing: "I can still conjure up the way this dress felt on my body. I loved to touch it and also the smell of it. It had a peculiar smell all its own. It was the first tailored suit I ever had. . . . It was nothing glamorous. I felt at home in it. It belonged to me in a deeper sense of the word."[40] Dichter applied what he learned from interviews to fashion projects, including advertising campaigns. To be compelling, an apparel advertisement had to capitalize on sensory pleasure, helping the reader to "'feel' the fabric, 'smell' the newness, etc."[41] Dichter brought an awareness of the deeply personal, sensuous nature of textiles to his work for DuPont.

One of the best-known IMR projects for DuPont, undertaken between 1965 and 1967, focused on "the peacock revolution," an emerging American menswear phenomenon in which the youth market cast aside traditional dowdy outfits and embraced colorful, expressive, sensual clothing.[42] The initial findings, publicized in a speech by Dichter at a DuPont-sponsored menswear symposium in Scottsdale, Arizona, in February of 1966, uncovered a growing taste for flashy fashion among young men and the role of sensory pleasure in their consumer choices. A longer, follow-up report, submitted to DuPont in December of 1966, explored the history of men's changing tastes, offered design suggestions for garments, and speculated on America's future role in global fashion. Finally, Dichter summarized the major characteristics of the peacock revolution in a second talk dating from January of 1967. The first speech, with its emphasis on the senses, is the focus of this analysis. To probe the inner workings of male youth culture, the IMR collected and analyzed data from interviews with clothing salesmen, observations in retail stores, and focus groups with consumers.[43]

The postwar menswear industry struggled with lethargic sales, a reality that stood in stark contrast to the expansive, energetic, and ever-changing women's ready-to-wear trade.[44] To modernize their lines, men's clothing manufacturers collaborated with textile mills on technical novelties such as "durable press" garments, the "no iron shirt," and the "drip dry" suit—but sales remained stagnant. With their eyes fixed on retail stores, DuPont marketing experts learned about a trend bubbling up among younger consumers. Throughout the West, young men ages seventeen to twenty-five were rejecting traditional styles in favor of fashions that expressed "their own individuality." Growing up in an affluent, media-saturated culture, American teenagers and young adults wanted to look like the celebrities on TV variety shows such as ABC's *Shindig!* and NBC's *Hullabaloo* or like "a rebel, 'swinger,' hot-rodder, surfer, beatnik, etc."[45] Some young men yearned to dress in the manner of movie heroes like James Bond, the stars of TV shows such as *I Spy* or *The Man from U.N.C.L.E*, or the fashion models in *Esquire* and *Playboy*.[46] These flashy preferences befuddled the conservative menswear trade, whose standard stock included British tweeds and grey flannel suits. DuPont marketers, looking to sell more synthetic fibers, intervened by hiring Dichter and the IMR "to unravel the secret of today's youth, . . . sociologically, psychologically and culturally."[47]

The IMR research on American peacocks was not the first study of postwar youth culture. A few years earlier in the United Kingdom, the sociologist Mark

Abrams surveyed the buying habits of British youngsters ages fifteen to thirty-four and published statistics about their hefty expenditures on fashion merchandise like men's shirts and ladies' lingerie.[48] The IMR studies differed from Abrams's work by foregrounding the senses, a major determinant in consumer choice. Decades earlier, DuPont and the Psychological Corporation had braved the territory of touch and textiles, but that effort paled next to the peacock studies and their focus on sensual pleasure among male consumers. The IMR's contention that men's shopping decisions were influenced by social class, ethnicity, and bodily experience is central to our story of synthetics and the senses.

The IMR identified the menswear upheaval of the sixties as "undeniably a lower class revolution" that originated with British blue-collar workers who sloughed off stuffy old bowler hats and tweed jackets for the slinky Mod styles of Carnaby Street.[49] The fad for colorful, form-fitting hipster gear then spread to other Western nations including Sweden, Holland, France, and the United States.[50] By December of 1966, flamboyant menswear was synonymous with the internationalization of Mod fashion, but there was more to the sartorial rebellion than the emulation of British style. "The Peacock Revolution is a revolution against the stereotyped clothing of the past," explained the IMR. "Each Peacock wishes to demonstrate his individuality, his creativeness, his ability to be different from other Peacocks."[51]

Back in 1958, Dichter had commented on the rising tide of American individualism, so the observations about the male penchant for self-expression were illuminating but not groundbreaking.[52] The novelty lies in the peacock's fashion choices being driven by sensory experience. The pursuit of sensual pleasure hallmarked the teenaged Baby Boomer, who saw himself as "an Adonis, a possessor of a young and beautiful body" who wore "clothes so as to show off that young body." Dressing in sensual attire was a means to cultural empowerment. "Not only is he an exhibitionist when he wears tight fitting clothes, but he is creating the illusion that he, the wearer, is the master—the clothing yields to him." Sensual clothing provided the wearer with confidence, providing a shield against external threats, both physically and mentally. "To the young man tight-fitting or tailored to the body contoured clothing gives him a feeling of security—he can feel his body and this feeling gives him the security of knowing that his body, his very self is intact."[53]

The level of sensual indulgence was determined by the consumer's ethnicity and social class. The working-class man was the most adventurous adult male, the epitome of the fan-tailing peacock. In Dichter's estimation, the average blue-collar American man was "of either Italian or Latin descent, representing groups who tend to be more concerned with personal appearance and to spend proportionally more on it, whether married or single." A decade later in 1977, this sensual being was personified by the fictional Brooklyn disco dancer Tony Manero, played by John Travolta, the Italian American actor, in the Hollywood film *Saturday Night Fever*. "This type is a very sensual being who likes to feel smooth, sleek fabrics," noted Dichter. "In his phantasies he sees himself exerting power over others, a reverse of his present situation."[54] With faith in the transformative power of clothing, blue-collar peacocks loved to try out new materials and styles. In contrast, white-collar men, whether high-school or college graduates, were stodgy and resistant to change. They preferred clothing that allowed them to blend in.[55]

Age was another factor that determined the degree of sensory indulgence. Younger males, whether they were high-school students or working adults under age thirty, "are more physically sensual than are we," noted Dichter, and "their sense of smell, touch, vision, hearing and taste are much more acute for their bodies are younger and fresher."[56] They had not yet learned to control their emotional responses and were thereby more open to self-expression. Regardless of social class, high-school boys yearned for a fashionable future filled with "stretch suits; open-toed shoes; clothes baring part of the body; iridescent colors in all types of attire; matching ties, socks and shirt sets in patterns; plunging shirts; fur lined shoes; tactically pleasing buttons." According to Dichter, the reason for this open-mindedness was that "the younger boy is much less inhibited *sensually*. He particularly enjoys tactual experiences. As we grow older we are taught, and quickly learn, that sophisticated people keep their hands to themselves, not so the young man. He is more likely to encourage you to feel his new sweater than to look at it."[57]

The IMR's research revealed that four of the senses—sight, smell, sound, and touch—loomed large in the young peacock's shopping experience. In the stores, the most important attractions were the displays, the packaging, and the clothes. Bright colors and novel textures intrigued the teen shopper who loved a "great variety of materials," including "velvet, fur, silk, hard fabrics, bumpy fabrics, fluffy fabrics, buttery textures and particularly fabrics with a different sensation on each side."[58] Smelling the merchandise was one of his favorite shopping indulgences. As a youngster browsed through jackets, trousers, sweaters, and ties on display in the store, he was "unconsciously exploring the odors, turning and twisting fabrics, breathing in deeply, wrinkling his nose in disgust or smiling slightly with pleasure."[59] As he tried on apparel in the dressing room, a youth listened to the sounds made by the taffeta in the jacket pockets, the trouser waistband, and the hat lining. For high-school boys, shopping for clothes was "an exciting tactual orgy—a new adventure."[60]

The projects on the peacock revolution provided DuPont marketers with a map of men's habits and tastes. The research highlighted the importance of sensuality and the concomitant trend "towards Apparel-Hedonism, the buying of clothes because it is fun to do so and not because one has to" among male Baby Boomers.[61] The research also showed that older American peacocks were far more pragmatic. One buyer in a men's clothing store noted, "Comfort has been great these last years. We have knitwear and stretch fabrics but still men want more comfort." A thirty-something teacher from Los Angeles envisioned a future with closets chock-full of relaxed apparel: "Clothing will be more like a second skin. Fabrics will be soft and I won't even be aware of wearing anything."[62]

The fashion concepts of "action clothes," "activity apparel," and "the ready-to-go look" reflected the ambitions of the sixties, the faster pace of life as embodied in automation, airplanes, and the Space Race.[63] "New fabrics, new designs and new styles will be necessary," noted the IMR, "as the restrictions on casual and work clothes breaks down and all clothing becomes action-oriented."[64] The movement toward soft, stretchable styles coincided with DuPont's commercialization of Lycra spandex and the fiber's growing acceptance as a reliable technology for endowing apparel with elasticity. Peacocks were fully aware of the relationship between fibers and ease of movement, as articulated by one consumer in his thirties: "The only thing I could think of that would give me more freedom would be a stretch material. . . . They have something like that now."[65]

Building on Dichter's peacock revolution studies, in 1967 DuPont sponsored a national menswear contest for student designers built around the question: "*What will the teen and early twenties group be wearing in 1970?*" Recognizing that half of the American population was under twenty-five years old, DuPont wanted to know more about these Boomer consumers. The DuPont advertising department received more than 500 entries, "a vision of apparel for the young that was sketched by the young." The contest confirmed the peacock studies, with many submissions suggesting that "the young man's wardrobe in the next decade will 'swing' with a lean, youthful sophistication."[66] Design students, male and female alike, submitted ideas for astronaut-inspired jumpsuits to be worn at formal events and Carnaby-style sports jackets for the office. There were a proliferation of turtleneck sweaters and a paucity of neckties. Olivia Lam, a student at the Philadelphia College of Textiles and Science (now Jefferson University), won the $250 first prize in the slacks category (Figure 11.3). She created a "slim, youthful silhouette" by combining a pair of boldly striped, tight-fitting, Lycra-belted

Figure 11.3. The happy-go-lucky young peacock, outfitted for the sensuous synthetic seventies in a turtleneck sweater and flared slacks made from DuPont materials. This prize-winning design by Olivia Lam, a student at the Philadelphia College of Textiles and Science, was submitted to a 1967 DuPont menswear competition that invited college-age designers to dress their own population cohort, the Baby Boomers, in youthful, forward-looking styles. Courtesy of the Hagley Museum and Library.

flared slacks with a thick turtleneck and slip-on shoes.[67] The casual look and the playful mood captured the zeitgeist. Here was the Baby Boomer peacock, ready to tackle the seventies in stylish, informal, comfortable clothes made from DuPont fibers.

With the help of psychological experts like Ernest Dichter, DuPont figured out the fast-paced consumer culture of postwar America. Over the course of the postwar era, DuPont gradually discontinued the manufacture of viscose and acetate yarns to focus on profitable, high-performance textile materials.[68] Strong global sales of Lycra spandex, the stretch fiber, showed that it was possible to make money by capitalizing on the senses.[69] In 1974, Gomer H. Ward, a veteran marketing specialist, provided one menswear trade conference with a précis of DuPont's position on synthetics and the senses. "Technology," he argued, "remains the ultimate answer to the continuing demand for new fabrics with acceptable aesthetics, easy care and high-performance quality."[70] Alexis Sommaripa, the father of fabric development in the man-made fibers industry, would have agreed.

Consumers and Comfort

Between the 1920s and the 1960s DuPont became the world's leading fiber manufacturer and marketer, known globally for its innovative products and lavish promotions. In this transformation, the firm looked to develop an "angle" that linked style and quality, the eye and the hand. That effort focused on bridging the gap between fiber science and sensory perception, on determining how to apply the firm's arcane knowledge of materials to the burgeoning consumer culture.

In the interwar years, Alexis Sommaripa set the stage for sensory research at DuPont, responding to the conservative nature and harried procedures of the American textile industry. In 1939, S. J. Kennedy of Pacific Mills described the frequent rush to introduce new designs and the disappointing sales that resulted. "In our industry we see every year fabric ideas launched on the market before finding out if the fabric is soundly enough constructed to meet consumer requirements," Kennedy wrote. "Successful industries do not leave the testing to the consumer, or assume that because a fabric 'will sell' they are justified in releasing it prematurely."[71] By establishing a bridge between scientific research, textile aesthetics, and sensory analysis, Sommaripa helped DuPont to build a strong customer-service orientation to the American textile industry and laid the groundwork for the sophisticated marketing research that emerged after World War II.

The acts of seeing, touching, smelling, and hearing had long guided consumers as they shopped for textiles and apparel. Sensory input helped the home seamstress to select yard goods for her new bedroom curtains, the fashion shopper to determine if a crepe dress matched the color of her favorite Easter handbag. In the postwar era, it became culturally acceptable for a newly identified market segment, the American peacock, to enjoy the sensual pleasures of textiles. Influences such as the British music and fashion invasions, lifestyle magazines, and outdoor leisure activities like golfing and sportscar driving encouraged men to think creatively about their appearance. To get a grip, DuPont expanded its commitment to market surveys, technical service, consumer psychology, and motivational research. The American peacock embraced clothes that permitted easy movement and thereby foregrounded the idea of comfort. As comfort became one of the most desirable attributes in textile merchandise, DuPont continued to interact with layers of customers—with weaving mills, converters, knitwear makers, garment cutters, and apparel retailers—always on the lookout for more and better information. The ultimate goal was to determine how sensory experience could be further demystified and exploited to sell more fibers.

CHAPTER 12

Feminine Touches

The Sensory World of Lady Hilton

MEGAN J. ELIAS

Four Moods

What mood are you in today? Could your mood be described as Continental, Latin, Eastern, or perhaps Island? You might think of different temperatures for Island and Continental, different soundscapes for Latin and Eastern, and different color palettes and perhaps flavors for each of the four. In 1968, Hilton Hotels corporation offered women guests these four moods in the form of four tiny bottles of perfume placed in certain hotel rooms.[1] The four scents were not just free perfume; they were an invitation to women guests to journey in their imaginations. By offering this sensory version of travel, Hilton emphasized the transformative potential of staying in a hotel, making the Hilton itself a destination. At the same time, they established the female guest as a special category of consumer with a particular sensory palate.

The perfumes were part of the Lady Hilton program, launched by Hilton Hotels in 1965. The program was designed for female guests traveling alone or with other women. The timing of the launch coincided with the increased mobility of American women in the postwar era, and their greater participation in the professional workforce. In a 1967 study of hotel guests, commissioned by the American Hotel and Motel Association, researchers found that while "for many years the commercial lodging market was considered by most to be a male market," this had begun to change and "during the last few years, the increase in women traveling alone or with their husbands has prompted increasing attention to the female segment of the market." Although women still were only 20 percent of hotel guests, this number provoked industry insiders to wonder if women might be "a unique market with special needs and preferences" and to ask their colleagues, "Is the proportion of women large enough to influence decorating schemes of sleeping rooms and/or public areas?"[2] Hilton Hotels had clearly decided the answer was yes.

The Lady Hilton program offered sensory experiences and material gifts in an attempt to please this traveler. How Hilton imagined the female travelers' sensory needs can help us to understand something about how consumer personas have been gendered and classed in the hospitality industry. This process posited different predilections based on gender identity which then delimited the consumer's own experience of gender in the space provided. If rooms arranged to appeal to purported feminine preferences did not please a particular woman, this potentially brought her into conflict with gender expectations. As it established a feminine aesthetic, Hilton Hotels simultaneously, and perhaps unintentionally, constructed the male traveler as someone who desired other sensory experiences, distinct from those offered for Lady Hilton. The hotel chain also ignored increasingly successful efforts to integrate hotels by exclusively representing the guest as white, sending Black guests the message that they were not welcome, even when they were able to register. Each choice that Hilton Hotels made in the Lady Hilton program conveyed messages about the cultural role of a hotel, the nature of travel and the traveler, and the place of gender in the commercial marketplace for experiences. This chapter explores those themes to understand how America's largest and most important postwar hotel chain—Hilton Hotels—appealed to the senses to construct the female traveler in the 1960s.

The Commercial Sensory World of Hotels

The Lady Hilton program was created within the already-complex sensory context of postwar twentieth-century hotels. Early in the century, the intertwined phenomena of urbanization, increased domestic travel, and industrialization had created a larger market for temporary lodging in cities. The twentieth century also saw the expansion of the resort market, but this chapter focuses on the urban hotel as these were the venues for the Lady Hilton program. Hotels were typically located close to train stations and in business districts. As the historian Molly Berger notes, by the 1920s some of the long-lasting standards of hotels as public spaces had been established. The hotel as an institution was frequently described as both "a self-regulating machine and as a city within a city." A building frenzy during the 1920s established norms in architecture and interior design for hotels that lasted until World War II. City hotels were typically built as solid towers with grand lobby spaces and several hundred guest rooms. On lower floors, a restaurant, a bar, and a few small retailers such as a cigar stand and a barber shop lured in nonguest dollars and kept travelers' money in-house. Responding to the rise of social clubs and professional associations, hotels also included spaces that could be used for large events such as banquets and conventions.[3] Inns and taverns had always been public spaces, as the historian Andrew Sandoval-Strausz argues, but the twentieth-century hotel offered ever more space to ever more public activities.[4] As such, modern American hotels moved beyond the relatively basic task of renting bedrooms and suites for sleeping. They began to deal in experiences.

The entrepreneur Elsworth Statler (1863–1928), founder of the Statler hotel chain, is credited as the creator of the modern hotel, building establishments where, "the small business man and the travelling salesman could enjoy a scaled-down version of the luxury hotel at a price they could afford."[5] The notion that the average traveler had a right to luxury, even scaled-down luxury, transformed the American hotel business and, gradually, the global hotel trade. The Statler jingle, "A room and a bath at a dollar and a half," offered transregional predictability in American lodgings in the precise moment when the standardization of sensory experience was emerging as a theme in American culture.[6] As Berger observes, Statler's hotel chain both "replicate[d] the structural plants" and offered "consistent decorating schemes" that helped the traveler achieve a sense of the familiar far from home.[7] In theory, the modern American standardized hotel was part of the new standardized world of American consumer products that included everything from prepackaged foodstuffs and flavorings to mass-produced clothing and children's toys. However, in reality, hotel chains that capitalized on aesthetic conformity did not become the norm until after World War II. Statler was an inspiration but also ahead of his time.

Through the twentieth century, the market for hotels grew, swelling first into overbuilding during the 1920s, a crash in the 1930s, and then rapid recovery after World War II. Conrad Hilton managed to hang on despite nearing bankruptcy in the Great Depression and was in a strong position when the war started. He rapidly expanded his chain at home and abroad during this era while also cultivating an international reputation. When Hilton bought Statler's whole chain from his widow in 1954, Hilton made his company the largest hotel chain in the world and also acquired Statler's reputation for reliably comfortable accommodations.

Postwar growth coincided with a revolution in hotel aesthetics, changing the guest's experience. As design historians Tom Avermaete and Anne Massey explain, "Twentieth-century mass tourism changed the status of the hotel from a venue for public display into a highly standardised and rationalised machine offering efficient accommodation for (often) large numbers of travelers."[8] Aesthetically, this was achieved with "a modernist, universal standard, providing not only predictable accommodation, but also a 'normalized' public environment: lobbies, bars and restaurants that were designed to be identical around the world."[9] In 1945, architect J. Gordon Carr and interior designer Elizabeth Z. Cutler explained the shift to readers of the industry journal *Hotel Management*: "The public seeks the lightness, simplicity and cleanliness of up-to-date hotels." In describing how to change décor to meet these new expectations, Carr and Cutler give us an idea of the sensory world that had fallen out of fashion: "Many hotels' traditional architecture can be changed quite simply. Ornately decorated walls and ceilings may be covered with smooth plaster. New lighting effects, both direct and indirect, may replace old-fashioned chandeliers and sconces. Light wood screens with textural interest may cover dark, heavy architectural details. Ornate posts may be encased in a simple smooth wooden frame or sometimes in mirror glass. High ceilings may be lowered, giving a feeling of intimacy and reducing heating costs."[10] Hotel spaces were still designed to promote a sensory reaction, but the concept of "grandness" was no longer bound up in traditions of the ornate. Now grandness was sleek.

Hilton Hotels International, established in 1948, became particularly well known in the postwar period for a consistent, modern, and clean aesthetic across properties and national borders.[11] Hilton contracted with noted architects to build in the International Style, recognizable by its signature use of concrete and glass, but relied on its own in-house design team, and local artisans, to create novel interiors. The design team incorporated themes and items of local design in the interior spaces to provide touchpoints of authenticity that did not disrupt the smooth operation of a modern American hotel. Thus, each Hilton was both obviously a Hilton, an American product, and also a reflection of the immediate surroundings. This combination was carried out in dining as well; guests could choose from a few local specialties on a menu otherwise comprised of "Continental" restaurant fare.

The growth in hotels in the first half of the twentieth century necessitated marketing and advertising that emphasized the customer's desires. The traveler was thus constructed publicly as a person with material and emotional expectations and standards that the hotel could meet. Repeat custom was the holy grail for managers, so hoteliers competed to come up with new services to attract and retain guests. As an essential part of this work, hotel owners and managers became dedicated to curating the sensory environment of their hotels. As early as 1926, an article in *Hotel Bulletin*, a journal for the hospitality industry, exhorted managers to pay attention to the "five senses of the guest.... See, taste, smell, feel, hear—these are the five ways in which guests become aware of conditions in a hotel that affect their comfort and pleasure." While most managers attended to the visual, the journalist warned, they often neglected smell and sound. Not only should a room not smell bad, but it could also actually smell good. "This does not mean that incense should be burned, or that heavily fragrant flowers should be displayed," noted the *Hotel Bulletin*. "It means, though, that effort should be made to provide a suitable fragrance for the season and the environment, which will be one thing in a bedroom, another in the lobby, still another in a dining room or décor." In other words, scent should be orchestrated. Attending to aural pleasure meant not only eliminating unpleasant noises like rattling elevators, but also producing pleasant sounds. Staff, for example, should wear shoes that generated footfall that was "firm" rather than "slouchy."[12] Imagining the guest as sensitive to small experiences such as the sound of leather heels on a polished floor added new layers to the concept of service.

Nearly forty years later, a 1963 advertisement for Comet cleanser published in the *Hotel World-Review* reflected the persistence of the idea of the sensitive guest. In this advertisement, a female guest in a suit and white gloves reached out to touch a bathroom sink. Through a doorway we can see a bedroom with a suitcase open on a luggage rack—clearly a hotel room. "This place is lovely," the woman says to a man waiting in the bedroom. "It's so shiny clean. So glad we stopped here." Because the woman is still holding her purse and her male companion still holds his hat, we get the sense that they have just arrived at the hotel, and the very first thing this guest wanted to do was to touch the porcelain fixtures. Commercial goods producers like Procter & Gamble, makers of Comet, perpetuated this ideal of the guest's hypercritical, sensory engagement with the hotel in order to sell goods.[13]

In the same year, Pittsburgh Paints alerted hotel industry readers to the psychology of colors, noting that "science has clearly established that... people respond more favorably to certain color treatments than to others." The company offered to help hoteliers use this science to their own benefit through the Pittsburgh Color Dynamics survey in consultation with a color specialist. The paint company promised to help hoteliers use "illusion, contrast, camouflage, tone, value, proportion, form" to make small rooms seem big, high ceilings seem low, and dark hallways look bright, manipulating the guest's sense of sight and experience of space. Because hotels needed to follow design trends but found redecoration to be costly and disruptive, such sensory tricks could both save and earn money for hoteliers.[14]

Once the hotel's interior decorator had established the hotel's look, it was up to the staff to maintain it. In larger facilities, the support team included not only the staff of the in-house laundries, but also seamstresses, carpenters, and upholsterers. Like a ship, the hotel had to be able to repair itself on the go. One advertisement for Utica Sheets, published in 1942, compared this work to the ongoing war. Declaring that hotel managing director H. P. Somerville had "a general's job in private life," it explained, "Mr. Somerville is a master strategist at martialing [sic] the forces of hospitality . . . supplying the armaments of comfort for the bivouac of sleep. He satisfies the critical, the harried, the leisurely, lavish and exacting." Listing the distinct kinds of travelers whom a hotel manager had to please, the advertisement spoke clearly to the insiders, those who knew how crucial long-wearing but still soft linens could be for sustaining business. In a 1963 advertisement for Martex towels, published in a trade journal, the company offered hotel managers "extra luxury, extra wear at no extra cost," combining the seemingly incompatible desires of guests for luxury with the hotel's need for durability.[15] This was a common combination in advertising to the hospitality industry, one that acknowledged the manager's role in orchestrating illusory sensory experiences—the feel of luxury at the price of a bargain. As hotel owners focused on the guest experience, they began to consider variations on the theme and niche markets for their services.

Women as Guests in Hotels

By the postwar period, the average hotel guest in America was still male and traveling for business. But the rise in domestic tourism and the growing number of women in the workforce and in public life meant that more women were traveling, either with family or by themselves.[16] Business historian Angel Kwolek-Folland identifies the year 1963, which witnessed the passage of the Equal Pay Act, as a watershed moment in American women's employment. The creation of the United States Equal Employment Opportunity Commission (EEOC) the next year also helped more women advance in business careers.[17] By the 1960s, travel was an important part of business culture, so to advance often meant to go on the road.

Hospitality, an industry obsessed with service and occupancy rates had previously framed female travelers as a distinct market segment and theorized about what women wanted. As far back as 1918, the Morrison Hotel in Chicago had advertised, "When my lady travels she wants that sense of security; of attentiveness; of unembarrassing guidance, that is an especial feature of Morrison service to women who make this hotel their headquarters for shopping, theatre, or business excursions to Chicago."[18] In this case, the Morrison employed a female staff member to serve as a guide for female guests who wanted to visit local tourist attractions. The implication was that a female guest could not ask a man for directions because a man would not know about female-focused attractions such as Chicago's famous department stores in the Loop. Worse, interaction with a strange man could even risk her safety.

Some hotels offered entire special floors with rooms and services "for women only." In 1926, Katherine Jordon Magoun, manager of the Women's Floor at the Palmer House in Chicago reported, "Each year brings a noticeable increase in the number of lady travelers. Most of the larger and finer hotels have set aside a special section for the exclusive use of lady guests, where they may secure every possible attention and that exclusiveness desired by so many refined women." While special service staff, such as manicurists sent up to the room and guides to local shopping could have been secured from any floor and sent to any room in the hotel, the availability of a secluded ladies' floor suggests that female guests could find proximity to unknown men disquieting. Was "exclusiveness" a code word for safety? If so, the all-women floors provided a sense of security that could be bodily—the release of that familiar physical tension experienced by women in situations that seem unsafe.

In these early examples of gender-based amenities, the female guest was constructed as a person entitled to special treatment and extra care. Katherine Jordon Magoun noted, however, that "there are many self-sufficient women quite capable of looking after themselves, who need no special attention—indeed, might resent any."[19] Women who had overcome obstacles to succeed in male-dominated fields or who bucked convention to travel alone might feel patronized by the implication that they needed help finding their way around the city. Even as Magoun's job title posited a difference in female and male travelers, her customers themselves undermined it.

The Great Depression and World War II battered the hotel industry, and special features for women travelers, pioneered in the 1920s, were scuttled. By the postwar period, however, as noted above, demographics shifted again to include more women traveling for business and, thanks to the growth of the middle class, for leisure. This new category of female travelers captured the eye of Hilton Hotels, who already had a director of women's services, Lucille Skerston. Skerston, who spent her career at Hilton, eventually becoming director of commercial sales, came up with the name for the Lady Hilton program, and the company selected a butterfly to be the logo (Figure 12.1).[20] The butterfly represented female guests as in transit but whimsically so, flitting from place to place rather than solely focused on matters of business. A guest might also imagine the Hilton as her cocoon, to rest in while beautifying.[21] The delicacy of the butterfly image implied that women guests needed gentle treatment.

Before launching the Lady Hilton program in 1965, the hotel chain surveyed the female guests in three of its most important hotels in Chicago and Los Angeles. Seventy-seven percent of the women who responded to the survey traveled on business. Of these, only 57 percent were married and more than 70 percent were over the age of forty, suggesting a cohort of experienced professionals, nearly half of whom prospered on one income.[22] The guests in the survey considered a hotel's location and its amenities to be top priorities in selecting their accommodations. The cost of the stay was listed last, indicating a cohort with expense accounts or disposable income. Even given the sparseness of this data, in retrospect, the butterfly does not seem an appropriate representation of the independent, well-off businesswoman who stayed at Hilton Hotels.

Each Hilton site that instituted the Lady Hilton program realized it in different ways. The program comprised a range of offerings, from full floors set aside for women to rooms specially decorated for women, ordinary rooms that included a selection of "female amenities," and services designed expressly for female guests.[23] Lady Hilton bedrooms were stocked with feminine items such as jewelry trays, special hangers for skirt suits, a sewing kit, dress hangers with rounded shoulders, hat and shoe racks, fresh flowers, and women's magazines. Lady Hilton bathrooms were equipped with magnifying mirrors, bath salts, shower caps, and the amenity "dearest to the dieting female's heart, a scale."[24]

While Lady Hilton rooms provided tools for the guest to beautify herself, the rooms were themselves the product of beautification campaigns. At the company's Waldorf Astoria Hotel in New York, a female interior designer redecorated nineteen rooms in the Lady Hilton mode. Each room was different from the others, but each had "a distinct aura of elegance and charm." As noted earlier, in 1965, hotel décor was in the midst of a revolutionary shift, from an older loosely Victorian style to a streamlined modernist look. Rooms with ornate

Figure 12.1. This pale-yellow pamphlet with white stripes and a butterfly illustration contained information for guests about the Lady Hilton program. Inside, the guest found lists of amenities. The outside cover set a tone for the guest experience that emphasized light and beauty. Author's collection. Courtesy of the Hilton Collection, Hilton College, University of Houston.

headboards, plump side chairs, and floral bedspreads were replaced with spaces outfitted with simple mattresses on frames under pattern-free coverlets. To augment the room's versatility, the beds converted into sofas. Desks and end tables were designed with straight lines and for functionality. As a writer in *The Architect's Journal* noted in 1970, "The trend is away from large, individually designed and finished apartments towards smaller rooms fitted with standard units of furniture, which allow economies in both capital outlay and space."[25] The décor of the Lady Hilton rooms seemingly resisted this transition, setting the rooms apart as a unique antimodernist aesthetic and sensory experience.

Rooms at the Waldorf included pink stationery with "Lady Hilton Wing" letterhead, so that guests could write from within their inner sanctum, using the pink paper to visually identify themselves as female to their correspondents. The story was much the same at the Palmer House in Chicago, another upscale Hilton property. "Opulent rooms are furnished in a uniquely feminine décor," noted a guest information packet about the Lady Hilton program. "Walls are covered in silk, curtains are exquisite brocade."[26] Such décor appealed to the sense of touch as much as to the eyes. We can compare the sensory cues in the Lady Hilton room to those in a room renovated for male use. In 1960, Hilton had renovated the Savoy Hotel in New York City, focusing particularly on the bar. As described in an industry journal, "The atmosphere to be created had to be somewhat rugged and of masculine appeal since the room is reserved for men only during luncheons." Working with the Hilton team, interior designer Tom Lee created a space that was windowless, wood paneled, narrow, and decorated with a mural created to look like stained glass that depicted dukes and kings of Savoy. In the dark space, the backlit mural bathed surfaces in jewel tones. The design posited a masculine aesthetics that blended "tradition" with the cleaner lines of modernist design.[27]

In the Lady Hilton rooms, the prevalence of the color pink and floral motifs helped to codify emerging stereotypes. As Regina Lee Blaszczyk notes in her history of color in America, pink had only begun to be associated with femininity in the immediate postwar period, when the venerable menswear company Brooks Brothers chose the shade for its first shirt for women. In the 1950s, pink became a popular color for all kinds of household items. Associating the color with rooms for women helped to build the connection.[28] These visual cues marked the Lady Hilton rooms as territories in which women could feel secure in their gender identity.[29] Even as it stereotyped female guests, the décor could also supply a fantasy of feminine supremacy for the traveling businesswoman who otherwise constantly encountered a world not made for her. The Palmer House alluded to this even in its invitation to women, noting that among the dining options on site was a steak house that had a "masculine atmosphere, with a welcome mat always out for the ladies."[30] There was no analogous dining option designed for women but also allowing men. The masculinity of the business world was rigidly policed so that women earned less, were recognized less, and faced possible harassment regularly with no recourse.[31] A comfortable space marketed specifically to women, no matter how essentializing its décor, probably had some appeal.

Hilton Hotels shared positive responses to the Lady Hilton program with a reporter for one of the hospitality industry's journals, *Hotel Management-Review*.

These responses both tell us something about the cohort of female travelers and how Hilton wanted to represent them. Reviewing a stay in a Lady Hilton room, one "government executive" noted, "I appreciate your little extras in the Lady Hilton rooms." The vice president of a bank said, "I have always felt hotels need 'the woman's touch' and in your case that touch certainly made our stay enjoyable."[32] Because this article was published in an industry journal, we can see that professionals in the field imagined and planned for women professionals who held positions of power in business and in communities, but also conformed to stereotypes reinforced through socialization such as women appreciating "special touches" that a man might not wish for or notice.

Feminine Touches

The "woman's touch" engaged the art of intuition—knowing what is wanted before anything is said. The terminology implies that Lady Hilton was created by women for women within the context of a shared notion of femininity. By 1965, the feminine appeal of the goods and services in the program had been well researched and commodified. The objects offered to guests functioned as "feminine touches" to construct the imagined female traveler. The objects were associated with beauty culture and fall loosely into two categories: self-improvement and self-care. Some objects found in the rooms embodied the contradictions inherent in Western beauty culture, suggesting that it was hard work to maintain the polished ideal image of a real-life Lady Hilton.

As the business historian Geoffrey Jones argues in his book on the global beauty industry, self-care products, such as face creams, were considered respectable long before color cosmetics, overtly used for self-improvement, were acceptable for the middle-class women of America. By 1941, however, cosmetic use was so widespread that the United States government "declared the production of lipstick a wartime necessity."[33] Jones notes that the wartime rationing of fabric had limited fashion choices—and helped to promote cosmetics as an alternate form of personal expression. As cosmetic use became normalized for all classes of women, what had once been risqué became de rigeur and the un-made-up face was only fit for private life. To appear in public, in hotels and at business meetings, American women had to spend time and employ skill creating faces that would express certain virtues—respectability, competence, compliance—and that would last through the day with only a few touch-ups factored into the daily schedule. By 1965, then, the Lady Hilton guest could be expected to apply a full face of makeup every morning and remove it at the end of the day. Hilton supplied guests some of the tools for this intimate work.

Self-Improvement

Items for self-improvement indicated to the guest that someone on the staff, and indeed someone in the global corporation, understood the work of performing femininity, work that required particular tools to achieve particular goals. Offering items designed specifically for beauty maintenance could be seen as both a sympathetic gesture and a goad to conformity. Items provided by the Lady Hilton service suggested to women guests what they needed to use in order to perform femininity properly. If a guest did not want the items, she potentially confronted her own dissonance with social norms for femininity.

This attention to the guest as a performer positioned the female traveler as a person not wholly at ease, unable literally to let her hair down even though she might be on vacation at a hotel. Shower caps were an important tool for maintaining appearances and creating allure in this era. Hairstyles that were popular in the 1960s were created and "set" at a salon, usually once a week. Once hair was set it remained mostly the same unless it happened to get wet. Water could quickly undo a hairstyle in which a woman had invested time and money, so shower caps were vital to preserving the coiffure. By providing this protective headgear, the designers of the Lady Hilton program told the guest that the hotel supported her work of maintaining appearances by restraining nature. The guest emerged from the bath or shower with her hair dry and a sense of being understood. She still had to do the work, but the hotel would help her to do it.

The bathroom scale performed similar work in that it acknowledged the female guest's fears that she would fail to conform to ideals of slim feminine beauty. The presence of the bathroom scale reminded the guest that it was her feminine duty to weigh herself on a daily basis and to watch her waistline. The scale's presence recognized and enabled the hard work she was supposed to do to control her appetite. It made women aware of their corporeality, notably at odds with the image of the butterfly who subsisted only on nectar. Ironically, the female customers consulted by market researchers for the Lady Hilton program had noted that they liked to eat and drink. Many had listed room service and the hotel cocktail bar among their top favorite amenities. Female guests were wont to indulge in corporeal pleasures while on the road, but the scale served to remind them of their cultural duty to remain slim and sexually attractive according to contemporary norms.

Lighted magnifying mirrors also helped women maintain appearances and perform their culturally sanctioned gender roles. As part of the sensory environment of Lady Hilton rooms, the makeup mirrors amplified the sense of sight to reveal textures of the skin and facilitated the application of cosmetics, highlighting some features and downplaying others. By magnifying so-called flaws, the mirrors used a kind of hyper-reality to help female guests work against nature. The makeup mirror, like the bathroom scale, emphasized the potential excesses of the body, calling for a calibrated response on the part of the lady traveler. Both could be experienced as a set of eyes trained on the body, searching it for failure. Altogether, three seemingly innocuous guest amenities—the shower cap, the magnifying mirror, and the scale—addressed the female traveler as a body under scrutiny. These tools were available to help the guest find hairs that were out of place, pores that were clogged, and flesh that might be expanding. These simple amenities thereby supported a regime of self-monitoring for public consumption. Far from a site for leisure, the Lady Hilton room was a workshop for the maintenance of femininity.

Self-Care

Mirrors and scales reminded the visiting Lady Hilton that restraint was her cultural responsibility. In contrast, another group of Lady Hilton amenities—bath salts, bottles of perfume, extra pillows, magazines, and fresh flowers—constructed the female guest as a body with pleasures, with the right to indulge, to retreat and change moods. These small gifts invited women to relax and indulge their senses, implying that the guest deserved treats and that it was proper for her to take time to herself. While the term "self-care" was not coined until the twenty-first century, the existence of spas (another type of hotel) and beauty salons created a market for middle- and upper-class female relaxation, suggesting that women's social roles created unique kinds of stress that was best treated with attention to the body. Crucially, the sensory indulgences Lady Hilton offered were private, reflecting lingering nineteenth-century middle-class associations of women with the private sphere and men with the public arena. Despite their own market research indicating that traveling women, just like traveling men, enjoyed going to the hotel bar, these items assumed that women guests would prefer to relax alone.

Nothing was more private or sensuous than the luxury bath salts provided in each Lady Hilton guest bathroom. Bath salts supposed a woman of action in need of relaxation. They offered her a combined experience of warmth and (typically) scent to undo the tensions accumulated through a busy business day full of appointments. Or, if she was in town as a tourist, the salts could make her forget any unpleasant dirt or odors encountered while walking around and seeing the sights. The presence of bath salts encouraged a female guest to enjoy the hotel as an escape from any claims on her time. Recuperative baths of course have a long history in human cultures, but modern developments in plumbing, packaging, and advertising had democratized access to luxury bathing by making it possible to create a mini-spa experience in an ordinary bathtub. For women who could not afford the money or time to visit a spa, a bottle of bath salts offered an experience associated with wealth and leisure culture.

Magazines conveyed a similar message, that the female guest deserved to take time for entertainment and specifically to focus on the world of women—at least as presented by journalism focused on popular consumer culture. The glossy covers that attracted the eye drew a reader into a world of fabrics, perfumes, and cosmetics, a visual sensory emporium. Although we do not know which magazines Lady Hilton provided, we can assume that they included some of the most popular women's monthlies of the day—*McCall's*, *Good Housekeeping*, and *Ladies' Home Journal*—which were mostly focused on domestic life. Since the magazines would have helped to establish the Lady Hilton guest's persona, it is reasonable to suspect that the selection also included fashion magazines such as *Harper's Bazaar* or *Vogue*. In large cities like New York and Chicago, female guests could ask the on-site Lady Hilton representative for directions to department stores or boutiques to shop for the fashions they saw depicted in the glamorous pages of the magazines.

While Hilton offered magazines to the guest as an aid to relaxation, the choice of reading material may have had the opposite effect. Woman's magazines may have disturbed the guest's sense of calm. In popular magazines, women readers encountered the many complexities of gender expectations. *Good Housekeeping* reminded a woman of all she was responsible for in the domestic sphere while *Harper's Bazaar* and *Vogue* offered outlandishly high expectations for beauty maintenance, showcasing the most expensive clothing and avant-garde style. Alongside the sensory pleasures of bright pages and the psychic adventure of imagining oneself in the latest fashions, magazines also reminded women of gender expectations for domestic competence and physical perfection.

As an amenity, fresh flowers were particularly luxurious, requiring extra care from the staff to remain in bloom, depending on the length of a guest's stay. In the 1960s, flowers were only sold at florists' shops, making them somewhat more special as a gift than they are today when they are available at grocery stores. Some of the larger and more expensive urban hotels rented space to florists. For the hotel, of course, this made it easier to supply bouquets to Lady Hilton rooms, and for travelers it may have helped to create a sense of luxury. A vase of flowers in the room indicated to the guest that the hotel thought she was worth the expense and attention. As sensory experience, fresh flowers introduced attractive fragrances and colors to a room and added an element of life, if not actually nature, to a space that could otherwise seem sterile and unremarkable.

Because they were only given to Lady Hilton guests, the set of tiny perfume bottles, the four moods, assumed that women were especially responsive to sensory experiences, able to travel in their imaginations (Figure 12.2). The four square bottles were each about one inch tall and nestled in a cardboard box decorated with a bronze metallic background and an illustration of a young white woman with long flowing hair and an armful of flowers. She wears wedding and engagement rings, an interesting detail that potentially signals security behind the implication of abandon in her loose hair and the flowers tumbling out of her arms. The illustration is in a pop art style derivative of Peter Max's modern version of art nouveau. The colors evoke luxury and the image suggests indulgence.

The scents seem to have been designed to reference perfumes that were widely known in 1968. The Hilton scent named Continental smelled very much like Chanel No. 5, while the Eastern fragrance had notes similar to Shalimar, from the French company Guerlain.[34] The moods available were, to some degree, preset through the popular culture of the moment, but also specific to the objectives of a hospitality company—making the person who sniffed them think about travel. Although the American perfume industry had recently begun to flourish, sparked by Elizabeth Arden's Youth Dew bath oil introduced in 1953, the most popular perfumes in America were still largely imported from France.[35] An olfactory reference to Chanel No. 5 could make a guest think about Paris. The hint of Shalimar, with its Orientalist advertising campaign, could make her imagine a trip to the Taj Mahal. The scent titled Island, with its notes of suntan lotion, would make her think of lying on a beach, perhaps at El Caribe, Hilton's hotel in Puerto Rico. Each of the Hilton knock-off scents was presented as a transporting experience, a trip within a trip for the Lady Hilton guest.

Because flowers and perfume were frequently given as gifts, these particular special touches could be experienced as tokens of love, corporatized. Even

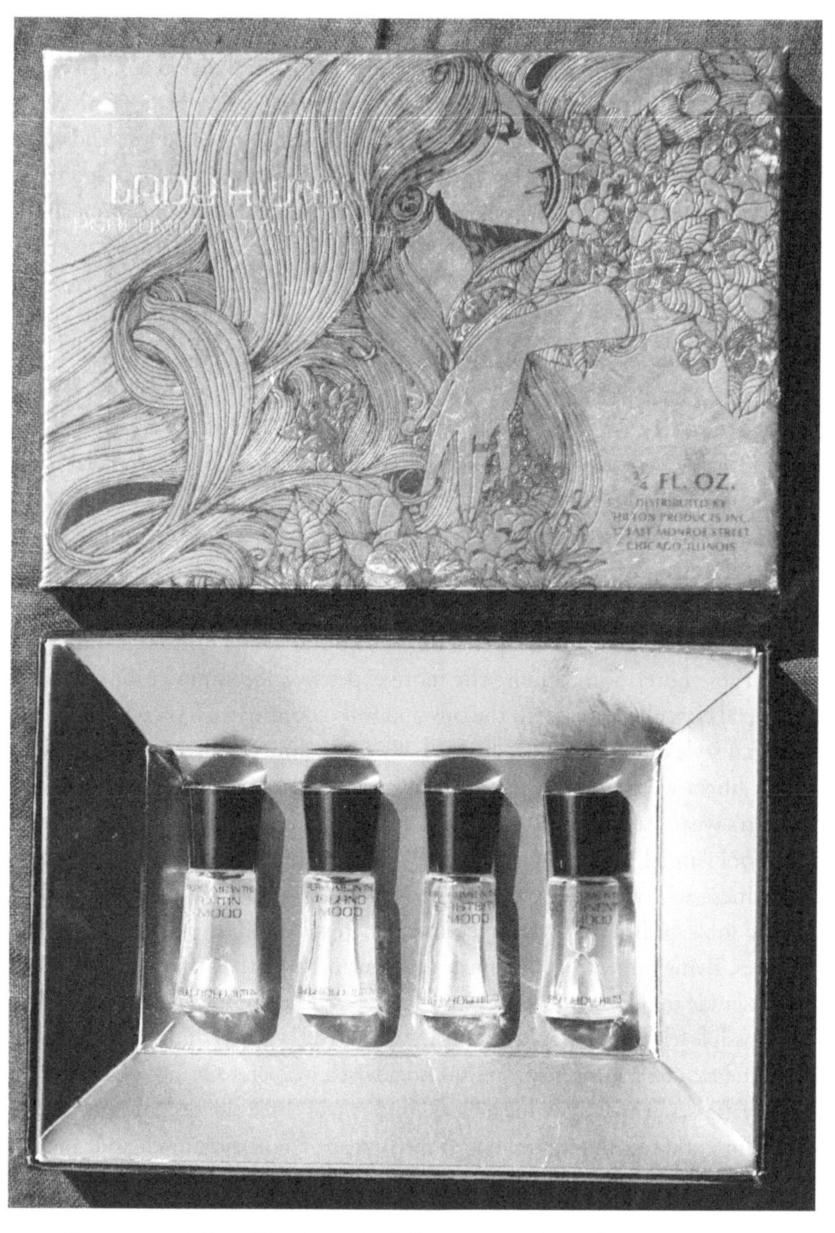

Figure 12.2. Hilton Hotels supplied the Four Moods perfumes to guests in some Lady Hilton rooms. The bottles were nestled in a small box decorated in flowing images executed in metallic inks. The four scents mimicked other perfumes popular at the time while the illustrations tapped into contemporary trends in graphic design that emphasized freedom and motion. Author's collection. Courtesy of the Hilton Collection, Hilton College, University of Houston.

better, this love affair came with "no strings attached"—beyond the hotel bill. As an informational flyer from the Palmer House in Chicago noted, "all women *are* special at Hilton hotels," whatever their experience might be at work or home.[36] Travel offered an opportunity to be appreciated and cared for. And when she took home the perfumes, the guest could reconnect to the travel experience through the scents, now not only smelling "Continental" and dreaming about Chanel in Paris but also remembering the Hilton.

Maintaining Appearances

Among the offers of new moods, relaxing experiences, and special treatment, one Lady Hilton amenity conflicted notably with the pervasive notion of care and indulgence: Lady Hilton guests could request irons and ironing boards. Hotels had long provided laundry and pressing services, and those amenities fit well within the category of care. The ironing boards that the Lady Hilton program offered, however, reconstituted the guest as a domestic laborer, perhaps the very thing she was traveling to escape. Women who stayed at a Hilton in the 1960s, when these hotels were among the more expensive accommodations, were of the social class associated with the tidy and fully coordinated look typified in the personal style of much-admired First Lady Jacqueline Kennedy. Although synthetic fibers were becoming more common in clothing, upper-middle-class women's wear was still far from casual and typically included silk, fine cotton, and wool flannel, all fabrics that could wrinkle easily in suitcases.[37] For women in business, who were still a small minority in the 1960s, it was especially important to look "pulled together" as so many men were still suspicious of women's abilities. Being pulled together meant presenting smooth surfaces.

A guide to packing for European travel, published in 1964, suggested "wherever possible [clothing] should be of the wash and dry variety" and noted that "synthetic fabrics are a great help," yet it also advised women to bring two suits, two "dressy dresses," three "daytime dresses," and two or three blouses, each potentially requiring extra touch-ups once out of the suitcase.[38] Another travel guide praised the new synthetics, but also advised women that "a suit with either sweaters or nylon blouses . . . should be the foundation of your wardrobe." When traveling, "you will find that you will practically live in it . . . A basic wool flannel in gray is suggested." Such an item would be versatile, but it would also require upkeep.[39]

Although the ironing board seems out of place with the notion of luxurious treatment, it remains a common feature in larger hotels today. The Lady Hilton experience provided a guest with some sense of sensuous luxury, but it also acknowledged the practical challenges to maintaining a professional, ladylike appearance, especially when away from home. Hilton offered female guests a special décor and special items that its executives guessed women would appreciate, but the offerings themselves established a template for the female traveler. She was constantly concerned with her appearance and knew the work required to stay within social norms for presentability—plucking her eyebrows, keeping her hair style dry, watching her weight, and pressing her placket smooth. She was also tired and in need of care. She would appreciate little luxuries such as perfumes and flowers and these would ideally promote her loyalty to the hotel itself, making a Hilton lady out of the Lady Hilton guest.

Conclusion

Hilton Hotels featured the Lady Hilton program for about a dozen years.[40] There are several likely reasons that it did not ultimately seem worth maintaining. The hotel business strives for full occupancy, and as such, it is clearly inefficient to keep rooms available for a particular set of guests who might or might not show up. It may also be that female guests were not exactly as Hilton had imagined them. They may have been more like the women Katherine Jordon Magoun described: self-sufficient and not amenable to suggestions that they needed help. As Lucille Skerston, who had named the Lady Hilton program, noted years later in 1983, "women began telling us they didn't want to be isolated or segregated." Still certain that women represented a unique niche in the market, Skerston reflected, "I'd like to round up large panels of traveling businesswomen and female opinion leaders and find out once and for all what they want us to do."[41] Writing in 2008, hotel analyst Bjorn Hanson argued, "By the mid-'80s, separate floors in hotels offended many women who were traveling on business. . . . They were trying to be C.E.O.'s but were looked on as the weaker sex. Women's floors became a kind of sexist thing instead of a polite offer."[42] The version of the program in which a hotel offered a menu of special items that could be added to the room was probably the most efficient as it allowed women to decide what they might need rather than being told what they wanted.

Another clue to the decline of the Lady Hilton program can be found in a comment found much earlier in *Hotel Management* about redecorating hotels after World War II. In 1945, industry journalist Virginia Komlos noted that rooms that had been decorated for women often ended up housing "bachelors."

Specifically, "some of these apartments have fluffy ruffles, ribbons and bowknots and delicate colors are used throughout, but nevertheless men seem to like them. This is one of the many paradoxes in hotel decorating."[43] By the end of the twentieth century with ever more women traveling for business, many of the so-called feminine touches that Lady Hilton offered became standard in hotel rooms: hair dryers, magnifying mirrors, sewing kits, and shower caps. In attempting to construct a female traveler, Hilton Hotels discovered that gendered expectations and sensory pleasures were not gendered in practice. Male and female travelers equally worried about how to present their bodies successfully in public and equally appreciated the sense that someone understood their anxieties. This was confirmed more recently as some large hotel chains began to again offer rooms and amenities marketed to women. The president of a company that managed three hotels described a new "woman's level" set aside in the hotel but then noted, "So much of what we do, by the way, is applicable to both men and women."[44] The concept of special touches was first associated with women but attractive to men, too. The story of the Lady Hilton marketing scheme, and of gendered programing in hotels in general, helps us to see how concepts of sensory engagement and personal care can challenge gender dichotomies within the capitalist marketplace for experiences.

NOTES

INTRODUCTION

The authors wish to extend a special thanks to Ai Hisano for her invitation to a Harvard Business School workshop that planted the seed for this project and to Roger Horowitz for his assistance with this introduction.

1. Clay Risen, "Louise Slade, Scientist Who Studied the Molecules in Food, Dies at 74," *New York Times*, November 1, 2021.

2. Colleen Walsh, "What the Nose Knows," *Harvard Gazette*, February 27, 2020, https://news.harvard.edu/gazette/story/2020/02/how-scent-emotion-and-memory-are-intertwined-and-exploited/.

3. Karl Marx, *Economic and Philosophic Manuscripts of 1844*, quoted in Karl Marx and Friedrich Engels, *The Marx-Engels Reader*, ed. Robert C. Tucker, 2nd ed. (New York: Norton, 1978), 89.

4. "Capitalism and the Senses," Harvard Business School, June 29, 2017, https://www.hbs.edu/faculty/research/seminars-conferences/Pages/event.aspx?conf=2017-capitalism-and-the-senses; "2020 Fall Conference: Capitalism and the Senses," Hagley Museum and Library, November 5–6, 2020, https://www.hagley.org/research/conference/2020-fall-conference.

5. We should note, however, that Chapters 6 and 11, by David Suisman and Regina Lee Blaszczyk, respectively, are not based on presentations from the conference.

6. Marx, *Economic and Philosophic Manuscripts of 1844* (emphasis in original); Georg Simmel, "The Metropolis and Mental Life," in *Classic Essays on the Culture of Cities*, ed. Richard Sennett (Englewood Cliffs, NJ: Prentice-Hall, 1969), 47–60; Walter Benjamin, "The Work of Art in the Age of Mechanical Reproduction," in *Illuminations*, ed. Hannah Arendt, trans. Harry Zohn (New York: Schocken, 1968), 217–51; Lucien Febvre, *The Problem of Unbelief in the Sixteenth Century, the Religion of Rabelais*, trans. Beatrice Gottlieb (Cambridge, MA: Harvard University Press, [1942] 1982); 423–36; Lucien Febvre, "Psychologie et histoire," in *Encyclopédie française*, vol. 8, *La vie mentale* (Paris: Société de gestion de l'Encyclopédie française, 1938); Lucien Febvre, "Comment reconstituer la vie affective d'autrefois? La sensibilité et l'histoire," *Annales d'histoire sociale* 3 (1941). Febvre's essays appeared in English in Lucien Febvre, *A New Kind of History: From the Writings of Febvre*, ed. Peter Burke, trans. K. Folca (New York: Harper & Row, 1973).

7. Alain Corbin, *The Foul and the Fragrant: Odor and the French Social Imagination* (Cambridge, MA: Harvard University Press, 1986).

8. Useful overviews of the history of the senses include David Howes and Constance Classen, *Ways of Sensing: Understanding the Senses in Society* (New York: Routledge, 2014); David

Howes, ed., *Empire of the Senses: The Sensual Culture Reader*, Sensory Formations Series (Oxford: Berg, 2005); Mark M. Smith, *Sensing the Past: Seeing, Hearing, Smelling, Tasting, and Touching in History* (Berkeley: University of California Press, 2008); Robert Jütte, *A History of the Senses: From Antiquity to Cyberspace* (Malden, MA: Polity, 2004).

9. Alain Corbin, "A History and Anthropology of the Senses," in *Time, Desire and Horror: Towards a History of the Senses*, trans. Jean Birrell (Cambridge, MA: Polity, 1995), 181–95.

10. Raymond Williams, *Keywords: A Vocabulary of Culture and Society*, rev. ed. (New York: Oxford University Press, 1983), 280–83, quotation at 281. See also Febvre, "Sensibility and History: How to Reconstitute the Emotional Life of the Past," in *A New Kind of History*, 12–26; William Empson, *The Structure of Complex Words* (New York: New Directions, 1951), 250–310; Sophia Rosenfeld, *Common Sense: A Political History* (Cambridge, MA: Harvard University Press, 2011).

11. Jütte, *A History of the Senses*, 35–42; Ian Ritchie, "Fusion of the Faculties: A Study of the Language of the Senses in Hausaland," in *The Varieties of Sensory Experience: A Sourcebook in the Anthropology of the Senses*, ed. David Howes (Toronto: University of Toronto Press, 1991), 194 and 192–202 passim; Fiona Macpherson, "Taxonomising the Senses," *Philosophical Studies* 153, no. 1 (2011): 127.

12. David Howes, "Historicizing Perception," in *Empire of the Senses: The Sensual Culture Reader*, ed. David Howes (Oxford: Berg, 2005), 56.

13. Mark S. R. Jenner, "Follow Your Nose? Smell, Smelling, and Their Histories," *American Historical Review* 116, no. 2 (April 2011): 350.

14. Monique Scheer, "Are Emotions a Kind of Practice (and Is That What Makes Them Have a History)? A Bourdieuian Approach to Understanding Emotion," *History and Theory* 51, no. 2 (May 2012): 193–220. Quotations at 201 and 194.

15. Karl Marx, *Capital* (New York: International Publishers, 1967), 1:425.

16. Karl Marx, *The Economic and Philosophic Manuscripts of 1844*, quoted in David Howes, "The Material Body of the Commodity: Sensing Marx," in *Sensual Relations: Engaging the Senses in Culture and Social Theory*, ed. David Howes (Ann Arbor: University of Michigan Press, 2003), 206–7. Emphasis in original.

17. Howes, "The Material Body of the Commodity," 207–8.

18. Howes, "The Material Body of the Commodity," 208.

19. Susan Strasser, *Satisfaction Guaranteed: The Making of the American Mass Market* (New York: Pantheon Books, 1989), 29–57. Quotation at 32.

20. For a summary of this historiography, see Regina Lee Blaszczyk and Philip B. Scranton, ed., *Major Problems in American Business History: Documents and Essays* (Boston: Houghton Mifflin, 2006).

21. Roland Marchand, *Advertising the American Dream: Making Way for Modernity, 1920–1940* (Berkeley: University of California Press, 1984); Roland Marchand, *Creating the Corporate Soul: The Rise of Public Relations and Corporate Imagery in American Big Business* (Berkeley: University of California Press, 2001).

22. Patricia Johnston, *Real Fantasies: Edward Steichen's Advertising Photography* (Berkeley: University of California Press, 1997).

23. Blaszczyk and Scranton, *Major Problems*.

24. See, for example, Regina Lee Blaszczyk, *Imagining Consumers: Design and Innovation from Wedgwood to Corning* (Baltimore: Johns Hopkins University Press, 2000), and Lisa Jacobson, *Raising Consumers: Children and the American Mass Market in the Early Twentieth Century* (New York: Columbia University Press, 2004).

25. Regina Lee Blaszczyk, *The Color Revolution* (Cambridge, MA: The MIT Press, 2012).

26. Kenneth J. Lipartito, "Connecting the Cultural and the Material in Business History," *Enterprise and Society* 14, no. 4 (December 2013): 686–704, and Kenneth J. Lipartito, "Reassembling the Economic: New Departures in Historical Materialism," *American Historical Review* 121, no. 1 (February 2016): 101–39. Also useful are Per H. Hansen, "Business History: A Cultural and Narrative Approach," *Business History Review* 86, no. 4 (Winter 2012): 693–717, and Philip Scranton and Patrick Fridenson, *Reimagining Business History* (Baltimore: Johns Hopkins University Press, 2013).

27. David Suisman, *Selling Sounds: The Commercial Revolution in American Music* (Cambridge, MA: Harvard University Press, 2009), quote at 16; "How Popular Song Factories Manufacture a Hit," *New York Times*, September 18, 1910; Timothy D. Taylor, *The Sounds of Capitalism: Advertising, Music, and the Conquest of Culture* (Chicago: University of Chicago Press, 2012); Jacques Attali, *Noise: The Political Economy of Music*, trans. Brian Massumi (Minneapolis: University of Minnesota Press, 1985), 53.

28. Roy Sheldon and Egmont Arens, *Consumer Engineering: A New Technique for Prosperity, Getting and Spending* (New York: Arno Press, [1932] 1976), 100–102; the authors emphasized "make it snuggle in the palm" by using the phrase as a subheading within the chapter on 101. See also Howes, "The Material Body of the Commodity," 211.

29. The Ernest Dichter collection is open for research at the Hagley Library; the finding aid is available at https://findingaids.hagley.org/repositories/3/resources/1071. The market research report portion of the collection is available in the digital database published by Adam Mathews, *American Consumer Culture: Market Research and American Business*. A Hagley conference devoted to assessing Dichter's influence generated the edited collection, *The Rise of Marketing and Market Research*, ed. Harmut Berghoff, Philip Scranton, and Uwe Spiekermann (New York: Palgrave Macmillan, 2012).

30. On the importance of calculation, see Max Weber, *The Protestant Ethic and the Spirit of Capitalism*, trans. Talcott Parsons (New York: Charles Scribner's Sons, 1958), 17–27.

31. On scientific management, see Frederick Winslow Taylor, *The Principles of Scientific Management* (New York: Harper & Brothers, 1911); Robert Kanigel, *The One Best Way: Frederick Winslow Taylor and the Enigma of Efficiency* (Cambridge, MA: The MIT Press, 2005).

CHAPTER 1

1. Jonathan Barnes, ed., *The Complete Works of Aristotle*, Revised Oxford Translation (Princeton, NJ: Princeton University Press, 1984), 1543.

2. Constance Classen, David Howes, and Anthony Synnott, *Aroma: The Cultural History of Smell* (New York: Routledge, 1994), 22–23.

3. Barnes, *The Complete Works of Aristotle*, 1544.

4. See Virginia Postrel, *The Substance of Style: How the Rise of Aesthetic Value Is Remaking Commerce, Culture, and Consciousness* (New York: HarperCollins, 2004).

5. Steven Shapin, "The Sciences of Subjectivity," *Social Studies of Science* 42, no. 2 (April 2012): 179.

6. Ella Butler, "Tasting Off-flavors: Food Science, Sensory Knowledge and the Consumer Sensorium," *The Senses and Society* 13, no. 1 (2018): 75–88.

7. Some scholars distinguish "feelings," "emotions," and "affects." I understand the historical and cultural specificity of each term, but in this chapter I mainly use "emotions" and "feelings"

interchangeably, following Jan Plamper's use of "emotions" as a meta-concept. Jan Plamper, *The History of Emotions: An Introduction*, trans. Keith Tribe (New York: Oxford University Press, 2015), 12.

8. See Constance Classen, *Worlds of Sense: Exploring the Senses in History and across Cultures* (New York: Routledge, 1993); David Howes and Constance Classen, *Ways of Sensing: Understanding the Senses in Society* (New York: Routledge, 2014); and Mark M. Smith, *Sensing the Past: Seeing, Hearing, Smelling, Tasting, and Touching in History* (Berkeley: University of California Press, 2008).

9. Jeffrey L. Meikle, *American Plastic: A Cultural History* (New Brunswick, NJ: Rutgers University Press, 1995); Mimi Sheller, *Aluminum Dreams: The Making of Light Modernity* (Cambridge, MA: The MIT Press, 2014).

10. Walter Benjamin, *The Arcades Project*, trans. Howard Eiland and Kevin McLaughlin (Cambridge, MA: Belknap Press of Harvard University Press, 1999).

11. Gernot Böhme, *Critique of Aesthetic Capitalism*, trans. Edmund Jephcott (Milan: Mimesis International, 2017); Andreas Reckwitz, *The Invention of Creativity: Modern Society and the Culture of the New*, trans. Steven Black (Cambridge, UK: Polity Press, 2017).

12. Rob Boddice and Mark Smith, *Emotion, Sense, Experience* (New York: Cambridge University Press, 2020), 30.

13. Ibid., 18, 56. See also Bettina Hitzer, "The Odor of Disgust: Contemplating the Dark Side of 20th-Century Cancer History," *Emotion Review* 12, no. 3 (2020): 156–67.

14. Plamper, *The History of Emotions*, 243–50. Plamper calls this coalition "critical neuroscience."

15. For a review of these studies, see Lisa Feldman Barrett, *How Emotions Are Made: The Secret Life of the Brain* (Boston: Houghton Mifflin Harcourt, 2017); Maria Gendron and Lisa Feldman Barrett, "Reconstructing the Past: A Century of Ideas about Emotion in Psychology," *Emotion Review* 1, no. 4 (October 2009): 316–39; and Plamper, *The History of Emotions*.

16. See Lisa Feldman Barrett, "Are Emotions Natural Kinds?," *Perspectives on Psychological Science* 1, no. 1 (March 2006): 28–58; Nico H. Frijda, "Emotion Experience and Its Varieties," *Emotion Review* 1, no. 3 (July 2009): 264–71; and Luiz Pessoa, "Emotion and the Interactive Brain: Insights from Comparative Neuroanatomy and Complex Systems," *Emotion Review* 10, no. 3 (July 2018): 204–16.

17. Barrett, *How Emotions Are Made*, 31.

18. Robert W. Levenson, "Reflections on 30 Years of *Cognition & Emotion*," *Cognition and Emotion* 33, no. 1 (2019): 8–13; Rainer Reisenzein, "Cognition and Emotion: A Plea for Theory," *Cognition and Emotion* 33, no. 1 (2019): 109–18.

19. Katie Hoemann and Lisa Feldman Barrett, "Concepts Dissolve Artificial Boundaries in the Study of Emotion and Cognition, Uniting Body, Brain, and Mind," *Cognition and Emotion* 33, no. 1 (2019): 67–76.

20. Nicole Eustace, Eugenia Lean, Julie Livingston, Jan Plamper, William M. Reddy, and Barbara H. Rosenwein, *AHR* Conversation: The Historical Study of Emotions, *American Historical Review* 117, no. 5 (December 2012): 1505. See also Barbara H. Rosenwein, "Worrying about Emotions in History," *American Historical Review* 107, no. 3 (June 2002): 821–45.

21. William M. Reddy, "The Unavoidable Intentionality of Affect: The History of Emotions and the Neurosciences of the Present Day," *Emotion Review* 12, no. 3 (July 2020): 172. See also William M. Reddy, "Saying Something New: Practice Theory and Cognitive Neuroscience," *Arcadia* 44, no. 1 (August 2009): 8–23.

22. See Rob Boddice, "The Developing Brain as Historical Artifact," *Developmental Psychology* 55, no. 9 (2019): 1994–96; Gendron and Barrett, "Reconstructing the Past"; and Constantina Papoulias and Felicity Callard, "Biology's Gift: Interrogating the Turn to Affect," *Body and Society* 16, no. 1 (March 2010): 29–56.

23. Monique Scheer, "Are Emotions a Kind of Practice (and Is That What Makes Them Have a History)? A Bourdieuian Approach to Understanding Emotion," *History and Theory* 51 (May 2012): 195. Emphasis in original.

24. Ibid., 209. See Brian Massumi, *Parables for the Virtual: Movement, Affect, Sensation* (Durham, NC: Duke University Press, 2002).

25. Rob Boddice, *A History of Emotions* (Manchester, UK: Manchester University Press, 2018); Rob Boddice, *A History of Feelings* (London: Reaktion Books, 2019).

26. Terry Eagleton, *The Ideology of the Aesthetic* (Malden, MA: Blackwell, 1990), 13.

27. Mary J. Gregor, "Baumgarten's 'Aesthetica,'" *Review of Metaphysics* 37, no. 2 (December 1983): 361.

28. Ibid., 357–85; Sven-Olov Wallenstein, "Baumgarten and the Invention of Aesthetics," *SITE* 33 (2013): 32–58.

29. Eagleton, *The Ideology of the Aesthetic*, 196.

30. Karl Marx, *Capital: A Critique of Political Economy*, trans. Ben Fowkes, vol. 1 (New York: Penguin Books, 1990), 552.

31. Karl Marx, *Economic and Philosophic Manuscripts of 1844 and the Communist Manifesto*, trans. Martin Milligan (Buffalo, NY: Prometheus Books, 1988), 118–19. Emphasis in original.

32. Wolfgang Fritz Haug, *Critique of Commodity Aesthetics: Appearance, Sexuality and Advertising in Capitalist Society*, trans. Robert Bock (Cambridge, UK: Polity Press, 1971), 8, 16.

33. Ibid., 16–17. Emphasis added.

34. Böhme, *Critique of Aesthetic Capitalism*, 14.

35. Gernot Böhme, *The Aesthetics of Atmospheres*, ed. Jean-Paul Thibaud (New York: Routledge, 2017); Böhme, *Critique of Aesthetic Capitalism*.

36. Ai Hisano, *Visualizing Taste: How Business Changed the Look of What You Eat* (Cambridge, MA: Harvard University Press, 2019).

37. Regina Lee Blaszczyk, "The Aesthetic Moment: China Decorators, Consumer Demand, and Technological Change in the American Pottery Industry, 1865–1900," *Winterthur Portfolio* 29, no. 2/3 (Summer–Autumn 1994): 121–53; Regina Lee Blaszczyk, *Imagining Consumers: Design and Innovation from Wedgwood to Corning* (Baltimore: Johns Hopkins University Press, 2000).

38. Thorstein Veblen, *The Theory of the Leisure Class* (New York: Oxford University Press, 2007); Jean Baudrillard, *The Consumer Society: Myths and Structures* (Thousand Oaks, CA: Sage, 1998).

39. See Postrel, *The Substance of Style*, v–vii.

40. Geoffrey Jones, *Beauty Imagined: A History of the Global Beauty Industry* (New York: Oxford University Press, 2010), 134–36.

41. Reckwitz, *The Invention of Creativity*, 2–3.

42. Ibid., 17.

43. Ibid., 105.

44. Regina Lee Blaszczyk, *The Color Revolution* (Cambridge, MA: The MIT Press, 2012); Hisano, *Visualizing Taste*.

45. Meikle, *American Plastic*.

46. Reckwitz, *The Invention of Creativity*, 89.

47. Thomas Dixon, *From Passions to Emotions: The Creation of a Secular Psychological Category* (New York: Cambridge University Press, 2009).

48. Boddice, *A History of Feelings*, 7.

49. See Bertil Hultén, *Sensory Marketing: Theoretical and Empirical Grounds* (New York: Routledge, 2017); Aradhna Krishna, ed., *Sensory Marketing: Research on the Sensuality of Products* (New York: Routledge, 2010); and Martin Lindstrom, *Brand Sense: Sensory Secrets behind the Stuff We Buy* (New York: Free Press, 2010).

50. Hultén, *Sensory Marketing*, 6.

51. Krishna, *Sensory Marketing*, 2.

52. Bertil Hultén, Niklas Broweus, and Marcus van Dijk, *Sensory Marketing* (New York: Palgrave Macmillan, 2009), 5.

53. Timothy de Waal Malefyt, "An Anthropology of the Senses: Tracing the Future of Sensory Marketing in Brand Rituals" in *Handbook of Anthropology in Business*, ed. Rita Denny and Patricia Sunderland (New York: Routledge, 2014), 714, 716.

54. Hultén et al., *Sensory Marketing*, 4–5.

55. Malefyt, "An Anthropology of the Senses," 712–13.

56. David Howes, "Day 2, Opening Keynote: The 'Race to Embrace the Senses' in Marketing: An Ethnographic Perspective," *Ethnographic Praxis in Industry Conference Proceedings* (2013), 13.

57. Ibid., 13–14.

58. Harry T. Lawless and Hildegarde Heymann, *Sensory Evaluation of Food: Principles and Practices*, 2nd ed. (New York: Springer, 2010), 1.

59. Herbert Stone and Joel L. Sidel, *Sensory Evaluation Practices*, 3rd ed. (San Diego, CA: Elsevier Academic Press, 2004), 13.

60. Jacob Lahne, "Standard Sensations: The Production of Objective Experience from Industrial Technique," *The Senses and Society* 13, no. 1 (2018): 15.

61. Jacob Lahne, "Sensory Science, the Food Industry, and the Objectification of Taste," *Anthropology of Food* 10 (2016), https://doi.org/10.4000/aof.7956.

62. "Odor by Specification," *Industrial Bulletin*, June 1927, Box 1, Arthur D. Little, Inc. records [hereafter ADL records], Series 3, Massachusetts Institute of Technology, Institute Archives and Special Collections (Cambridge, MA).

63. ADL, "Development of Pea Soup Flavoring," Report for A. A. Walter and Co., C-57331, March 20, 1944, Box 8, ADL records, Series 4.

64. Lahne, "Sensory Science," 9; Christopher J. Phillips, "The Taste Machine: Sense, Subjectivity, and Statistics in the California Wine World," *Social Studies of Science* 46, no. 3 (2016): 461–81.

65. ADL, "Progress Report on Artificial Cinnamon," Report for D & L Slade Company, C-57238, February 5, 1942, Box 4; ADL, "Progress Report of Improvement of PARD Dog Food," Report for Swift, C-57386, December 13, 1943, Box 10; ADL, "Study of Advantages of Glass Containers and Refrigeration for Keeping Coffee in the Home," Report for Owens-Illinois Glass, C-57186, July 25, 1941, Box 2, all in ADL records, Series 4.

66. Howes, "The Race to Embrace the Senses," 15.

67. Sara Korzen and Jesper Lassen, "Meat in Context: On the Relation Between Perceptions and Contexts," *Appetite* 54 (2010): 274–81; Jacob Lahne, Amy B. Trubek, and Marcia L. Pelchat, "Consumer Sensory Perception of Cheese Depends on Context: A Study Using Comment Analysis and Linear Mixed Models," *Food Quality and Preference* 32, Part C (March 2014): 184–97.

68. See Nadia Berenstein, "Designing Flavors for Mass Consumption," *The Senses and Society* 13, no. 1 (2018): 19–40.

69. Hisano, *Visualizing Taste*, chapter 4.

CHAPTER 2

This work was supported by the Chemical Heritage Foundation, Beckman Center (Doan fellowship 2016), Riksbankens Jubileumsfond (grant number P16-0411:1), and the Swedish Research Council (grant number 2019-02897). The author also wishes to thank the coeditors of this volume as well as the external reader for their generous assistance and constructive comments.

1. Ernest C. Crocker and Washington Platt, "Food Flavors—A Critical Review of Recent Literature," *Food Research* 2, no. 3 (1937): 184.

2. Hans-Jörg Rheinberger, *Toward a History of Epistemic Things: Synthesizing Proteins in the Test Tube* (Stanford, CA: Stanford University Press, 1997), 27–31.

3. See, for example, Steven Shapin, "The Sciences of Subjectivity," *Social Studies of Science* 42, no. 2 (2011): 170–84; Steven Shapin, "A Taste of Science: Making the Subjective Objective in the California Wine World," *Social Studies of Science* 46, no. 3 (2016): 436–60; Christopher J. Phillips, "The Taste Machine: Sense, Subjectivity, and Statistics in the California Wine World," *Social Studies of Science* 46, no. 3 (2016): 461–81; Nadia Berenstein, "Flavor Added: The Sciences of Flavor and the Industrialization of Food in America," (PhD diss., University of Pennsylvania, 2017).

4. Koray Çalışkan and Michel Callon, "Economization, Part 2: A Research Programme for the Study of Markets," *Economy and Society* 39, no. 1 (2010): 1–32.

5. Fabian Muniesa, Yuval Millo, and Michel Callon, "An Introduction to Market Devices," *Sociological Review* 55, no. 2 (2007): 1–12.

6. For examples, see Benjamin R. Cohen, "Analysis as Border Control: Chemists along the Boundary Between Pure Food and Real Adulteration," *Endeavour* 35, nos. 2–3 (2011): 66–73.

7. Crocker and Platt, "Food flavors," 192; Ernest C. Crocker, *Flavor* (New York: McGraw-Hill, 1945), chapter 14.

8. Washington Platt, "Some Fundamental Assumptions Pertaining to the Judgment of Food Flavors," *Food Research* 2, no. 3 (1937): 240–41.

9. Robert K. Hower, "Flavor Testing in a Baking Company," in *Flavor Research and Food Acceptance: A Survey of the Scope of Flavor and Associated Research, Compiled from Papers Presented in a Series of Symposia Given in 1956–1957*, ed. Arthur D. Little (New York: Chapman & Hall, 1958), 219–21.

10. Washington Platt, "Rational Methods of Scoring Food Products," *Food Industries* 3, no. 3 (1931): 108–10.

11. See, for example, Armand V. Cardello, Howard G. Schutz, and Alan O. Wright, "History of Food Acceptance and Sensory Research on Military Rations," in *Military Food Engineering and Ration Technology*, ed. Ann H. Barrett and Armand V. Cardello (Lancaster, PA: DEStech Publications, 2012), 349–50.

12. For Dove's unicorn project, see W. Franklin Dove, "Artificial Production of the Fabulous Unicorn," *Scientific Monthly* 42, no. 5 (1936): 431–36.

13. W. Franklin Dove, "Appetite Levels of Food Consumption: A Technique for Measuring Foods in Terms of Psychological and Nutritional Values Combined," *Human Biology* 15, no. 3 (1943): 199–220; W. Franklin Dove, "Developing Food Acceptance Research," *Science, New Series* 103, no. 2668 (1946): 190.

14. W. Franklin Dove, "Food Acceptability—Its Determination and Evaluation," *Food Technology* 1 (January 1947): 39–44.

15. About the "pineapple ester," see Berenstein, "Flavor Added," chapter 1.

16. Crocker and Platt, "Food Flavors," 191.

17. See Magni Martens, "A Philosophy for Sensory Science," *Food Quality and Preference* 10, no. 4–5 (1999): 233–44; Harry T. Lawless and Hildegarde Heymann, *Sensory Evaluation of Food: Principles and Practices* (New York: Springer, 2010), 20–21.

18. Platt, "Rational Methods of Scoring Food Products," 108–10.

19. Rose-Marie Pangborn, "Sensory Evaluation of Foods: A Look Backward and Forward," *Food Technology* 18, no. 9 (1964): 1310.

20. Dove, "Food Acceptability," 44, 47.

21. N. H. Pronko and J. W. Bowles, "Identification of Cola Beverages: First Study," *Journal of Applied Psychology* 32, no. 1 (1948): 304–12.

22. See David R. Peryam, "Sensory Difference Tests," in *Flavor Research and Food Acceptance: A Survey of the Scope of Flavor and Associated Research, Compiled from Papers Presented in a Series of Symposia Given in 1956–1957*, ed. Arthur D. Little (New York: Chapman & Hall, 1958).

23. See Phillips, "The Taste Machine."

24. Ernest E. Lockhart, "Flavor and Food Acceptance Methodology," in *Flavor Research and Food Acceptance*, 123.

25. Crocker, *Flavor*, 10–14, 43–44.

26. Stanley E. Cairncross and Loren B. Sjöström, "Flavor Profiles—A New Approach to Flavor Problems," *Food Technology* 4, no. 8 (August 1950): 308.

27. Jean F. Caul, Stanley E. Cairncross, and Loren B. Sjöström, "The Flavor Profile in Review," in *Flavor Research and Food Acceptance*, 65–74.

28. Loren B. Sjöström, "The Descriptive Analysis of Flavor," in *Food Acceptance Testing Methodology*, ed. David R. Peryam, Francis J. Pilgrim, and Martin S. Peterson (Chicago: United States Quartermaster Food and Container Institute, 1953), 26–27.

29. See Nadia Berenstein, "Designing Flavor for Mass Consumption," *The Senses and Society* 13, no. 1 (2018): 19–40; Lawless and Heymann, *Sensory Evaluation of Food*, 231–34.

30. R. B. Dustman, "The Storage of Black-Walnut Kernels," *Food Research* 1, no. 3 (1936): 250.

31. A. S. Richardson, "Report of Committee on the Kreis Test for Rancidity," *Journal of the American Oil Chemists' Society* 8, no. 7 (1931): 269–70.

32. Keith D. Bartle and Peter Myers, "History of Gas Chromatography," *Trends in Analytical Chemistry* 21, nos. 9–10 (2002): 547–56; Christy Spackman, "Perfumer, Chemist, Machine: Gas Chromatography and the Industrial Search to 'Improve' Flavor," *The Senses and Society* 13, no. 1 (2018): 41–59.

33. J. F. Mateson, "Olfactometry: Its Techniques and Apparatus," *Journal of the Air Pollution Control Association* 5, no. 3 (1955): 167–70.

34. O. W. Lang, L. Farber, and F. Yerman, "The 'Stinkometer'—New Tool," *Food Industries* 17, no 1 (1945): 8–9, 116, 118.

35. K. P. Dimick and J. Corse, "Gas Chromatography—A New Method for the Separation and Identification of Volatile Materials in Foods," *Food Technology* 10, no. 8 (1956): 360.

36. W. H. McFadden et al., "Volatiles from Strawberries: II. Combined Mass Spectrometry and Gas Chromatography on Complex Mixtures," *Journal of Chromatography* 18 (1965): 10–19.

37. E. A. Day, D. A. Forss, and S. Patton, "Flavor and Odor Defects of Gamma-Irradiated Skimmilk. II. Identification of Volatile Components by Gas Chromatography and Mass Spectrometry," *Journal of Dairy Science* 40, no. 8 (1957): 932–41.

38. Loren B. Sjöström, "Correlation of Objective-Subjective Methods as Applied in the Food Field," in *Correlation of Subjective-Objective Methods in the Study of Odors and Taste*, ed. W. H. Stahl (Philadelphia: American Society for Testing and Materials, 1968), 8.

39. George H. Fuller, R. Steltenkamp, and G. A. Tisserand, "The Gas Chromatograph with Human Sensor: Perfumer Model," *Annals of the New York Academy of Sciences* 116, no. 2 (1964): 711–24.

40. Shapin, "A Taste of Science," 449.

41. Sjöström, "Correlation of Objective-Subjective Methods as Applied in the Food Field," 14.

42. J. R. Magness and George F. Taylor, "An Improved Type of Pressure Tester for the Determination of Fruit Maturity," *United States Department of Agriculture: Department Circular 350* (Washington, D.C.: Government Printing Office, 1925); Alice M. Child and Mary Baldelli, "Press Fluid from Heated Beef Muscle," *Journal of Agricultural Research* 48, no. 12 (1934): 1127–34.

43. Nikolaus N. Volodkevich, "Apparatus for Measurements of Chewing Resistance or Tenderness of Foodstuffs," *Food Technology* 3, no. 2 (1938): 221.

44. Ibid., 221–25.

45. Aaron L. Brody, "Masticatory Properties of Foods by the Strain Gage Denture Tenderometer" (PhD diss., Massachusetts Institute of Technology, 1957), 25–56.

46. Ibid., 11, 184, 220, 232, 240, 244.

47. Elaine Z. Skinner et al., "A Tribute to Dr. Alina Surmacka Szczesniak," *Journal of Texture Studies* 12, no. 2 (1981): ix–xiii.

48. Alina S. Szczesniak, "Texture is a Sensory Property," *Food Quality and Preferences* 13, no. 4 (2002): 215–25. Quotation at 217.

49. For expanded discussion, see Anthony Acciavatti, "Ingestion: The Psychoreology of Everyday Life," *Cabinet* 48 (2012): 12–16; Ingemar Pettersson, "Mechanical Tasting: Sensory Science and the Flavorization of Food Production," *The Senses and Society* 12, no. 3 (2017): 301–16.

50. Anna Krzywoszynska, "Wine Is Not Coca-Cola: Marketization and Taste in Alternative Food Networks," *Agriculture and Human Values* 32, no. 3 (2015): 491–503.

51. David Howes, "Hyperesthesia, or, the Sensual Logic of Late Capitalism," in *Empire of the Senses: The Sensual Culture Reader*, ed. David Howes (Oxford: Berg, 2005), 284.

52. Eric R. Kandel, "The Molecular Biology of Memory Storage: A Dialogue Between Genes and Synapses," Nobel Lecture, December 8, 2000, https://www.nobelprize.org/uploads/2018/06/kandel-lecture.pdf.

53. Jacob Lahne and Christy Spackman highlight the social and economic agency of sensory science by framing it as "sensory labor," see Jacob Lahne and Christy Spackman, "Introduction to Accounting for Taste," *The Senses and Society* 13, no. 1 (2018): 4.

54. Crocker and Platt, "Food Flavors," 184.

55. Bernard H. Smith, "Modern Trends in Flavors," *Food Research* 2, no. 3 (1937): 251.

CHAPTER 3

1. David P. Szatmary, *Rockin' in Time: A Social History of Rock-and-Roll*, 8th ed. (Boston: Pearson, 2014), 244.

2. Simon Frith, *Sound Effects: Youth, Leisure and the Politics of Rock 'n' Roll* (New York: Pantheon, 1981), 31–33.

3. Recording Industry Association of America, "Inside the Recording Industry: A Statistical Overview" (Washington, DC: RIAA, 1985).

4. "Der Staatsfeind Nummer Eins," *Deutschlandfunk*, May 28, 2009, http://www.deutschlandfunk.de/der-staatsfeind-nummer-eins.1295.de.html?dram:article_id=193317.

5. Dieter Wiedemann, "Kulturell-künstlerische Interessen und Verhaltensweisen," in *Die Freizeit der Jugend*, ed. Peter Voß (Berlin: Dietz, 1981), 135.

6. Sven Kube, "Born in the U.S.A. / Made in the G.D.R.: Anglo-American Popular Music and the Westernization of a Communist Record Market" (PhD diss., Florida International University, 2018), 170, 249.

7. Alexei Yurchak, *Everything Was Forever, Until It Was No More: The Last Soviet Generation* (Princeton, NJ: Princeton University Press, 2006), 191.

8. Steffen Könau (music journalist), in discussion with the author, August 2021.

9. Könau, in discussion with the author.

10. Michael Rauhut, *Beat in der Grauzone: DDR-Rock 1964 bis 1972* (Berlin: BasisDruck, 1993), 96.

11. Ole Krüger (amateur musician), in discussion with the author, September 2021.

12. Könau, in discussion with the author.

13. Raymond G. Stokes, *Constructing Socialism: Technology and Change in East Germany, 1945–1990* (Baltimore: Johns Hopkins University Press, 2000), 180–85.

14. Joachim Garten (Director of Technology at VEB Deutsche Schallplatten), in discussion with the author, April 2015.

15. Stephan Trepte, "Erinnerungen" in *Rockszene DDR: Aspekte einer Massenkultur im Sozialismus*, ed. Olaf Leitner (Reinbek, Germany: Rowohlt, 1983), 71–73.

16. Christian "Kuno" Kunert, "Schau mich nicht so schüchtern an, weil ich Dich gut leiden kann: Rock in der DDR," in *Rock Session 2*, ed. Jörg Gülden and Klaus Humann (Reinbek, Germany: Rowohlt, 1978), 203.

17. Krüger, in discussion with the author.

18. Lynn Wheelwright, "Ro-Pat-In Electric Spanish: Granddaddy to the Stars!," *Vintage Guitar Magazine Online*, July 2008, http://www.vintageguitar.com/3588/ro-pat-in-electric-spanish.

19. Richard R. Smith, *The History of Rickenbacker Guitars* (Anaheim, CA: Centerstream Publications, 1987), 9, 12.

20. Paul Oliver, *The Story of the Blues* (Boston: Northeastern University Press, 1998), 192–95.

21. Steve Waksman, *Instruments of Desire: The Electric Guitar and the Shaping of Musical Experience* (Cambridge, MA: Harvard University Press, 1999), 45–46.

22. Tony Bacon, "The British Guitar Embargo: When Brits Were Banned from Buying American," *Reverb*, April 5, 2018, https://reverb.com/news/the-british-guitar-embargo-when-brits-were-banned-from-buying-american.

23. András Simonyi, *Rocking Toward a Free World: When the Stratocaster Beat the Kalashnikov* (New York: Grand Central, 2019), 25.

24. *Flying V*, directed by Peter Hansen (2020; Foresthill, CA: MetalRock Films, 2020), DVD.

25. Volkmar Andrä (record producer), in discussion with the author, September 2021.

26. Klaus Peter Albrecht (record producer), in discussion with the author, September 2021.

27. Sören Marotz, "E-Gitarren aus dem Vogtland: Fotonachlese einer Ausstellung," *Schlaggitarren*, November 2008, *http://www.schlaggitarren.de/home.php?text=historie&kenn=8*.

28. Sören Marotz, "Stromgitarren in der DDR: Die E-Gitarren der Musima," *DDR Museum*, March 5, 2015, https://www.ddr-museum.de/de/blog/archive/stromgitarren-der-ddr-die-e-gitarren-der-musima.

29. Krüger, in discussion with the author.

30. Leitner, *Rockszene DDR*, 63.

31. Rauhut, *Beat in der Grauzone*, 54.

32. Leitner, *Rockszene DDR*, 401.

33. Krüger, in discussion with the author.

34. Timothy W. Ryback, *Rock Around the Bloc: A History of Rock Music in Eastern Europe and the Soviet Union* (New York: Oxford University Press), 56–57.

35. Jeff Chang and DJ Kool Herc, *Can't Stop Won't Stop: A History of the Hip-Hop Generation* (London: Picador, 2005), 17–21.

36. Gordon Reid, "The History of Roland, Part 2: 1979–1985," *Sound on Sound*, December 2004, https://www.soundonsound.com/people/history-roland-part-2.

37. Ikutaro Kakehashi with Robert Olsen, *I Believe in Music: Life Experiences and Thoughts on the Future of Electronic Music by the Founder of the Roland Corporation* (Milwaukee, WI: Hal Leonard, 2002), 62.

38. *808*, directed by Alexander Dunn (2015; Los Angeles, CA: You Know Films, 2016), Stream.

39. Jason Anderson, "Slaves to the Rhythm," *Canadian Broadcasting Corporation News*, November 27, 2008, https://www.cbc.ca/news/entertainment/slaves-to-the-rhythm-1.771508.

40. Chris Norris, "The 808 Heard around the World," *New Yorker*, August 13, 2015, https://www.newyorker.com/culture/culture-desk/the-808-heard-round-the-world.

41. Peter Wells, *A Beginner's Guide to Digital Video* (London: Bloomsbury, 2004), 16.

42. Elias Leight, "8 Ways the 808 Drum Machine Changed Pop Music," *Rolling Stone*, December 6, 2016, https://www.rollingstone.com/music/music-news/8-ways-the-808-drum-machine-changed-pop-music-249148.

43. "Interview mit Amiga," *Melodie und Rhythmus* (April 1980), 4.

44. Könau, in discussion with the author.

45. Andrä, in discussion with the author.

46. Daniel Harrison, "After Sundown: The Beach Boys' Experimental Music" in *Understanding Rock: Essays in Musical Analysis*, ed. John Covach and Graeme M. Boone (New York: Oxford University Press, 1997), 41–43.

47. Albrecht, in discussion with the author.

48. Trevor Pinch and Frank Trocco, *Analog Days: The Invention and Impact of the Moog Synthesizer* (Cambridge, MA: Harvard University Press, 2002), 53–56.

49. Peter Kirn, *The Evolution of Electronic Dance Music* (Milwaukee, WI: Hal Leonard, 2011), 2–8.

50. *Synth Britannia*, directed by Ben Whalley (2009; London: British Broadcasting Corporation, 2009), Stream.

51. David Keenan, "Hypnagogic Pop: Childhood's End," *Wire Magazine*, August 2009, 26.

52. John M. Chowning, "Synthesis of Complex Audio Spectra by Means of Frequency Modulation," *Journal of the Audio Engineering Society* 21, no. 7 (1973): 530.

53. Pinch and Trocco, *Analog Days*, 6.

54. Paul Lehrman, "A Talk with John Chowning Part II: Making Electronics Sing," *Mix Magazine* (March 2005), 26.

55. John Twells, "The 14 Most Important Synths in Electronic Music History and the Musicians Who Use Them," *Fact*, September 2016, https://www.factmag.com/2016/09/15/14-most-important-synths; Jim Betteridge, "Track Record: West End Girls," *International Musician & Recording World*, March 1986, 114–15.

56. Kunert, "Schau mich nicht so schüchtern an," 203.

57. Stokes, *Constructing Socialism*, 166–67.

58. Bernhard Lösener, "Vintage Park: Vermona Synthesizer," *Keyboards*, November 3, 2016, https://www.keyboards.de/equipment/vermona-synthesizer-1983/.

59. Leitner, *Rockszene DDR*, 201–2.

60. Albrecht, in discussion with the author.

61. Jürgen Balitzki, "Rezension: Computer-Karriere," *Melodie und Rhythmus* (December 1982), 18.

62. Robert Andrä, "Karat: Der blaue Planet," (Seminar paper, Humboldt-Universität zu Berlin, 2003), 6–7.

63. Andrä, in discussion with the author.

64. Leitner, *Rockszene DDR*, 200.

CHAPTER 4

I would like to thank Regina Blaszczyk and David Suisman for their helpful comments and suggestions. I would also like to acknowledge the members of the Gender and Sexualities Research Cluster at UCSB who participated in the session where I workshopped these ideas. Special thanks to Uttathya Chattopadhyay, Nicole de Silva, Jarett Henderson, John Majewski, Alice O'Connor, Erika Rappaport, and Sherene Seikaly.

1. Ai Hisano, *Visualizing Taste: How Business Changed the Look of What You Eat* (Cambridge, MA: Harvard University Press, 2019), 1–2.

2. For other analyses of multidimensional processes of sensory knowledge creation, see Regina Lee Blaszczyk, *The Color Revolution* (Cambridge, MA: The MIT Press, 2012) and Regina Lee Blaszczyk and Uwe Spiekermann, eds., *Bright Modernity: Color, Commerce, and Consumer Culture* (London: Palgrave Macmillan, 2017).

3. Vance Packard, *The Hidden Persuaders* (New York: Pocket Book Edition, 1958), 8–9; Lawrence R. Samuel, *Freud on Madison Avenue: Motivation Research and Subliminal Advertising in America* (Philadelphia: University of Pennsylvania Press, 2010), 5, 8, 28–29, 50; Sarah Igo, *The Averaged American: Surveys, Citizens, and the Making of a Mass Public* (Cambridge, MA: Harvard University Press, 2007), 103–49.

4. Samuel, *Freud on Madison Avenue*, 15, 38. For excellent analyses of how Dichter advised clients in other industries, see Erika Rappaport, *A Thirst for Empire: How Tea Shaped the Modern World* (Princeton, NJ: Princeton University Press, 2017), 369–74, 388–90; Laura Shapiro, *Something from the Oven: Reinventing Dinner in 1950s America* (New York: Penguin Books, 2004), 63–64, 75–77; Amy Bentley, *Inventing Baby Food: Taste, Health, and the Industrialization of the American Diet* (Berkeley: University of California Press, 2014), 82–83; and the essays in *Ernest Dichter and Motivation Research: New Perspectives on the Making of Post-War Consumer Culture*, ed. Stefan Schwarzkopf and Rainer Gries (Hampshire, UK: Palgrave Macmillan, 2010).

5. Samuel, *Freud on Madison Avenue*, 30, 32.

6. "Whisky Jitters," *Business Week*, April 12, 1947, 76; "The Whiskey Rebellion," *Fortune* 35 (June 1947): 140.

7. "Ready-Mix Woos the Drinker," *Business Week*, September 17, 1960, 152, 154.

8. Ernest Dichter, "Proposal for a Research Study on the Sales and Advertising Problems of Imperial Whiskey," July 1951, 5, in *American Consumer Culture: Market Research and American Business, 1935–1965*, Adam Matthew Digital, 2014 [hereafter cited as *ACC*]; Ernest Dichter, "A Psy-

chological Survey of the Sales and Advertising Problems of Lord Calvert Whiskey," April 1950, 12, *ACC*.

9. Ernest Dichter, "Sales and Advertising Problems of Lord Calvert Whiskey," 14.

10. Institute for Motivational Research, "A Pilot Study of Certain Aspects of Old Fitzgerald Sales and Advertising," July 1955, 36, *ACC*.

11. Institute for Motivational Research, "A Motivational Research Study on the Sales and Advertising Problems of Old Cabin Still," June 1956, 99, *ACC*.

12. Dichter, "Sales and Advertising Problems of Lord Calvert Whiskey," 24–25.

13. Ernest Dichter, "A Preliminary Psychological Study of Consumer Reactions to Three Feathers' Merchandising and Advertising," June 1949, 5, *ACC*.

14. Ernest Dichter, "Three Feathers' Merchandising and Advertising," 5.

15. Institute for Research in Mass Motivations, "Old Fitzgerald Bourbon Progress Report," 1954, 15, *ACC*.

16. "Calvert Taste Test Kit," c. 1953 (in author's possession); Sales Promotion Department, *The Calvert Taste Test Kit: Getting Down to Cases* (New York: Calvert Distillers Corporation, 1953), Box 200, Series III, accession 2173, Seagram Museum Collection, Hagley Museum and Library, Wilmington, DE [hereafter SMC].

17. Reid Mitenbuler, *Bourbon Empire: The Past and Future of America's Whiskey* (New York: Penguin Books, 2015), 217.

18. Ernest Dichter, "A Psychological Research Study on the Sales and Advertising Problems of Schenley Reserve," May 1953, 13, 51, *ACC*.

19. Dichter, "Sales and Advertising Problems of Schenley Reserve," 25–26.

20. Dichter, "Sales and Advertising Problems of Schenley Reserve," 18.

21. Dichter, "Sales and Advertising Problems of Schenley Reserve," 15, 24, 32, 57, 76–84.

22. Melissa L. Caldwell, "Digestive Politics in Russia: Feeling the Sensorium Beyond the Palate," *Food and Foodways* 22, nos. 1–2 (2014): 112–35 (quotations, 115, 121).

23. Dichter, "Sales and Advertising Problems of Schenley Reserve," 48–49.

24. Dichter, "Sales and Advertising Problems of Schenley Reserve," 32.

25. David E. Sutton, *Remembrances of Repasts: An Anthropology of Food and Memory* (New York: Berg, 2001), 90, 97.

26. Carolyn Korsemeyer, *Making Sense of Taste: Food and Philosophy* (Ithaca, NY: Cornell University Press, 1999); Jeffrey M. Pilcher, "The Embodied Imagination in Recent Writings on Food History," *American Historical Review* 121 (June 2016): 861–87; Patricia Parkhurst Ferguson, "The Senses of Taste," *American Historical Review* 116 (April 2011): 371–84; Gerard J. Fitzgerald and Gabriella M. Petrick, "In Good Taste: Rethinking American History with Our Palates," *Journal of American History* 95 (September 2008): 392–404; Charles C. Ludington, "The Standard of Taste Debate: How Do We Decide What Tastes Best?" in *Food Fights: How History Matters to Contemporary Food Debates*, ed. Charles C. Ludington and Matthew Morse Booker (Chapel Hill: University of North Carolina Press, 2019); David Courtwright, *The Age of Addiction: How Bad Habits Became Big Business* (Cambridge, MA: Belknap Press of Harvard University Press, 2019), 186; Hisano, *Visualizing Taste*.

27. Sutton, *Remembrance of Repasts*, 17.

28. Michael M. Cohen, "Jim Crow's Drug War: Race, Coca Cola, and the Southern Origins of Drug Prohibition," *Southern Cultures* 12 (Fall 2006): 55–79; Daniel Okrent, *Last Call: The Rise and Fall of Prohibition* (New York: Scribner, 2010), 42–46.

29. For one such example, see Wanda Webster, "Army Jim Crow in Texas Assailed," *Chicago Defender*, July 24, 1943, 14.

30. For an analysis of the gendering of *Gourmet*, see Megan J. Elias, *Food on the Page: Cookbooks and American Culture* (Philadelphia: University of Pennsylvania Press, 2017), 72–104.

31. "Betting on Blends," *Business Week*, September 22, 1951, 50; "The Trend to Straights Quickens," *Business Week*, January 22, 1955, 42–44; Ira U. Cobleigh, "Of Bonds and Blends," *Commercial and Financial Chronicle* 192 (November 24, 1955), 4.

32. Institute for Research in Mass Motivations, "Old Fitzgerald Bourbon Progress Report," 4, 9.

33. Institute for Research in Mass Motivations, "Old Fitzgerald Bourbon Progress Report," 3, 5; Dichter "Motivational Research Study on . . . Old Cabin Still," 10–11, 13, 65.

34. Institute for Motivational Research, "Motivational Research Study on . . . Old Cabin Still," 21–23, 26–27.

35. Institute for Motivational Research, "Motivational Research Study on . . . Old Cabin Still," 17, 23–25.

36. For more on how mass marketers use "product complements" to connect goods with particular class identities or cultural lifestyles, see Grant McCracken, *Culture and Consumption: New Approaches to the Symbolic Character of Consumer Goods and Activities* (Bloomington: Indiana University Press, 1990), chapter 8.

37. Institute for Motivational Research, "Motivational Research Study on . . . Old Cabin Still," 18.

38. Institute for Motivational Research, "Pilot Study of . . . Old Fitzgerald Sales and Advertising," 12, 14; Institute for Motivational Research, "A Pilot Survey on Attitudes Toward Scotch Whiskey," September 1961, 12, 21, *ACC*.

39. In the mid-twentieth century, Black marketers also struggled to persuade white-owned firms to cultivate the Black consumer market. See Robert E. Weems, *Desegregating the Dollar: African American Consumerism in the Twentieth Century* (New York: New York University Press, 1998); Susannah Walker, *Style and Status: Selling Beauty to African American Women, 1920–1975* (Louisville: University of Kentucky Press, 2007); Jason Chambers, *Madison Avenue and the Color Line: African Americans in the Advertising Industry* (Philadelphia: University of Pennsylvania Press, 2009); Brenna Wynn Green, *Represented: The Black Imagemakers Who Reimagined African American Citizenship* (Philadelphia: University of Pennsylvania Press, 2019), 200–13; and Adam Green, *Selling the Race: Culture, Community, and Black Chicago, 1940–1955* (Chicago: University of Chicago Press, 2007), chapter 4.

40. Institute for Motivational Research, "Proposal for a Motivational Research Study Aimed at Expanding the Sales Leadership of Old Crow Bourbon," August 1958, 2, 4, 10, *ACC*; Institute for Motivational Research, "An Outline Proposal for a Motivational Research Study on the Sales, Advertising, and Packaging Problems of Lord Calvert Whiskey," November 1955, 2–4, *ACC*.

41. For more on the connections between synesthesia and the evocative power of food, see Sutton, *Remembrances of Repasts* and David E. Sutton, "Food and the Senses," *Annual Review of Anthropology* 39 (2010): 209–23.

42. Institute for Motivational Research, "Pilot Study of . . . Old Fitzgerald Sales and Advertising," 21.

43. Institute for Motivational Research, "A Motivational Research Study of the Market Potential for Vat 69 Classic Light," June 1963, 30–31, *ACC*.

44. Institute for Motivational Research, "Pilot Study of . . . Old Fitzgerald Sales and Advertising," 30.

45. Dichter, "Motivational Research Study of . . . Vat 69 Classic Light," 29–30.

46. Sarah Hand Meacham, *Every Home a Distillery: Alcohol, Gender, and Technology in the Colonial Chesapeake* (Baltimore: Johns Hopkins University Press, 2009), 133–34.

47. Elaine Parsons, *Manhood Lost: Fallen Drunkards and Redeeming Women in the Nineteenth-Century United States* (Baltimore: Johns Hopkins University Press, 2003), 63, 69–74.

48. Dichter, "A Psychological Survey of . . . Lord Calvert Whiskey," 39.

49. "Drinkers Seek the 'Light,'" *Business Week*, February 23, 1963, 81.

50. Adam Mack, "The Senses in the Marketplace: Commercial Aesthetics for a Suburban Age," in *A Cultural History of the Sense in the Modern Age*, ed. David Howes (New York: Bloomsbury Academic, 2019), 77–100.

51. Institute for Research in Mass Motivations, "Old Fitzgerald Bourbon Progress Report," 21.

52. Dichter, "Pilot Survey on Attitudes Toward Scotch Whiskey," 41.

53. Alex Gochfeld, "Preliminary Findings on Scotch Liquor Survey," August 23, 1961, 4, *ACC*.

54. Korsemeyer, *Making Sense of Taste*, 101, 143.

55. Richard De Grandpre, *The Cult of Pharmacology: How America Became the World's Most Troubled Drug Culture* (Durham, NC: Duke University Press, 2006).

56. Institute for Motivational Research, "Creative Memorandum on Liquor," October 1962, 22–23, *ACC*.

57. Timothy Leary, the psychologist and psychedelic researcher, coined the term "set and setting." For more examples of how "set and setting" influence the effects of food-drugs, see Courtwright, *Age of Addiction*, 186.

58. Packard, *Hidden Persuaders*, 25.

59. Samuel, *Freud on Madison Avenue*, 57.

60. Samuel, *Freud on Madison Avenue*, 66.

61. Dichter, "A Psychological Survey of . . . Lord Calvert Whiskey," 114.

62. Dichter, "Proposal for a Research Study on . . . Imperial Whiskey," 4.

63. Dichter, "Sales and Advertising Problems of Schenley Reserve," 52.

64. Dichter, "A Psychological Survey of . . . Lord Calvert Whiskey," 36, 39.

65. Lori Rotskoff, *Love on the Rocks: Men, Women, and Alcohol in Post-World War II America* (Chapel Hill: University of North Carolina Press, 2002); Michelle L. McClelland, *Lush Ladies: Gender, Alcohol, and Medicine in Modern America* (New Brunswick, NJ: Rutgers University Press, 2017).

66. Dichter, "A Psychological Survey of . . . Lord Calvert Whiskey," 39.

67. James Gilbert, *Men in the Middle: Searching for Masculinity in the 1950s* (Chicago: University of Chicago Press, 2005), 34–61; David Riesman, Nathan Glazer, and Reuel Denney, *The Lonely Crowd: A Study of the Changing American Character* (New Haven, CT: Yale University Press, 1950); Barbara Ehrenreich, *The Hearts of Men: American Dreams and the Flight from Commitment* (New York: Anchor Books, 1983), 29–40.

68. Institute for Motivational Research, "Proposal for a Motivational Research Study on . . . Lord Calvert Whiskey," 4–5.

69. "Drinkers Seek the 'Light,'" 81.

70. Gochfeld, "Preliminary Findings of Scotch Liquor Survey," 3.

71. Jesse Berrett, "Feeding the Organization Man: Diet and Masculinity in Postwar America," *Journal of Social History* 30 (Summer 1997): 808; Carolyn de la Pena, *Empty Pleasures: The History of Artificial Sweeteners from Saccharin to Splenda* (Chapel Hill: University of North Carolina Press, 2010); R. Marie Griffith, *Born Again Bodies: Flesh and Spirit in American Christian-*

ity (Berkeley: University of California Press, 2004); Peter Stearns, *Fat History: Bodies and Beauty in the Modern West* (New York: New York University Press, 2002).

72. "Drinkers Seek the 'Light,'" 81.

73. Peter Bart, "'Soft Whisky' Campaign to Open," *New York Times*, April 19, 1963, Calvert Extra Meets the Press Scrapbook, March–May 1963, Box 800, Record Group 2, SMC.

74. Jack Crellin, "Calvert Introduces a New 'Soft' Whisky," *Detroit News*, March 14, 1962, Calvert Extra Meets the Press Scrapbook, SMC.

75. For earlier examples of this advertising tactic, see Lisa Jacobson, "Navigating the Boundaries of Respectability and Desire: Seagram's Advertising and the Muddled Meanings of Moderation After Repeal," *Social History of Drugs and Alcohol* 26 (Summer 2012): 122–46.

76. "New Calvert whisky features 'soft taste,'" *Newark Star Ledger*, March 31, 1963, Calvert Extra Meets the Press Scrapbook, SMC.

77. Calvert Extra advertisement, *Time*, May 14, 1965, Calvert Extra advertisements, 1960s, Box 86, Series III, SMC.

78. "Ready-Mix Woos the Drinker," *Business Week*, September 17, 1960, 152, 154.

79. Steven Shapin, "The Tastes of Wine: Towards a Cultural History," *Rivista di Estetica* 51 (March 2012): 49–94; Steven Shapin, "Changing Tastes: How Things Tasted in the Early Modern Period and How They Taste Now," Hans Rausing Lecture 2011, Uppsala Universitet, Uppsala, Sweden, Salvia Småskrifter, no. 14, 7–48, https://www.idehist.uu.se/digitalAssets/636/c_636622-l_3-k_salvia_2011.pdf.

80. Ludington, "The Standard of Taste Debate," 102. See also S. Margot Finn, *Discriminating Taste: How Class Anxiety Created the American Food Revolution* (New Brunswick, NJ: Rutgers University Press, 2017).

CHAPTER 5

This work was supported by the Colombian Ministry of Science, Technology and Innovation through a postdoctoral fellowship at Universidad Nacional de Colombia [Contract 838-2020]. I thank Regina Lee Blaszczyk and David Suisman for their critical reading and generous editing.

1. As Erica Fretwell describes, psychophysics only appears sparingly as a precursor to experimental psychology in histories of pragmatism and psychoanalysis. Erica Fretwell, *Sensory Experiments: Psychophysics, Race, and the Aesthetic of Feeling* (Durham, NC: Duke University Press, 2020). Today, it is difficult for a scientist to build a career in psychophysics, and as I was told during my fieldwork among some scientists there is the perception that rigorous training in psychophysics is not fundamental to carry out experiments with humans.

2. Edwin Boring, *Sensation and Perception in the History of Experimental Psychology* (New York: Appleton-Century-Crofts, 1942), 36.

3. For a detailed account of the development of sensory methods since the 1930s see Ingemar Pettersson in this volume; and Nadia Berenstein, "Flavor Added: Synthetic Flavors, the Industrialization of Food, and the Sciences of Flavor in America" (PhD diss., University of Pennsylvania, 2017), chapter 3. For how, since the 1930s, the modern marketplace, as represented by the figure of the supermarket in the United States, set to engage all five senses in their commercial strategy, see Adam Mack, "'Speaking of Tomatoes': Supermarkets, the Senses, and Sexual Fantasy in Modern America," *Journal of Social History* 43, no. 4 (2010): 815–42.

4. Recent historical studies have examined the central role of sensory attributes and sensory skills for the making and commerce of particular commodities and industries. See Regina Lee Blaszczyk, *The Color Revolution* (Cambridge, MA: The MIT Press, 2012); Ai Hisano, *Visualizing Taste: How Business Changed the Look of What You Eat* (Cambridge, MA: Harvard University Press, 2019); Berenstein, "Flavor Added"; David Singerman, "Inventing Purity in the Atlantic Sugar World, 1860–1930" (PhD diss., Massachusetts Institute of Technology, 2014).

5. Steven Shapin, "The Sciences of Subjectivity," *Social Studies of Science* 42, no. 2 (April 2012): 170–84, 177. For ethnographic or historical accounts of sciences and expert practices of subjectivity see for example: Alexios Tsigkas, "Tasting Ceylon Tea: Aesthetic Judgment Beyond 'Good Taste,'" *Food, Culture & Society* 22, no. 2 (2019): 152–67; Ella Butler, "Tasting Off-Flavors: Food Science, Sensory Knowledge and the Consumer Sensorium," *The Senses and Society* 13, no. 1 (2018): 75–88; Jacob Lahne, "Standard Sensations: The Production of Objective Experience from Industrial Technique," *The Senses and Society* 13, no. 1 (2018): 6–18; Ingemar Pettersson, "Mechanical Tasting: Sensory Science and the Flavorization of Food Production," *The Senses and Society* 12, no. 3 (2017): 301–16; Christy Spackman, "Perfumer, Chemist, Machine: Gas Chromatography and the Industrial Search to 'Improve' Flavor," *The Senses and Society* 13, no. 1 (2018): 41–59; Ana María Ulloa, "The Aesthetic Life of Artificial Flavors," *The Senses and Society* 13, no. 1 (2018): 60–74.

6. Carolyn Korsmeyer, *Making Sense of Taste: Food and Philosophy* (Ithaca, NY: Cornell University Press, 1999); Robert Jutte, *A History of the Senses: From Antiquity to Cyberspace* (Cambridge, UK: Polity Press, 2005); Ophelia Deroy, "The Power of Tastes: Reconciling Science and Subjectivity" in *Questions of Taste: The Philosophy of Wine*, ed. Barry Smith (New York: Oxford University Press, 2007).

7. Erica Fretwell, *Sensory Experiments*, 6–12.

8. Johnathan Crary, *Techniques of the Observer: On Vision and Modernity in the Nineteenth Century* (Cambridge, MA: The MIT Press, 1992), 70.

9. Fechner's biographers tell of a deep nervous crisis, initiated by chronic demand and exhaustion in 1839, that made him retire from his professional duties in the physics department for five years. Sensitivity to light (he induced damage to his eyes after prolonged contemplation of the sun through colored glasses), impaired hearing, and an accompanying mental illness that came with mania, psychosis, and depression, were his most acerbated symptoms. It was after overcoming this crisis that Fechner wrote in 1860 his famous *Elements of Psychophysics*. For a full account of Fechner's life, see Michael Heidelberger, *Nature from Within: Gustav Theodor Fechner and His Psychophysical Worldview* (Pittsburgh, PA: University of Pittsburgh Press, 2004).

10. Ruth Benschop and Douwe Draaisma, "In Pursuit of Precision: The Calibration of Minds and Machines in Late Nineteenth-Century Psychology," *Annals of Science* 57, no. 1 (2000): 1–25.

11. Singerman, *Inventing Purity in the Atlantic Sugar World.*

12. Singerman, *Inventing Purity in the Atlantic Sugar World.*

13. David Howes, "The Senses: Polysensoriality," in *A Companion to the Anthropology of the Body and Embodiment*, ed. F. E. Mascia-Lees (Oxford: Blackwell, 2011), 435–50. See also Graham Richards, "Getting a Result: The Expedition's Psychological Research 1898–1913," in *Cambridge and the Torres Strait: Centenary Essays on the 1898 Anthropological Expedition*, ed. A. Herle and S. Rouse (Cambridge, UK: Cambridge University Press, 1998), 158–80.

14. George Gescheider, *Psychophysics: The Fundamentals*, 3rd ed. (Mahwah, NJ: Lawrence Erlbaum Associates, 1997).

15. Weber, founding father of experimental psychology, conducted several studies on sensation and touch and came up with the concept of just-noticeable difference to measure

differences in weight. Weber's influence on Gustav Fechner was crucial for the development of psychophysics.

16. Stanley Stevens, "To Honor Fechner and Repeal His Law," *Science, New Series*, 133, no. 3446 (1961): 80–86; Stanley Stevens, "Quantifying the Sensory Experience," in *Mind, Matter, and Method: Essays in Philosophy and Science in Honor of Herbert Feigl*, ed. Paul K. Feyerabend and Grover Maxwell (Minneapolis: University of Minnesota Press, 1966), 215–36.

17. Stanley Stevens, "On the New Psychophysics," *Scandinavian Journal of Psychology* 1 (1960): 27–35.

18. Stanley Stevens, "Measurement, Psychophysics and Utility," in *Measurement: Definitions and Theories*, ed. C. W. Churchman and P. Ratoosh (New York: John Wiley, 1959), 25.

19. Howard Moskowitz, "The Intertwining of Psychophysics and Sensory Analysis: Historical Perspectives and Future Opportunities—A Personal View," *Food Quality and Preference* 14 (2002): 88.

20. Stevens, "Quantifying the Sensory Experience," 230.

21. Deborah Coon, "Standardizing the Subject: Experimental Psychologists, Introspection, and the Quest for a Technoscientific Ideal" *Technology and Culture* 34, no. 4, (1993): 757–83.

22. Fretwell, *Sensory Experiments*, 22.

23. Henry Lawless, "Olfactory Psychophysics," in *Tasting and Smelling: Handbook of Perception and Cognition*, ed. Gary Beauchamp and Linda Bartoshuk, 2nd ed. (San Diego, CA: Academic Press, 1997).

24. Stanley Stevens, "The Direct Estimation of Sensory Magnitudes: Loudness," *American Journal of Psychology*, 69, no. 1, (1956): 1–25.

25. Moskowitz, "The Intertwining of Psychophysics and Sensory Analysis."

26. Howard Moskowitz, *Consumer Testing and Evaluation of Personal Care Products* (New York: Marcel Dekker, Inc, 1995).

27. Edwin Boring, "A History of Introspection," in *Psychological Bulletin* 50, no. 3 (1953): 182.

28. Taste panels developed within the academia-industry nexus, as part of research on food acceptance carried out at the U.S. Army Quartermaster Corps—the army branch in charge of logistics and food service in the second half of the twentieth century. The laboratory attracted prominent researchers (mainly statisticians, psychologists, and physiologists) in charge of developing a scientific basis for sensory evaluation, becoming one of the first places in which a panel facility was constructed (with booths and special lights) for sensory studies carried out with experts, trained panelists, and consumers. Moreover, the army's food research program housed a strong Behavioral Sciences Division that allowed for the coupling of basic psychophysics and food acceptance research. For a detailed history of the making of the flavor profile and the use of taste panels see Nadia Berenstein, "Designing Flavors for Mass Consumption," *The Senses and Society* 13, no. 1 (2018): 19–40. See also Pettersson in this volume.

29. Christy Spackman and Jacob Lahne, "Sensory Labor: Considering the Work of Taste in the Food System," *Food, Culture & Society* 22, no. 2 (2019): 142–51. See also Spackman, "Perfumer, Chemist, Machine."

30. See Fabian Muniesa and Anne-Sophie Trébuchet-Breitwiller, "Becoming a Measuring Instrument," *Journal of Cultural Economy* 3, no. 3 (2010): 321–37; Spackman, "Perfumer, Chemist, Machine"; Nadia Berenstein, "Flavor Added," chapter 3.

31. David Howes, "The Science of Sensory Evaluation: An Ethnographic Critique," in *The Social Life of Materials: Studies in Materials and Society*, ed. Adam Drazin and Susanne Küchler (London: Bloomsbury, 2015), 81–98; Ella Butler, "Mouth Work: Bodily Action in Sensory Science," *Food, Culture & Society* 22, no. 2 (2019): 224–36; Lahne, "Standard Sensations."

32. Sarah Besky, "Tea as Hero Crop? Embodied Algorithms and Industrial Reform in India," *Science as Culture* 26, no. 1 (2016): 1–21.

33. Lahne, "Standard Sensations."

CHAPTER 6

1. "Kennedy to Press Supersonic Plane for Airline Flights," *New York Times* (hereafter *NYT*), June 6, 1963; "The Russians Lead with the SST," *NYT*, January 5, 1969. On the moon landing, see, e.g., Roger D. Launius, *Reaching for the Moon: A Short History of the Space Race* (New Haven, CT: Yale University Press, 2019).

2. David Suisman, "The American Environmental Movement's Lost Victory: The Fight Against Sonic Booms," *Public Historian* 37, no. 4 (November 2015): 120.

3. David Suisman, "The Oklahoma City Sonic Boom Experiment and the Politics of Supersonic Aviation," *Radical History Review*, no. 121 (January 2015): 171.

4. "Price of SST," *NYT*, August 30, 1967.

5. The most comprehensive analysis appears in Mel Horwitch, *Clipped Wings: The American SST Conflict* (Cambridge, MA: The MIT Press, 1982). Other notable accounts include Erik Conway, *High-Speed Dreams: NASA and the Technopolitics of Supersonic Transportation, 1945–1999* (Baltimore: Johns Hopkins University Press, 2005); and James R. Hansen, "What Went Wrong? Some New Insights into the Cancellation of the American SST Program," in *From Airship to Airbus: The History of Civil and Commercial Aviation*, ed. William Leary (Washington, DC: Smithsonian Institution Press, 1995), 1:168–89.

6. On leadership in aviation since World War II and balance of trade, see "Kennedy to Press Supersonic Plane for Airline Flights." On "Another Sputnik," see, e.g., "Air Experts Back Supersonic Plane," *NYT*, January 28, 1960; "Who Will Win the Supersonic Race," *NYT*, August 23, 1964. On costs, see "The Russians Lead with the SST."

7. "Kennedy to Press Supersonic Plane for Airline Flights."

8. *Mission: Sonic Boom* (N.p.: United States Air Force and United States Navy, 1959), https://archive.org/details/MissionSonicBoom.

9. See, e.g., "B-58 Sets 3 Records in Crossing U.S. Twice in 4 Hours 42 Minutes," *NYT*, March 6, 1962.

10. Curt Kanow to William Proxmire, February 14, 1962, box 168, folder 65, William Proxmire Papers, Wisconsin Historical Society. Proxmire's papers contain scores of letters in this vein.

11. Dwight Eisenhower, "Farewell Address," January 17, 1961, American Experience, PBS, https://www.pbs.org/wgbh/americanexperience/features/eisenhower-farewell/.

12. "There's a Ssst, a Boom and a Lot of Bah," *Washington Post*, June 11, 1967.

13. "Boeing's Winning Bid on SST Snapped a Long Losing Streak," *Los Angeles Times*, July 10, 1967.

14. Horwitch, *Clipped Wings*, 72–73.

15. Suisman, "The Oklahoma City Sonic Boom Experiment," 173–85 passim.

16. "There's a Ssst, a Boom and a Lot of Bah"; Horwitch, *Clipped Wings*, 143.

17. *Teacher's Guide for SST..T..T (Sound, Sense, Today, Tomorrow, Thereafter)* (Washington, D.C.: Federal Aviation Administration, 1969); *Milwaukee Sentinel*, June 24, 1971; "Supersonic Teaching," *Time*, February 21, 1972.

18. Horwitch, *Clipped Wings*, 280–81. George C. Eads called Magruder "an excellent salesman," quoted in Henry Lenhart, Jr., "Transportation Report: SST Foes Confident of Votes to Clip

Program's Wings Again Before Spring," *National Journal* 3, no. 2 (January 9, 1971): 47; "hell of a presentation" from George Alderson, interview by David Suisman, September 25, 2011; Joyce (Teitz) Wood, interview by David Suisman, May 4, 2012; "William Magruder, Headed SST Project," *NYT*, September 12, 1977.

19. *You and Me . . . and the SST*, produced by Boeing Company (ca. 1970), https://www.youtube.com/watch?v=73ohKzBgu6c.

20. For a summary of the political contest over the SST ca. 1970–71, see, e.g., Joel Primack and Frank Von Hippel, "Scientists, Politics and SST: A Critical Review," *Bulletin of the Atomic Scientists* 28, no. 4 (April 1972): 24–30. On Earth Day, see Adam Rome, *The Genius of Earth Day: How a 1970 Teach-in Unexpectedly Made the First Green Generation* (New York: Hill & Wang, 2013). On Earth Day's impact on the SST debate: George Alderson, interview; and George Liebmann, interview by David Suisman, May 14, 2012.

21. Suisman, "The American Environmental Movement's Lost Victory," esp. 122–29.

22. See John M. Picker, *Victorian Soundscapes* (New York: Oxford University Press, 2003); Emily Thompson, *The Soundscape of Modernity: Architectural Acoustics and the Culture of Listening in America, 1900–1933* (Cambridge, MA: The MIT Press, 2002); Raymond W. Smilor, "Cacophony at 34th and 6th: The Noise Problem in America, 1900–1930," *American Studies* 18, no. 1 (1977): 23–38; Raymond W. Smilor, "Toward an Environmental Perspective: The Anti-Noise Campaign, 1893–1932," in *Pollution and Reform in American Cities, 1870–1930*, ed. Martin V. Melosi (Austin: University of Texas Press, 1980), 135–51; Karin Bijsterveld, *Mechanical Sound: Technology, Culture, and Public Problems of Noise in the Twentieth Century* (Cambridge, MA: The MIT Press, 2008), esp. 91–136.

23. For broader histories of noise, see Hillel Schwartz, *Making Noise: From Babel to the Big Bang and Beyond* (New York: Zone Books, 2011); Mike Goldsmith, *Discord: The Story of Noise* (Oxford: Oxford University Press, 2012); David Hendy, *Noise: A Human History of Sound and Listening* (New York: Ecco, 2014).

24. Had commercial supersonic aviation developed as planned, sonic booms would have touched hundreds of millions of Americans from coast to coast. William Shurcliff estimated that "a typical town [anywhere in the continental United States] would be struck by about 10 to 50 sonic booms per day." William A. Shurcliff, *S/S/T and Sonic Boom Handbook* (New York: Ballantine Books, 1970), 53. See also the map on 54–55.

25. Stuart Hall and Doreen Massey, "Interpreting the Crisis: Doreen Massey and Stuart Hall Discuss Ways of Understanding the Current Crisis," *Soundings*, no. 44 (Spring 2010): 57. For a useful prolegomenon to conjunctural analysis, see Jeremy Gilbert, "This Conjuncture: For Stuart Hall," *New Formations: A Journal of Culture/Theory/Politics* 96, no. 1 (2019): 5–37.

26. Sarah E. Igo, *The Known Citizen: A History of Privacy in Modern America* (Cambridge, MA: Harvard University Press, 2018), 152–67; *Griswold v. Connecticut*, 381 U.S. 479 (1965).

27. John Neary, "The Big Snoop: Electronic Snooping, Insidious Invasions of Privacy," *Life*, May 20, 1966, 38–43.

28. Igo, *The Known Citizen*, 67–74; Samuel D. Warren and Louis D. Brandeis, "The Right to Privacy," *Harvard Law Review* 4, no. 5 (1890): 193–220; *Olmstead v. United States*, 277 U.S. 438 (1928); *Katz v. United States*, 389 U.S. 347 (1967). *Katz*, it should be noted, was not the last word on sound, intimacy, and the government. The following year, the Congress passed the Omnibus Crime Control and Safe Streets Act the following year, which restored legal authority for wiretapping but with much stricter limitations than had existed previously. On *Katz*, see, e.g., Robert F. Scoular, "Wiretapping and Eavesdropping Constitutional Development from *Olm-*

stead to *Katz*," *Saint Louis University Law Journal* 12 (1967–1968): 513–49. On the history of wiretapping, see Brian Hochman, *The Listeners: A History of Wiretapping in the United States* (Cambridge, MA: Harvard University Press, 2022).

29. Christopher Sellers, "Body, Place and the State: The Makings of an 'Environmentalist' Imaginary in the Post-World War II U.S.," *Radical History Review*, no. 74 (1999): 31–64, esp. 32–34 and 59n5. Sellers's use of the term "environmental imaginary" draws on Richard Peet and Michael Watts, "Towards a Theory of Liberation Ecology," in *Liberation Ecologies: Environment, Development, Social Movements*, ed. Richard Peet and Michael Watts (New York: Routledge, 1996), 267–68.

30. Rachel Carson, *Silent Spring* (Boston: Houghton Mifflin, 1962).

31. On Fluxus and Lucier, see, e.g., Douglas Kahn, *Noise, Water, Meat: A History of Sound in the Arts* (Cambridge MA: The MIT Press, 2001), 224–40; Brandon LaBelle, *Background Noise: Perspectives on Sound Art*, 2nd ed. (New York: Bloomsbury, 2015), 49–66, 125–30.

32. R. Murray Schafer, *The New Soundscape: A Handbook for the Modern Music Teacher* (Don Mills, Ontario: BMI Canada, 1969); R. Murray Schafer, *The Tuning of the World* (New York: Knopf, 1977); Ari Y. Kelman, "Rethinking the Soundscape: A Critical Genealogy of a Key Term in Sound Studies," *The Senses and Society* 5, no. 2 (2010): 212–34.

33. "Noise Control Here Is Aim of New Group," *NYT*, January 9, 1967.

34. "Symposium Today to Study Noise Pollution Rise," *NYT*, February 28, 1969.

35. Theodore Berland, *The Fight for Quiet* (Englewood Cliffs, NJ: Prentice-Hall, 1971); Robert Alex Baron, *The Tyranny of Noise* (New York: St. Martin's Press, 1970); Henry Still, *In Quest of Quiet: Meeting the Menace of Noise Pollution: Call to Citizen Action* (Harrisburg, PA: Stackpole Books, 1970); "The Tyranny of Noise," *NYT*, November 29, 1970; "Noise Pollution: Symptom or Disease?" *Wall Street Journal*, December 2, 1970.

36. The phrase "national resource" was the *Post*'s, not Udall's. See "Would SST Peril U.S. Tranquility?" *Washington Post*, December 20, 1967; "Udall Begins Study of 'Noise Pollution,'" *NYT*, December 21, 1967; "News in Brief," *Science* 158, no. 3809 (December 29, 1967): 1655; John C. Calhoun, Jr., *Report of the Secretary of the Interior of the Special Study Group on Noise and Sonic Boom in Relation to Man* (Washington, D.C.: Department of the Interior, November 4, 1968).

37. "Excessive Noise Termed Unsuspected Health Peril," *NYT*, June 23, 1966; "Park Ridge Supports Bill Against Jet Noise," *Chicago Tribune*, February 18, 1968; "House Votes for Curbs on Plane Noise," *Chicago Tribune*, June 11, 1968.

38. "Industrial Headache," *Wall Street Journal*, June 14, 1972.

39. "Philadelphia Noise Called a Problem for Bicentennial," *NYT*, April 30, 1972.

40. "Highway Traffic Noise," Federal Highway Administration, accessed July 19, 2016, http://www.fhwa.dot.gov/environment/noise/.

41. "Panel Urges Rules on Noise Pollution," *NYT*, March 21, 1971; "New Standards to Fight Noise Pollution Urged," *Los Angeles Times*, March 21, 1971; "Fight Noise Pollution, U.S. Urged," *Chicago Tribune*, March 21, 1971.

42. "2 U.S. Agencies Form Noise Abatement Office," *NYT*, October 24, 1971; "Noise-Pollution Bill Sent to Nixon at Last Minute," *Wall Street Journal*, October 19, 1972.

43. "Clamor Against Noise Rises Around the Globe," *NYT*, September 3, 1972.

44. "The Next Noise You Hear," *Wall Street Journal*, April 26, 1966.

45. Quoted in Joel Primack and Frank Von Hippel, *Advice and Dissent: Scientists in the Political Arena* (New York: Basic Books, 1974), 17.

46. See, e.g., "Showdown for the SST," *NYT*, November 28, 1970; "Senate Bars Funds for SST, 51-46," *NYT*, March 25, 1971; "Twin Towers of Power," *Seattle Times*, September 29, 1996.

47. See miscellaneous documents in Box 45, Folder 16, Henry S. Reuss Papers, Wisconsin Historical Society; "Blame for the SST Defeat: A Search for Scapegoats," *National Journal* 3, no. 2 (January 9, 1971): 54–55.

48. William Proxmire, *Report from Wasteland: America's Military-Industrial Complex* (New York: Praeger, 1970). Other books condemning the military-industrial complex published that year include Seymour Melman, *Pentagon Capitalism: The Political Economy of War* (New York: McGraw-Hill, 1970), and Sidney Lens, *The Military-Industrial Complex* (Philadelphia, PA: Pilgrim Press, 1970). For a contrasting view see John Stanley Baumgartner, *The Lonely Warriors: Case for the Military-Industrial Complex* (Los Angeles, CA: Nash, 1970). A review of all four of these books appeared in "Report from Wasteland," *NYT*, May 24, 1970.

49. Henry Lenhart, Jr., "Transportation Report: SST Foes Confident of Votes to Clip Program's Wings Again Before Spring," *National Journal* 3, no. 2 (January 9, 1971): 43–58; John Lear, "Teaching in the Big School," *Saturday Review* 54, no. 1 (January 2, 1971): 63–66.

50. "Federal Jet Noise Control Needed," *Los Angeles Times*, February 12, 1968; "Transport News: Air Noise Dispute," *NYT*, February 26, 1968; "Pilots' Group Quits Noise Control Unit; 3d to Leave in Year," *NYT*, July 10, 1968.

51. Horwitch, *Clipped Wings*, 265, 286–87; "Private Interests Behind the SST: Serious Gaps in a United Front," *National Journal* 3, no. 2 (January 9, 1971): 52–53; Hansen, "What Went Wrong," 1:168–89, esp. 177–78.

52. Brock Evans, "Environmental Campaigner: From the Northwest Forests to the Halls of Congress," an oral history conducted in 1982 by Ann Lage, in *Building the Sierra Club's National Lobbying Program 1967–1981* (Berkeley, CA: Regional Oral History Office, The Bancroft Library, 1985), 132–33.

53. Gary Soucie, interview by David Suisman, August 7, 2011.

54. "Senate Bars Funds for SST, 51-46," *NYT*, March 25, 1971.

55. For a breakdown of appropriations over the entire life of the SST project, see "Congress Ends U.S. Funding of Supersonic Aircraft," in *CQ Almanac 1971*, vol. 27, *CQ Almanac Online Edition* (Washington, D.C., United States: Congressional Quarterly, 1972).

56. See Howard Moon, *Soviet SST: The Techno-Politics of The Tupolev-144* (New York: Orion, 1989).

57. Kenneth Owen, *Concorde and the Americans: International Politics of the Supersonic Transport* (Washington, D.C.: Smithsonian Institution Press, 1997).

58. Horwitch, *Clipped Wings*, 288; "Top Economists Oppose SST As Unwise, Fulbright Declares," *NYT*, September 16, 1970; Gary Soucie, interview.

59. See, e.g., Horwitch, *Clipped Wings*, 300–301. The potential economic ramifications of banning commercial supersonic flights over land were by that time well established. See, e.g., Calhoun, Jr., *Report of the Secretary of the Interior of the Special Study Group on Noise and Sonic Boom in Relation to Man*.

60. See, e.g., Andrew J. Hawkins, "Fifteen Years after Concorde, Supersonic Jets Are Booming Back into Style," The Verge, November 13, 2018, https://www.theverge.com/2018/11/13/18089300/supersonic-jet-concorde-boom-aerion-carbon-us-laws; "Aerion, Boom Taking Different Paths to Supersonic Economics," Avionics, November 13, 2018, https://www.aviationtoday.com/2018/11/13/aerion-boom-taking-different-paths-supersonic-economics/.

CHAPTER 7

For their generous feedback on earlier versions of this chapter, I am grateful to Regina Blaszczyk, David Suisman, Shannon Mattern, Max Ritts, Daniel Fisher, Trevor J. Pinch, Stefan Helmreich, and audiences at the Hagley Conference, the Annual Meeting of the Society for Social Studies of Science, and the New Media Working Group at University of California, Berkeley.

1. A recording of these sounds may be heard here: https://soundcloud.com/user-253244136/cendrillon-metal.

2. For more on the sonic experiences of seafarers, see Penny McCall Howard, "Feeling the Ground: Vibration, Listening, Sounding at Sea," in *On Listening*, ed. Angus Carlyle and Cathy Lane (Axminster, UK: Uniformbooks, 2013), 61–66.

3. David Novak, "Noise," in *Keywords in Sound*, ed. David Novak and Matt Sakakeeny (Durham, NC: Duke University Press, 2015), 125.

4. Interestingly, Ingold deploys a maritime metaphor in his description of ensoundment: "Sound, like breath, is experienced as a movement of coming and going, inspiration and expiration. If that is so, then we should say of the body, as it sings, hums, whistles or speaks, that it is *ensounded*. It is like setting sail, launching the body *into* sound like a boat on the waves. . . ." Tim Ingold "Against Soundscape," in *Autumn Leaves: Sound and the Environment in Artistic Practice*, ed. Angus Carlyle (Paris: Double Entendre, 2007), 12.

5. The idea that sound studies is a transdiscipline rather than an interdiscipline comes from Michael Gallagher, Anja Kanngeiser, and Jonathan Prior, "Listening Geographies: Landscape, Affect, and Geotechnologies," *Progress in Human Geography* 41, no. 5 (August 2016): 618. Sound studies scholarship that suggests sound is difficult to theorize includes James A. Steintrager and Rey Chow, "Sound Objects: An Introduction," in *Sound Objects*, ed. James A. Steintrager and Rey Chow (Durham, NC: Duke University Press, 2019); Jean-Luc Nancy, *Listening*, trans. Charlotte Mandell (New York: Fordham University Press, 2007).

6. Despite these etymological issues, I deploy the terms *theory* and *speculation* in a fairly conventional manner throughout this chapter, for two reasons. First, because practically these are the best terms available to describe what I am trying to do here. And second, because the fetishization of etymology is itself integral to the project of theorization I want to resist.

7. Though see Mark A. Johnstone, "Aristotle on Sounds," *British Journal for the History of Philosophy* 12, no. 4 (July 2013): 631–48.

8. Steintrager and Chow, "Sound Objects," 12.

9. Though see Jean-Luc Nancy's contention that sound does not dissolve form but "rather enlarges it; it gives it an amplitude, a density, and a vibration or an undulation whose outline never does anything but approach," in Nancy, *Listening*, 2.

10. "The Humble Hero," *The Economist*, May 18, 2013, http://www.economist.com/finance-and-economics/2013/05/18/the-humble-hero. Publications that focus explicitly on the shipping container and containerization include: Frank Broeze, *The Globalisation of the Oceans: Containerisation from the 1950s to the Present* (Liverpool, UK: Liverpool University Press, 2000); Brian Cudahy, *Box Boats: How Container Ships Changed the World* (New York: Fordham University Press, 2006); Marc Levinson, *The Box: How the Shipping Container Made the World Smaller and the World Economy Bigger* (Princeton, NJ: Princeton University Press, 2006); Rose George, *Ninety Percent of Everything: Inside Shipping, the Invisible Industry That Puts Clothes on Your Back, Gas in Your Car, and Food on Your Plate* (New York: Metropolitan Books, 2013); Craig Martin, *Shipping*

Container (London: Bloomsbury, 2016); Alexander Klose, *The Container Principle: How a Box Changes the Way We Think* (Cambridge, MA: The MIT Press, 2015).

11. Levinson, *The Box*.

12. Martin Parker, "Containerisation: Moving Things and Boxing Ideas," *Mobilities* 8, no. 3 (2013): 371.

13. Greg Miller, "How Three Chinese Companies Cornered Global Container Production," *American Shipper*, May 24, 2021, https://www.freightwaves.com/news/how-three-chinese-companies-cornered-global-container-production.

14. Nippon Steel provides a detailed technical overview of Cor-Ten in "Cor-Ten," Nippon Steel Corporation, accessed September 8, 2021, https://www.nipponsteel.com/product/catalog_download/pdf/A006en.pdf.

15. "Frequently asked questions about corten weathering steel," Corten.com, accessed September 8, 2021, https://www.corten.com/frequently-asked-questions.html.

16. Robert A. Hadfield, "Faraday and his Metallurgical Researches: with Special Reference to Their Bearing on the Development of Alloy Steels," *Nature* 129 (1932): 259–60.

17. M. Morcillo, I. Díaz, B. Chico, H. Cano, and D. de la Fuente, "Weathering Steels: From Empirical Development to Scientific Design. A Review," *Corrosion Science* 83 (June 2014): 6–31.

18. "It is an odd fact that steel was not understood by science until the twentieth century," points out the materials scientist Mark Miodownik. Mark Miodownik, *Stuff Matters: Exploring the Marvelous Materials that Shape Our Man-Made World* (Boston: Houghton Mifflin Harcourt, 2013), 3. Thanks to an anonymous reviewer for this reference.

19. *Official Proceedings of the Railway Club of Pittsburgh* 34, no. 1, (November 22, 1934), https://archive.org/embed/officialproceedi33rail.

20. *Railway Club*, 24.

21. *Railway Club*, 31.

22. "Stop Using Half of Your Power to Pull Deadweight," Republic Steel Corporation advertisement, *Railway Mechanical Engineer* 119, no. 11 (November 1945): 154–55, https://archive.org/embed/sim_railway-locomotives-and-cars_1945-11_119_11.

23. "180,000 Freight Cars Have Been Built Better with USS COR-TEN Steel Since 1933," United States Steel advertisement, *Railway Locomotives and Cars* 128, no. 4, (April 1954): 30–31, https://archive.org/embed/sim_railway-locomotives-and-cars_1954-04_128_4.

24. "What is U.S. Steel Doing About Art and Architecture?," United States Steel advertisement, *Pittsburgh Post-Gazette*, October 13, 1970, 5.

25. Grace Glueck, "Sculptor's Ordeal with Steel: It's Pretty but Temperamental," *New York Times*, August 22, 1991.

26. David Seidner, "Interview: Richard Serra," *Bomb Magazine*, 42, January 1, 1993. https://bombmagazine.org/articles/richard-serra/; see also, Richard Serra, *Writings/Interviews* (Chicago: University of Chicago Press, 1994).

27. Barnaby Lewis, "Boxing Clever—How Standardization Built a Global Economy," International Standards Organization, September 11, 2017, https://www.iso.org/news/ref2215.html.

28. "Customs Convention on Containers," Customs Co-Operation Council, the United Nations/International Maritime Organization, December 2, 1972, http://www.wcoomd.org/-/media/wco/public/global/pdf/about-us/legal-instruments/conventions-and-agreements/containers/pf_txt_containers_contract.pdf.

29. ISO 668, which governs the classifications, dimensions, and ratings of freight containers, was most recently revised in 2020, following previous updates in 2013, 1995, and 1988.

30. Karl Marx, *Capital: A Critique of Political Economy*, vol. 1, trans. Ben Fowkes (London: Penguin Books, 1990), 255.

31. Research on what Alfred Sohn-Rethel calls "real abstraction" is particularly relevant here. See Alfred Sohn Rethel, *Intellectual and Manual Labour: A Critique of Epistemology*, trans. Martin Sohn-Rethel (Leiden, Netherlands: Brill, 2021); Alberto Toscano, "The Open Secret of Real Abstraction," *Rethinking Marxism* 20, no. 2 (2008): 273–87.

32. Stefano Harney and Fred Moten, *The Undercommons: Fugitive Planning and Black Study* (Wivenhoe, UK: Minor Compositions, 2013), 90.

33. The Iron and Bronze Ages are the latter two periods in the influential tripartite division of ancient human history introduced in the first half of the nineteenth century. Increasingly the distinctions between the three ages (Stone, Iron, Bronze) have been critiqued by historians and archaeologists alike. See, for instance, Kristian Kristiansen and Michael Rowlands, *Social Transformations in Archaeology: Global and Local Persepectives* (London: Routledge, 1998).

34. Gray Brechin, *Imperial San Francisco: Urban Power, Earthly Ruin* (Berkeley: University of California Press, 2006), 17.

35. Brechin, *Imperial San Francisco*, 19.

36. A more thoroughgoing exploration of the relationship between metal and capitalism might include Siegfried Giedion, *Mechanization Takes Command: A Contribution to Anonymous History* (New York: Oxford University Press. 1948); Robert Kanigel, *The One Best Way: Frederick Winslow Taylor and the Enigma of Efficiency* (Cambridge, MA: The MIT Press, 2010); John Law, *Aircraft Stories: Decentering the Object in Technoscience* (Durham, NC: Duke University Press, 2002); Mimi Sheller, *Aluminum Dreams: The Making of Light Modernity* (Cambridge, MA: The MIT Press, 2014); Jonathan Waldman, *Rust: The Longest War* (New York: Simon and Schuster, 2015).

37. Andrew Barry, "Materialist Politics: Metallurgy," in *Political Matter: Technoscience, Democracy, and Public Life*, ed. Bruce Braun, Sarah J. Whatmore, Isabelle Stengers, and Jane Bennett (Minneapolis: University of Minnesota Press, 2010), 93.

38. Max Weber, *The Protestant Ethic and the Spirit of Capitalism*, trans. Talcott Parsons (London: Routledge, 1992), 123.

39. Peter Baehr, "The 'Iron Cage' and the 'Shell as Hard as Steel': Parsons, Weber, and the *Stahlhartes Gehause* Metaphor in the Protestant Ethic and the Spirit of Capitalism," *History and Theory* 40, no. 2 (2001): 161–62.

40. Giedion, *Mechanization Takes Command*, 98.

41. See Luc Boltanski and Eve Chiapello, *The New Spirit of Capitalism*, trans. Gregory Elliott (London: Verso, 2005); Mark Fisher, *Postcapitalist Desire: The Final Lectures*, ed. Matt Colquhoun (London: Repeater Books, 2021).

42. Marx, *Capital*, 1:168–69.

43. Guy Debord, *The Society of the Spectacle*, trans. Donald Nicholson-Smith (New York: Zone Books, 1995), 11. With regard to sound and Debord's spectacle, Steintrager and Chow ask, "Why is there so much talk about the society of the spectacle and not that of the . . . sonic what? We seem to lack an equivalent term." See Steintrager and Chow, "Sound Objects," 6.

44. One could argue that Allan Sekula made a career of trying to see inside containers and other opaque logistical systems. See Allan Sekula, *Fish Story* (Rotterdam, Netherlands: Richter Verlag, 1995). Alternately, Shannon Mattern, like me, turns away from vision and toward sound in an effort to apprehend the complexity of maritime logistics. See Shannon Mattern, "The Pulse of Global Passage: Listening to Logistics," in *Assembly Codes: The Logistics of Media* (Durham, NC: Duke University Press, 2021), 75–92.

45. Quoted in Robert Fink, Zachary Wallmark, and Melinda Latour, "Introduction—Chasing the Dragon: In Search of Tone in Popular Music," in *The Relentless Pursuit of Tone: Timbre in Popular Music*, ed. Robert Fink, Zachary Wallmark, and Melinda Latour (New York: Oxford University Press, 2018), 5. The phrase "structures of feeling" is from Raymond Williams, *Marxism and Literature* (Oxford: Oxford University Press, 1977), 128–35.

46. Imaginative listening thus intersects with other creative methods, including Fredric Jameson's "cognitive mapping" and Saidiya Hartman's "critical fabulation." See Fredric Jameson, *Postmodernism, or, The Cultural Logic of Late Capitalism* (Durham, NC: Duke University Press, 1997); Saidiya Hartman, "Venus in Two Acts," *Small Axe* 26 (June 2008): 1–14.

47. Stuart Hall, "The Problem of Ideology—Marxism Without Guarantees," *Journal of Communication Inquiry* 10, no. 2 (1986): 28–44.

48. Cornelia Fales, "Hearing Timbre: Perceptual Learning Among Early Bay Area Ravers," in *The Relentless Pursuit of Tone: Timbre in Popular Music*, ed. Robert Fink, Zachary Wallmark, and Melinda Latour (New York: Oxford University Press, 2018), 29.

49. Brian Kane, "The Fluctuating Sound Object," in *Sound Objects*, ed. James A. Steintrager and Rey Chow (Durham, NC: Duke University Press, 2019), 68.

50. The term "interpellation," as deployed by Louis Althusser, describes the process whereby a capitalist subject becomes a subject by imbibing capitalist ideology, and thus reproducing the relations of production in capitalist society. Althusser writes, ". . . all ideology hails or interpellates concrete individuals as concrete subjects. . . ." See Louis Althusser, "Ideology and Ideological State Apparatuses (Notes towards an Investigation)" in *Lenin and Philosophy and other essays*, trans. Ben Brewster (New York: Monthly Review Press, 1971), 127–88. Quotation at 173.

CHAPTER 8

1. Sidney W. Mintz, *Sweetness and Power: The Place of Sugar in Modern History* (New York: Penguin Books, 1986); Elizabeth Abbott, *Sugar: A Bittersweet History* (New York: Overlook Press, 2008); Richard P. Tucker, *Insatiable Appetite: The United States and the Ecological Degradation of the Tropical World* (Berkeley: University of California Press, 2000).

2. Hannah Landecker, "A Metabolic History of Manufacturing Waste: Food Commodities and Their Outsides," *Food, Culture & Society* 22, no. 5 (October 2019): 530–47.

3. Claas Kirchhelle, *Pyrrhic Progress: The History of Antibiotics in Anglo-American Food Production* (New Brunswick, NJ: Rutgers University Press, 2020); Nancy Langston, *Toxic Bodies: Hormone Disruptors and the Legacy of DES* (New Haven, CT: Yale University Press, 2011).

4. Nancy Tomes, *The Gospel of Germs: Men, Women, and the Microbe in American Life* (Cambridge, MA: Harvard University Press, 1999); Melanie A. Kiechle, *Smell Detectives: An Olfactory History of Nineteenth-Century Urban America* (Seattle: University of Washington Press, 2017).

5. Susanne Elizabeth Freidberg, *Fresh: A Perishable History* (Cambridge, MA: Harvard University Press, 2009).

6. Emily Pawley, "Feeding Desire: Generative Environments, Meat Markets, and the Management of Sheep Intercourse in Great Britain, 1700–1750," *Osiris* 33, no. 1 (October 2018): 47–62; Susan Schrepfer and Philip Scranton, ed., *Industrializing Organisms: Introducing Evolutionary History* (New York: Routledge, 2003); Susan D. Jones, *Valuing Animals: Veterinarians and Their Patients in Modern America* (Baltimore: Johns Hopkins University Press, 2003); William Boyd, "Making Meat: Science, Technology, and American Poultry Production," *Technology and Culture* 42, no. 4 (October 2001): 631–64.

7. Katy Overstreet, "How to Taste Like a Cow: Cultivating Shared Sense in Wisconsin Dairy Dorlds," *Why Food Matters: Critical Debates in Food Studies*, ed. Melissa Caldwell (New York: Bloomsbury, 2021), 313–24.

8. Radhika Govindrajan, *Animal Intimacies: Interspecies Relatedness in India's Central Himalayas* (Chicago: University of Chicago Press, 2018).

9. This is with exception to felines, who do not recognize sweet flavors due to an evolutionary mutation. See Thomas Brown and Patricia Wallace, *Physiological Psychology* (New York: Academic Press, 1980), 174.

10. Paul Lindenmaier and Morley Kare, "The Taste End-Organs of Chicken," *Poultry Science* 38, no. 3 (1959): 545–50.

11. Some sources that explore these points include, Sunaura Taylor, *Beasts of Burden: Animal and Disability Liberation* (New York: New Press, 2017); Nicole Shukin, *Animal Capital: Rendering Life in Biopolitical Times* (Minneapolis: University of Minnesota Press, 2009); Donna J. Haraway, *When Species Meet* (Minneapolis: University of Minnesota Press, 2007); Harriet Ritvo, "Border Trouble: Shifting the Line Between People and Other Animals," *Social Research* 62, no. 3 (1995): 481–500.

12. While scientists in the Progressive Era cited herbivore/omnivore distinctions, later studies focused on neuro receptors and taste have shown cattle respond enthusiastically to not only sweetness but umami flavor: Cécile Ginane, René Baumont, and Angélique Favreau-Peigné, "Perception and Hedonic Value of Basic Tastes in Domestic Ruminants," *Physiology & Behavior* 104, no. 5 (October 2011): 666–74.

13. Emily Pawley, "The Point of Perfection: Cattle Portraiture, Bloodlines, and the Meaning of Breeding, 1760–1860," *Journal of the Early Republic* 36, no. 1 (2016): 37–72.

14. "Drift-Wood Along the Railroads," *Vermont Journal*, February 22, 1856, 1.

15. "Report on Mill Feeds," *Boston Post*, June 23, 1880; "Grasses," *New England Farmer*, June 25, 1881.

16. "Startling Exposure of the Milk Trade of New York and Brooklyn," *Frank Leslie's Illustrated Newspaper*, May 8, 1858. See also Catherine McNeur, *Taming Manhattan: Environmental Battles in the Antebellum City* (Cambridge, MA: Harvard University Press, 2014); Kendra Smith-Howard, *Pure and Modern Milk: An Environmental History Since 1900* (New York: Oxford University Press, 2013).

17. See the case of Utah, in particular, cited in *Pure Food Legislation: Hearings Before the Committee on Interstate and Foreign Commerce of the House of House of Representatives on Bills H.R. 3109, 12348, 9352, 276 and 4342* (Washington, D.C.: GPO, 1902), 495; George Ehret, *Twenty-Five Years of Brewing: With an Illustrated History of American Beer, Dedicated to the Friends of George Ehret* (New York: Gast Lithograph & Engraving Company, 1881), 66.

18. F. A. Gulley, *Silos, Silage, and Cattle Feeding* (Dallas: Texas Farm and Ranch Publishing Co., 1890); Henry Stephens and James Macdonald, *Stephen's Book of the Farm* (William Blackwood and Sons), 1908.

19. W. W. Crane. "Ensilage: A New and Important Subject Treated by One Who Speaks from Expertise," *Dayton Herald*, December 30, 1889.

20. A. A. Borland, "Raising a Dairy Calf," Third Annual Meeting of the Granite State Dairyman's Association Proceedings, 1915, 66.

21. See Kendra Smith-Howard, "Hard [Butter] Times in Canada: What Buttergate Reveals about Environmental and Food History," The Otter Blog of the Network in Canadian History and Environment, March 24, 2021, https://niche-canada.org/2021/03/24/hard-butter-times-in-canada-what-buttergate-reveals-about-environmental-and-food-history/.

22. Nicole Welk-Joerger, "Milk: A History of Tasting What Cows Eat," *Nursing Clio*, April 6, 2017, https://nursingclio.org/2017/04/06/milk-a-history-of-tasting-what-cows-eat/.

23. "Molasses as Feed," *The News* (Frederick, MD), September 21, 1901; "Sugar as Cattle Food," *Yorkshire Herald*, October 11, 1884; "Feeding Sweets to Stock," *Newport Mercury* (RI), April 7, 1888.

24. Carob bean is also known as "locust bean" and was commonly known in the early twentieth century as "St. John's bread." The carob tree is native to the Mediterranean, which emphasizes how economically global manufactured feed stuffs were by the late nineteenth and early twentieth centuries. Today, carob bean is often used as a chocolate substitute. For a source from this period, see Ira J. Condit, *The Carob in California* (Berkeley: University of California Press, 1919).

25. Larry Wherry, *The Golden Anniversary of Scientific Feeding* (Milwaukee, WI: Business Press, 1947), 109.

26. This is based on advertisements found in Wisconsin newspapers advertising Blatchford's Calf Meal in 1888, Kansas papers in 1892, and New Jersey papers in 1895. See *Chippewa Herald*, March 30, 1888; *Hopewell Herald*, April 4, 1895; *Kansas Farmer*, April 27, 1892.

27. "Molasses as a Food for Farm Animals," *Farmer's Bulletin* 13, no. 107 (1899): 17–19.

28. "Molasses for Mule Feed," *Louisiana Planter and Sugar Manufacturer*, May 12, 1900, 290.

29. *Pure Food Legislation*, 358.

30. *Pure Food Legislation*, 187.

31. Wherry, *The Golden Anniversary of Scientific Feeding*; Landecker, "A Metabolic History of Manufacturing Waste."

32. William Lloyd Fox, "Harvey W. Wiley's Search for American Sugar Self-Sufficiency," *Agricultural History* 54, no. 4 (1980): 516–26.

33. Benjamin R. Cohen, *Pure Adulteration: Cheating on Nature in the Age of Manufactured Food* (Chicago: University of Chicago Press, 2019).

34. Lewis Sharpe Ware, *Cattle Feeding with Sugar Beets, Sugar, Molasses, and Sugar Beet Residuum* (Philadelphia, PA: Philadelphia Book Company, 1902).

35. "Feed Jobbers to Organize," *Flour and Feed*, May 1920, 32.

36. A. G. Winter, quoted in "Feed Manufacturers Organize," *American Hay, Flour, and Feed Journal*, April 1909, 50a. The organization dissolved in 1910, and some sources say it either merged with the American Feed Manufacturers Association or the National Grain and Feed Association. The latter was founded in 1896.

37. "Feed Manufacturers Organize," *American Hay, Flour, and Feed Journal*, April 1909, 50b.

38. For a comprehensive analysis of the professionalization of doctors in the early twentieth century, see Paul Starr, *The Social Transformation of American Medicine: The Rise of a Sovereign Profession and the Making of a Vast Industry* (New York: Basic), 1984.

39. *Flour and Feed*, September 1918, 39.

40. Col. A. G. Winter, "Out of the Past," *Flour and Feed*, January 1918, 26.

41. Earley Vernon Wilcox and Clarence Beaman Smith, *Farmer's Cyclopedia of Live Stock* (New York: Orange Judd Company, 1908).

42. "Cane vs. Beet Molasses," *Breeder's Gazette*, March 8, 1905, 471; earlier reports of the effects of beet molasses over cane molasses were published in the 1890s, when Wiley conducted his research. See "Molasses for Cattle Food," *Galveston Daily News* (Galveston, Texas), March 9, 1894.

43. "Use Molasses as Feed Roughage," *Sedalia Democrat* (Sedalia, Missouri), February 26, 1935.

44. "Adulteration of Mixed Feeds Hearing" (Washington, D.C.: Government Printing Office, 1918), 4.

45. "Adulteration of Mixed Feeds Hearing," 18.

46. "Adulteration of Mixed Feeds Hearing," 97

47. "Adulteration of Mixed Feeds Hearing," 119–20.

48. "Feed Pilot Wheel Feed," *Country Gentleman*, March 16, 1918, 41.

49. *Report of the Federal Trade Commission on Commercial Feeds*, March 29, 1921 (Washington, D.C.: Government Printing Office, 1921), 160.

50. "Adulteration of Mixed Feeds Hearing" (Washington, D.C.: Government Printing Office, 1918), 111.

51. Susan Strasser, *Satisfaction Guaranteed: The Making of the American Mass Market* (Washington, D.C.: Pantheon Books, 1989); *Flour and Feed*, February 1918, 3.

52. "Laboratory Tested Feed," *The Evening News* (Harrisburg, PA), October 6, 1919, 3.

53. "Buy Feeds Now," *Flour and Feed*, July 1918, 51.

54. G. F. McMillen, "Service-Merchandising," *Feedstuffs*, July 1924, 12.

55. "Service-Merchandising," 13.

56. "This Man Depends on You," *Feedstuffs*, September 1924, 23.

57. "Ralston Purina Company: A Motivational Research Study on the Sales and Advertising Problems of Purina Feeds, 1955," Ernest Dichter Papers, Accession 2407, Box 14, Hagley Museum and Library.

58. "Sugar as Cattle Food," *Yorkshire Herald* (York, UK), October 11, 1884, 18.

59. Deborah Kay Fitzgerald, *Every Farm a Factory: The Industrial Ideal in American Agriculture* (New Haven, CT: Yale University Press, 2003).

60. Price list for Agri-Flavors Company (2020), Agri-Flavors, Inc., accessed October 27, 2021, http://agriflavors.com/.

61. "Market Research Report: Feed Flavors and Sweeteners Market by Type (Feed Flavors and Feed Sweeteners), Livestock (Ruminants, Swine, Poultry, Aquatic Animals), Form (Dry and Liquid), Source (Natural and Synthetic) and Region—Global Forecast to 2022," September 2017, Markets and Markets, https://www.marketsandmarkets.com/Market-Reports/feed-flavors-sweeteners-market-101817133.html.

62. See, for example, Nadia Berenstein, "Designing Flavors for Mass Consumption," *Senses & Society* 13, no. 1 (March 2018): 19–40.

63. See for example, Andrew Griffin, "American Farmers Secretly Feed Cows Defective Skittles Because They Are Cheaper Than Corn, Truck Crash Reveals," *Independent*, January 20, 2017, https://www.independent.co.uk/climate-change/news/skittles-cows-corn-truck-crash-american-farmers-wisconsin-dodge-county-a7536731.html.

64. Diane Nelson, "Can Seaweed Cut Methane Emissions on Dairy Farms?," UC Davis, May 24, 2018, https://www.ucdavis.edu/news/can-seaweed-cut-methane-emissions-dairy-farms; Jeff Mulhollem, "Seaweed Feed Additive Cuts Livestock Methane but Poses Questions," Penn State News, June 17, 2019, https://news.psu.edu/story/578123/2019/06/17/research/seaweed-feed-additive-cuts-livestock-methane-poses-questions.

CHAPTER 9

Thanks to the editors of this volume, and to the British Academy/Leverhulme for funding this research.

1. Georg Simmel, "Das Problem des Stiles," *Dekorative Kunst. Illustrierte Zeitschrift für Angewandte Kunst* 11, no. 7 (1908): 307–16, 309, quoted in Siegfried Gronert, "Simmel's Handle: A Historical and Theoretical Design Study," *Design and Culture* 4, no. 1 (2012): 55–71, 62.

2. See, for example, *Senses and Sensation: Critical and Primary Sources* ed., David Howes, vol. 4, *Art and Design* (London: Bloomsbury, 2018); Ian Heywood, ed., *Sensory Arts and Design* (Abingdon, UK: Routledge, 2018).

3. David Howes, "HYPERESTHESIA, or, The Sensual Logic of Late Capitalism" in *Empire of the Senses: The Sensual Culture Reader*, ed. David Howes (Abingdon, UK: Routledge, 2005), 281–303. Quotations at 282, 283.

4. Carroll D. Wright, "Preface', *13th Annual Report of the Commissioner of Labor 1898: Hand and Machine Labor*, vol. 1, *Introduction and Analysis* (Washington, D.C.: Government Printing Office, 1899), 6. This study was based on fieldwork begun in November 1894. The author of the preface was the U.S. Commissioner of Labor.

5. Wright, *13th Annual Report*, 1:5.

6. Wright, *13th Annual Report*, 1:11.

7. Roger Kneebone, *Expert: Understanding the Path to Mastery* (London: Viking, 2020). See, for example, the work of Lee McQueen, for his own label Alexander McQueen and for the Givenchy couture house.

8. Glenn Adamson, *Fewer, Better Things: The Hidden Wisdom of Objects* (London: Bloomsbury, 2018).

9. Lewis Mumford, *Technics and Civilization* (New York: Harcourt, Brace & World, 1963), 12. For a broader definition of technics which includes "blood and sinew" see Lewis Mumford, "An Appraisal of Lewis Mumford's *Technics and Civilization* (1934)," *Daedalus* 88, no. 3 (1959): 527–36.

10. Lewis Mumford, *The Condition of Man* (New York: Harcourt, Brace and Company, 1944).

11. Mumford, *Technics and Civilization*, 372.

12. Siegfried Giedion, *Mechanization Takes Command* (New York: Norton, 1948), back cover, 2–3, 10–11.

13. Lewis Mumford, "Man Takes Command: Notes on Siegfried Giedion's Comprehensive Study of Mechanization," *Progressive Architecture* 39 (July 1948): 48, 108, 110, 112. On p. 10, Mumford's phrase "the realm of technics" may refer to his own work. His comments point to one explanation for why Giedion did not reference Mumford's earlier text, even though he had moved from Switzerland to the United States to research and write his book at that time.

14. Giedion, *Mechanization Takes Command*, 41.

15. Giedion, *Mechanization Takes Command*, 46.

16. Giedion, *Mechanization Takes Command*, 714.

17. Giedion, *Mechanization Takes Command*, 723. "Humanscale" is the name of a design resource developed from Henry Dreyfuss's *Measure of Man*. See Niels Diffrient, Alvin R. Tilley, and Joan C. Bardagjy, *Humanscale 1/2/3: A Portfolio of Information* (Cambridge, MA: The MIT Press, 1974); Niels Diffrient, Alvin R. Tilley, and Joan C. Bardagjy, *Humanscale 4/5/6: A Portfolio of Information* (Cambridge, MA: The MIT Press, 1981). It also the name of a design studio for which Diffrient has designed ergonomic seating.

18. Douglas Tallack, "Siegfried Giedion, Modernism and American Material Culture," *Journal of American Studies* 28, no. 2 (1994): 149–67, esp. 151, 157. See also Marshall McLuhan, *The Mechanical Bride: Folklore of Industrial Man* (London: Routledge, 1967).

19. H. Marshall McLuhan, "Encyclopedic Unities," *Hudson Review* 1 (1948): 599–602.

20. Marshall McLuhan, *Understanding Media: The Extensions of Man* (London: Routledge Classics, 2001), 165. This text was originally published in 1964.

21. Marshall McLuhan, *The Mechanical Bride: The Folklore of Industrial Man* (New York: Vanguard Press, 1951), 53.

22. Neil MacGregor, *A History of the World in 100 Objects* (London: Penguin, 2010), 30.

23. Eugene S. Ferguson, "The Mind's Eye: Nonverbal Thought in Technology," *Science*, n.s., 197, no. 4306 (August 26, 1977), 827–36. Quotation at 835.

24. "Museum of Modern Art Exhibits Revolutionary Type of Handle Designed to Fit the Hand," New York: Museum of Modern Art, press release for exhibition March 2–May 16, 1948, https://www.moma.org/calendar/exhibitions/3232 [hereafter cited as MoMA press release].

25. Julian Stair filmed by Paul Craddock for the V&A Research Institute, "International Symposium—Encounters on the Shop Floor: Embodiment and the Knowledge of the Maker," Victoria and Albert Museum, London, June 26–28, 2019.

26. For instance, "Where Today Meets Tomorrow: General Motors Technical Center," Public Relations Staff (Detroit, MI: General Motors, 1956).

27. MoMA press release.

28. Henry Hagert, "Biographical Sketches of 1953 I.D.I. Honors," Industrial Designers' Institute, May 26, 1953, in accession 2181: Thomas Lamb Papers, Manuscripts and Archives Department, Hagley Museum and Library, Wilmington, DE.

29. Hagley Museum and Library, "Universal Design: Thomas Lamb–The Handle Man," accessed March 11, 2022, https://www.hagley.org/research/digital-exhibits/thomas-lamb-handle-man.

30. On the Lim-Rest and similar solutions, see Cara Kiernan Fallon, "Walking Cane Style and Medicalized Mobility," in *Making Disability Modern: Design Histories*, ed. Bess Williamson and Elizabeth Guffey (London: Bloomsbury, 2020), 45–60, esp. 52–53.

31. Allen, "Tom Lamb: The Handle Man," *Industrial Design* 1, no. 1 (1954): n.p.

32. Allen "Tom Lamb."

33. Hagley Museum and Library, accession 2181: Thomas Lamb Papers [hereafter cited as Lamb Papers], finding aid.

34. Advertisement, "The Exclusive Handle with the 'Feel Appeal,'" in *Blade* [Cutco newsletter] undated clipping, ca. 1950–1959, Series 1, Subseries B, Box 4, Lamb Papers. For visual evidence of Lamb's work environment, see Lamb Box 4 Tom Lamb Photographs, undated, Thomas Lamb Papers, 1916–1988 (Accession 2181), Hagley Museum and Library, Wilmington, DE 19807.

35. E. J. Kahn Jr., "Profiles: Come Let Me Clutch Thee," *New Yorker*, May 29, 1954, 33.

36. Rachel Elizabeth Delphia, "Design to Enable the Body: Thomas Lamb's 'Wedge-Lock' Handle, 1941–1962" (master's thesis, University of Delaware, 2005), 52–53.

37. Delphia, "Design to Enable the Body," 52–53.

38. Allen, "Tom Lamb." Prototype handles. Thomas Lamb Papers, 1916–1988, Accession 2181, Hagley Museum and Library, Wilmington, DE 19807.

39. Allen, "Tom Lamb."

40. Ferguson, "The Mind's Eye," 828.

41. Ferguson, "The Mind's Eye," 828.

42. Ferguson, "The Mind's Eye," 834 cites *Dictionary of American Biography* (New York: Scribner, 1928–36).

43. Kahn "Profiles," 33.

44. Rudolf Arnheim, *Visual Thinking* (Berkeley: University of California Press, 1969), 3, cited by Ferguson, "The Mind's Eye," 831.

45. Ferguson, "The Mind's Eye," 834.

46. Eugene S. Ferguson, *Engineering and the Mind's Eye* (Cambridge, MA: The MIT Press, 1994), 58.

47. Ferguson, *Engineering and the Mind's Eye*, 3–4.

48. Ferguson, *Engineering and the Mind's Eye*, 59.

49. Ferguson, "The Mind's Eye," 827.

50. J. Christopher Jones, "Handles: The Ergonomic Approach," *Design* 72 (December 1954): 34–38, 36.

51. Delphia, "Design to Enable," 67.

52. See, for instance, "Lamb Wedge-Lock Handle," Standard Handle Co. promotional leaflet, cover. Undated. Thomas Lamb Papers, 1916–1988, Accession 2181, Hagley Museum and Library, Wilmington, DE.

53. Jennifer Frank Tantia, ed., *The Art and Science of Embodied Research Design: Concepts, Methods and Cases* (Abingdon, UK: Routledge, 2021).

54. Pamela H. Smith, Amy R. W. Meyers, and Harold J. Cook, eds., *Ways of Making and Knowing: The Material Culture of Empirical Knowledge* (Chicago: University of Chicago Press and Bard Graduate Center, 2018).

55. For example, Sarah Barber and Corinna Peniston-Bird, eds., *History Beyond the Text: A Student's Guide to Approaching Alternative Sources* (London: Routledge, 2009).

56. Grace Lees-Maffei, "The Production-Consumption-Mediation Paradigm," *Journal of Design History* 22, no. 4 (2009): 351–76, esp. 366–67.

57. Jeffrey L. Meikle, "Writing About Stuff: The Peril and Promise of Design History and Criticism," in *Writing Design: Words and Objects*, ed. Grace Lees-Maffei (London: Berg, 2012), 23–32. Quotations at 23.

58. Ferguson, "The Mind's Eye," 835.

59. Ralph Caplan, "I.D. Magazine, 1954–2009," AIGA, January 5, 2010, https://web.archive.org/web/20210205104618/https://www.aiga.org/i-d-magazine-1954–2009.

60. Thomas Lamb, "The Story of the Lamb Lim-Rest," 10–12, Lamb papers.

61. Business Papers, 1916–1996, Box 2; Wedge-lock Handle, Box 4; Crutch—Technical article and correspondence with the New York State Department of Health, March 9–April 13, 1950; Handle sketches—pots and pans, April 1, 1945-December 16, 1947, Box OS 5; Hands and Handles, June 4, 1945–June 23, 1963, Box OS 7; Baggage, Luggage, and Carrier Handles, Box 17; Series II: Artifacts—Baggage, etc., Box 17A, Lamb papers.

62. Delphia, "Design to Enable," 57–58. It is not clear whether Delphia is reporting on her own "hands-on experience" and whether she is "the user" mentioned. Arguably, embodied research necessitates a first-person register, because otherwise the researcher risks normatively extrapolating from her own experiences the generalized potential experiences of others. Critics of Lamb's approach might claim that he did this in design, too. Nevertheless, the editors of this volume have requested that this chapter report on archival research in the third person.

63. Delphia, "Design to Enable," 99.

64. Beiyuan Guo, Linzhi Tian, and Weining Fang, "Effects of Operation Type and Handle Shape of the Driver Controllers of High-speed Train on the Drivers' Comfort," *International Journal of Industrial Ergonomics* 58 (2017): 1–11.

65. Delphia, "Design to Enable," 29.

66. "Foreword" in "The Story of the Lamb Handle," September 8, 1954, 9, Lamb Papers, Series 1, Subseries A, Box 4.

67. "Editorial Plan," December 12, 1948, Lamb Papers, Series 1, Subseries A, Box 4. Underlining in original.

68. "Facts Concerning Lamb Handle Cutlery," January 1953, Lamb Papers, Series 1, Subseries A, Box 4.

69. "The Lamb Handle: A Perfect Mate for Every Hand," in Wear-Ever Aluminium, Inc., Cutco Division, *Blade* 12, no. 12 (March 21, 1960): 2, in Lamb Papers, Series 1, Subseries B, Box 4. Capitalization in the original.

70. Delphia, "Design to Enable," xii. Delphia's comment echoes that of Kahn, "Profiles," 33. "Come Let Me Clutch Thee" is a quotation from Macbeth's dagger soliloquy in the eponymous play by William Shakespeare (1603–1606).

71. Hagley Museum and Library, "Universal Design."

72. Bess Williamson, "Getting a Grip: Disability in American Industrial Design of the Late Twentieth Century," *Winterthur Portfolio* 46, no. 4 (2012): 213–36. Quotation at 214.

73. Williamson, "Getting a Grip," 217.

74. Bess Williamson, *Accessible America: A History of Disability and Design* (New York: New York University Press, 2019), 156.

75. Aimi Hamraie, *Building Access: Universal Design and the Politics of Disability* (Minneapolis: University of Minnesota Press, 2017), 255–61.

76. Williamson, "Getting a Grip," 218.

77. Hamraie, *Building Access*, 19–39.

78. Caroline Criado-Perez, *Invisible Women: Exposing Data Bias in a World Designed for Men* (London: Chatto & Windus, 2019), 157.

79. Criado-Perez, *Invisible Women*, 161.

80. Aaron M. Yoder, Ann M. Adams, and Elizabeth A. Brensinger, "Designing Agricultural Tools and Equipment for Women," poster for the Women in Agriculture Educators National Conference, Indianapolis, IN, April 3–4, 2014, https://agrisk.umn.edu/Conferences/Presentation/designing_agricultural_tools_and_equipment_fo cited in Criado-Perez, *Invisible Women*, 121.

81. Criado-Perez, *Invisible Women*, 121–22, cites Wendy Davis, ex-director of the U.K. organization, the Women's Design Service (1987–2012), and the New York Committee for Occupational Safety and Health (NYCOSH), "Risks Facing Women in Construction," September 2014, https://nycosh.org/wp-content/uploads/2014/09/Women-in-Construction-final-11-8-13-2.pdf.

82. Urška Puh, "Age-Related and Sex-Related Differences in Hand and Pinch Grip Strength in Adults," *International Journal of Rehabilitation Research* 33, no. 1 (2010): 4–11; Kerith K. Zellers and M. Susan Hallbeck, "The Effects of Gender, Wrist and Forearm Position on Maximum Isometric Power Grasp Force, Wrist Force, and Their Interactions," *Proceedings of the Human Factors and Ergonomics Society Annual Meeting* 39, no. 10 (1995): 543–47.

83. D. Leyk, W. Gorges, D. Ridder, et al., "Hand-grip Strength of Young Men, Women and Highly Trained Female Athletes," *European Journal of Applied Physiology* 99 (2007): 415–21.

84. For instance, on the craftwork of leisured upper-class Englishwomen as what she calls "ladies' work" see Constance Classen, "Feminine Tactics: Crafting an Alternative Aesthetics in the Eighteenth and Nineteenth Centuries" in *The Book of Touch*, ed. Constance Classen (Abingdon, UK: Routledge, 2005), 228–39.

CHAPTER 10

This research was generously funded by a Social Sciences and Humanities Research Council of Canada Insight Development Grant.

1. On the relationship between the Salon's actors and charitable pursuits, see Catherine Hindson, "Offstage Labour: Actresses, Charity Work, and the Early Twentieth-Century Theatre

Profession," in *Stage Women, 1900–50: Female Theatre Workers and Professional Practice*, ed. Maggie B. Gale and Kate Dorney (Manchester, UK: Manchester University Press, 2019), 94–117.

2. J. Douglas Porteous, "Smellscape," *Progress in Physical Geography: Earth and Environment* (September 1985): 359–60; Victoria Henshaw, *Urban Smellscapes: Understanding and Designing City Smell Environments* (New York: Routledge, 2014), 5.

3. Erika D. Rappaport, "The Senses in the Marketplace: Stimulation and Distraction, Gratification and Control," in *A Cultural History of the Senses in the Age of Empire*, ed. Constance Classen (London: Bloomsbury 2014), 69–88; Constance Classen, *The Deepest Sense: A Cultural History of Touch* (Urbana: University of Illinois, 2012), 191–97; Serena Dyer, "Shopping and the Senses: Retail, Browsing and Consumption in Eighteenth-Century England," *History Compass* 12, no. 9 (2014): 694–703.

4. Jon Stobart, Andrew Hann, and Victoria Morgan, eds., *Spaces of Consumption: Leisure and Shopping in the English Town, C. 1680–1830* (London: Routledge, 2007); Claire Walsh, "Shop Design and the Display of Goods in Eighteenth Century London," *Journal of Design History* 8 (1995): 157–76; Erika D. Rappaport, *Shopping for Pleasure: Women in the Making of London's West End* (Princeton, NJ: Princeton University Press, 2000).

5. Constance Classen, David Howes, and Anthony Synnot, *Aroma: The Cultural History of Smell* (New York: Routledge, 1994), 186–92. See also Alain Corbin, *The Foul and the Fragrant: Odor and the French Social Imagination* (Cambridge, MA: Harvard University Press, 1996); William Tullett, *Smell in Eighteenth-Century England: A Social Sense* (New York: Oxford, 2019).

6. Mark M. Smith, *Sensing the Past: Seeing, Hearing, Smelling, Testing, and Touching in History* (Berkeley: University of California Press, 2007), chapter 1.

7. Classen et al., *Aroma*, 3–5 and 169–70; Jonathan Reinarz, *Past Scents: Historical Perspectives on Smell* (Chicago: University of Illinois Press, 2014), chapter 6.

8. "An 'All-British' Shopping Week," *The Times of London*, January 13, 1911.

9. "'All-British' Shopping Week Commences Today," *Exeter and Plymouth Gazette*, March 27, 1911.

10. "The 'All British' Shopping Week," *The Times*, February 10, 1911.

11. Thomas Richards, *The Commodity Culture of Victorian England: Advertising and Spectacle, 1851–1914* (Stanford, CA: Stanford University Press, 1990); Lynda Nead, *Victorian Babylon: People, Streets and Images in Nineteenth-Century London* (New Haven, CT: Yale University Press, 2000), 58.

12. Rappaport, *Shopping for Pleasure*, 147, 158–60.

13. See, for example, Classen et al., *Aroma*, 5; Classen, *The Deepest Sense*, 182.

14. "Of Interest to Women. All-British Shopping Week," *Daily Mirror*, March 28, 1911; "Of Interest to Women. All-British Shopping Week," *Daily Mirror*, March 29, 1911.

15. Hindson, "Offstage Labour," 100.

16. On the actors' careers onstage, see Hindson, "Offstage Labour," 106–7. On actors as fashionable exemplars, see Marlis Schweitzer, "American Fashions for American Women: The Rise and Fall of Fashion Nationalism," in *Producing Fashion: Commerce, Culture, and Consumers*, ed. Regina Lee Blaszczyk (Philadelphia: University of Pennsylvania Press, 2008), 134.

17. "Actresses As Shopgirls," *Evening Telegraph*, March 29, 1911. Emphasis mine.

18. On perfumers, see Geoffrey Jones, *Beauty Imagined: A History of the Global Beauty Industry* (New York: Oxford University Press, 2010); Jessica P. Clark, *The Business of Beauty: Gender and the Body in Modern London* (London: Bloomsbury, 2020), chapter 4.

19. Rappaport, *Shopping for Pleasure*; Rappaport, "The Senses," 70; Michael Ball and David T. Sunderland, *An Economic History of London* (London: Routledge, 2001), 139–41.

20. Georg Simmel, "The Metropolis and Mental Life," in *Metropolis: Center and Symbol of our Times*, ed. Philip Kasinitz (New York: New York University Press, 1995), 30–45.

21. Rappaport, "The Senses," 73–76; and Ian MacLachlan, "A Bloody Offal Nuisance: The Persistence of Private Slaughter-Houses in Nineteenth-Century London," *Urban History* 34, no. 2 (2007), 228.

22. Classen et al., *Aroma*, 79–80.

23. Classen, *The Deepest Sense*, 193; Rappaport, "The Senses," 71.

24. Harrods floorplans, early twentieth century, Harrods Corporate Archives, Hammersmith, London.

25. Lindy Woodhead, *Shopping, Seduction, & Mr. Selfridge* (New York: Random House, 2013), 112. See also Rappaport, *Shopping for Pleasure*, chapter 5.

26. See Harold Whitehead, *Principles of Salesmanship* (New York: Roland Press Company, 1920), 57.

27. F. Standish, "Arranging the Perfume Department," *Bulletin of Pharmacy* 28 (1914): 420–23.

28. "Parfumerie Harrods," c. 1913, Harrods Corporate Archives, Hammersmith, London.

29. Anne McClintock, *Imperial Leather: Race, Gender and Sexuality in the Colonial Contest* (New York: Routledge, 1995), chapter 5; Lori Loeb, *Consuming Angels: Advertising and Victorian Women* (New York: Oxford University Press, 1994), 152–53.

30. "Some Aspects of Modern Advertising, by 'Observer,' III-Perfumery," *Perfumery and Essential Oil Record* (hereafter *PEOR*) 1 (April 1911): 81–82.

31. Tom Zelman, "Language and Perfume: A Study of Symbol-Formation," in *Advertising and Popular Culture: Studies in Variety and Versatility*, ed. Sammy Richard Danna (Bowling Green, OH: Bowling Green State University Popular Press, 1992), 109.

32. Classen et al., *Aroma*, 195.

33. "Editorial. Fashion in Perfumes," *PEOR* 8 (November 1917): 91; Catherine Maxwell, *Scents and Sensibility: Perfume in Victorian Literary Culture* (London: Oxford, 2017), 213n54.

34. John M. Mackenzie, *Propaganda and Empire: The Manipulation of British Public Opinion, 1880–1960* (Manchester, UK: Manchester University Press, 1984), 16.

35. Advertisement for Gosnell's Society Eau de Cologne, nd, John Gosnell & Co. Archives, Lewes, East Sussex.

36. Clark, *Business of Beauty*, chapter 4.

37. "Reports on Mitcham Oils, 1913," *PEOR* 4 (August 1913): 290.

38. See John C. Umney, "Essential Oils: their Constitution and Commerce," *PEOR* 3 (July 1912): 170–75.

39. "A German Industry Passing into British Hands," *Manawatu Standard*, April 10, 1902, quoted in "Luce's Eau de Cologne," *Jerripedia*, https://www.theislandwiki.org/index.php/Luce%27s_Eau_de_Cologne.

40. John C. Umney, "Perfumery—Part II," *PEOR* 5 (November 1914): 17.

41. "Eau de Cologne," *PEOR* 6 (November 1914): 129; and Maxwell, *Scents and Sensibility*, 97.

42. William Whiteley Ltd., *General Price List, October 1913*, Foreign Edition—Section I (London: 133–159 Queen's Road, 1913), 470.

43. "Editorial. Fashion in Perfumes," 91.

44. Anandi Ramamurthy, *Imperial Persuaders: Images of Africa and Asia in British Advertising* (Manchester, UK: Manchester University Press, 2003), 15, 20.

45. "Parfumerie Harrods," c. 1913, Harrods Corporate Archives, Hammersmith, London.

46. Jones, *Beauty Imagined*, chapter 1.

47. Umney, "Perfumery—Part II," 14.

48. Jones, *Beauty Imagined*, 22; G. W. Septimus Piesse, *The Art of Perfumery* (Philadelphia, PA: Lindsay and Blakiston, 1857), 119–23; and Eugène Rimmel, *The Book of Perfumes* (London: Chapman and Hall, 1865), 253.

49. See "Editorial," *PEOR* 5 (November 1914): 397–98; and "Processes Pertaining to Perfumery Products," *PEOR* 8 (May 1917): 116–44.

50. A. M. Kirk, "Japonisme and Femininity: A Study of Japanese Dress in British and French Art and Society, c. 1860–c.1899," *Costume* 42 (June 2008): 111–29.

51. Catherine Hall and Sonya Rose, "Introduction: Being at Home with Empire," *At Home with Empire: Metropolitan Culture and the Imperial World*, ed. Catherine Hall and Sonya Rose (New York: Cambridge University Press, 2006), 5, 13.

52. "Editorial," *Colonial Advertising and Commodity Racism*, ed. Wulf D. Hund, Michael Pickering, and Anandi Ramamurthy (Zurich, Switzerland: Lit, 2013), 14; John M. MacKenzie, *Imperialism and Popular Culture* (Manchester, UK: Manchester University Press, 1986).

53. Ramamurthy, *Imperial Persuaders*, 11; and David Ciarlo, "Advertising and the Optics of Colonial Power at the Fin de Siècle," *Empires of Vision: A Reader*, ed. Martin Jay and Sumathi Ramaswamy (Durham, NC: Duke University Press, 2014), 190.

54. *The Sphere*, October 2, 1915; *The Graphic*, April 17, 1915; "Shem-el-nessim," *Illustrated London News* (hereafter *ILN*), August 20, 1910.

55. See, for example, Classen et al., *Aroma*, 165–69; Reinarz, *Past Scents*, chapter 3; Connie Y. Chiang, "Monterey-by-the-Smell: Odors and Social Conflict on the California Coastline," *Pacific Historical Review* 73 (2004): 183–214.

56. "Shem-El-Nessim," *ILN*, August 14, 1909; and "Shem-el-nessim," *ILN*, May 14, 1910.

57. Sadiah Qureshi, *Peoples on Parade: Exhibitions, Empire, and Anthropology in Nineteenth-Century Britain* (Chicago: University of Chicago Press, 2011), 34–38, 44–46.

58. Judith R. Walkowitz, "The 'Vision of Salome': Cosmopolitanism and Erotic Dancing in Central London, 1908–1918," *American Historical Review* 108 (April 2003): 337–76.

59. "Shem-el-nessim," *ILN*, August 20, 1910; "Shem-El-Nessim," *ILN*, December 7, 1912.

60. Qureshi, *Peoples on Parade*.

61. Ramamurthy, *Imperial Persuaders*, 18–19.

62. "J. Grossmith & Son," *ILN*, September 14, 1912.

63. "Shem-el-nessim," *ILN*, August 20, 1910.

64. Hall and Rose, "Introduction: Being at Home with Empire," 7; Ramamurthy, *Imperial Persuaders*, 17–19.

65. Classen et al., *Aroma*, 91.

66. Maggie Angeloglou, *A History of Make-Up* (New York: Macmillan, 1970), 115.

67. Berta Ruck, *Miss Million's Maid* (New York: A. L. Burt, 1919), 144.

68. Clark, *Business of Beauty*, 36–37; and Carol Dyhouse, *Glamour: Women, History, Feminism* (London: Zed Books, 2010), 19–22.

69. Hindson, "Offstage Labour," 94.

CHAPTER 11

1. E. I. du Pont de Nemours and Company, advertisement, "I believe it's better," *Women's Wear Daily* (hereafter cited as *WWD*), September 11, 1945. Image produced by ProQuest LLC as part of ProQuest® Women's Wear Daily Archive, www.proquest.com.

2. Classic works include Jeffrey L. Meikle, *Twentieth Century Limited: Industrial Design in America, 1925–1939*, 2nd ed. (Philadelphia, PA: Temple University Press, 2001), and Roland Marchand, *Advertising the American Dream: Making Way for Modernity, 1920–1940* (Berkeley: University of California Press, 1985).

3. See, for example, Regina Lee Blaszczyk and Véronique Pouillard, eds., *European Fashion: The Creation of a Global Industry* (Manchester, UK: Manchester University Press, 2017).

4. Alfred D. Chandler Jr., *Strategy and Structure: Chapters in the History of the Industrial Enterprise* (Cambridge, MA: The MIT Press, 1962), chapter 2; David A. Hounshell and John K. Smith Jr., *Science and Corporate Strategy: DuPont R&D, 1902–1980* (New York: Cambridge University Press, 1988).

5. Regina Lee Blaszczyk, *American Consumer Society, 1865–2005: From Hearth to HDTV* (Hoboken, NJ: John Wiley & Sons, 2009).

6. Ibid.

7. Amory M. Sommaripa, *Diary of a Mad Russian: A Tribute to Alexis Sommaripa, 1900–1945* (New York: iUniverse, 2005), 1–12; Nashua Manufacturing Company, *Annual Report for the Fiscal Year Ending October 31, 1924*, [4].

8. Melissa Murphy, Baker Library Special Collections, Harvard Business School, email to author, May 13, 2019.

9. Blaszczyk, *American Consumer Society*.

10. Unless otherwise noted, my discussion of DuPont is based on Regina Lee Blaszczyk, *The Synthetics Revolution* (Cambridge, MA: The MIT Press, 2024).

11. Charles H. Rutledge, DuPont Company, to Curtis R. Troeger, *New York Times*, November 12, 1965, box 7, accession 1193-ADD: Charles H. Rutledge Collection, Hagley Museum and Library, Wilmington, DE (hereafter cited as HML).

12. "How Did Rayon Get Its Name?" *Rayon Textile Monthly* (hereafter cited as *RTM*) 26 (January 1945): 56; A. G. Scroggie, "Why the Word 'Rayon' Should Not Be Adopted as a Generic Term for All Man-Made Fibers," *RTM* 26 (January 1945): 57–58.

13. Alexis Sommaripa, "Milestones of Rayon Technology," *RTM* 19 (July 1938): 37–39, 44. Quotations at 37.

14. Alexis Sommaripa, "Beauty . . . Softness . . . Economy," *DuPont Magazine* (hereafter cited as *DM*) 21 (June 1927): 7 ("softness").

15. Ibid. ("advantages").

16. "Canadian Viewpoint on Rayon," *Rayon* 3 (September 15, 1926): 20–27, 34. Quotations at 22.

17. A. Stuart Hunter, "Measuring the Luster of Rayon Yarns," *RTM* 17 (September 1936): 111–12.

18. "Rayon Dresses in the Summertime," *Rayon Journal and Cellulose Fibers* 2 (September 1927): 23–24, 42–43.

19. Alexis Sommaripa, "Progress in Spun Rayon Fabrics Here and Abroad," *RTM* 17 (September 1936): 34–35, 37.

20. William L. Bird Jr., *"Better Living": Advertising, Media and the New Vocabulary of Business Leadership, 1935–1955* (Evanston, IL: Northwestern University Press, 1999).

21. "DuPont Reproduces Sheer Dress Wools in Spun Rayon," *WWD*, May 10, 1937.

22. Psychological Corporation, "A Word of Explanation about the Psychological Corporation," ca. 1943, in box 4, accession 1662: Papers of Lammot du Pont, HML.

23. How Sommaripa connected with the Psychological Corporation is unknown, but DuPont's advertising department kept the consultants on retainer as part of an effort to "apply more

research methods to our promotion problems." See William A. Hart, Advertising Department, DuPont Company, to Executive Committee, April 18, 1938, and Hart to Lammot du Pont, Aug. 18, 1939 ("apply"), both in box 4, accession 1662: Papers of Lammot du Pont, HML.

24. Earnest Elmo Calkins, "Beauty, the New Business Tool," *The Atlantic*, August 1927, https://www.theatlantic.com/magazine/archive/1927/08/beauty-the-new-business-tool/376227/.

25. Regina Lee Blaszczyk, *The Color Revolution* (Cambridge, MA: The MIT Press, 2012), chapter 5.

26. Rowena Ripin and Paul F. Lazarsfeld, "The Tactile-Kinaesthetic Perception of Fabrics with Emphasis on Their Relative Pleasantness," *Journal of Applied Psychology* 21 (April 1937): 198–224 (198, "hedonic"); Ferdinand C. Wheeler et al., "Progress in Marketing Research," *Journal of Marketing* 2 (October 1937): 155 ("visual").

27. Ripin and Lazarsfeld, "Tactile-Kinaesthetic," 223 ("no question").

28. "Feel of Fabric Key to Success," *News Journal* (Wilmington, DE), February 17, 1938.

29. "Fabric Styles Set by Consumer," *Wilmington Morning News* (DE), February 17, 1938 ("Particularly").

30. "Feel of Fabric Key to Success."

31. Blaszczyk, *Color Revolution*.

32. "Fabric Styles Set by Consumers."

33. "Future of Spun Rayon Yarns Held Up to Spinner, Weavers," *WWD*, October 7, 1937 ("Rayon").

34. "Interesting Statistics of Finished Rayon Goods," *RTM* 26 (January 1945): 58.

35. Francis A. Adams, "More Rayons for Civilians," *RTM* 26 (July 1945): 49.

36. Unless otherwise notes, this section draws on Regina Lee Blaszczyk, "Styling Synthetics: DuPont's Marketing of Fabrics and Fashions in Postwar America," *Business History Review* 80 (Autumn 2006): 485–528.

37. Andrew E. Buchanan Jr., "Textile Progress from Fundamental Research," paper presented at the Twentieth Annual Meeting of the Textile Research Institute, New York, December 2, 1949, 5, box 81, accession 1771: Records of the Textile Fibers Department, E. I. du Pont de Nemours and Company, HML (hereafter cited as TF-HML).

38. These reports are found in TF-HML.

39. Arthur M. Saunders Jr., "Selling Becomes Marketing Under the Impact of the Man-Made Fibers," *American Fabrics* 57 (Summer 1962): 88 ("relatively").

40. "'Chuse Thy Cloaths by Thine Own Eyes, Not Another's," 4–5 (quotations), undated typescript, Ernest Dichter papers, collection of Hedy Dichter, Peekskill, New York (hereafter cited as ED). I used Ernest Dichter's office files in 2006 when they were in the private hands of his widow. Subsequently, in 2007, the family donated the papers to HML, which processed the collection as accession 2407: Ernest Dichter Papers.

41. Ernest Dichter, typescript on advertising and fashion, undated, 4 (quotations), ED.

42. Regina Lee Blaszczyk, "Ernest Dichter and the Peacock Revolution: Motivation Research, the Menswear Market and the DuPont Company," in *Ernest Dichter and Motivation Research: New Perspectives on the Making of Post-War Consumer Culture*, ed. Stefan Schwarzkopf and Rainer Gries (New York: Palgrave Macmillan, 2010), 126–39.

43. Ernest Dichter, "The Peacock Revolution: The Psychology of the Young Men's Market," speech delivered in Scottsdale, AZ, February 18, 1966; Institute for Motivational Research (hereafter cited as IMR), "Down with the Barriers: The Continuation of the Peacock Revolution," December 1966; Ernest Dichter, "Down with the Barriers: The Peacock Revolution Continues," January 26, 1967, all in ED.

44. Blaszczyk, "Ernest Dichter and the Peacock Revolution," 133–34.

45. Dichter, "Peacock Revolution," 2 ("durable press"), 4 ("individuality," "rebel").

46. Ibid., 37.

47. Ibid., 5 ("unravel").

48. Regina Lee Blaszczyk, "What Do Baby Boomers Want? How the Swinging Sixties Became the Trending Seventies," in *The Fashion Forecasters: A Hidden History of Color and Trend Prediction*, ed. Regina Lee Blaszczyk and Ben Wubs (London: Bloomsbury Academic, 2018), 112–13.

49. IMR, "Down with the Barriers," 19 ("undeniably").

50. Ibid., 17.

51. Ibid., 130 ("Peacock Revolution").

52. Blaszczyk, *American Consumer Society*, 186.

53. Dichter, "Peacock Revolution," 11 ("Adonis"; "clothes"; "Not only"), 11–12 ("To the young man").

54. Ibid., 15 ("Italian"; "This type").

55. Ibid., 16–18.

56. Ibid., 25 ("physically sensual").

57. Ibid., 19 ("stretch suits"; "younger boy").

58. Ibid., 20 ("great variety"; "velvet").

59. Ibid., 26 ("unconsciously").

60. Ibid., 20 ("tactile orgy"), 26–27.

61. Ibid., 58 ("Apparel-Hedonism").

62. IMR, "Down with the Barriers," 121 ("Comfort"; "second skin").

63. Dichter, "Peacock Revolution," 33 ("action"; "ready-to-go"); IMR, "Down with the Barriers," 81 ("activity apparel").

64. IMR, "Down with the Barriers," 81 ("New fabrics").

65. Ibid., 86 ("only thing").

66. "Sartorial Styles for the Seventies," *DM* 61 (September–October 1967): 10–13 (10, "*What*" and "young"; 11, "vision").

67. Ibid., 12 ($250); DuPont Product Information Service, "Du Pont First Place Award for Slacks," 1967 ("slim"), 1984259_010313_143, in folder 22, box 27, accession 1984.259: DuPont Textile Fibers Product Information Photographs, Audiovisual Collections and Digital Initiatives Department, HML.

68. Donald F. Holmes, "History of Textile Fibers Department," rev. ed. (1982), 48–51, box 81, TF-HML.

69. DuPont Company, Textile Fibers Department Annual Report, December 1981, 10, in box 2: accession 2091: DuPont Company Executive Committee Records, HML.

70. Polly Rayner, "New Male Look Casual, Yet Dressy," *Morning Call* (Allentown, PA), June 24, 1974 ("Technology").

71. J. S. Kennedy, "A Solution to Customer Complaints Through Consumer Research," *RTM* 20 (February 1939): 33–35 (33, "In our industry").

CHAPTER 12

1. Justia Trademarks, "LADY HILTON Trademark - Registration Number 0902759 - Serial Number 72293384 :: Justia Trademarks," accessed September 5, 2020, https://trademarks.justia.com/722/93/lady-hilton-72293384.html.

2. Robert L. Blomstrom, *The Commercial Lodging Market* (East Lansing, MI: Michigan State University, 1967), 19.

3. Molly W. Berger, *Hotel Dreams: Luxury, Technology, and Urban Ambition in America, 1829–1929* (Baltimore: Johns Hopkins University Press, 2011), 181.

4. A. K. Sandoval-Strausz, *Hotel: An American History* (New Haven, CT: Yale University Press, 2007).

5. Arthur White, *Palaces of the People* (New York: Taplinger Publishing Company, 1968), 166.

6. White, *Palaces of the People*, 166.

7. Berger, *Hotel Dreams*, 211.

8. Tom Avermaete and Anne Massey, *Hotel Lobbies and Lounges* (London: Routledge, 2013), 1.

9. Avermaete and Massey, *Hotel Lobbies and Lounges*, 1.

10. J. Gordon Carr and Elizabeth Z. Cutler, "Ideas on Post-War Decoration," *Hotel Management*, (May 1945).

11. Annabel Jane Wharton, *Building the Cold War* (Chicago: University of Chicago Press, 2001), 197.

12. "The Five Senses of the Guest," *Hotel Bulletin* 36, no. 6 (June 1926): 474.

13. "Ad for Comet," *Hotel World-Review* 143, no. 2 (January 23, 1963): 17.

14. For more about Pittsburgh Paint's "Color Dynamics," see chapter 9 in Regina Lee Blaszczyk, *The Color Revolution* (Cambridge, MA: MIT Press, 2012).

15. "Ad for Martex Towels," *Hotel World-Review* 143, no. 1 (January 9, 1963): 10.

16. For a discussion of the rise of domestic tourism, see Marguerite S. Shaffer, *See America First: Tourism and National Identity, 1880–1940* (Washington, D.C.: Smithsonian Institution Press, 2001).

17. Angel Kwolek-Folland, *Incorporating Women: A History of Women and Business in the United States*, Twayne's Evolution of Modern Business Series (New York: Prentice Hall International, 1998), 173.

18. Morrison Hotel, "When My Lady Travels," *Hotel World* 87, no. 2 (July 13, 1918): 24.

19. "Caring for the Ladies," *Hotel Bulletin* 36, no. 4 (April 1926): 332.

20. "Lady Hilton: Determined Effort to Win the Fair Sex," *Hotel Management - Review* (July 1965): 30–31.

21. I thank Regina Blaszczyk for this insight.

22. "Lady Hilton: Determined Effort to Win the Fair Sex," 30.

23. Elizabeth Adams and Virginia Washburn, "Travel Service Deparment," *Town & Country* 119, no. 4513 (August 1965): 96–98.

24. "Lady Hilton: Determined Effort to Win the Fair Sex," 31.

25. The Architect's Journal, *Principles of Hotel Design* (London: The Architectural Press, 1970).

26. "Lady Hilton Information Packet," c.1965, collection of the author.

27. "The Traditional Meets the Modern," *Bar Management* 10, no. 2 (February 1960): 11.

28. Regina Lee Blaszczyk et al., *The Color Revolution* (Cambridge, MA: The MIT Press, 2012), chapter 11, http://ebookcentral.proquest.com/lib/bu/detail.action?docID=3339497.

29. For further explorations of how pink came to be associated with femininity, see Valerie Steele et al., *Pink: The History of a Punk, Pretty, Powerful Color* (New York: Thames & Hudson, 2018).

30. "Lady Hilton Promotional Folder," c 1965, collection of the author.

31. Kwolek-Folland, *Incorporating Women*; Vicki Schultz, "Telling Stories About Women and Work: Judicial Interpretations of Sex Segregation in the Workplace in Title VII Cases Rais-

ing Lack of Interest Argument," *Harvard Law Review* 103, no. 1749 (June 1990) in Mary Yeager, ed., *Women in Business*, vol. 3 (Cheltenham, UK: Elgar Reference, 1999).

32. "Lady Hilton: Determined Effort to Win the Fair Sex," 31.

33. Geoffrey Jones, *Beauty Imagined: A History of the Global Beauty Industry* (Oxford, UK: Oxford University Press, 2010), 164.

34. *Lady Hilton Perfumes in Four Moods*, n.d., collection of the author. Although all perfumes change over time, the scents in my collection have retained strength and distinct notes.

35. Jones, *Beauty Imagined: A History of the Global Beauty Industry*, 164.

36. "Lady Hilton Promotional Folder." Emphasis in original.

37. Regina Lee Blaszczyk, "Styling Synthetics: DuPont's Marketing of Fabrics and Fashions in Postwar America," *Business History Review* 80, no. 3 (2006): 485–528.

38. Myra Waldo, *Myra Waldo's Travel Guide to Europe* (New York: The Macmillan Company, 1964), 16–17.

39. Harvey S. Olson, *Aboard and Abroad* (Philadelphia: J. B. Lippincott Company, 1961), 36.

40. "Hilton History Timeline," accessed September 30, 2020, https://newsroom.hilton.com/assets/BCM/images/Hilton100/Docs/Hilton-History-Timeline.pdf. This Hilton Hotels official timeline provides a date for the beginning of the program but not its end. Materials in the company archives (currently closed to researchers) will likely help to explain when and how the program was phased out. Some clues can be found in Paul Burnham Finney's article about the revival of hotel services for women referred to below.

41. "Hotel Industry Baffled by Women Travelers," *Santa Cruz Sentinel*, June 26, 1983.

42. Paul Burnham Finney, "Women-Friendly Hotel Floors Return, With Modern Twists," *New York Times*, August 5, 2008, https://www.nytimes.com/2008/08/05/business/05women.html.

43. Virginia M Komlos, "Resourceful Ways in Which War-Weary Hotels Can Be Redecorated," *Hotel Management* XLVIII, no. 3 (September 1945): 28 & ff.

44. Finney, "Women-Friendly Hotel Floors Return, With Modern Twists."

CONTRIBUTORS

NICHOLAS ANDERMAN is PhD candidate in the Department of Geography at the University of California, Berkeley, and an editor at *Qui Parle*, a journal of critical humanities and social sciences published by Duke University Press.

REGINA LEE BLASZCZYK is professor of business history and Leadership Chair in the History of Business and Society at the University of Leeds in the United Kingdom. She is the author or editor of twelve books on design and innovation in the creative industries, consumer society, the history of color, the fashion business, and the cultural dimensions of the chemicals industry. Two of her books—*The Color Revolution* (The MIT Press, 2012) and her current project, *The Synthetics Revolution*—engage with the history of the senses. She divides her time between Leeds and Philadelphia.

JESSICA P. CLARK is associate professor in the Department of History at Brock University in Canada. She is the author of *The Business of Beauty: Gender and the Body in Modern Britain* (Bloomsbury, 2020), and has published articles on British beauty culture, consumption, and luxury. Her current book project, "Scents of Change: Experiencing Modernity in Britain, 1880–1930," is funded by the Social Sciences and Humanities Research Council of Canada (SSHRC).

MEGAN J. ELIAS is associate professor of practice and director of the Gastronomy Program at Boston University. She has published five books on food and American popular culture, including *Food on the Page: Cookbooks and American Culture* (University of Pennsylvania Press, 2017), and has contributed to anthologies and academic journals.

AI HISANO is associate professor at the Graduate School of Interdisciplinary Information Studies at the University of Tokyo. Her first book, *Visualizing Taste: How Business Changed the Look of What You Eat* (Harvard University

Press, 2019), won the Hagley Prize in Business History (Business History Conference) and the Shimizu Hiroshi Book Award (Japanese Association for American Studies).

LISA JACOBSON is associate professor in the Department of History at the University of California, Santa Barbara. Her publications include *Raising Consumers: Children and the American Mass Market in the Early Twentieth Century* (Columbia University Press, 2004) and *Capitalism's Hidden Worlds* (University of Pennsylvania Press, 2019), an anthology edited with Kenneth J. Lipartito. Her current book project is "Fashioning New Cultures of Drink: Alcohol and the Politics of Pleasure after Prohibition."

SVEN KUBE is a historian of culture, business, and technology with special interest in popular music. Trained at German, Canadian, and American universities, he is completing his first book on pop records as a cultural commodity in Cold War competition. His article "Shop of the Pops" won the 2022 Russel B. Nye Award for the Outstanding Article published in the *Journal of Popular Culture*. Kube is currently a National Endowment for the Humanities research fellow at the Hagley Museum and Library.

GRACE LEES-MAFFEI is professor of design history at the University of Hertfordshire in the United Kingdom and director of DHeritage, the professional doctorate in heritage. She is the author or editor of eight books and numerous peer-reviewed journal articles in design history and material culture studies, and she is currently writing a book about hands in the history of design. Grace is chair of the editorial board of the *Journal of Design History* (Oxford University Press), the leading humanities journal in its field, and coeditor of the Cultural History of Design book series for Bloomsbury Academic.

INGEMAR PETTERSSON is a historian of science and technology in the Department of Economic History at Uppsala University in Sweden. He is currently involved in three funded research projects, supported by Swedish research councils, on research policy in Sweden and on industrial production and the senses. He has published peer-reviewed journal articles, books, and book chapters on Swedish research policy, industrial and agricultural sciences, and on the history of flavor science and food production.

DAVID SUISMAN is associate professor of history at the University of Delaware, where he specializes in cultural history, the history of music, sound studies, war and society, and the history of capitalism. His books include *Selling Sounds: The Commercial Revolution in American Music* (Harvard University Press, 2009), recipient of numerous awards and honors, and *Sound in the Age of Mechanical Reproduction* (University of Pennsylvania Press, 2010), coedited with Susan Strasser. His articles and reviews have appeared in the *Journal of American History, Social Text, Radical History Review, The Believer, American Historical Review, Journal of Social History*, and other publications. From 2010 to 2021, he was associate editor and book review editor of the *Journal of Popular Music Studies.*

ANA MARÍA ULLOA received her PhD in anthropology from The New School University in New York and is currently an assistant professor of anthropology at Universidad de los Andes in Bogotá, Colombia. Her articles have appeared in *The Senses and Society, Gastronomica: The Journal of Critical Food Studies*, and *Food, Culture, and Society.*

NICOLE WELK-JOERGER is the deputy director of the Center for 21st Century Studies at the University of Wisconsin-Milwaukee. She completed postdoctoral appointments at North Carolina State University and Princeton University and earned her PhD in the history and sociology of science at the University of Pennsylvania. She is at work on her first book, "Rumen Nation: Consuming Sustainability in the United States."

INDEX

Page numbers in italics refer to illustrations.

Printed and bound by CPI Group (UK) Ltd, Croydon, CR0 4YY

23/12/2024

14617254-0001